D0744586

324.243
M452

# The German Greens

## PARADOX BETWEEN MOVEMENT AND PARTY

EDITED BY

## Margit Mayer *and* John Ely

Translations by Michael Schatzschneider

WITHDRAWN

Temple University Press

Philadelphia

TEMPLE UNIVERSITY PRESS, PHILADELPHIA 19122
Copyright © 1998 by Temple University. All rights reserved
Published 1998
Printed in the United States of America

♾ The paper used in this book meets the requirements of the American National Standard for Information Sciences—Permanence of Paper for Printed Library Materials, ANSI Z39.48-1984

Text design by Gary Gore
Chapters 3–9 and 11–13 were translated from the German by Michael Schatzschneider.

Library of Congress Cataloging-in-Publication Data
The German Greens : paradox between movement and party/[edited by]
Margit Mayer and John Ely; translations by Michael Schatzschneider.
    p.    cm.
    Includes bibliographical references (p.    ) and index.
    ISBN 1-56639-515-1 (cloth : alk. paper).—ISBN 1-56639-516-X
paper : alk. paper)
    1. Die Grünen (Political party)—History.    2. Green movement—Germany—History.
I. Mayer, Margit.    II. Ely, John.
JN3971.A98G723293    1997
324.243'08—dc20                  96-30656

# Contents

# I

# Introduction

## Chapter 1

Cᴧᴜ

# Success and Dilemmas of Green Party Politics

MARGIT MAYER AND JOHN ELY

The German Greens have captured the American imagination over the last decade. For a "movement party" to enter the political mainstream is a remarkable feat that has inspired the efforts of movements with similar goals around the world. When more than two million West Germans gave their vote to the Greens on March 3, 1983, the new social movements that had appeared all over the country during the 1970s achieved parliamentary representation for the first time. For two legislative periods, the Green Party represented progressive and ecological politics on the national political stage, giving hitherto marginalized movement politics an enviable edge of effectiveness.

Over the course of the 1980s, the Green Party significantly altered the political landscape of the Federal Republic of Germany (FRG); the effects are still apparent in the new united Germany. After reunification and the temporary exclusion of the West German Greens from the reunited nation's first parliament, the party has a more secure position within the German party system than ever before. It is active in a variety of state and local parliaments and participates in many governing coalitions on the local level as well as in three state governments.

Bündnis 90/Die Grünen (Alliance 90/the Greens), as the merged party of Eastern and Western Greens has called itself since 1993, has consolidated as an ecological reform party with an unambiguous aspiration toward government. This transformation into a pragmatic and more centrist parliamentarian party was less a result of unification than the outcome of a process already on its way in the late 1980s; unification was merely the catalyst. That process—the attempt to find a form for bringing movement politics into party politics—is the focus of this book. It looks back at the first 10 years of Green Party development in a country in many ways typ-

3

ical of advanced capitalist nations. Though the Green Party is embedded in a specifically *West* German political culture, the experiment of translating the "new issues" of ecology, gender, and grassroots democracy into the organizational form of a political party is applicable to similar efforts in other nations. The quick transition to parliamentary party politics—two years after their founding the Greens were sent to Bonn—did not allow them much space to explore the party form for the new politics. But their history reveals the possibilities and structural constraints facing such projects in any western country.

The contributors to this book deal with the particular conditions in the West German political system of the 1970s that allowed an ecological–radical democratic–socialist mixture to cohere under the green label. The German electoral system requires a party has to receive at least 5 percent of the vote to be represented in the legislature. The 5 percent clause—rather than a common political agenda—pressured these diverse tendencies to unite into one party. Over its first 10 years, however, the Green Party shed both "single-issue" and "movement" characteristics and took a secure place, as a political party, in the Federal Republic's political system. The Greens have forced the question of who is to pay for the costs of solving environmental problems and insisted on asking this question in social terms. They have drafted legislation to end discrimination against women (the Antidiscrimination Law), proposed steps toward disarmament, criticized existing refugee and immigrant policies, and developed programs for restructuring the industrial base of society. They have effectively translated demands originally voiced by various social movements into concrete positions and legislative proposals, thus exerting considerable pressure on the large established parties. But their successes have been limited. Even in the ecological sphere, Green-sponsored environmental protection measures fall far short of original ambitions, and ecological thinking is far from assuming a central role in the formulation of governmental policy.

This book explores the significance of the Greens on a deeper level than just the successful implementation of "green" principles. In the analyses presented here, one can see the gradual changes in Green definitions of politics and the changes in radical discourse that result from the pressures of parliamentarization and party competition. The contradictions between the forms and the logic of movements and those of parties account for both the party's successes and the conflicts that have often threatened to tear it apart. The debate on the chances for a new politics in German parliaments and the effects of parliamentarization on the Green Party has been wide-ranging and intense among German scholars and activists. Yet little of this debate has been available to American readers. Because Americans involved in environmental and other grassroots movements frequently look to the German Greens as a model for translating social movements into effective legislative action, understanding the costs and contradictions of this process of parliamentarization is crucial.

## Emergence from a Multitude of Social Movements

It was far from self-evident that the social movements of the 1970s would produce a political *party*. The German social movements of the 1960s and 1970s shared a grassroots orientation and a strong antiparliamentarian bias, which was reinforced by the political constellations at the time. A growth coalition of political, corporate, and labor leaders that was closed and exclusive, and a political system that was characterized by bureaucratized and statist "people's parties," tended to encourage strong antistate and anti-institutional orientations among those it excluded. The basis of this central corporatist accord (called "Model Germany")[1] was unfettered economic growth that allowed for welfare state redistributive measures. Its focus on centralized, large industrial projects directed toward competition on the world market ran roughshod over local interests and countered civic opposition with security state measures. By the end of the decade the term "Model Germany" had Orwellian overtones in the milieus of the new social movements. Joachim Hirsch's studies of the postwar "German Model" (which he summarizes in Chapter 9 in this volume) show how the crisis of this model weakened the reformism of the German Social Democratic Party (SPD). At the same time, the ecology, antinuclear, and peace movements experienced state repression and came to see the limits of mass protest. After the spectacular success of the antinuclear movement in Wyhl, where activists prevented the construction of a nuclear power plant through site occupations and massive regional opposition, and after further escalations of protest at the Grohnde and Brokdorf construction sites in 1976 and 1977, mass demonstrations and militancy could scarcely be stepped up. The ruling parties increasingly cited this militancy in their efforts to delegitimate the ecological and antinuclear movements and critique. In this situation, the movements hesitantly explored electoral politics as a means to increase their leverage. This trend was reinforced by the "German Autumn" of 1977, which brought home the futility of raising militancy to the level of terrorist actions. Electoral politics ultimately appeared as the most promising route for expanding the options of the new social movements.

During this period, the ideologically diverse social movements also experienced something like a "greening" of their diverse protest motives: ecology became a common denominator for the many protests that citizen initiatives and movements were engaged in. This emphasis on ecology involved a fundamental critique of mainstream growth politics at the same time that it unified heterogeneous oppositional motives and transformed the demand of many citizen initiatives from, as the Americans put it, NIMBY ("Not in my backyard!") to NANBY ("Not in anybody's backyard!"). Where movements were particularly strong, green-alternative slates began fielding candidates for local elections. Horst Mewes describes the development from these early (local and regional) coalitions to the founding of the national Green Party in Chapter 2. The effort to build a national party was led by a small group of activists, mostly former leftists intent upon using environmentalism as a new unifying force. As the founding documents assembled in Chapter 11 illustrate, the ideological backgrounds of the different coalitions active in local and state elections were frequently quite at odds with the national party builders. Nonetheless, these coalitions formed the basis of the national party.

In spite of this heterogeneity of ideological orientations, writers have in the past emphasized one tendency over the others, depending on their own preferences and sometimes at the expense of historical accuracy.[2] The slogan "We are neither left nor right, but in front" enjoyed popularity and wide dissemination, but ample empirical research suggests that the primary structuring processes of the Green Party have been conflicts between right and left; the compromise over the ecological issues has remained rather vague and unelaborated.[3] The party quickly discovered that environmentalism did not readily resolve powerful political differences of long standing. While the ecology and the peace movements were catalysts for the emergence of the Green Party out of a broader spectrum, they never achieved a synthesis of the different traditions. Marxists of the student movement and party-building phase, conservationists, anthroposophists[4] and other groups seeking a "third way" between communism and capitalism, environmentalists, alternative movements, and feminists all entered into this party project because, as extraparliamentarian movements, they had reached the limits of confrontational politics within the political opportunity structure of the FRG.

What these ideologically heterogeneous elements had in common was a fundamental critique of progress: they challenged both the traditional leftist ideas of progress and the industrial productivism and the patriarchal structures of capitalist society. The question was how to fold such a critique of progress and a politics of social and political opposition into a concept of concrete politics and a parliamentarian politics of reform.

## Movement Rationality versus Party Rationality

During the early expansion phase of the Green Party, a broad spectrum of positions and tendencies worked together to create a rainbow of constituencies and supporters. The very concrete and particular demands of the heterogeneous electoral base contrasted sharply with the lukewarm, broad, and overgeneralized programs of the large established parties. However, the very first attempts to synthesize these disparate claims into an actual program made it obvious that some priorities had to be selected. A first casualty of the debate over the program was the bourgeois-conservative wing. The conservatives' exit meant that the party could no longer claim to transcend the traditional left-right division (Rudolf Bahro called it the historic compromise of red and green). Under the pressures of party competition, the Green Party decided to become a *program* party, rather than limiting itself to representing extraparliamentarian protest in parliament as, for example, the Partido Radicale did in Italy. In fact, and rather quickly, the Green Party shed the image of being a single-issue "ecological lobby." While it was perceived as standing to the left of social democracy, the necessities of the 5 percent clause forced the wide spectrum of positions—from eco-socialist to eco-capitalist—to cohere. Although "eco" was the ever-present modifier/prefix, it did not ideologically define the party.

The transition from "movement" to "political party" was not accompanied by a clear distinction between movement politics and party politics. Rather, the concept of a "new politics" blurred the boundaries between the two. The Green Party has remained connected to the left-libertarian movement milieus in the topics it addresses, its political style, and the omnipresence of movement discourse; indeed, these features appear to be keys to the nature of the new problems—ecological devastation, gender discrimination, and so on. But while movements need not worry about the 5 percent barrier and electoral success, a party does. Early on the party responded to this dilemma by developing its program through a strategy of addition, taking care not to exclude any movement demands. The 500-page program of the North Rhine–Westphalia Greens, exhaustively calling for the abolition of every identified problem, testifies to this encyclopedic approach to accommodation and compromise.

The attempt to embrace the relevance of *all* issues and simultaneously pursue the requirements of electoral and coalition strategies soon immobilized the Greens. "Identification" with all movements did not resolve the asymmetrical relationship between movements and party. Although movements and party share similar interpretations of the problems of ecology, peace, and gender, they differ significantly in the actions they can undertake effectively. For parties, electoral behavior, coalitions, and legislation are the criteria of success; furthermore, parties expect movements to follow the imperatives of voter mobilization and adapt to the logic of bargaining tactics. Movements, however, soon rebelled against being instrumentalized for voter mobilization or, in the case of Hesse's early red-green coalition, against being used for the cycle of coalition negotiations. In Hesse, social movements objected to the politics of the Green minister for environmental affairs as overly incremental and piecemeal and frequently demonstrated against them. The so-called fundamentalist Greens, who presented themselves as the spokespeople for the radical ecological critique and rejected piecemeal reformism altogether, capitalized on the movements' objections. Determining what kind of relationship to maintain to the "base," or "grassroots" (that is, the social movements), while trying to mature into an effective political party, became a key issue for the competing factions.

Competition and struggle between the different tendencies soon dominated party life. After an early phase characterized by efforts to criticize and make public the devastating effects of "the system," the period from 1984 to 1988 was dominated by ideological conflict between the fundamentalists and realists ("Fundis" and "Realos" in the language of the scene), a conflict that escalated over the question of SPD and Green Party coalition. It was not until 1989 that the party developed an elaborate program to "restructure" industrial society. This was, however, well prepared by the Green faction in parliament, the *Bundestagsfraktion*.[5]

In their empirically grounded analysis in this volume (Chapter 3), Roland Roth and Detlef Murphy describe the substance of these factional controversies. While the media have often presented only the opposition of fundamentalists versus *realpolitiker*, with the feminists on the side, Murphy and Roth identify four distinct factions: eco-socialists, eco-libertarians (formed in 1983/84 in reaction to the former group), radical ecologists (i.e., fundamentalists), and Realos. They describe how in 1987 these tendencies were complemented and partially superseded by the formation of the centrist "Green Awakening '88" (Grüner Aufbruch '88) by an alliance of pragmatic leftists and softer Realos. Founded to overcome the antagonism of the factions, it became an additional faction. In November 1988 yet another political current, the Left Forum (Linkes Forum), gathered some of the independent leftists (mainly from the eco-socialists) and sought to overcome the paralyzing contest between Fundi and Realo positions. Roth and Murphy's profile suggests that all factions, including the feminists, acted within the programmatic framework defined by the four "classic" currents. They analyze the composition, politics, distinctive positions, and power bases of these factions before and after the power shift of 1988, when the national executive committee, which used to be the (left) counterweight to the Realo-dominated Bundestagsfraktion, was voted out. The composition of the new national executive committee, including one Reala, one Aufbruch, and one left feminist, reflected the new alignment: no longer did the left hold a clear majority.

Indicating the erosion of the left/right fronts, the power shift of 1988 was yet another expression of the difficult relationship between social movements and the Green Party. While the Greens derive energy and innovative impulses from the new social movements, they derive their political power from elections and their ability to function effectively within political institutions. The Greens addressed this tension by designing organizational structures to resist and preclude their integration into the iron law of oligarchy. These principles of internal organization (gender equality, rotation of offices, and the imperative mandate)[6] had limited success; in some ways, they even served to intensify informal power hierarchies, as Claudia Pinl shows for men (in Chapter 6)[7] and Lilian Klotzsch, Klaus Könemann, Jörg Wischermann, and Bodo Zeuner show for the parliamentarian groups on both state and national levels (Chapter 5). Alex Demirović examines in Chapter 7 how the open, unbureaucratic design of the party meetings—which was supposed to guarantee permeability to the grassroots—resulted in time-consuming rules-of-order debates that were then tactically manipulated by informal power groups. On the federal level, the rotation principle was soon abolished, but the struggle between "professionals" and "grassroots dilettantes" did not subside. Even after the 1987 electoral success, when the number of Green Party delegates increased from 28 to 44 and many "rotated" stars returned to the Bundestag, it remained a source of conflict.

## Dilemmas of Makeup and Structure

Green voters differ from those voting for other parties in many respects, Lutz Mez argues in Chapter 4. Not only do the statistics reveal the Green Party as a "middle-class" party; they also show strong political interests and affinities with progressive social movements. The middle-class label is misleading, however, because the demands and interests associated with ecology, gender relations, technocracy, or peace cannot be traced from the social composition of either the new social movements or the Green Party. Instead, the unintended consequences and side effects of the old arrangements have become politicized. What are perceived and articulated as new inequalities (of gender, of spatial segmentation, of risk) are *not* middle-class issues by nature; it is middle-class groups who have articulated them simply because they have the resources and skills to do so.

Voters' closeness to social movements is manifested in the Green Party's curious and unique imbalance of office-holders, members, and voters. The party membership (about 42,000)[8] is but a fraction of electoral support (3,126,000 in the 1987 national election); the ratio of members to supporters is much lower than that of other parties. Worse, one in six of those 42,000 members holds an office at the local, state, or national level! The need to fill positions often overwhelms the membership pool, and relatively few have never held a party or elected office. A 1989 survey found that of the 5,000 Hessian Greens, 4,000 were functionaries and mandate-holders![9] This problem is especially severe among women activists. With the feminists' success in establishing the 50 percent quota, staffing needs far exceed the resources of the approximately 3,000 female party activists. Moreover, in spite of all the devices installed to ensure grassroots input and participation, most regular party members are more interested in their own extraparliamentarian or movement problems than in day-to-day legislative problems or in controlling their delegates. Reservations about party politics sometimes severely restrict grassroots input.

These ratios indicate that Green Party work is primarily work in councils and parliaments. As a consequence, parliamentary work—which commands richer resources[10]—dominates party debates. The "parliamentarization" of the Green Party, a term introduced by Klotzsch and her co-authors, refers to the preponderance of the parliamentarian faction: it drastically restricts the introduction of movement themes and demands into the official political sphere and favors instead mutually instrumentalist relations and clientelism. The imbalance of membership and office-holders has also kept the Green Party from developing an organizational culture expressive of its grassroots-democratic claims. The powerful parliamentary factions have no real counterweight in the party, while they feel keenly the pressures of their daily parliamentary tasks.

Additionally, this imbalance means that the bulk of Green Party work takes place at the *local* level. At that level, the party has about 7,000 elected positions (as opposed to 170 delegates to state parliaments and eight to the European parliament). This strong local presence was for a long time hardly reflected in debates over programs or political strategy.[11] This may be due to the variety of situations in different localities. In Frankfurt, for example, movements are strongly oriented toward their representatives in parliament, but in other places they keep their distance. As a result, a wide variety of clientelist and instrumental relations exist between local movement scenes and "their" Green Party.

Most experiments with red-green governing coalitions take place in municipalities, but they, too, have rarely been discussed in the supralocal political debate. This is due, of course, to the instability of such coalitions through the 1980s,[12] and the Greens/Alternatives have actually implemented a very limited number of issues.[13] Typically, local Green politics is geared to the pragmatic and feasible, with an emphasis on concrete ways of doing things differently. This pragmatization of environmental, feminist, or energy politics allows the established parties to "steal" elements of such policies and integrate them into their own platforms (frequently helping them to regain lost voters).

The first green slates emerged and succeeded in places where strong social movements had mobilized around regional conflicts. After the founding of the national party, these states became widespread phenomena. In most local elections, the Greens are now the third-strongest party. "Progressive local politics," although it has evolved a particular German shape,[14] has not developed either its own identity or extensive coordinating networks and institutions. A few supraregional conferences have addressed such local issues as housing, waste disposal, and public transport; an equally pragmatic monthly publication exists,[15] and an association of Green councilpersons has formed to facilitate discussion of shared practical problems. But there is no strategic debate on the status of green-alternative local politics.[16]

As in most advanced industrial nations, numerous systemic and financial constraints preclude the implementation of radical change on the local level. For example, the kind of resolution that made Berkeley, California, a "nuclear free zone" would be, in the Federal Republic, constitutionally impossible. The local state has even fewer prerogatives than is the case in the United States, and in both countries the direction of economic as well as social politics is decided on higher levels both inside and outside the nation state. But the problems increasingly accumulate and are articulated on the local level.

Many municipalities have adapted to the dilemma of increasing problems and decreasing finances with a search for innovative (i.e., cheap but effective) policies. Established parties have entered coalition governments with the Greens in part in order to tap the newcomers' innovative energy: especially in sectoral politics, local parties in need of new programs have sought the cooperation of pragmatic Green councillors. In many towns and cities, Greens have been placed in charge of supervising waste disposal or given the offices of environmental affairs, women's affairs, or (multi)cultural politics.

In local governing coalitions as well as in the state governments of Hesse, Lower Saxony, and Berlin, the Greens were able to negotiate for small concessions for movement groups. Since the political system privileges parties with a whole array of resources, the Green Party has redistributed at least some of those resources toward movement groups via eco-funds, a Rainbow Foundation, and access to jobs in the public administration. The new clientelist relations with the social movements have their basis here.

### Bringing New Politics into Old Parliaments

The development of the party organization on the federal and local level highlighted the contradiction between movement politics and party politics. Movements began to turn into competing clients of the party, and the organizational procedures installed to safeguard grassroots democracy within the party often backfired. These conditions do not exactly encourage the translation of the "new politics" into the party organization and party life. It is one thing to bring flowers, a new dress code, or direct language into parliament, or even to challenge traditional styles of love-making in a parliamentary speech (see Waltraud Schoppe' speech in Chapter 13)[17] but quite another to *realize* gender equality in an atmosphere where party delegates and staff compete to make their points. Notwithstanding the all-women leadership in the Bundestagfraktion in 1984/85, the "zipper principle" in all electoral lists (which alternates women and men in consecutive order on the slate), and the strong statements in the Women's Program and in the draft legislation to end discrimination against women,[18] important party posts and positions are all too frequently distributed according to an old boys' network. The difficulties of implementing the new politics are most visible in the case of feminist politics.

The party did not begin to develop a feminist profile until 1983/84, when women's affairs officers (*Frauenreferentinnen*) and "working groups on women" were established at the national and state levels (respectively the Bundesarbeitsgruppe [BAG] Frauen and the Landesarbeitsgruppe [LAG] Frauen). An ambitious program of affirmative action was started (highlighted in the antidiscrimination legislation proposal), and internal party quotas were implemented. On the parliamentary level, a sixth *Arbeitskreis* ("working circle"), the so-called AK 6 or AK Frauen, was created. It comprised all women affiliated with the parliamentary group, including those who had not been elected to parliament. Of the six parliamentary working groups, this was the only one not directly linked to a parliamentary committee, which meant that the delegates could invest only part of their energy here, in women-specific legislation and programs, as they also were active in the "regular" working groups linked to the parliamentary committees.

Feminist parliamentarians face unique dilemmas. In addition to their day-to-day parliamentary work, the competition between party factions that dominated party life after 1984 forced feminists to choose between building a feminist faction of their own or working within one of the existing currents. Many influential women chose to work within the different currents, especially on the left. For Regina Michalik, "the realist tendency and the strategy of the 'Aufbruch,' too, exclude feminism."[19] As with the demands of the ecology movement, leftist feminists have bemoaned the fact that radical demands of the women's movement cannot be furthered in parliament, let alone in a red-green government. To them, the feminist group is of subordinate interest, used merely as a tactic for placing women candidates on the ballot and gaining electoral advantage. But since it deals exclusively with women-specific issues, rather than developing an agenda on *all* issues from a feminist perspective, it has succumbed to the pull of the general factions. As with "ecology," the new politics of "gender relations" did not provide a sufficiently clear focus for the unification of divergent political interests within the Green Party. Gender relations are so intricately enmeshed in the structure of society that feminist (like ecological) politics always raises questions of how society as a whole ought to be transformed.

The differences on this question were dramatically brought to the fore in the controversy surrounding the so-called Mothers' Manifesto, published in March 1987. Here, a group of Green Party women argued for the establishment of another federal working group for women, this one to represent the interests of mothers (see Chapter 14). BAG Frauen, the existing federal working group for women,[20] argued that it was adequately representing the interests of women with children, and thus its members voted against the establishment of an additional autonomous BAG. They were outvoted by a narrow margin. A subgroup called "Mothers' Politics" was established with a speaker and financial resources of its own.[21]

This split expressed competing concepts of women's emancipation. The manifesto calls for overcoming the inequality between men and women by valorizing women's reproductive labor. It argues that reducing feminist politics to affirmative action, quota systems, and the right to abortion will not deliver justice to the majority of women, described as "not career women." Moreover, arguing that the existing feminist politics of emancipation and antidiscrimination remains within the logic of the industrial system, this feminist position presented itself as the more "ecological." Mothers' work is played out against industrial production: women who yield to the temptations of the (male) labor market contribute (if unintentionally) to the destruction of the planet because they no longer have time to organize ecological households.[22] Consequently, the Mothers' Manifesto attacks the Green draft for an antidiscrimination law, and its goal of a 50 percent quota in all positions that provide access to power, money, and influence, calling them "unecological."

These feminists aligned themselves with the fundamentalists in the party. The opposing faction, claiming a "realist" position, argued that women, roughly half of the population, under current conditions perform about two-thirds of societal labor: one-third of the wage labor total, plus almost all housework and family work. This position (see the Statement on the Mothers' Manifesto in Chapter 14) asserts that the gendered division of labor in society has to be overcome, and with it the ascription of certain (traditionally female) qualities exclusively to women. They assume that the more women (with or without children) enter positions in the public world, the more easily male-defined competitive structures may be transformed. They envision a society in which the division of labor between "one gender being responsible for nourishing, care, and intuition, the other for subjecting the earth" no longer exists.

The concrete demands with which the Mothers' Manifesto ends did not extend beyond the existing Green program. The draft of legislation to regulate working hours (*Arbeitszeitgesetz*) and the antidiscrimination legislation (*Antidiskriminierungsgesetz*, ADG) already incorporated such demands as independent and adequate finances for children ("at every street-corner") and other caretaking tasks (ADG, Article 1, Paragraph 8), financing for neighborhood centers and "mothers' centers" (although this latter formulation is new), drastic shortening of the workweek, re-entry opportunities for all jobs, and equal wages for equal work. The *Umbau* ("rebuilding") program and the Green Party resolution for a guaranteed basic income had already raised the demand for a minimum income (*Mindestrenten*). Indeed, the Umbau program (see Chapter 14) is even more radical on the issue of part-time work and flexible working hours than the Mothers' Manifesto, leaving the timing of working hours strictly up to the employees.

Nonetheless, the "mothers' position" succeeded remarkably in mobilizing people's emotions. At the second Federal Women's Conference of the Green Party (November 1987), the "mothers" provoked vehement debate by demanding installation of a sixth forum next to the five planned ones on the variety of female life models. Here, as in many other debates, the life paths of mothers (but only mothers who do not participate in the labor market) were set over and against those of other women, who were located in the "ghetto of nonmothers" or the "aquarium of career women."[23] They successfully capitalized on the grievances of nonworking women with small children, who are disadvantaged at every point in a society that valorizes only paid labor. The conflict with the other feminist tendency was over whom to hold responsible for this discrimination: career women or men and the patriarchal system. As Pinl shows in Chapter 6, the ideological differentiation within the feminist camp has continued.

The feminist movement, and Green feminists in parliament, share with the other new social movements ambivalent and at times contradictory expectations about the state and its laws. For example, when feminists called for tougher legislation to punish rape in marriage (Paragraph 177), the (mostly female) Bundestagsfraktion, aware of the longstanding movement critique of the prison system, resisted the demand.[24] The fundamentalist federal executive (*Bundesvostand*), presumably closer to the "grassroots," leapt into the expected attack against the parliamentary faction for not coming out in support of a feminist demand: once again, women's issues were arranged along customary antagonistic factional lines.[25]

These contradictory assumptions about the state are more systematically explored in Alex Demirović's analysis of Green Party grassroots democracy (*Basisdemokratie*) in Chapter 7. He traces the dilemma to the movements' critique of parliamentarianism in the 1960s and 1970s, the failure of the "grassroots democracy" these debates prescribed, and the Green Party's ultimate retreat from the goal of procedural democratization. He shows how and why the principle of grassroots democracy did not and could not prevent the professionalization and "normalization" of the Green Party, as Klotzsch and co-authors and Pinl have found for different areas. Because their critique of parliamentarianism is so abstract, he argues, the Greens are caught between parliamentarian representation and grassroots-democratic mechanisms, and blinded by their programmatic definition of grassroots democracy to the various potentials of the capitalist state. Social movements are not the only representatives of universal general interests; the narrowness and abstraction of the Greens' concept of the state keeps them from acknowledging how this state represents some very real general interests, too. Essentially, Demirović demonstrates how conceptual confusion limits the effectiveness of the institutional precautions the party established to guarantee grassroots democracy. These institutional mechanisms were revised only in response to the devastating electoral results of December 1990.

The contradiction between the demands of social movements and the requirements of parliamentary politics is even more strikingly evident in the debates over the legitimacy of the "state's monopoly on force," triggered by the militant struggles of antinuclear activists in the late 1980s and the hunger strikes of imprisoned militants of the Red Army Faction (RAF). As the activism of broad-based (mainly peace) movements of the early 1980s ebbed, with Green politics being criticized by many as piecemeal and reformist, the radical and anarchist wings of the social movements developed a counterweight. At demonstrations the *Autonomen* would flaunt their distinctive costume and the tactic of the "black block," so called after their practice of wearing black leather uniforms and black woolen facemasks and forming tight defensive formations.[26] While these militants saw disruptive and illegal actions as a legitimate form of opposition to an expansive and destructive state, state authorities used such actions to justify widened police powers and surveillance capacities. The state modernized riot equipment on a large scale and introduced computer-readable identification cards; legislation was passed prohibiting so-called passive weapons at demonstrations—including motorcycle helmets and water canteens to wash tear gas out of one's eyes. In 1987 the state used RAF violence as a pretext for broadening the definition of terrorism (Paragraph 129a) to include elements of the antinuclear movement; in this way, it blurred the lines between the tactics of the RAF and more popular and widely accepted forms of civil protest. The escalating dynamic of violence and repression running through the post-1968 history of the Federal Republic has produced what the Aufbruch leader Antje Vollmer called the movements' "collective experience" with violence. The Greens have been strongly supportive of movement activists imprisoned under the terrorism laws.[27] By the mid-1980s, however, the Greens were caught in the crossfire between widespread sympathy for the militant protesters and the need they felt as a party to fit into the constitutional order.

In the heated context of 1985, which saw the death of a demonstrator at an anti-Nazi protest in Frankfurt and constant violent confrontations between antinuclear demonstrators around a planned nuclear reprocessing plant at Wackersdorf, Vollmer started a debate by calling for dialogue between the Greens and members of the RAF, emphasizing the shared New Left roots of both groups. Otto Schily, also a Green member of parliament but at that time the most moderate national figure in the party (he has since joined the SPD), publicly argued that the Greens must accept the "legitimate monopoly on force" on the part of the state.[28] Schily thereby pushed debates about the nature of politics in a direction foreign to the founding discourse of the party, which was based both on nonviolence and on challenging the state's illegitimate authority. Connecting to this heritage, party leftists such as Thomas Ebermann argued that those who claimed to be advocates of "nonviolence" ought not to support a state's "monopoly claim on the legitimate use of violence." On the other hand, Joschka Fischer and other supporters of Schily struggled to dissociate the Greens from the militant sectors of the movements and adamantly supported nonviolence as a binding party doctrine.

There is no unambiguous solution to this problem. "Freedom with Security: 16 Theses on Green Legal and Domestic Policy" (Chapter 14), produced by the federal parliamentary faction in 1989, opposed police expansion and state intrusion into the affairs of the individual.[29] But this strategy only shifted the debate onto a legal level and failed to resolve the question of the need for societal coordination and the conditions under which the state might organize this in a democratic fashion.

## The Greens within the German Party Spectrum

In the political landscape of the Federal Republic, the (previously) vacant space to the left of the Social Democrats, which gave rise to the Green Party, has become smaller. The established parties, especially the conservative ones, have begun to address issues of environmental destruction, gender relations, and political alienation. At the same time, however, the party spectrum has expanded on the right as xenophobia and demands to stiffen the laws regulating foreigners and refugees grew markedly between 1986 and 1988. In January 1989, a new right-radical party, the Republicans, enjoyed sudden electoral success in the city-state elections in Berlin.

With the SPD losing working-class constituencies to the increasing nationalism and strength of the new right, the Greens became the most adamant party voice for a "multicultural" society, a franchise for immigrants, the "right to remain" in Germany for those who so choose, and minority rights.[30] This increasing emphasis on civil liberties strengthened the Realo wing of the party, which has consistently advocated a republic that is liberal and multiethnic as well as ecologically sound, but has shown less interest in social justice.[31] The development of the right wing also improved conditions for a coalition between Social Democrats and Greens on the national level. While unification and the subsequent decline of the right have dampened this possibility, the structural conditions leading to the success of the far right have by no means disappeared.

Even though the elections for the first all-German parliament in December 1990 disrupted the trend, the broader tendencies that emerged in the West German political system during the 1980s will likely prevail. Local and state elections as well as the 1994 national election have suggested that there are no clear, reliable majorities in the new six-party system. The traditional large parties can no longer count on "their" constituencies, small parties capitalize on the increasing fluctuation of political orientations, and the Green Party (joined on some issues by the Party of Democratic Socialism, the PDS) continues to articulate movement demands within the system.

For all of its shortcomings and difficulties, the Green Party has transformed the political landscape of Germany. Demands considered unconventional, marginal, and utopian in the 1970s—ending nuclear energy and linear economic growth, unilateral disarmament, proportional representation of women in all spheres—are now discussed and even demanded by other parties in the political mainstream.

The diffusion in society of "green thinking" and the takeover of "green" issues by the established parties has, however, made the Greens' survival as a successful party more difficult. Not only has the party lost the monopoly on ecological issues; at least for a period, the leading position in processes of political change has gone to the "revolutionaries of 1989" in the East. Both factors have made it imperative that the Green Party resolve the paradox of being an "antiparty." While this paradox was a source of vibrancy and electoral support during its initial years, the difficulties experienced since 1990 made continued vacillation on this issue suicidal.

To resolve this paradox, different scenarios have been developed both inside and outside the party. In the spectrum of these scenarios, Joachim Hirsch and Claus Offe represent opposite positions. Offe (and many in the Realo wing) envision a more clear-cut division of labor between social movements and the party (see Chapter 8). While social movements may cultivate the rituals and roles of protest, the party should confront the task of capitalizing on that protest. Hence Offe advocates a process of self-rationalization in terms of organizational politics, social programs, and relationship to the constitution and the state's monopoly on force.[32] Hirsch, in contrast, interprets such "maturation" processes as essentially denying the democratic coordination of general with particular interests, especially when they lead to acceptance of the state monopoly on force. Instead, he advocates the "reappropriation of politics by society."[33] The Green Party, to critics like Hirsch, may be heading for a future as a "postmodern" or alternative "yuppie party." In fact, since Hirsch wrote Chapter 9, the eco-libertarian position has dissipated into the majoritarian Realo and Aufbruch positions. While this might be read as indication that the Green Party is well on the way to participating, more or less consciously, in the (eco-)modernization of capitalist society, the verdict is not yet in. As long as both utopian-fundamentalist and pragmatic-realist demands remain in the Green Party, the situation is open. While the events around the collapse of the Eastern communist regimes and German reunification have certainly strengthened desires for *Realpolitik*, radical and disruptive politics are still practiced by the party, as illustrated, for example, by the campaign for desertion from the military during the build-up for the Gulf War.[34]

## The Green Party after German Unification

Many Germans were initially skeptical about or even opposed to unity. During the postwar decades, the two societies had moved further and further apart, so that when the Eastern regime collapsed in October and November of 1989, almost everyone conceived of the solution to the German Question in terms of two separate states slowly moving toward confederated structures. The Ten-Point Plan proposed by Chancellor Helmut Kohl on November 28 sought to establish unity on such a basis. But the popular pressures for unification were much stronger. Although the momentum surprised all of Germany's political parties, the Green Party's response led to its devastating electoral defeat on the national level and its temporary exodus from Bundestag. Selecting *Klimakatastrophe* ("climatic catastrophe") as central issue for the electoral campaign leading up to the first all-German elections can only be interpreted as an expression of denial, an attempt to avoid bidding farewell to the leftist myth of the socialist state. In any case, the problems raised by unification radicalized the contradictions within the "movement party" in new ways.

Initially, the Greens were excited by the rise of opposition movements that led to the toppling of the East German totalitarian system. In many ways, they appeared similar to the new social movements that had given rise to the Greens themselves. But soon it became clear that the dissident groups that formed into political parties under the pressure of state elections in the East represented very different issues and agendas, shaped by the totalitarian past (hence the emphasis on civil liberties) and by the economic and social problems bequeathed by the dissolution of the old regime. The ecological and feminist consciousness shaping West German political culture and represented in the Western Green Party did not (and still does not) exist to the same degree in the East.

Increasingly aware of these differences and intent on implementing democratic process, the Greens sought a gradual, grassroots-up federation of Eastern and Western groups, in contrast to all the other parties, which swallowed up their East German counterpart whole, virtually expropriating the East German electoral process. The partner groups with whom the Greens engaged were a set of essentially movement federations, the so-called "citizens' movements" that had carried out the East German revolution. Within a matter of a month or two, these dissident groups were forced to transform themselves into electoral parties while still having to devote considerable energy to guarding the closed offices of the State Security Police (Stasi). Consequently, they were insufficiently developed to succeed in the first free elections in the German Democratic Republic (GDR) in March 1990.[35] In preparing for the all-German elections of December 1990, the West German Greens respected the independence of the Eastern groups and their combined slate of "Alliance' 90" and the Eastern Green Party[36] and postponed the process of assimilation and merging until after the elections. The results of this running separately are well known: the Eastern ticket won slightly more than the required 5 percent,[37] while the Western Greens fell short with only 4.8 percent. A party unified like the others might have responded to the real constraints of representation, but this was precluded by the Greens' rigid grassroots conception of democracy.

At the same time, the debates over a new constitution again radicalized the concept of grassroots democracy. Like several other groups on the left, the Greens had attempted to combine unification with demands for constitutional provisions for a multicultural, nonnationalistic Germany. Voters of the new Germany, however, were less interested in an (ecological or postmaterialist) critique of growth than in growth guaranteed. And the nationalist fervor of the period gave no advantage to a cosmopolitan, antinationalist party that had advocated a two-state solution for too long.[38]

Events eventually compelled the Greens to abandon the two-state proposal.[39] Needing to rescue his government from the erosion of public support suggested by the electoral breakthrough of the radical right, and forced to do something about the immense refugee problem generated by the disintegration of the Eastern regime, Chancellor Kohl decided to place himself and his party in the vanguard of the movement for German unification. The West German government rapidly shifted from a policy of confederation to one of "union"—that is, absorption of the GDR via economic and monetary union. While using the power of his office to promote unification, the chancellor also made it clear that financial assistance would be tied to conditions the Modrow-Round-Table government could not fulfill.

In this context, the Greens aligned themselves with Modrow's plan for a confederation in several stages; they demanded that negotiations be slowed down and opposition groups represented in the negotiations. The poor showing of movement parties and electoral lists in the Volkskammer elections made it obvious that these positions left the Greens isolated and practically irrelevant to the processes of development in the GDR. Furthermore, splits over the two-state position were developing in the party itself. While some radicals left to join the Radical Left,[40] others, mainly eco-socialists, defected to the successor of the East German Communist Party, the Party of

Democratic Socialism (PDS).[41] These developments prepared the ground for the party finally, at its federal congress in June 1990, to approve a first joint statement of Green and alternative parties and movements from the two Germanys. While rejecting the state treaty signed by the finance ministers of the two Germanys in May 1990, it expressed explicit support for German unification. The adoption of this Joint Declaration on the State Treaty satisfied both realist and radical intentions: it moved the party back into the center of politics, while its insistence on accomplishing unification through drawing up a new constitution kept it connected to more radical-democratic aspirations.

While Realos had been more likely to recognize the legitimacy of the East Germans' desire for a material quality of life on par with that enjoyed by the West Germans, eco-socialists expressed bitterness about the "servile" desires of the former East Germans.[42] Their rejection of the East Germans' plebiscite for unification complicated the good reasons for insisting on the independence of the German states with a fundamental mistrust of the German people, and in this way betrayed an elitist and paternalistic conception of democracy (cf. Demirović's comments in this volume). Characterizing the East Germans as susceptible to Western conservative parties' promises of economic stability, or the PDS as a means of revitalizing the Greens' anti-capitalist profile,[43] was insulting to East German voters, to whom the Christian Democratic Union (CDU) appeared as a substantial and welcome improvement over "real, existing" socialist state-security agencies.

Only a year later, in March 1991, mass demonstrations (reviving the tradition of the Monday demonstrations that toppled the old regime) targeted the CDU government. Instead of the promised improvements, people in the East have been faced with a daunting array of problems. Increasingly, they hold the Bonn government responsible for delaying the business investment needed to modernize the backward productive infrastructure in the former GDR and for throwing its citizens into situations of extreme social and economic insecurity.

The eight delegates of Alliance '90/Greens[44] in the all-German parliament were overwhelmed with trying to represent the concerns of the new second-class citizens. The rump of the old West German Green Party, meanwhile, began to carry out radical reform of the party organization at the federal level. Centrists in the Realos and Left Forum used the loss of the 44 Bundestag seats along with all the resources that came with them to advance the party's "maturation process": the party convention in Neumünster in 1991 sealed the basic compromise between Realos and the Left Forum, saw the exodus of the radical ecologists associated with Jutta Ditfurth, and left behind all variants of fundamentalism. Individual leadership as well as professionalization were explicitly acknowledged, the federal executive was trimmed, and the principle of participatory democracy was abolished, while the party organization itself was democratized by the introduction of a party plebiscite. After extensive and careful negotiations—Alliance '90, with fewer than 3,000 members, had to fear being swallowed up by the 40,000-member Western sister party—the merger was completed and ratified at the Leipzig convention in May 1993. In time for the 1994 national elections, party leaders unveiled a detailed program concentrating on 10 reform projects that were to be presented to a possible red-green government. Thus professionalized, pragmatic, and centrist, the "reformed" Green party won 7.3 percent of the vote (49 delegates) and became the third-largest *Fraktion* after the CDU and SPD.[45] At least in the West, where their vote share increased from 4.8 percent in 1990 to 7.9 percent in 1994, their future as an established party is no longer in doubt. In the East, however, the party's vote total dropped from 5.9 percent in 1990 to 4.3 percent: the PDS significantly outpolled the Greens, pushing them to fourth place in the East. While the fall 1995 elections in Berlin woke new hopes (10 percent of the vote in East Berlin went to Alliance '90/Greens), the sociocultural milieus that form the constituency for the Greens in the West remain far weaker in the East or are absorbed by the PDS.[46]

The continued or even growing importance of the Greens has been confirmed by the gains in the 1995 state elections (in the West), where they polled 11.2 percent in Hesse, more than 13 percent in the city-state of Bremen, and 10 percent in North Rhine–Westphalia, producing a red-green governing coalition in Germany's largest state. While the chances for a red-green governing coalition on the federal level were dimmed by the simultaneous big losses of the SPD, the Greens are now securely established as a left-wing ecological reform party. To understand how and why they got here, their first 10 years are of crucial importance.

This book is organized into six sections. The following section presents the history of the Green Party, the political positions of its factions, and the composition of its electoral and grassroots support. Part III examines the formation of the Green Party's identity. In this section, engaged German social scientists and activists analyze such pillars of Green Party identity as grassroots democracy and feminism, and the party's relationship to the extraparliamentary social movements. Part IV confronts the debate about the role of the Green Party in German politics. Claus Offe and Joachim Hirsch, both sympathetic social scientists, defend rather opposite conclusions. Together, Chapters 2 through 9 explore a central contradiction: that the Green Party has served to retraditionalize political orientations and to strengthen parliamentarism as such, while also achieving real gains for progressive movements. Part V looks beyond the German horizon. In Chapter 10, John Ely explores how the several European green parties have linked up in the European parliament and the ways in which American politics might be informed by the German Green experience.

Part VI consists of documents. This section includes original manifestos, speeches, and position papers covering the diverse positions represented in the founding efforts of the Green Party, the different currents within the party, the provocative and dramatic nature of the new themes raised in the old parliaments, and some of the controversial positions, heatedly debated, that make up the political identity of the Green Party.

These primary texts as well as the political posters reproduced illustrate the flavor and texture of the Greens' first 10 years better than any analytic text could: their raucous public arguments and their innovative campaign tactics, the heat as well as the background of the intense controversies within the party, the rich sources and innovative energy of the Greens' political struggle but also the gradual erosion of many of their original goals.

## NOTES

Special thanks go to Joan Vidal and Jane Barry, without whom this project would not have been completed, and to Steve Katz, without whom it would not have gotten started.

1. "Model Germany" was originally the political slogan of the Social Democratic Party's state-guided industrial modernization program. Through the 1970s this label came to stand for the central corporatist accord directed by political, business, and labor leaders. Cf. Joachim Hirsch, *Der Sicherheitsstaat: Das "Modell Deutschland," seine Krisen und die neuen sozialen Bewegungen* (Frankfurt: Europäische Verlagsanstalt, 1980).

2. Cf. Chapter 10, by John Ely, in this volume.

3. Cf. Joachim Raschke, *Krise der Grünen: Bilanz und Neubeginn* (Marburg: Schüren, 1991).

4. Anthroposophy (the wisdom of humanity) is a spiritual science wherein nature is deduced from the nature of humanity. It was founded by Rudolf Steiner (1860–1925). The Anthroposophical Society was formed in 1913 to study his writings and to support the Waldorf school.

5. In the German parliamentary system, the delegates of a party form a *Fraktion*. While formally similar to the delegation of Republicans or Democrats in the U.S. Congress, a *Fraktion* has a much higher profile and is more formally organized because of the greater importance of parties in parliamentary government under a system of proportional representation.

6. The so-called imperative mandate binds parliamentarians to party resolutions, allowing party members to directly control the parliamentarians' work. "Rotation" was practiced until 1987. All representatives (with the exception of Petra Kelly, who refused to "rotate") stepped down for their office in mid-term and were succeeded by the next person on the electoral list. This "rotation principle" was applied to both parliamentary and party functions in order to prevent the emergence of a political elite pursuing its own professional interests.

7. Cf also Pinl's "Was auch die grüne Welt im innersten zusammenhält: Notizen über ein

Prinzip: Seilschaften," originally in Die Grünen, eds., *Reader zur 2. Bundesfrauenkonferenz der Grünen* (Bonn: Die Grünen, 1987). The conference was held on November 28–29, 1987, in Cologne.

8. Between 30 and 35 percent of the members are women, about 13,000. Of those, maybe 5,000 are feminists.

9. Cf. Klaus-Peter Klingelschmitt, "Parteifunktionäre unter sich? Hessens Grüne auf der Suche nach der Basis," *die tageszeitung,* November 30, 1989, p. 11.

10. The richest source of jobs and resources has been the Bundestag, where the Greens were entitled to fill about 80 full-time posts, and where the *Fraktion* employed about 150 persons. The pattern also holds true on the level of state and local parliaments, where the resources are not as plentiful, however.

11. Neither the journal *Kommune,* in which all currents find expression, nor the Green-Alternative yearbooks of 1986/87 and 1988 deal with issues of local politics. (See the introduction to the German-language bibliography in this volume.)

12. The more experienced and professional way in which the state government coalitions between SPD and Greens in Lower Saxony (1990) and Hesse (1991) were initiated indicates that the precarious and tension-ridden initial phase of red-green coalitions has come to an end.

13. For an evaluation of local red-green governing coalitions in the state of Hesse, see Udo Bullmann, "Mehr als nur der Unterbau: Die Zusammenarbeit von Sozialdemokraten und Grünen in den Kommunen," in Richard Meng, ed., *Modell rot-grün? Auswertung eines Versuchs* (Hamburg: VSA, 1987) 54–90; for a study of Berlin's brief red-green state government, see Gudrun Heinrich, *Rot-Grün in Berlin: Die AL Berlin in der Regierungsverantwortung 1989–1990* (Marburg: Schüren, 1993); and for a survey of red-green collaborations on the local level, see Bodo Zeuner and Jörg Wischermann, *Rot-Grün in den Kommunen* (Opladen: Leske & Budrich, 1995).

14. On American progressive local politics, see Pierre Clavel, *The Progressive City* (New Brunswick: Rutgers University Press, 1986).

15. The publication *Alternative Kommunalpolitik (AKP)* has appeared regularly since 1985. That year its editorial board also published a comprehensive *Handbook for Alternative Local Politics,* which has been updated since.

16. Cf. Roland Roth, "Städtische soziale Bewegungen und grün-alternative Kommunalpolitik," in Hubert Heinelt and Hellmut Wollman, eds., *Brennpunkt Stadt* (Basel: Birkhäuser, 1990) 167–86.

17. Note, however, that these colorful actions and provocative issues were introduced into the German Bundestag primarily in the early stages.

18. The latter two are translated in Eva Kolinsky, ed., *The Greens in West Germany* (Oxford: Berg, 1989) 250–52.

19. Interviewed in *tageszeitung,* February 13, 1989, p. 9. After serving for four years in the party leadership, Regina Michalik has turned away from party work to return to the women's movement.

20. BAG Frauen was established in 1983 and played an important role in preparing the antidiscrimination legislation as well as the quota regulations.

21. Mothers' Politics was established at the National Delegates' Congress, May 1–3, 1987.

22. Gisela Erler, *Frauenzimmer: Für eine Politik des Unterschieds* (Berlin, 1985) 115. Erler was the theoretical leader of the Mothers' faction in the Green Party.

23. See "Mothers' Manifesto" in Chapter 14, and Mechthild Jansen, "'Motherhood Is Beautiful'—Ein Beitrag zur Auseinandersetzung um das Mütterkonzept," *Kommune* 5, no 6 (1987) 66–71; Claudia Pinl, "Neue (grüne) Mütterlichkeit—Eine ökologische Frauenpolitik,"

in Die Grünen, ed., *Frauen und Ökologie: Gegen den Machbarkeitswahn* (Cologne: Kölner Volksblatt, 1987); Barbara Bussfeld, "Grüne Frauenpolitik in der Krise: Anmerkungen zur 2. Bundesfrauenkonferenz," *Kommune* 6, no. 1 (1988) 54.

24. A special section on prisoners in the 1980 program of the Green Party challenges the justice of West German legal procedures and sees prisoners as victims of a repressive system of law enforcement.

25. Cf. Martha Rosenkranz, "Das Ende eines Kavaliersdelikts," presentation on the debate over the minimum sentence for rape, reprinted in *die tageszeitung,* June 10, 1989.

26. Besides militant demonstrations, the Autonomen also engaged in other militant activities, such as cutting down high-tension lines to challenge government and corporate energy policies. Geronimo, *Feuer und Flamme: Zur Geschichte und Gegenwart der Autonomen* (Berlin: Edition ID-Archiv, 1990), provides background on the Autonomen.

27. See, for example, Benny Härlin's campaign statement in Chapter 13.

28. Antje Vollmer and Otto Schily, "Sonst sehe ich schwarz für die Grünen," *Der Spiegel,* March 25, 1986, pp. 66–81.

29. See Chapter 14. Note that in European states "domestic" policy, as well as the office of minister of the interior, deals with internal law and order, not social policy or a country's national parks.

30. The party made these calls at a party congress in May 1989, just after the radical right repeated its success in the local elections in the state of Hesse.

31. Fischer spearheaded the transformation of the realist wing into an "ecological civil rights" orientation in contrast to a leftist "social ecological" position. Cf. also his speech on political asylum in Chapter 13.

32. For a more elaborate version see his "Reflections on the Institutional Self-Transformation of Movement Politics: A Tentative Stage Model," in Russell J. Dalton and Manfred Kuechler, eds., *Challenging the Political Order* (Oxford: Basil Blackwell/Polity, 1990) 232–51.

33. For the background of this position, see Joachim Hirsch and Roland Roth, *Das neue Gesicht des Kapitalismus* (Hamburg: VSA, 1986). A brief English summary may be found in Joachim Hirsch, "The Crisis of Fordism: Transformations of the 'Keynesian' Security State, and New Social Movements," *Research in Social Movements, Conflict, and Change* 10 (1988) 43–55.

34. The Green Party leaflets asking soldiers to desert were confiscated by the attorney general, thus publicizing both the issue and the campaign. See *Der Spiegel,* November 19, 1990, p. 100.

35. The parties that came to power in East Germany were essentially extensions of the West Germany political system, and the extensions of Bonn's governing coalition were in a clear majority.

36. "Bündnis '90" joined the "Initiative for Peace and Human Rights" (a civil rights group active since 1985) and the two more recently founded (September 1989) citizens' groups New Forum and Democracy Now, whose memberships had exploded during 1989. The (Eastern) Green Party (founded in November 1989) and an Independent Women's Association (UFV, founded in February 1990) formed another electoral coalition (Bündnis Grüne Partei/Unabhängiger Frauenverband). The two coalitions ran separately in the first free elections in East Germany in March 1990 (Grüne/UFV: 1.96 percent, 8 seats; B '90: 2.9 percent, 12 seats), but formed one parliamentarian faction within the short-lived East German government. They ran one ticket (Bündnis '90/Grüne) for the all-German elections in December 1990.

37. Because of the 5 percent barrier, the movement alliance, which did not campaign in the West, would have been excluded if the Supreme Court had not ruled that the votes in the first post-unification national election would be tallied separately for the East and West.

38. The declaration released by the party's federal executive committee in Saarbrücken in November 1989 argued that only recognition of the GDR as a sovereign state would advance the cause of reform; reunification would amount to annexation and a defeat of the democratic movement. The SPD also favored the two-state solution for too long, contributing to the wide margin with which East German voters chose CDU Chancellor Kohl in their referendum on unification.

39. They abandoned the two-state proposal at the federal party congress in Dortmund in June 1990.

40. This group, founded in April 1989, not only criticized the process of unification as pushed through by the CDU government in Bonn but engaged in directly antiunification activities.

41. Having lost the battle over governing coalitions with the Realos, many in this camp had been looking for a way to leave the party. A truly "anticapitalist" party appealed to the Maoist roots; the substantial financial resources of the old East German Communists may have helped to bring about these defections.

42. Cf. "Deutschland erwache?—Lieber nicht!" the February 2, 1990, position paper of the (eco-socialist-dominated) Hamburg Green-Alternative List, in *grüner basis-dienst*, February 1990, pp. 8–9.

43. For example, Jutta Österle-Schwerin, "Dennoch—die Grünen" and Gerd Hickmann, "Moderne und postmoderne Parteien: Die PDS als Chance zur neuen ökologischen Profilbildung der Grünen," *Kommune* 8, no. 11 (November 1990) 44–45.

44. Only two of the delegates were members of the Green Party, which is, in spite of the extraordinary environmental problems in the East, significantly weaker (1,246 members in 1992) than the dissident citizens' movements in the ex-GDR (membership estimates varied between 3,000 and 5,000).

45. The "reformed" Greens had already done well at the 1993 and 1994 state elections (Hamburg 13.5 percent; Lower Saxony 7.4 percent) as well as in the elections for the European Parliament (10 percent).

46. In the fall elections of 1994 the Eastern Greens lost three of four state parliamentary fractions; currently they are represented in only one of the five state parliaments.

# II

## Emergence and Characteristics of the West German Green Party

## Chapter 2

ॐ

# A Brief History of
# the German Green Party

HORST MEWES

January 1990 saw the tenth anniversary of the German Green Party. There were no joyous celebrations. True, the party had outlived predictions of its impending demise, and the elections to the European Parliament in June 1989, in which the Greens received 8.4 percent of the vote, seemed to assure their immediate future as a small party. For many Greens, however, the party, after only a decade, was ossifying,[1] while unresolved internal struggles limited it as an effective political force. Furthermore, it appeared that recent political events were relegating the Greens to the political sidelines. The dramatic changes in Eastern Europe, together with the November 1989 revolution in the German Democratic Republic, had brought to the forefront the problem of German national unification and the future balance of power in Europe—a problem for which the Greens, more than any other party, were ideologically and politically unprepared.

But these political developments merely exacerbated a problem intrinsic to the Green Party since its inception. A ubiquitous sense of "crisis" has accompanied it from the beginning. The Greens, more than other parties were preoccupied with internal debates over their common platform.[2]

This perpetual identity crisis can be said to result from the Greens' enormously ambitious original goals, as well as from the political and intellectual diversity of their constituent parts. Together, these factors have made for a volatile history of faction formation and struggles over priorities and strategy. The party never followed the stereotypical developmental pattern of a conventional political party in a Western industrial democracy. It certainly never conformed easily to the rules of constitutionally ordained party government in the Federal Republic. Though some might view this "failure" as one of the Greens' greatest accomplishments, it also necessarily limited the party's ability to realize its political goals.[3]

29

The ambitious, and in some respects unprecedented, goals of the early Green Party can be summarized as follows.

1. As an *environmental party* (their primary identification), the Greens intended to inaugurate a "new politics" whereby ecological politics would supersede and take precedence over traditional ideological and interest politics. This "postmaterialist" politics clearly failed, despite the growing urgency of environmental issues, as environmental politics became the captive of traditional ideological struggles between left-leaning groups within the party.

2. The Greens also intended to become a *"social movement party,"* reflecting and representing the interests of movement activists ranging from antinuclear and peace groups to feminists, countercultural "alternative groups," senior citizens (Gray Panthers), gays, and others. This aim not only raised questions about the power relations and organizational links between the parliamentary party and various external groups and movements, but also raised anew longstanding questions about the party's priorities in the face of conflicting demands by rival social movements.[4] Many Greens have charged that defining themselves as a social movement party has turned the party organization itself into a fiefdom of various groups intent upon defending their particular interests rather than creating a party consensus and a party program capable of attracting a wider body of potential voters.

3. The commitment of the Greens to principles of *participatory democracy,* however undefined, strengthened the tendency mentioned above. This important and admirable practice opened the party organization to participation by representatives of various social movements and citizen initiatives, but it has hindered the kind of oligarchization typical of "establishment" mass political parties, though other kinds of elite formation are evident. Adherence to this principle has also meant that party decisions are subject to shifting majorities at party conferences, thus preventing centralized party decisions. More importantly, as mentioned above, it has not been able to prevent fractionalization.

The Greens' pursuit of these goals has been marked by continuous conflict between the advocates of *Realpolitik* and the "fundamentalists." Fundamentalists like Jutta Ditfurth refuse to enter political alliances with the Social Democrats for fear of compromising the long-range aim of wholesale changes in industrial society, and for fear of becoming prisoner of the establishment's "political game." Reformists, on the other hand, clearly in the ascendency after 10 years, believe in the necessity, especially for a small party, of entering alliances and realizing in small increments what otherwise would remain politically ineffective "utopian" goals.[5] Environmental politics, insofar as it entails revolutionary changes in society and economics, thus leads to the formation of "extremists" and "moderates" similar to those of earlier revolutionary movements. But these labels also reflect basically different attitudes toward politics: many Green fundamentalists, whether out of personal conviction or the judgment that representative democracy is part of the socioeconomic system that causes ecological suicide, simply do not trust the political process and the politicians running it.[6]

## The Origins of the Green Party

Widespread awareness of environmental deterioration emerged almost simultaneously toward the end of the 1960s in the United States, Europe, and Japan. Characteristically, public concern expressed itself first as grassroots protest over isolated local environmental threats.[7] Within a short time, the danger was officially recognized as a global problem by the United Nations, and many governments of the industrial world passed their first comprehensive environmental legislation, without, however, eliminating almost continuous public protests during the 1970s. On the contrary, governments, increasingly succumbed to economic pressures. In the aftermath of the oil crisis of 1973, and the subsequent decline of economic growth and rising inflation, questions of future energy supplies and problems of "reindustrialization" took priority over environmentalism.

In Germany, concern for environmental decay spawned thousands of local, independently acting citizen groups ( *Bürgerinitiativen*). By 1979 an estimated 50,000 such groups existed, rivaling in total membership the approximately 1.6 million registered members of political parties.[8] This degree of spontaneous participation in protest actions was unprecedented in the political history of modern Germany. Even during the student protests and anti–Vietnam War demonstrations of the late 1960s, this "extraparliamentary opposition" was unable to establish patterns of continuous local action. Instead, the remnants of the student protests broke up into a multitude of leftist factions isolated from the rest of the population. Still, while the formation of citizen action groups was an expression of a wider democratization of German life, we should not underestimate the role of the extraparliamentary opposition as a precursor of such citizen activism.

Above all else, it was the issue of nuclear energy that was increasingly to serve as catalyst and rallying point for citizen concern. The government's plans to focus on nuclear power in response to the energy crisis triggered local, regional, and finally national protest. The potential threat of a "nuclear security state" served as the negative symbol of the first nationwide protest movement.[9] Significantly, not until the rise of the European and German peace movements toward the beginning of the 1980s did the protest against nuclear power stations also turn against the stationing of nuclear weapons on German soil. The first national protest against the nuclear reactor at Wyhl—held in 1975 and joined by local farmers, citizens, and young protesters from all parts of Germany—still consciously avoided the problem of nuclear weapons in order to remain politically neutral.

National organization of local protest groups followed quickly. In 1972, 16 citizen groups founded the Federal Association of Environmental Citizen Initiatives (Bundesverband Bürgerinitiativen Umweltschutz, BBU), which would soon comprise more than a thousand affiliated action groups and more than 300,000 individual members. Though intended as a nonpartisan organization, the BBU was more than a mere national clearinghouse for environmentalists. It perceived itself, instead, as a citizen initiative at the national level, able to mobilize and coordinate support on pressing national environmental issues. Thus, the BBU put into practice the concept of cooperative citizen groups as a new national force operating independently of parliament and established parties. As the new manifestation of participatory democracy, and as the advocate of the principles of "simplification, decentralization, and deconcentration" in the name of more "humane power," the BBU conjured up the memory of traditional socialist council-democracy in the new context of ecological politics.[10] It was the BBU that first proposed joint action between ecologists and peace protesters, and together with Protestant church groups it led in organizing the first major German peace conference in Hamburg in June 1981.[11]

Although a BBU member, Petra Kelly, was a central figure in the discussions leading to the founding of a national Green Party, the BBU itself was not officially involved. Under the leadership of Jo Leinen, it had kept a critical distance from the new party, though it cooperated with the Greens in public protest actions. Leinen, a member of the Social Democratic Party (and minister for the environment in the state of Saar from 1985 til 1994), advocated wider alliances in a "nonpartisan" spirit of environmentalists with political parties and trade unions. He remained critical of the concept of a separate ecology party, and later charged that the Greens as a party unwittingly served to discourage independent grassroots action.[12]

Loose coalitions of independent citizen groups made their first attempt to enter electoral and party politics in 1977. In retrospect, the steps toward founding an environmental protest party can be construed as obeying the developmental sequence of the movement itself.[13] According to this view, a party organization was necessary first to express the unity intrinsic in ecological politics and second to provide continuity and coherence to dispersed citizen groups who otherwise might lose their direction and dynamics. Another, probably more significant reason was the prominence of political parties in the German political system itself. Since the major established parties dominate access to politics and indeed the public realm itself, the temptation to challenge them on their own terms tended to be strong. Furthermore, since the public tends to equate legitimacy as a spokesperson for political interests with being an elected party member, protesters seized the opportunity to legitimize themselves and their protest and challenge the established parties on their own terms. These motives at least appear to have been operating in some of the earliest efforts to start Green parties at the state level, as for instance in Lower Saxony in 1977. There, antinuclear organizers and environmentalists concerned about the pollution of the North Sea won 3.6 percent of the vote in June 1978.[14]

In the traditionally Social Democratic city-state of Bremen, a coalition of former Social Democrats, environmentalists, independent leftists, and antinuclear groups established the "Bremen Green Lists" in the spring of 1979. As was to be the case in other major urban areas like Hamburg and Berlin, the effort to establish an ecology party involved lengthy and heated debates among left-wing factions, including unorthodox communists interested in utilizing the new issue of ecology for their own more traditional political advancement. In Bremen, efforts at cooperation failed, and such unorthodox communists established an "Alternative List" that competed with the Greens in the state elections of 1979. However, many prominent independent leftists supported the Green list; the former student leader Rudi Dutschke, for instance, campaigned personally for the new primacy of ecological politics and supported the Greens. The election results in that fall caused a small sensation in Germany when for the first time the Greens rose above the 5 percent minimum vote barrier and entered a state parliament.[15]

While the Greens in Bremen were primarily left-leaning environmentalists, advocating "ecology, decentralization, participatory democracy, and nonviolence," ecology was secondary in the process of party formation in Hamburg and Berlin. (Such differences contained the seeds of the internal conflicts of the national Green Party, which would be founded a few years later.) In Hamburg, for instance, the candidate list of March 1978 was backed by a coalition of about 200 small, independent "liberation" and emancipation groups, ranging from unorthodox Maoist communists to autonomous radical feminists. Again, the Greens refused to cooperate with communists and campaigned independently. When in early 1980 a small but influential Maoist party, the Communist League, split into Marxist-Leninist and independent democratic factions, the latter joined the Greens. For the 1982 Hamburg elections, Greens and "alternatives" still dominated by Marxist-Leninists formed a successful electoral coalition, guaranteeing equal status to each. Environmental and social issues were to carry equal political weight. Some of the unorthodox Greens from Hamburg, notably Thomas Ebermann and Rainer Trampert, were later to play leading roles in the national Green Party.

Berlin's "Alternative List for Democracy and Environmental Protection," founded in October 1978, was to become the most "radical" of all state parties. Dominated by some Marxist-Leninist and Maoist groups, as well as independent Marxists and socialists, the Berlin party in addition represented various feminist, gay liberation, and countercultural groups, including squatter activists. The party's preoccupation with "Marxist" issues was less characteristic of other Green state parties. In May 1981, the Berlin Alternative list received 7.2 percent of the vote and moved into the legislature.[16] Two years later, during the federal election campaign of March 1983, the Alternative List split over the issue of violent protests. While the federal party proclaimed nonviolence as a fundamental principle, the Berlin party refused to go along. In addition, many Greens expressed concern that the alternative groups in Berlin and Hamburg were intent upon subverting the new party into a leftist social democratic entity that would link up with the left wing of the Social Democrats. Clearly, Green Party factional struggles began the moment the party was founded.[17]

In stark contrast to the developments in the northern urban centers, the Green Party in the southwestern, politically more conservative state of Baden-Württemberg was founded by rather eclectic circles not easily fitted into traditional categories of left and right. Aside from regionally influential anthroposophic circles like the Achberger Kreis, concerned with finding a "third way" between communism and capitalism, the party was mainly founded by conservative environmentalists with a bent for radical activism, and by independent nationalists. The conservative environmentalists had gathered together in a party called Green Action Future (Grüne Aktion Zukunft, GAZ), founded by Herbert Gruhl, former Christian Democrat and prominent author of an early bestseller on global environmental destruction. The independent nationalists, a tiny middle-class party under the direction of August Haussleiter, had been advocating ecological socialism since 1974. In March 1980 the new Green Party received 5.3 percent of the vote and has since then established itself as one of the most "moderate" of the various state parties under the early influence of Wolf-Dieter Hasenclever. Hasenclever resigned from his party post in 1985, mainly over differences concerning the party's rotation principle.[18]

Simultaneously with, but mostly independently of, the formation of Green parties in individual states, individuals and groups launched the laborious process of founding a national environmental party. From the outset, the process was strongly influenced by former leftists and independents intent upon utilizing environmentalism as a new unifying force transcending traditional political divisions. Throughout the 1970s, independent Marxists and socialists, including former student protesters like Dutschke and the Czech emigrant Milan Horacek, debated the possibility of founding a "free, independent, and undogmatic" socialist party. In the spring of 1977, Horacek explored the possibilities of uniting various leftist circles and ecologists, but with little success. In meetings at Vlotho (fall 1977), Troisdorf (1978), and Kassel (1978) a diverse group including Horacek, Haussleiter, Gruhl, the artist Joseph Beuys, Petra Kelly, Ossip K. Flechtheim, Rudolf Bahro, and others continued the effort to create an alliance of environmentalists spanning the political spectrum from right to left, from "Gruhl to Dutschke." With anthroposophists and ecologists from northern Germany, this group established the Political Association of Greens (Sonstige Politische Vereinigung Die Grünen), which received 3.2 percent of the vote in the elections to the European parliament in 1979.

It was this group and its supporters who were instrumental in founding the Green Party, "Die Grünen."[19] Bahro, who was to leave the party in protest during 1985, was perhaps the key figure in creating a theoretical as well as practical bridge between German socialists and the new ecological perspective. Bahro rose to prominence as an East German dissident by publishing a critical analysis of the communist regime from a humanist Marxist perspective. Immediately after his release from prison in the German Democratic Republic (GDR) in October 1979, he moved to the Federal Republic and involved himself in the new politics of ecology. At a socialist conference in May 1980 in Kassel, Bahro invited about 1,200 delegates from most independent leftist groups to discuss "ecology and Marxism." For him the ecological crisis would usher in the final demise of capitalism, but it had also made the old Marxist class analysis obsolete, since workers as consumers participated in the destruction wrought by advanced capitalist society. Not class interest but the species interest of humankind was now to guide revolutionary strategy. This, according to Bahro, required an unprecedentedly broad coalition of all groups suffering from the destructive forces of capitalist society. The coalition would be led by those whose spiritual values could overcome the cross materialism of the modern consumer economy.[20]

Bahro's grand vision of a coalition including the "overwhelming majority" of the population never got off the ground. In fact, the new Green Party was not even to include the environmental conservatives who participated in its planning. The Greens emerged as a national party from a series of meetings at Offenbach, Karlsruhe, Saarbrücken, and Dortmund during late 1979 and early 1980. About 1,000 delegates from local and regional green groups and

250 representatives from "alternative" and countercultural groups agreed, after vituperative debates, to create a party by January 1980. The basic party program, passed in March 1980, contained an array of concrete proposals for environmental policy, framed in what was ultimately a "utopian" design for a pacifist, environmentally compatible welfare state, with totally emancipated, self-governing green republics existing autonomously in a pacified world of international mutual assistance and political harmony.[21]

But the small group of original "founders" had failed to attain what to them had been the most crucial goal. The "historical compromise" between political conservatives and leftists, between "Christians and socialists" for the rescue of human and Western civilization, in Bahro's words, did not materialize.[22] His solidarity with conservatives like Gruhl did not bring them into the new party. A heated controversy arose over the admission to the convention of sectarian Marxist groups and various alternative lists. Old-fashioned political conservatives and moderates feared the politics of these groups more than they trusted the ability of "environmentalism" to transcend such politics. Further, differences developed immediately about the economic and foreign policy implications of the various conceptions of "ecological politics." The concept, it was discovered very quickly, was not sufficient to blend "traditional" political differences into a new harmonious unity.

A majority of Green delegates supported cooperating with independent Marxists and other radical groups, while excluding Moscow-oriented and authoritarian, doctrinaire ones. At Karlsruhe it was also decided to prohibit dual party membership for Green Party members, to prevent "infiltration" by outside organized forces. At Saarbrücken, however, sympathizers of the left and counterculture groups prevailed in determining the content of the new party platform. Political conservatives saw these groups as repackaging the traditional leftist social program under the new label of an environmental party. Most objectionable was the leftists' tendency to view "all political problems, especially ecological problems . . . from the perspective of class struggle." The conservative Gruhl considered the economic part of the new party platform to be a "fairytale utopia," sharing the technocratic thinking of establishment parties.[23] In addition, instead of prognosticating an age of scarcity, the new program simply presented a new ecological version of the old leftist promise of a perfect, harmonious society. All prominent conservatives had resigned from the new party by the summer of 1980. After being defeated in an election for the new party executive committee, Gruhl formed his own Ecological Democratic Party. It never won any offices.

In October 1980, the Greens received 1.5 percent of the vote in their first federal election, well below the minimum 5 percent required to enter parliament. But the party quickly began to show more electoral success at the state level. It moved into the state legislature of Baden-Württemberg during March 1980, with 5.3 percent of the vote. In May 1981 the Berlin Alternative List received 7.2 percent. In 1982, the Greens succeeded in Hamburg (7.7 percent), Lower Saxony (6.5 percent), and Hesse (8.0 percent). Bremen followed with 5.4 percent in September 1983. These successes in more than half of the German states prepared the Greens for the federal elections of March 1983, when the party improved its performance to 5.6 percent of the popular vote and, for the first time, sent 27 members to the Bundestag.

Prior to this milestone election, the party conventions at Offenbach (1981) and Hagen (1982), together with the election congress at Sindelfingen in January 1983, had set the trend for the internal party conflicts of the future. Members of various Alternative Lists and unorthodox Marxist groups clearly expanded their influence in the party committees at the expense of those favoring a more nonpartisan ecological orientation. The party was inexorably moving toward a position to the left of the Social Democrats. At Hagen, Rainer Trampert from Hamburg, formerly an unorthodox communist, was elected head of the federal executive committee.

Since Trampert favored an eventual working relationship with the Social Democratic Party, the question of a possible alliance with the SPD quickly became the main point of contention; it was to continue to preoccupy the Greens over the years. At first, it was Trampert versus Bahro. The latter favored a broad coalition including conservatives over a narrower orientation toward social democracy. But the convention at Hagen did pass a catalogue of eight points as preconditions for a possible left-wing coalition. It included demands for an immediate shutdown of all nuclear plants and a stop to the introduction of cruise missiles and Pershing 2's into Germany by the North Atlantic Treaty Organization (NATO). In the area of economic policy, however, the Greens were unable to reach agreement, as various leftist proposals clashed with ecological perspectives or more conventional defenses of free-market economics from liberal Greens hailing from southern Germany.

The controversy over the state's monopoly on force was raised at these early party meetings. At a convention in Hannover during June 1983, Trampert proposed that the Greens break with the "state-mandated legality" principle and participate in general strikes and blockades against rocket bases as part of the peace movements' battle against NATO.[24]

## After the 1983 Elections

Given the uncertainties surrounding the dangers of environmental destruction—How urgent was the need for action? How fundamentally did modern society have to be reformed?—disagreements about political strategy were to be expected. But in the years after the Greens became members of the Bundestag, disappointment and even resignation grew. The party had spent most of its energy on forging compromises between the various factions that had founded it and was capable of only limited and often confused action.

By the fall of 1985, the Greens found themselves in their deepest crisis since their founding.[25] Official party membership (around 30,000) had stagnated. Constant fighting between the leadership of the parliamentary party and the federal executive committee caused demoralization, and some of the novelty of a "green" party had worn off. Many Greens complained that the party had lost its ability to mobilize citizen action groups. Independent activity among citizen initiatives had seriously declined, apparently vindicating those who had warned that a federal party would stifle citizen activism. Early enthusiasm and exaggerated hopes had dissipated. Contributing to the crisis was the apparent ascendency of the SPD. At the federal level, the Social Democratic leadership publicly condemned the Greens as a party paralyzed by factions yet unreliable and unpredictable.[26]

Bahro left the party in disgust that year because the party would not condemn all experimentation with animals. More liberal members like Hasenclever in Baden-Württemberg refused to run for office again. Others associated mainly with the peace movement, like the former military general Gert Bastian, left the party in protest over the "reigning incompetence."[27] And while many party members rationalized the "chaos" as a necessary transitional stage for a protest movement that was attempting to transform itself into a political party, the lack of a "consensus of power" became increasingly debilitating. It detracted from the fact that the Greens *had* introduced a refreshing degree of participatory democracy into German political life, that they *had* brought some color into an otherwise dull parliamentary routine, and that they *did* advance not only the cause of environmentalism, but also those of feminism and disarmament. Other parties had a token woman in a high position; only the Greens elected women to all six party-spokesperson positions for the party Bundestag faction in April 1984. Even women of the establishment parties congratulated the Greens.[28]

As a small party, the Greens never had any of their legislative proposals accepted by the Bundestag. Nevertheless, the general population quickly began to identify them as the party most concerned with ecological problems. The Greens, more than anyone else in Germany, introduced environmentalism into the political dialogue and brought it to the attention of a mass public.[29] But they quickly experienced the limits of their appeal: Greens and German environmentalists in general were greatly disappointed when, in the aftermath of the Chernobyl nuclear plant disaster in the summer of

1986, the party registered only insignificant gains in a state election in Lower Saxony. Instead, the conservative government reaped political gains by appointing the first federal minister for the environment, a symbolic gesture that hid the lack of real action.

At the state level, the Greens' fortunes fluctuated. In April 1984, they showed considerable gains in the conservative state of Baden-Württemberg, where they moved ahead of the Free Democrats. In Heidelberg, Freiburg, Tübingen, and some other university towns the Greens became the second-largest party, ahead of the Social Democrats, with 14 to 20 percent of the vote.[30] On the other extreme, the party had to come to terms with two crucial losses in the traditionally Social Democratic states of Saarland and North Rhine–Westphalia. In March 1985 the Social Democrat Oskar Lafontaine won the election after a strong environmental campaign directed at young voters and against the Greens. The Greens' lackluster campaign, dominated by apolitical fundamentalists who rejected any cooperation with Lafontaine, won them only 2.5 percent of the vote. The outcome was considered a dangerous precedent by the Greens' political realists: by usurping the environmental issue, the Social Democrats could prosper while ignoring the Greens entirely.[31]

Two months later, in May 1985, the Greens were decisively beaten by another Social Democrat, Johannes Rau, and again fell below the 5 percent minimum in the state of North Rhine–Westphalia. Once again, the political realists blamed the fundamentalists who had dominated the campaign and failed to appeal to the traditionally social democratic electorate.[32] Instead, the party had, with great media attention, catered to small bands of eccentrics, like a group demanding legalized sex with minors. Political realists warned that the party was in danger of succumbing to some of the most erratic and uncontrollable members of the new social movements. Even the more legitimate concerns of certain Greens contributed to this general impression. Thus, Antje Vollmer, without the support of the parliamentary party caucus, had initiated a widely publicized discussion with incarcerated members of the Red Army Faction (RAF), a terrorist group, who had gone on hunger strike to protest against the conditions of their imprisonment. Her intention was to reintegrate former terrorists into society by visiting them in their high-security prisons and engaging them in a discussion about their ideological views, yet to many political realists her action served only to identify the Greens with the political concerns of extremists and highly controversial fringe groups.[33]

The question of a working alliance or formal coalition between the SPD and the Greens divided the Social Democrats as much as the Greens themselves. At the Green party convention in Hamburg in December 1984, the newly elected federal executive committee was equally divided between fundamentalists like Jutta Ditfurth and realists like Hubert Kleinert and Joschka Fischer. The party leadership therefore decided not to decide: collaboration with "other parties" was left entirely to the local, regional, and state parties.[34] Local cooperation was at this point unproblematic, and the Greens participated in the governing of literally hundreds of villages and towns. The only state, however, where a political alliance with the SPD was even a remote possibility was Hesse.

The Greens had already entered the state parliament of Hesse in September 1982 with 8.0 percent of the vote. A year later, they dropped down to 5.9 percent, again mainly because of the vehement infighting between fundamentalists opposing work with the SPD and realists supporting it. The bargaining position of the Greens improved dramatically when the SPD, under the leadership of Holger Börner, became the largest party without being able to govern against a coalition of Conservatives and Free Democrats. Börner himself, who during the election campaign had condemned and dismissed the Greens as a chaotic bunch of misfits, was adjusting to the new political realities. By December 1983, serious talks began between the parties. Neither side, however, was prepared to enter into negotiations for a formal governing alliance; conservative Social Democrats balked at collaborations with Greens and the party itself, like the Conservatives, was under heavy criticism for illegal party financing practices in a scandal known as the Flick affair.[35]

In 1984 the Greens in Hesse agreed to a *Duldungsvertrag* with the Social Democrats whereby they would tolerate an SPD minority government and support it by judging each issue and legislative proposal independently. This agreement was canceled by the party caucus and the state convention in November 1984 over a controversy involving nuclear power plants. The Social Democratic minister for economics had permitted two very controversial manufacturers of nuclear materials for power plants in Hesse to continue their operations. The Greens not only opposed the civilian use of nuclear energy in general but demanded the closure of these particular manufacturers (Nukem and Alkem) because of their apparently serious safety violations and irregular disposal of nuclear waste.[36]

Conflict over political strategy continued throughout the following years. At the party convention of June 1985 in Hagen, no one faction managed to garner a majority of delegates. Every conceivable position found advocates, from a Green opposition role to coalition with the SPD to attempting to gain a Green majority, with leftist groups predominating over those from southern Germany who sympathized with an ecologically compatible free-market economy. The official party line that finally emerged insisted that political coalitions should be entertained only if important demands of the Greens could thus be realized.

After the next Hesse state election in October 1985, Social Democrats and Greens once again negotiated a possible coalition. The SPD had gained enough votes to win 51 percent of the seats but needed the Greens to overcome the slight advantage of the combined conservative-liberal vote. Against the vote of the speaker of the national executive committee, the Hesse state party finally decided to enter a joint government with the Social Democrats. The well-known Green political realist Joschka Fischer became the first Green state minister for environmental and energy affairs. Fischer had been a participant in the 1960s student protest movement, had served on the Frankfurt city council, and had been a member of the Bundestag after 1983.[37]

## After the 1987 Federal Elections

The federal elections of January 1987 preserved the conservative-liberal coalition government: despite the worst election showing by the Christian Democratic Union (CDU) since 1949, the liberal Free Democratic Party (FDP) managed sufficient gains to save the government. In light of the Social Democrats' stagnating share of the vote (37 percent), the gains of the Greens (from 5.6 percent in 1983 to 8.3 percent) could not create even a hypothetical alternative to the conservative coalition. The Greens were forced to continue their opposition role for another legislative period. More importantly, shortly after the election the two attempts at coalition government between Greens and the Social Democrats in Hesse and Hamburg fell apart. These failures of the realist strategy to gain political influence by means of alliances with the SPD encouraged the fundamentalist forces within the party and undoubtedly contributed to their victories during the summer of 1987. The new star of the Greens was to be the fundamentalist from Frankfurt, Jutta Ditfurth. She and the fundamentalist majority in the federal executive maintained their position until the defeat of the fundamentalists at the Karlsruhe party convention in December 1988.

At the Duisburg party convention in May, Ditfurth was elected speaker of the federal executive committee by a vote of 381 out of 600 delegates. The fundamentalists managed to take eight out of 11 committee positions. Otto Schily, a well-known political realist, feared that the fundamentalist victory had seriously damaged the party, and he charged Ditfurth herself with having encouraged enmity between party factions and general fanaticism among all members. Ditfurth announced that the new course of the party would consist of substantive confrontation of the value-conservative ideologies dominating the conservative-reactionary political establishment—with no further efforts at political coalitions. Members of the Bundestag party caucus, including Antje Vollmer and the realist Waltraud Schoppe, undertook some attempts at mediation between fundamentalists and realists but to no avail. The realists, convinced that the majority of Green voters were behind them, interpreted the fundamentalist victory as a takeover by a minority that could well lead to the political demise of the Greens.[38]

At the moment, however, events appeared to support the opponents of political coalitions. In February 1987, Holger Börner, the SPD minister of Hesse, fired Minister for the environment Joschka Fischer. The ostensible reason was Fischer's claim before his state party convention that he no longer had any confidence in the Social Democrats' willingness to compromise in the dispute over whether to licence Alkem, the controversial plutonium manufacturer. The real reason was the unwillingness of the SPD right wing to continue cooperation with the "radical" Greens. The strategy backfired for the Social Democrats, as well as for those Greens who opposed the coalition. In the April elections, the Hesse conservatives together with the liberals won a safe majority, and the SPD were the big losers. Again, and despite their substantial gains (from 5.9 to 9.4 percent), the Greens were left out in the cold. Their relative victory nonetheless transformed itself into a loss for the Greens' realists.[39]

May elections in Hamburg also produced a substantial loss for the Green-Alternative List. The GAL had forced the election by refusing cooperation with the Social Democrats. The electoral results presented the Greens with 7.0 percent of the vote (down from 10.4 percent) and a victory coalition of Social Democrats and liberals. The GAL, whose parliamentary faction in Hamburg consisted entirely of leftist fundamentalist women, had lost its opportunity to govern with the SPD. Leftist fundamentalists like Thomas Eberman argued that the Greens should encourage or simply anticipate various social and economic forces that were bound to heighten social conflicts and ultimately drive the Social Democrats into a crisis situation.

By December 1987, conflicts between the various party factions had reached yet another point of crisis. Open battle between the fundamentalist party executive committee and Speaker Ditfurth, on one hand, and the mainly realist Bundestag party caucus of Green elected representatives, on the other, led to widespread protests among the grassroots membership. To deal with the crisis, the Bonn parliamentary party called for a meeting in Bonn between the party executive committee, the parliamentary party representatives, and heads of all state party organizations.

One major dilemma concerned the party's official attitude toward the use of violence against persons or property during antinuclear and antigovernment demonstrations, and toward fringe groups committed to breaking the state's "monopoly" on force. Despite appeals to reach a party consensus while maintaining diversity of opinion, and despite the effort to form a new coalition, Green Awakening '88 (Grüner Aufbruch '88), between the two main factions, no agreement could be reached during the often tumultuous meeting.[40]

The party did, however, agree to hold a conference in May 1988 to discuss "perspectives" (*PerspektivenKongreß*), not only to shift the discussion of basic positions back to the grassroots and away from the deadlock between parliamentary party and party executive committee, but, more importantly, to rejuvenate the party by returning to the original, founding task of defining the identity and goals of the party. The discussion was to air attitudes toward the state, toward the party system, and toward radical change and its potential for realization. Only such a debate, it was believed, would overcome the party's loss of confidence, membership, and enthusiasm.

The Perspectives Congress in Bad Godesberg, near Bonn, turned into a celebration of resistance, protest, subversion, and revolution against capitalism. It was as if the spirit of the 1960s was rising once again, with its hope of a leftist cultural revolution against the Western capitalist societies. The tone was set by Jutta Ditfurth's visit to Cuba and her praise of Castro and his brand of revolutionary communism. The realists were clearly outnumbered. Their "Manifesto for a Realistic Green Politics" nevertheless pointed to the problems entailed by the pursuit of what they called the "sectarian struggles" of leftist splinter groups. The outcome would be political isolation at best, political suicide at worst. According to the realists, the Greens represented the first attempt in the Federal Republic to "organize the new questions concerning the survival of the human species into questions of practical politics of reform." But the "old New Left" refused to realize that the classic left strategy of conquering the state in order to assert control of the economic system no longer applied. The struggles between a multitude of leftist groups and their refusal to attempt new ways to get involved in realizable strategies of change attested to the failure of their view. In the eyes of the realists, the situation of the Greens was absurd: although they had been the first to make society aware of the new, impending danger of ecological disaster, the mainstream established parties had taken over their main themes while the Greens returned to the infighting of the sixties and seventies.[41]

Despite the apparent isolation of the realists during the summer and fall of 1988, however, the tide was turning their way. The fundamentalists around Ditfurth were clearly out of touch with the party membership and their interests in environmentalism and reform politics, and they were no longer needed to balance the now dissolved Realo-SPD government in Hesse. This, together with suspicions that fundamentalists at the national level had been involved in the misappropriation of party funds, led to the defeat of the fundamentalists at the party convention at Karlsruhe in December. With the support of "moderates" associated with Vollmer's Awakening '88, the realists voted the fundamentalists out of the party executive committee. Many leftists withdrew from national Green politics altogether. But this hardly meant the total defeat of the fundamentalists or a clear victory for the realists around Joschka Fischer, Otto Schily, and Hubert Kleinert. Aufbruch '88 demanded that the debate about the basic party orientation continue in the form of a future membership vote on the various manifestos and plans published by the different party factions.[42]

The next year brought further successes for the Greens' political realists. In March 1989, at the party convention in Duisburg, they elected a new federal executive committee constituting a mix of Aufbruch (Ralf Fücks), realists (Micha Hammerbacher), and fundamentalists (Verena Krieger). The founding phase of the party was proclaimed to be over. Political trends in the first half of 1989 also seemed to favor the "new spirit" of the party.[43] In January, elections in Berlin created a situation where the Social Democrats under Walter Momper needed a coalition with the Alternative List (i.e., the Berlin Greens) in order to govern. The Alternatives, usually counted among the more radical urban groups, agreed on a coalition government. They also consented to acknowledge the state's monopoly on the use of force and accept the Allied status of the Berlin government as well as its ties to the Federal Republic: all demands formerly rejected by many Berlin radicals. In March, Momper presented a new cabinet with eight women and five men, with the ministries for schools, environment, and women, family, and youth all going to Alternative women.[44] In April, the Greens also agreed to enter a governing coalition with Volker Hauff, the Social Democratic candidate for mayor of Frankfurt. The symbolic value of this coalition in the financial headquarters of Germany, the largest city of the state of Hesse where a previous coalition had failed, did not escape the political public. Neither did the appointment of Daniel Cohn-Bendit, the former leader of the French student rebellion of 1968, as honorary head of the Office of Multicultural Affairs.[45]

Throughout the summer of 1989, looking ahead to the elections of 1990 and the expected defeat of the Kohl government, speculations about a possible coalition with the Social Democrats filled the air. In May, at the party convention at Münster, Ralf Fücks, the speaker of the executive committee, set the tone by proclaiming that a majority of voters were in favor of a coalition between Greens and Social Democrats. On the other hand, it was apparent that even after the political isolation of the fundamentalists Ditfurth and Ebermann, the political consensus of the party was quite shaky. The Left Forum, a new leftist faction, was at best willing to "tolerate" a Social Democratic minority government. A proposal to form working groups to design a possible program for a coalition government was turned down. And under no circumstances was a majority ready to enter a government consisting of Social Democrats and Free Democrats.

The possibility of such a government coalition in 1990 became more realistic after the results of the elections for the European parliament were in. The June elections brought a decline of 8 percent in support for the conservatives (down to 37.8 percent) and roughly the same vote for the Social Democrats (37.3 percent). They also brought onto the national scene the rightist radical Republicans with 7.1 percent (14.6 percent in Bavaria), who in their first nationwide election thus drew uncomfortably close to the Greens' showing of 8.4 percent. This shift toward the right brought with it open speculations about the possibility of a Social Democratic, Free Democratic, and Green coalition in 1990. In fact, at the end of June a number of realist Greens met " in secret" with members of the Social Democrats to discuss the likelihood and conditions of possible future collaboration. When this meeting of Fischer, Schily, Hammerbacher, and Alfred Mechtersheimer with the Social Democrats was publicized, a storm of protest broke out among other Green leaders. It was made clear that Fischer and company did not represent a consensus within the party. The question of political strategy was as controversial as ever, although its advocates were clearly taking the initiative this time.[46]

By the fall of 1989, however, and especially after the peaceful November revolution in the GDR, coalition talks between the Greens and the SPD became an exercise in futility. This was especially clear after the first free elections in the GDR on March 18, 1990, brought an overwhelming victory not for the SPD, as had been widely predicted, but for the conservative alliance under the aegis of Kohl and the West CDU. An overwhelming majority of East Germans appeared to be in favor of the most rapid road toward German unification. The initial Green position advocating a confederation of two independent German states in the framework of a confederative united Europe was clearly a minority view. As usual, the party position was a compromise: the Greens of Hesse, for example, had stated that if a majority of East German citizens freely voted for unity with the Federal Republic, "no one in the FRG could politically reject or prevent this." But the party as a whole remained undecided as to whether a German confederation, a two-state solution, or a federal republic (*föderalistischer Bundesstaat*) should develop.

Before the March GDR election, a new independent Green Party ("Grüne Partei") had been founded there. Its platform of February 1990 committed it to a broad program of environmental protection and international cooperation. Specifically, it wanted to join "free-market control mechanisms" with overall economic planning. Capital should be subject to democratic controls. Broad democratic controls should guarantee the environmental compatibility of economic developments. German unification should take place only in the context of European unity.[47] In an election alliance with a feminist party, the GDR Greens received about 1.8 percent of the vote.

It is impossible to predict the consequences for the Greens in the Federal Republic of the process of German unification and the politics of a united Germany. Most Greens are deeply suspicious of the forces of nationalism, and justifiably so. Furthermore, the economic unification of Germany seems likely to strengthen big industry and corporations, tending to hinder rather than promote effective environmental policies. In addition, leftist groups within the Green Party have been weakened by the loss of credibility for alternative economic routes modeled after "humanist socialism." And while this does not necessarily entail the demise of the "left," it does not make the future orientation of the Greens any easier.

## NOTES

1. See Joschka Fischer, Hubert Kleinert, Udo Knapp, and Jo Müller, "Sein oder Nichtsein: Entwurf für ein Manifest grüner Realpolitik," manuscript (summer 1988).

2. The "Perspectives Congress" of June 1988 at Bonn–Bad Godesberg, and that of November 1989 at Saarbrücken, with their proliferation of proclamations and manifestos and vociferous public debates, showed that the Greens were, after 10 years, still preoccupied with the question of their own identity. Cf. Erwin Jurtschitsch, Alexander Rudnick, and Frieder Otto Wolf, eds., *Grüne Perspektiven: Grünes und Alternatives Jahrbuch 1988* (Cologne: Kölner Volksblatt, 1988); Klaus Gotto and Hans-Joachim Veen, eds., *Die Grünen: Partei wider Willen* (Mainz: Hase & Koehler, 1984); Gerd Langguth, *The Green Factor in German Politics* (Boulder: Westview Press, 1984); Thomas Kluge, ed., *Grüne Politik: Der Stand einer Auseinandersetzung* (Frankfurt: Fischer, 1984). See also PerspektivKongreß, June 16–19, 1988, Bonn–Bad Godesberg, Programm (Die Grünen, Bundesgeschäftsstelle, Bonn); Ludger Volmer et al., "Schutt wegräumen: Undogmatische Linke zu Lage und Perspektive der Grünen Partei, manuscript (June 17, 1988). In addition, *Umbruch im Osten: Im Westen nichts Neues?*, Second PerspektivKongreß, November 17–19, 1989, Saarbrücken (Die Grünen, Bundesgeschäftsstelle, Bonn, January 1990).

3. Cf. Sabine Stamer, ed., *Von der Machbarkeit des Unmöglichen: Politische Gespräche über grüne Praxis und grüne Perspektiven* (Hamburg: Junius, 1985).

4. See Klaus von Beyme, "Neue soziale Bewegungen und politische Parteien," in *Aus*

*Politik und Zeitgeschichte,* November 1, 1986, pp. 30–39; Karl-Werner Brand, Detlef Büsser, and Dieter Rucht, eds., *Aufbruch in eine andere Gesellschaft: Neue soziale Bewegungen in der Bundesrepublik* (Frankfurt: Campus, 1984); Karl-Werner Brand ed., *Neue soziale Bewegungen in Westeuropa und den USA* (Frankfurt: Campus, 1985).

5. Joschka Fischer, *Von grüner Kraft und Herrlichkeit* (Reinbek bei Hamburg: Rowohlt, 1984).

6. Thomas Ebermann and Rainer Trampert, *Die Zukunft der Grünen: Ein realistisches Konzept für eine radikale Partei* (Hamburg: Konkret Literatur, 1984).

7. Cf. Joseph M. Petulla, *American Environmentalism* (College Station: Texas A&M University Press, 1980); Steven R. Reed, "Environmental Politics: Some Reflections Based on the Japanese Case," in *Comparative Politics* 13 (April 1981) 253–71; James R. McDonald, "Environmental Concern and the Political Process in France," *Environmental Professional* 4 (1982).

8. Cf. Klaus von Beyme, *Das politische System der BRD* (Munich: Piper, 1979), 93.

9. Cf. Dorothy Nelkin and Michael Pollack, *The Atom Besieged* (Cambridge, Mass.: M.I.T. Press, 1981).

10. Cf. Rudolf Brun, ed., *Der grüne Protest* (Frankfurt: Fischer, 1978). Council-democratic movements (such as the Paris Commune of 1871 and the Russian revolutions of 1905 and 1917) are characterized by grassroots-democratic organizational forms. In the socialist tradition this organization took place on the shop floor, underlining the significance of labor and of production for the relationship of man and nature. Eds.

11. Cf. Hans A. Pestalozzi, *Frieden in Deutschland* (Munich: Goldmann, 1982) 25–32.

12. Cf. Petra Kelly and Jo Leinen, *Prinzip Leben: Ökopax—die neue Kraft* (Berlin: Olle & Wolter) 15–20.

13. Cf. Bernd Guggenberger, *Bürgerinitiativen in der Parteiendemokratie* (Stuttgart: Kohlhammer, 1980).

14. Cf. Jörg Mettke, ed., *Die Grünen* (Hamburg: Rowohlt, 1982), and esp. the essay "Im Parlament und auf der Straße: Die Doppelstrategie der Grünen Niedersachsen," by Martin Mombaur, 135–46.

15. Ibid. 159–79.

16. Cf. ibid. 82–101.

17. *Die Zeit,* March 11, 1983.

18. Cf. Mettke, *Die Grünen,* 101–20; also, Wolf-Dieter and Connie Hasenclever, *Grüne Zeiten* (Munich: Kösel, 1982).

19. Cf. Milan Horacek, "Zwischen uns und den Etablierten liegen Welten: Die Grünen im Frankfurter Rathaus," in Mettke, *Die Grünen,* 120–35.

20. Cf. Rudolf Bahro, *Elemente einer neuen Politik: Zum Verhältnis von Ökologie und Sozialismus* (Berlin: Olle & Wolter, 1980).

21. Die Grünen, *Das Bundesprogramm,* (Bonn: Die Grünen, 1982).

22. Cf. Bahro, 120–21.

23. Cf. Rolf Meyer, "Die Grünen vor der Wahl," *Aus Politik und Zeitgeschichte,* September 6, 1980, pp. 3–22.

24. Cf. Gerd Langguth, *Protestbewegung: Die Neue Linke seit 1968* (Cologne: Verlag Wissenschaft und Politik, 1983) 267–69.

25. *Der Spiegel,* September 16, 1985, pp. 30–32.

26. *Der Spiegel,* October 28, 1985, pp. 29–34.

27. *Der Spiegel,* February 20, 1984, pp. 25–26.

28. *Der Spiegel,* April 9, 1984, pp. 18–22.

29. Cf. Hans-Joachim Veen, "Wer wählt grün?" *Aus Politik und Zeitgeschichte,* Septem-

ber 1, 1984, pp. 3–17; also, Marie-Luise Weinberger, "Ende des grünen Zeitalters?" *Aus Politik und Zeitgeschichte,* November 9, 1985, 19–29.

30. *Der Spiegel,* April 12, 1984, pp. 48–58.
31. *Der Spiegel,* March 18, 1985, pp. 27–34.
32. *Der Spiegel,* May 20, 1985, pp. 31–34.
33. *Der Spiegel,* March 25, 1985, pp. 66–81.
34. *Der Spiegel,* December 3, 1984, pp. 62–66.
35. *Der Spiegel,* October 10, 1983, pp. 17–34.
36. *Der Spiegel,* November 26, 1984, pp. 19–22.
37. *Der Spiegel,* November 4, 1985, pp. 24–59.
38. *Der Spiegel,* May 11, 1987, pp. 24–40.
39. *Der Spiegel,* April 13, 1987, pp. 17–26.
40. Cf. Bundesgeschäftsstelle die Grünen, "Die Krisen-Klausur im 'Pantheon'. Protokoll der gemeinsamen Sitzung des Bundeshauptausschusses der Grünen mit VertreterInnen der Landesvorstände und den Abgeordneten der Grünen im Bundestag am 12. Dezember 1987 in Bonn" (Bonn, March 1988).
41. Cf. PerspektivKongreß, 1988; *Der Spiegel,* June 27, 1988, pp. 26–27.
42. *Der Spiegel,* December 12, 1988.
43. *Der Spiegel,* March 13, 1989, pp. 10–12.
44. *Der Spiegel,* March 20, 1989, pp. 27–30.
45. *Der Spiegel,* April 10, 1989.
46. *Der Spiegel,* July 24, 1989, pp. 16–18.
47. Green Party, Basic Program, passed at the First Party Convention on February 10, 1990, in Halle, Central Office Green Party of the GDR, House of Democracy, Friedrichstr. 165, Berlin.

## Chapter 3

# From Competing Factions
# to the Rise of the Realos

ROLAND ROTH AND DETLEF MURPHY

When we look at the first 10 years of the Green Party, four historic markers stand out. The federal party Congress held in Karlsruhe in 1980 saw the assertion of a left wing (labeled "fundamentalists" or "Fundis" in the party language), consisting of eco-socialists, radical ecologists, and feminists, against "Realos" ("realists") pushing for reformist policies and participation in government. Karlsruhe 1988 stands for the end of this dominance. Just after midnight at this extremely dramatic party congress, the defeated and dazed left retreated into a dark corner of the building and spoke of betrayal and schism. Only a year earlier in Duisburg during the election of the federal executive committee (Bundesvorstand), they had triumphed over their Realo opponents. Duisburg 1987 confirmed their national dominance over a party in whose parliamentary groups and state sections Realos had already begun to erect bulwarks. Duisburg 1989 brought to a close developments that had begun 1988 in Karlsruhe: the intraparty fronts had begun to move, as old groupings became differentiated and new ones formed. A nonhomogeneous majority came together to put an end to the paralyzing and—with respect to the 1990 Bundestag elections—unpleasant Fundi–Realo dispute.

In 1989 the party enthroned a federal executive committee based on equal representation. The Greens' "classic" left fell into isolation. After a governmental coalition between the Berlin Alternative List (AL) and the Social Democratic Party (SPD) was formed in one of their bastions, their only political home remained with the Hamburg Green-Alternative List (GAL). The final fall from power came in October 1989 when the federal executive committee decided to deny their Old Guard the prominent placement they sought within the Congress on Future Perspectives. Although the decision was extremely controversial, it shows that the nomination of formerly prominent figures such as Jutta Ditfurth and Thomas Ebermann was no longer guaranteed and thus underscores how much the Greens changed within a spell of only two years.

For a long time, entrenched ideological battles and opportunistic jockeying for positions—struggles that in form and content hardly embodied the much-praised "new political culture"—left the impression that the Greens had reached the final stage of in-group formation: intraparty paralysis and political immobility. But the Bundestag election in January 1987 (in which the Greens won 8.3 percent of the vote and 16 new mandates) showed that they remained unaffected by the second aspect of this stage of development: the loss of electoral popularity. An unusually tolerant electoral base allowed them to present the problem of factionalism as the virtue of pluralism.[1] Taking advantage of this switch, the delegates to the Duisburg federal congress in May 1987 allowed themselves a group of executive speakers who, in conjunction with the Bundestag group and several state sections, followed a line of increasing polarization. But as the next Bundestag elections approached, this sanguine attitude disappeared. Within this process of eroding optimism, a state election played a crucial role. On May 8, 1988, the Greens' second failure to gain parliamentary representation in the Schleswig-Holstein state elections and, even more, their fall from a meager 3.9 percent of the vote to a shameful 2.9 percent, evoked protests within the party. While the federal executive blamed the Realos' lack of commitment during the election campaign for the debacle, the latters' speakers held the federal executive responsible and demanded that penalties be imposed for this "bankruptcy of fundamentalism." One Green Bundestag parliamentarian even sent a congratulatory telegram to the victorious SPD-candidate: "Given the political course of the Greens in Schleswig-Holstein, I would have voted for the SPD too, to make sure of toppling the Christian Democratic Union from power."[2]

The fear that polarization could get out of hand and that pluralism could become excessive and overtax their electorate—despite its remarkable tolerance—loomed larger and larger. Centrism (the takeover of power by a "neutral" center group) and the *Feminat* (an organizational principle based on exclusively female committees and groups representing all factions) were discussed and practiced. Simple party members were more and more irritated, and displeasure with the top echelons went hand in hand with an increasing apathy. In 1988 for the first time the party lost members. An explosive mix of general resignation, a tendency to withdraw (into communal politics, into movement activities, into a membership card existence, or from the party altogether), displeasure with the "Promis" (prominent politicians), who had destroyed what had been built up by the grassroots, and a strong antifactionalist desire for harmony merely required a spark—or a group that understood how to light a fuse without being branded as arsonists. Karlsruhe 1988 brought both; in its wake, after the smoke had cleared, the task of Duisburg 1989 was one of limiting the damage and beginning the reconstruction. Pluralism was contained at a level that was electorally acceptable.

Whether the federal congresses of Karlsruhe 1988 and Duisburg 1989 actually introduced the second, so-called postfundamentalist phase of the Greens (as the Realos hoped), whether it was just a temporary lull in the internal conflict before the coming Bundestag elections, or whether the breakup of the red-green coalition in Berlin would again evoke polarization was not immediately clear. Orderly and consequential reform party, radical movement mouthpiece, or both simultaneously: the Greens are not yet stable enough for us to make more than a well-educated guess. The 5 percent barrier is still an important topic for the Greens, as it still holds together a party spectrum reaching from ecological socialists to ecological capitalists, even if these labels are no longer or not yet used by the different factions. The Fundi-Realo conflict has become a left-right conflict that is both less intense and programmatically clearer.[3]

## Points of Conflict

Greens' transformation into a national organization in 1979 and 1980 was depicted by Rudolf Bahro, at that time the most prominent advocate of a Green political federation, as a West German "historical compromise" in which "red and green go together well"—an analogy to the Italian prototype. Indeed, the early Greens encompassed a wide spectrum of groups and tendencies from widely differing ideological camps.

The breakaway of the conservative wing soon after the official founding brought an end to a conflict that had troubled the new party from the outset and had only been put aside for a short time for the sake of participating in the Bundestag elections. The party's ideological-programmatic center thereby moved somewhat to the left. And while the founding compromise expressed itself in slogans such as "neither left nor right, but in front," and the desire to overcome the left–right paradigm, the Greens were by the early 1980s viewed both by their voters and by a majority of their members as a party clearly left of the SPD.

Despite this programmatic narrowing, the reduced internal spectrum left room for intense conflicts between competing factions. Six years after founding, conflicts emerged in Hesse that seemed to foretell split in the eyes of both party members and external observers. The hardening contradictions between Fundis and Realos were most prominently displayed in the mayoral elections in Frankfurt in August 1981, when the fundamentalist city council members refused to vote for the candidate favored by the majorities of both the party and the parliamentary group, and when a Realo state parliamentarian refused to abide by the party rule of "mandatory rotation" of parliamentary seats, which in this case would have enthroned a member of the fundamentalist wing.

The background for the escalation of this factional dispute was the coalition government between the Greens and the SPD in West Berlin. As before in Hamburg, where the GAL had temporarily supported an SPD minority government, the conflict between Fundis and Realos centered on the concrete conditions under which the Greens were willing to take part in coalition governments with the SPD, which was no longer able to govern alone. Only on the surface was the conflict one of tactical and strategic differences concerning the number and nature of "essentials" for Green governmental participation. Although such "conditions for coalition" became the focus of debate more and more often as electoral successes and increasing votes from SPD members put the Greens into a position of real power, underlying this debate were the questions of whether the SPD's reformist politics were credible, whether they could be influenced and altered, and how open and innovative the political decision-making process really was. We can draw an analogy to the social democratic debate on revisionism, all the way to the formation of a centrist group within the Green Party ("Zentralos"), who sought to bridge the widening gap between the competing wings by pairing reformist practice with verbal radicalism.

Besides the radicalism-versus-reform dimension of the conflict, a Green variety of the classical left–right dispute also developed and was seen as such by the protagonists. Joschka Fischer, a leading figure within the Realo wing and Hesse's minister for the environment from December 1985 to February 1987, distinguished the conflict over "coalition and identity" on one hand from the "left–right conflict between eco-libertarians and eco-socialists" on the other hand.[4] Self definition as Green "socialists," "liberals," or "libertarians" was not the only sign of programmatic traditions; the formation (initially in Hesse) of the "left within the Greens" demonstrated the revival in "the new kind of party" of old ideological lines that many thought had been overcome in the euphoria of party founding. In this way, the eco-libertarians, who had formed a faction in early 1984, represented the right within the Green continuum, whereas the eco-socialists viewed themselves as the nucleus of a left-wing party grouping.

These power relationships led to a situation—seen most clearly in Hamburg and Hesse—where all areas of factional conflict were ultimately connected to the question of cooperation with the SPD: the debates over fundamental goals, the type of society envisaged, the so-called system question, the appraisal of parliamentarianism, the relationship to the new social movements, the party model, and the stance toward unions. Divergent positions on these issues came to the fore most clearly for external observers as the lines of struggle within the party hardened. The dispute over the Hesse model of red-green coalitions, especially, created divisions that were to reach far into the future. This dispute tested the resilience of the "new political culture" of the Green Party hailed by many, even as the established parties gloatingly depicted its demise.

The new phase was signaled less by the election at Duisburg in 1989 of a new federal executive and the concomitant shift of power at the top echelon than by the way the delegates at that federal congress treated the second red-green experiment at state level: the newly installed SPD-AL coalition in West Berlin. Whereas the Offenburg federal congress in 1985 saw long and heated debates over Green governmental participation in Hesse and re-elected Jutta Ditfurth, an explicit opponent of Green coalitions, to the federal executive by a two-thirds majority, three years later the new coalition sparked hardly any controversy at all. Moreover, the AL delegate who had come to seek support became the star of the convention:

> The applause turned into a standing ovation. The debate over the Berlin experiment, originally scheduled for 60 minutes, was canceled; the congregation is already converted. The coalition issue, for many years good for a litmus test, is acknowledged by mere acclamation. This is the real defeat of the Fundi wing, and it will remain to be seen whether Berlin is already, "the opportunity of the century," as Joschka Fischer maintained, who also pointed to the coming 1990 state elections in the Saarland, North Rhine–Westphalia, and Lower Saxony."[5]

## A Map of the Green Currents

Observers invariably found the Greens's diversity somewhat confusing, and the self-imposed and externally imposed labels actually made things worse. At a Green Party congress in late 1984, one observer made out seven factions: "extreme fundamentalists," "radical fundamentalists," "moderate fundamentalists," "mediators," "eco-socialists," "Realos" and "eco-libertarians."[6] Realos were occasionally called "Koalos" or "radical reformers." The *tageszeitung,* a newspaper close to the Greens, at times distinguished between "anarcho-Realos" and "fundamental-Realos." Other media reduced the spectrum to the simple dualism of fundamentalists and Realos. This convenient mode of classification, whose use in Party jargon provoked the concerted resistance of the radical wing (self-labeled as "the left"), often covered up the existing configuration of four or more less clearly distinguishable factions. This by now classical constellation set the eco-socialists and radical ecologists on the left wing and the Realos and eco-libertarians on the moderate wing. Whether women would be able to constitute their own wing with an independent and self-imposed programmatic-ideological profile was uncertain for a long time. However, the so-called *Müttermanifest*[7] of 1986 indicated that women too would be unable to resist the forces of factionalization (a resistance that many had no interest in anyway). The conflict over intraparty opportunities for the participation of Green mothers pressed the feminists more firmly into cooperation with the eco-socialists and radical ecologists, while their opponents—following the dualist automatism—found themselves siding with the Realos. As early as 1987, "independents," "neutralists," and the "nonaligned" launched centrist attempts at overcoming factional dispute by integrative means—a strategy only occasionally propagated before that date. Predictably, their efforts led to the formation of a new wing, even if this one was conceived of as an antifaction wing. The first public meeting of this group, called Green Awakening '88 (Grüner Aufbruch '88), took place in January 1987. The formal founding followed soon after at the first working meeting. While the eco-socialists had already experienced some losses, the "undogmatic" or "pragmatic" left eventually formed the Left Forum (Linkes Forum). The factional wings began to move and the old quartet temporarily turned into a sextet.

Until the phase of factional re-formation began in 1987, four factions formed the reservoir used by the factional newcomers. The old distinguishing criterion now increasingly irrelevant—was the position on coalitions with the SPD.

The *eco-socialist* regional nucleus and bastion was Hamburg, where the influence of activists from so-called K-groups such as the Kommunistischer Bund in the antinuclear movements and the resulting Bunte Liste ("Rainbow List") made itself felt early on. Their activists had gained considerable organizational experience in the New Left, in early extraparliamentary protest, and in union activities. Although critical of unions, eco-socialists were never in opposition to them, which distinguished from them the radical ecologists with whom they otherwise co-operated closely.

Beginning in 1980, the eco-socialists gathered around the quasi-factional periodical *Moderne Zeiten* and in the Initiative Sozialistische Politik, from which important impulses toward the nationwide formation of the Green left emanated. A book entitled *Die Zukunft der Grünen* (1984) was widely regarded as the eco-socialists' programmatic manifesto both inside and outside the party.[8] In it, Thomas Ebermann and Rainer Trampert sketch the "political demands standing in opposition to the old socialist promises" and attempt to "revive the debate over true societal and individual wealth, a debate long lost to Marxist tradition." In the ecological movement the authors see an "aspiring toward the appropriation of the societal forces of production" that can take place only by extraparliamentary mass mobilization and not in the halls of parliament—least of all in a coalition with the SPD. In contrast to other factions, the eco-socialists see a central role for the new social movements *and* for the working class in creating a nonoppressive and ecological society. The working class has to be freed from two elements integrated into capitalism: Social Democracy and the unions. This requires that the "ecological problematic must be seen by the producers of societal 'wealth'—the workers—and resolved in successive struggles. Our aim, the transformation of production, the closing down of production areas or the abandonment of certain production techniques, can be realized only with them."[9] A wide mass mobilization must go beyond the new social movements to encompass an old social movement that has departed from the wrong path of industrialism and been revitalized.

The eco-socialists adhered to a strategic concept of "toleration," making their support for an SPD government dependent upon "crucial changes in social, ecological, and military policies." This concept differs decisively from a coalition "in which a comprehensive program of governmental politics would have to be carried mutually." And even in the case of a not improbable and even calculated failure of toleration, the eco-socialists see the possibility of a "clarifying enlightenment about what the SPD is really like."[10] The strategic difference between this policy and the coalition policy of the Realos lies in the eco-socialists' intention of unmasking and their orientation toward the extraparliamentary mobilization potential; they can be distinguished from the Fundis in the weight they give the working class as a target group and the productive sector as a field of action.

The *eco-libertarians* were the programmatic opposites of the eco-socialists. They presented the clearest contrast to the "Hamburg concept" with regard to societal goals, the "system question," and the envisaged socioeconomic structures, and also with regard to coalition policy, the relationship to the new social movements, and the party model. The eco-libertarians formed explicitly to keep the eco-socialists from becoming too powerful. "Against the Doomsday Mood"—subtitled "For a Free Political Dialogue"—was the title prominent Greens from Berlin, Baden-Württemberg, and Schleswig-Holstein gave their November 1983 "Theses on the Situation of the Green Party."[11] Their intraparty line of action, even if for-

mulated mildly, did not lack clarity. The authors criticize the spread of political functionaries, with "experience grounded in the sect-like organizational structures of the past decade or directly in Social Democracy," a fact
that contributed to making the new party an "elite club of tough political
professionals." They also diagnose a "teutonically colored Jacobinism" in
the Greens that "had a long tradition in the German left" and would eventually lead to "pedagogical dictatorship."

The faction's founding statement, published in February 1984, was
clearer still. It describes the eco-socialist program as a "dangerous combination" of "biological ecologism" and a "pedagogical-dictatorial socialist
Jacobinism" contrasting these labels with their own "free ecological politics." Personal responsibility, individuality, privatization, debureaucratization and self-help are the bases of the eco-libertarians' political concept,
whereas control over the means of production and the social question are
"problems of second degree." Soviet-democratic models are strictly rejected. They would "fail due to imminent structural deficits" and "the whole
complex and sensitive engine for coordinating millions of decisions over
production, distribution, and consumption now taking place via the market
would come to a standstill."[12] Not surprisingly, the eco-libertarians viewed
representative democracy and parliamentarianism as the "central locus of decision making" and favored abandonment of grassroots principles, the rotation of mandates, and the imperative mandate. They wanted to end the
Greens' unproductive existence as a "hermaphrodite, half-party, half-
movement." Remoteness from the grassroots and an electoral as well as parliamentary orientation characterize the eco-libertarian political strategy.
Genuine libertarian traditions can still be found occasionally in their official
program, but libertarian elements are suppressed in favor of an orientation
toward a bourgeois electorate.[13]

The *fundamentalists* gained prominence mainly through their struggle
against Realo tendencies within the Greens, upholding the banner of the
new social movements against parliamentarians supposedly detached from
the grassroots. Their program and strategy stem from a radically pessimistic
diagnosis of a bankrupt industrial system, whose catastrophe can be neither
postponed nor averted in the long term. Resistance to and withdrawal from
the system are the key terms characterizing the Fundis' attitude to industrial
society in both its capitalist and its socialist variants.

These radical ecologists (in contrast to the eco-socialists, who are close
to them in the party ideological continuum) view themselves as a "force beyond the old left–right paradigm."[14] They focus exclusively on the *new* social movements as an oppositional force and label themselves protagonists
of a "path between reformism and armed militancy."[15] In their view, the

working class has for the most part lost its potential for mobilization. At most, the Fundis' strategic concept regards parliamentary work and party politics as a feeder for extraparliamentary mass mobilization independent of the party. Parliament serves as a "platform" for the furtherance of protest. The Greens themselves are visualized as part of the new social movements, an advanced post within the established political system; they will not—as the Realos do—let themselves be coopted with a pseudo participation in power, parliaments not being the true locus of power anyway. *Ersatz* electoral successes distract activists from the only really meaningful field of activity: resistance by the persons affected and local protest. Fundis perceive only a technical distinction between formal coalitions and the toleration of minority rule; for them, coalition with the Social Democratic section of the "ruling bloc" just serves to suck the Greens into a "corrupting basic consensus" that obscures the real structure of power: "Cynicism, bourgeoisification, squareness, centralization, isolation as well as a concentration of information, authority, and ruling power describe the SPD and characterize Green Realo politics."[16]

In order to counteract this pull toward integration, the radical ecologists, more than any other party faction, insisted on securing the mechanisms embedded in the Green grassroots organizational structure: rotation of mandates, the imperative mandate. These rules offer the only way to control the top echelons and the parliamentary groups and maintain a strong bond with the party grassroots and the new social movements.

The differences between the radical ecologists and the eco-socialists arise from different political backgrounds and can be clearly seen in their self-chosen labels. Whereas the ecological self-destruction of the industrial system is crucial for the radical ecologists' societal critique, the eco-socialists focus strongly on the more traditional areas of a leftist diagnosis, such as economic exploitation, unemployment, and poverty. The eco-socialists therefore do not turn away from modern production structures, and their critique of technology is not so radical. Their call for only marginal disengagement from industrial society corresponds to an only relative strategic rejection of parliamentary participation (again, the radical ecologists go further) as the eco-socialists maintain that parliaments are "not mere 'platforms'" but have a "special relevance as central organs for the development of political will within and between the various societal groups."[17] The radical ecologists have a somewhat more limited strategic repertoire when it comes to target groups, mobilization efforts, and areas of activity, a fact that, however, has not affected their common front against the Realo faction.

In contrast to the other factions, the Green *realists*, or Realos, did not make many public programmatic statements in their early days. Naturally,

they formed and demonstrated their identity in local political practice
(mostly in parliaments) and in their defense against the Fundi critique. Their
most prominent speakers are usually Greens with successful political careers.
Realos view parliaments as effective fields of activity, and electoral gains are
their measure of the success of Green politics. For this reason, they regard
too close a relationship to the new social movements as counterproductive.
They see the professionalization of party work as urgent; while other Greens
perceive their party as a "super-citizen initiative" (Otto Schily), for Realos
this self-conceptualization disregards the actual possibilities of parliamentary
party work as well as the level of institutionalization that has been reached.

The Realo faction laid down its position in a countermotion to the leading motion of the Fundi-dominated federal executive at the Hamburg federal congress in December 1984.[18] They spelled out their goal of an "ecological and social conversion of capitalist-industrial society," to be attained
by a "politics of ecological reform," and they criticized the "fundamental
opposition to the system" formulated in the leading motion as a "step backward into the old sectarian positions of the 70s," positions that in the end
would lead to an "oppositional ghetto with all its illusions of disembarking
from the system and denial" and a general refusal to take into account "the
actual course of the ecological crisis and the arms race." The change of federal government in 1983 was a decisive starting point for the Realos' strategic conception: "For all those who are endangered by social marginalization,
a 'red-green coalition' has become a new hope, because without parliamentary majorities a dismantling of the social system cannot be prevented . . .
Just by itself, the red-green alternative as a sign of hope will call into question the conservative-reactionary change of values." The Realos, in contrast
to the Fundis, do not regard the SPD and CDU alike as "nuclear and economic growth parties." In view of the urgency of coping with the problems
emanating from industrialization, they consider "the hope that the continuing ecological crisis will lead to a concomitant linear growth of the ecological movement and the Greens as illusionary, timid, and irresponsible."

"What counts is not a new edition of old socialist models but the eco-
logical future of capitalism. . . . We need a mixture of regulative policies me-
diated by the state as well as an ecological economy with market elements."
Hubert Kleinert, a prominent Realo, told an interviewer for *Stern* magazine
(April 4, 1988). These widely publicized statements brought the Realos into
a programmatic terrain that only the eco-libertarians had explored before.
But by breaking the taboo on "ecological capitalism," in the Fundi view, the
Realos had exposed their true nature as the "right" wing of the Greens. One
year later, Joschka Fischer published *Der Umbau der Industriegesellschaft*
("The Reconstruction of Industrial Society"), considered to be a late reply

to Ebermann's and Trampert's 1984 book. In it, he maintains that "capitalism has won, socialism has lost. . . . So if the left heart bleeds or even bleeds to death, the above shows that the framework and the decisive instruments of an ecological reform of the industrial system will be determined by the existing economic mode of Western capitalism." Fischer sees "a whole left model of politics in a fundamental crisis," since "the basic assumption that the economy can be reshaped more equitably, made more socially acceptable and ecologically efficient by way of political power rather than by using the forces of the market, is today more than ever questionable. This, then, has eliminated the common basis of left politics, regardless of its manifold colorings."[19] Here was the most radical departure yet of a prominent Green from the central element of consensus regarding party identity, a consensus that had reached from the eco-socialists and radical ecologists all the way to the Realo faction. It marks one extreme in the party's internal left–right conflict in which the "postfundamentalist" left—even if it no longer rejected red-green coalitions—still viewed these in terms of a "rejection of capitalist modernization" and an "offensive left project."[20]

The Realo faction's members—with the exception of Frankfurt's metropolitan nonorthodox leftists—come from rural states such as Hesse, Baden-Württemberg, Bavaria ("the Realo south"), and Lower Saxony, while the eco-socialists had their main bastions in city-states such as Hamburg and Berlin as well as in the industrial belt of North Rhine-Westphalia. These bastions are slowly being taken by the undogmatic left, just as organized Realo minorities have expanded in Hamburg and Berlin.

Almost from the beginning, forces in the Greens criticized the internal conflict over policy direction as "unproductive," "without content," and damaging to the party. These forces—most of whom refused to identify themselves with any specific faction—labeled themselves the Green Middle, Zentralos or Constructivos and called for an end to the polemical debate over strategy and a return to programmatic work and thereby to a minimal Green consensus: "The political center of the Party will shift. We will no longer focus our attention only on the main characters of the coalition debate. . . . Those that lead the counterdiscourse and those that pit a concrete alternative conception against the critique of reality will make up the new party center. They constitute the Zentralo faction. The break between Realo and Fundi can be neutralized by bringing together those 'enlighteners' of both poles who think innovatively on issues with the neutral specialists standing in between."[21] Both conflicting groups viewed such attempts at integration as enemy maneuvers.

The centrist tendencies could not be suppressed in the long run, however, and 1987 saw the crumbling of old fronts. Conflict between women concerning the "Mothers' Manifesto" (*"Müttermanifest"*; see Chapter 14) heralded a factional reformation, as did the start of a retreat by some of the Green left from eco-socialist dominance (whereby old internal contradictions from pre-Green times re-emerged). While the undogmatic left only gradually began to break away from the hardened factional fronts, the center began—at first only negatively—to set itself apart from both factions. As of September 1987, quite a few leading state and federal politicians began the "search for a third path" (Ralf Fücks), a "difficult path between the factions" (Thea Bock), toward an "Awakening (*Aufbruch*) from the deadend of the Greens' bloc logic" (Lukas Beckmann).[22] An open letter to the increasingly restless and critical grassroots it was signed by both Realo independents and moderate-pragmatic factional politicians from both wings. The 23 Green representatives in the Bundestag, who all signed, announced they would not take part in efforts to split their parliamentary group. The leading figures of the new factions who had publicly called for a clarification of the Greens' relationship to violence as well as their position regarding parliamentarianism "on the basis of comprehensive concepts" on November 27, 1987, emerged from this circle of signatories. The hardliners of both classical factions (people like Ebermann on the one hand and Kleinert on the other) were not signatories. Grüner Aufbruch '88 emerged as a result of the cooperation between the Bonn leaders of the independents (Antje Vollmer and Lukas Beckmann) and the group surrounding Ralf Fücks in Bremen. This group was formally constituted during their first public meeting on January 9, 1988. The Aufbruch group was soon leading the critique of the polarizing effects of "the old factional disputes," and it echoed the concerns of the grassroots, those "people who have to look on, angry, resigned, or helpless," as Antje Vollmer said during a crisis meeting of the Bundestag group with the state executive committees in December 1987.[23]

"Delegating responsibility back to the grassroots" was the goal of an *Urabstimmung*[24] concerning different factional manifestos that was developed by Working Group Green 2000. The group's center was Beckmann, the former speaker of the federal executive committee, and the propagated *Urabstimmung* was the main reason the new group was formed. It wanted not merely to serve the grassroots, however, but also to profit from the restlessness. Critics saw the *Urabstimmung* as a populist strategy by which responsibility was formally to be returned to the grassroots only to be usurped once more by a victorious Aufbruch manifesto.

Although it was aimed at alleviating party disunity and taking the edge off the factional conflicts, the discussion about the *Urabstimmung* initially produced the opposite effect. First, the pressure to produce the manifesto (in which both the "old left" (eco-socialists) and the "new left" (radical ecologists) categorically refused to participate) accelerated the formation of fronts and deepened the gap between factions. Second, the minimum requirement for an *Urabstimmung* (a third of all *Kreisverbände* or country organizations: i.e., about 120) had the effect of transferring factional competition from the party's federal and state congresses down to the grassroots meetings. The Aufbruch group—formed in the name of antifactionalism—thus further factionalized the Greens, even if only for a short time. For the competitors, the party's Perspectives Congress in June 1988 was just another forum, while for the grassroots it was an outlet for venting displeasure. Manifestos had been presented: the eco-libertarians' "Von der Größe des Kleinen: Über Perspektiven Grüner Politik" ("The Largeness of the Small: On Perspectives of Green Politics"), the Realos' "Sein oder Nicht-Sein': Entwürfe für ein realpolitisches Manifest" ("To Be or Not to Be: Outlines for a *Realpolitik* Manifesto"), and, of course, the Aufbruch group's "Manifest: Grüner Aufbruch '88" ("Manifesto: Green Awakening '88"). The independent left, which was in the process of constituting itself, presented "Langweilige Bekenntnisse zu einer nicht-illusionistischen Bestandsaufnahme" ("Boring Confessions for a Nonillusionist Inventory"), a position paper signed mainly by members from Hamburg, Berlin, and Cologne. This group got together during the congress.

Instead of producing a manifesto, the eco-socialists published an advance copy of an article designated for publication in *Konkret* in which their spokesmen Ebermann and Trampert sharply attacked the Realos' manifesto ("loyal to the state and to capital") and labeled the Aufbruch group as green Machiavellians: "They recast serious controversies over contents and strategy as 'disputes between the wings.' The Aufbruch group in actual fact cultivates the dispute or the crisis, as its *raison d'être* is based thereon."[25]

The new group nevertheless presented itself to party members as an honest intermediary in the factional dispute and articulated a concern for the well-being of the party and a wish to bring together the best of both wings: "Our politics in substance is more fundamentalist, and we are more Realo in our rejection of dogmatism and stubbornness."[26]

Linkes Forum, a new faction of the independent left created during a working session in November 1988, also set itself apart from both sides of the Fundi–Realo dispute: "Completely against its intentions, the effect of fundamentalism was to strengthen the SPD and weaken the influence of the Greens, while the effect of the cabinet-wing's strategy[27] was to subordinate the Greens to the SPD, to push the constellation of political power to the right, thus leading to a solidification of conservative hegemony in society. . . . . Realos and Fundis are afflicted by an extreme overestimation of the Greens' capacities: where 'all' is demanded, 'nothing' is the result.[28]

The fundamentalist majority in the federal executive committee sensed a "merciless campaign" with the aim of making the Greens "a normal Western parliamentary party and cleansing them of all 'fundamentalist relics.'"[29] Only days before the Bonn congress, the committee, in the name of guarding the endangered party program, mounted a counterattack unique in the history of West German political parties. On May 27, 1988, it placed a one-page advertisement in the *Frankfurter Rundschau* newspaper carrying the statement: "The Green Bundestag group no longer represents its party grassroots!" In this reaction to the group's position on the penalty for rapists, the committee was backed by three state sections (those of Hamburg, the Saarland, and Berlin) as well as nine Bundestag members. The Realo-colored sections of Bavaria, Hesse, and Baden-Württemberg, and also the North Rhine-Westphalia section, condemned the ad.

On June 13, 1988, the current affairs weekly *Der Spiegel* featured a story on supposed financial manipulations by the federal executive committee and irregularities in the renovation of the party's federal headquarters near Bonn. Although these accusations were immediately withdrawn after the threat of a libel suit and an internal investigative committee was instated, the Green "financial scandal" grew in the ensuing months to become the central focus of the factional dispute. The party leadership turned out to be especially vulnerable here, as the questionable handling of financial affairs produced moral outrage among the Green grassroots.

Four months passed before the federal executive committee accepted "full political and legal responsibility" for the confirmed violations of tax and labor laws that had occurred during the refurbishment of the Villa Wittgenstein. At the same time, however, the committee maintained: "There is no reason to speak of a 'financial scandal.'" Rather, the whole issue was an attempt at "political character assassination" and should be seen as a "series of preconvictions."[30]

In early November, a national meeting of the Realo faction decided to back the Aufbruch group's campaign for an *Urabstimmung* and offered the latter a coalition for the envisaged federal party congress in Karlsruhe. On November 20, the Bavarian state party congress called on the federal executive committee to resign. Realo and Aufbruch spokespeople endorsed this demand, adding that similar circumstances had led to the resignation of the state executive committee of North Rhine-Westphalia. The state executive committee of Baden-Württemberg demanded that a discussion of "finances" be added to the agenda of the next party congress, set for November 2–4, which was supposed to have focused on the theme of Europe.

Against the opposition of the federal executive committee, a heated debate of several hours duration erupted in Karlsruhe, where Realo-Aufbruch coalition had placed the financial issue on the agenda. Shortly before midnight on November 2, delegates passed (214 to 186) a motion for the resignation of the federal executive committee, which accepted this demand a short while later. That night the congress dissolved into meetings of the various factions in which the losers discussed the consequences of their defeat and the winners discussed the new power constellations. But instead of exploiting their newly gained power and thereby provoking the breakaway of the defeated eco-socialists and radical ecologists, the new majority decided on an "institutional solution" and instated the *Bundeshauptausschuß*[31] as an interim federal executive committee.

Compare Duisburg 1987 and Duisburg 1989. In 1987, a Realo gave up his membership in the federal executive committee in response to the Fundis' triumph in the election of speakers to that committee; in 1989, a radical ecologist withdrew as a candidate because she was "disgusted by the majority of delegates' horny desire for a coalition." In 1987, Jutta Ditfurth was elected speaker of the federal executive committee with 387 out of 600 votes, and triumphantly waved the gratulatory flowers she received. During the federal party congress two years later she had a hard time even presenting her report of activities, designed as a rebuke to her opponents within the party, in an atmosphere colored by lack of interest, pity, and cries of "Beat it." She refused with a contemptuous gesture, to accept the flowers she was offered. The change of power was complete; the path was open for the new majority.

"The federal executive committee should no longer be an instrument of factional struggle but must respect the real pluralism within the Greens, must attempt to further discourse between the various positions"—that is how Ralf Fücks described the changed function of that committee just before the 1987 congress. Fücks was the Aufbruch group's candidate for one of the three speaker positions on the committee. The committee's old task, as it had been propagated and practiced by the left, was to function as an opposite pole to the Realo-colored group in the Bundestag. Now, even within the left wing, which had met shortly before the Duisburg congress, there was no longer a consensus of opinion.[32] The Aufbruch group's seriousness about the willingness to cooperate with different party factions asserted in its manifesto was evidenced in late January 1989, when the group entered into a center-left coalition against the Realo candidate Schily in a regular vote for membership in the Bundestag group's own executive committee. Whereas the defeated eco-socialists and radical ecologists had criticized a center-right coup in the wake of the Karlsruhe party congress, it was now the Realo group in the Bundestag that felt "pushed out" by the "negative coalition" between the Aufbruch group and the left.

The Party Congress of March 3–5, 1989, was marked by a desire for harmony and internal conciliation. In a symbolic rebuttal of the behavior that had intensified polarization two years earlier at the same location, the victors of Karlsruhe dispensed with marching through the hall. The delegates installed a federal executive committee that no longer included radical ecologists and explicit eco-socialists but gave a slim majority to the "new" party left, consisting of the Left Forum and left feminists. The committee's three-person speaker group reflected the new main tendencies: elected were a Realo representative, a member of the Aufbruch group, and a feminist who regarded herself as an "independent left-wing" candidate. All committee members were experienced state or federal politicians, and all were professionalized—that is, paid by the party—after returning their mandates, in line with a motion the delegates had taken.

The process of depolarization had thus come to an end. This process began with the development of a "bloc-free center" in which the new Aufbruch group had installed itself. This center had a suction effect upon the two factions, based on already existing fissures, which caused the independent left to distance itself from the eco-socialists and the radical ecologists. The newly formed Left Forum drew the necessary conclusions from the fact "that a certain form—I repeat, a certain form—of left politics within the Greens is no longer accepted,"[33] canceled its taboo on coalitions, and put the "system question" (in its Realo version) on the agenda of a de-escalated internal debate. Evolution of a comparable process on the other wing, with a differentiation between "soft" and "hard" Realos is what the centrists hoped for, and it was still possible.

The envisaged *Urabstimmung* had functioned as a catalyst for the reorganization and new formation of factions and was backed by the necessary number of county organizations by spring 1989. It was stopped by the Greens' *Bundesschiedsgericht* (party court) just prior to the closing date for manifestos because of a motion by a single county organization. In early May, the party court confirmed its initial directive with the explanation that the *Urabstimmung* had the status of an uncommitting "members' consultation" that could be resolved—if at all—only by a federal party congress or by the *Bundeshauptausschuß*. Only the Aufbruch group protested; the other group did not seem to care much about the project. It had served its purpose. The Realos did not need it any longer; the "old" and "new" left had rejected it anyway.

### Factionalism and Party Development

The Greens' tendency to lean toward the Realo wing in some cities and the eco-socialist wing in others has a lot to do with local traditions prior to party formation: political and cultural milieus that developed along with or in the aftermath of the student protest movement, local traditions of opposition in conjunction with the youth sections of labor organizations or with the political protests of the 1950s and 1960s. The locally dominant political powers must also be seen as an important factor. These differences were not leveled out in the movement surges and political experiments that followed, but intensified and overlapped in many ways. Ideological differentiation in accordance with local traditions has been shown with regard to earlier neo-communist party-building projects of the "proletarian turnaround" and also for the women's movement. New nationwide themes are colored by the experiences of these local milieus.

Hamburg and Frankfurt illustrate the powerful influence of prior local political history on the orientation and stability of politically dominant groups within the Greens and, at the same time, the inadequacy of a simple hypothesis of continuity of original local orientations within the new party. The continuity hypothesis is untenable for the dominant powers in Frankfurt's green-alternative milieu—a milieu that broke with the "revolutionary struggle" and the squatters' movement of the early 1970s and moved on into the "Sponti milieu" of autonomous anarchist movements and the Realo or eco-libertarian wing. The hypothesis is quite valid, however, for the development of Hamburg's Kommunistischer Bund into the eco-socialist wing. In any case, the reasons for continuity or change can be found more in the analysis of collective learning processes than through a personalized focus on individual biographies.

The path from a radicalized left-wing milieu to a green *Realpolitik* in Frankfurt was shaped in part by the logic of factionalism. During the formation phase in Frankfurt, the Green Party's left wing was already occupied by fundamentalist forces. Early attempts to overtake these by being even more radical failed; a high "right-wing" profile in the struggle for internal dominance was the only promising tactic. Another influence can be found in the preferred political style of the Frankfurt scene, which put a premium on a committed, even existential engagement and easily broke with its own political past as political options changed. This helps explain how resolute street fighters became resolute professional politicians with a tendency to act in accordance with the rules of *Realpolitik* in party and parliament.

The short existence of the Greens justifies interpreting the conflict between competing groups as a process of party development allowing various perspectives. Should the ongoing factionalism be regarded as an inevitable adolescent crisis of a young party on the way to its own identity? Does the factionalism symbolize the "wings of maturity" in the sense of intraparty alternatives with a long-term future? Or should it be viewed as a sign of a political experiment doomed to failure? Looking back into the phase of formation, we can discern lines of tradition that are clearly shaped by the original historical constellation. The trauma of the "German Autumn" had an unleashing effect.[34] The battle against terrorism hardened the domestic political fortress mentality, leading to a massive containment of oppositional movements, including citizen initiatives and the movement against nuclear power. None of these lines of conflict were articulated in parliament, street protest was repressed, and the countermobilization of the unions in the nuclear power conflict left people with the impression, that extraparliamentary protest was a deadend. The march into local and state parliaments and the Bundestag thus began with a whole bundle of motives, in which institutional critique was intermeshed with a desire for representation and an acknowledgment of the new political topics inspiring the politically aware public. The critique of parliamentarianism and the recourse to movement politics was the downpayment for a party that also wanted to obtain a parliamentary voice as the only real opposition against an all-party cartel.

This oppositional stance against the "old parties" cartel was strengthened time after time by new practices of discrimination and marginalization by the "old parties": banning the Greens from parliamentary control commissions, calling into question the party's constitutionality when it debated mandatory rotation or when violent demonstrations occurred. Nevertheless, the mere presence of the Greens and, later, the (oppositional) Social Democrats has helped to overcome this marginalization. By 1990, "Green" issues were echoed in the progammatic debates of all parties. And as a result of their own parliamentary work, the Greens' institutional critique lost much of its earlier sharpness. The "avant-garde mentality" of earlier years and the oppositional gathering of different factions have increasingly come under the pressure of party competition. The intensified infighting in the still-young party can be interpreted as an attempt to come up with a clearer party profile after a many-sided formation phase. "Identity" has become a key term in the disputes.[35]

The party's political identity, defined by programs and political concepts, is always in danger of putting someone off or even ignoring the electoral base activated in the new social movements. The party's selective linkage to the movement milieus has so far held on, and the movements' internal homogeneity has allowed manifold relations with intra-party tendencies. The new social movements' political forms and goals can, for instance, be differentiated in the political process with respect to their capacity for negotiation and compromise. Opposition to nuclear energy seemed to be nonnegotiable (and therefore essential for the political identity of the Greens); in the face of the anticipated risk, opposition to nuclear power was not a quantitative matter of "more or less." (This stance was eased through temporally undefined exit scenarios condensed in the formula "the beginning of the end of nuclear power," coined by the Social Democrats in the wake of the Chernobyl crisis.) A similar situation exists with respect to the feminist "autonomy" thesis and critique of ruling political forms. The antinuclear and the radical feminists movements can thus be regarded as a "natural" base for the Greens' fundamentalist wing, and parliamentary and intraparty politics does in actual fact play a central role in factional infighting with respect to nuclear energy installations.

On the other hand, local alternative and project milieus (especially those where professionalized labor market and social-political services are offered) and that section of the women's movement dependent upon "public money" (e.g., houses for battered women), present themselves as "natural" coalition partners of the Realo wing.[36] Financial concessions to this part of the movement sector are thus basic negotiation issues of local "red-green coalitions" and the experiment in Hesse. There, the fundamentalists charged, the Realos entered a coalition "for a song"—women's representatives and alternative projects.

Seen in this perspective, the Realo wing's rise within the Party coincides with a "project phase" of several years duration within different areas of the new social movements—a development many observers have interpreted as a demise.[37] In retrospect, it seems reasonable to apply Alberto Melucci's concept of an alternation between latency and visibility to the drop in visible movement activities after the mass mobilization of the peace movement during the fall of 1983.[38] Phases in which a milieu is stabilized alternate with new surges in mobilization in conjunction with new challenges and topics. The "invisible" activity in the latency phase creates the networks and infrastructures necessary for carrying out new campaigns. Speaking for the validity of this concept is the renewed protest dynamic that emerged in West Germany in the wake of the Chernobyl nuclear catastrophe, with diverse activities protesting against Chernobyl-caused levels of radiation, mass demonstrations at the building site for the nuclear reprocessing plant in Wackersdorf (Bavaria), and in the fall of the same year, a plethora of peace actions against the newly deployed mid-range cruise missiles.

The relationship of individual groups within the Greens to specific segments of other movements has, however, become increasingly complicated. The new party—as the movements' parliamentary arm—is the preferred recipient of Realpolitik expectations. Obviously the party backs equal opportunity institutions, advisory bureaus for alternative projects offering jobs in the "second labor market," independent ecological research groups, and women's shelters. But the Greens by now have a lot of competition. In all parties we can now find forces that—even if they have different goals and frequently employ only modest material means—support movement projects and institutions. The Greens—in contrast to other parties—put a considerable part of their public funds into movement projects ("eco-funds"), but the political effects are less clearcut.[39]

An exclusive clientelistic bond between the project milieu and the Green Party has not yet developed. Self-help institutions independent of parties continue to play an important role in political initiatives emanating from the movements. What is more, dependence upon public funding (and thereby political backing through interested parties) seems to vary strongly within different project areas. The Greens have clearly contributed to shift away from the radical rejection of "public funding" that was the norm in alternative milieus during the late 1970s. The projects' material difficulties, the fundamental claim for paid professional work in various institutions of the women's movement, and political attempts to take over this clientele by other parties seem to be more important for this development than a conscious attempt to form a "Green" clientele. Close clientelistic relationships are more scattered and relatively rare. Significantly, however, *Realpolitik* expectations addressed to the Greens are no longer looked down upon, as is documented in the debates concerning the creation of a foundation trust close to the Greens. Economic marginalization and long-term unemployment too have added a survival mentality to the movement milieus' broad political goals. Such processes found an ideological basis in Realo and eco-libertarian circles.[40]

Not the demise of but differentiation within the new social movements thus makes possible the specific clientelistic and grassroots relationships within the diverse Green groups. As success in central issues such as nuclear energy, disarmament, and ecological economics can be achieved only in the long term, the tension between the radical and Realo factions will continue even if the clientelistic relationships to the project milieu should intensify.

If the internal dispute over the party's direction is—as we suggest—determined by the dynamics of new social movements much more than the opponents allege, then the topic of party development as a catalyst takes on greater importance. Green parliamentary groups have adapted quickly to institutional rules. Provocative actions that called into question the legitimacy of institutional practices remained—for all Party groupings—exceptional. Initiatives pertaining to the organizational form of the political parties, too, stayed within the limits of "constructive opposition." Greens must be given credit for (partly unintentionally) enlivening and strengthening the legitimacy of West German parliamentarianism.[41] The party's present direction is neither an inevitable consequence of the requirements of institutional politics nor a necessary product of the movement sector. Even the "electoral will" in its demoscopic reading has not become a reliable or even a heeded reference point. Electoral results have supported both Realo options (majorities among Green voters favored "red-green coalitions"; the "moderate" Bavarian Greens won good results) and Fundi experiments (the women's ticket of the Hamburg GAL gained double-digit support). This dual option was confirmed by the results of the 1987 Bundestag elections, which were factionally neutral.

In the search for causes and consequences of the Greens' factional disputes, the development of the party's organizational structures has received increasing attention. One obvious issue here is the party's extreme imbalance (compared with other parties) between those holding parliamentary mandates, members, and voters. The extremely small membership of about 40,000 in 1987, which has been stagnating for years, has led to a situation in which every sixth member holds some kind of parliamentary mandate. Green Party work is thus in the main parliamentary work, and the latter, absorbing most of the party's resources, strongly influences the issues and contents of internal debates. A party base that is active in communal politics exacts substantial pressure on the party. The first wing that emerged from the factionalist dynamics in the Green Party successfully instrumentalized this pressure in the form of dissatisfaction with polarizing factional elites. Green Centrism portrayed itself as an organized self-reflectivity, as *the* force mobilizing the party's (decentralist) self-healing powers for the welfare of all: "It has again become obvious that the Green Party landscape can be understood neither from the vantage point of the headquarters of political blocs nor from the few big cities in which it has been easy for the political scene of the seventies to hibernate. It was especially the 'Green countryside' that profited from the initiative for an *Urabstimmung*, in conjunction with those cities that had attempted to circumvent the Realo–Fundi dispute and do their own thing all along."[42]

The Aufbruch group—whether its members were truly an antifactional wing or merely the populist profiteers of the polarization crisis that their opponents accused them of being—was the endogenous answer to the Greens' structural problem of having to follow the path of parliamentary representation despite being a party of the new social movements. The central paradox remains: a party deriving its energy and innovative impulses from the social movements' extraparliamentary and institutionally critical practices, but at the same time deriving the political power necessary for realizing its policies from elections and institutional representation. Whether the new factional constellation can consolidate the envisaged model of a "party of a new kind,"[43] or whether it must already be seen as a departure from this model, is yet to be seen.

NOTES

1. By "factions" we mean ideological currents that are *organized* into camps within a political party: that is, they have their own journals, conferences, and other organizational infrastructure.

2. See *die tageszeitung,* May 10, 1988.

3. The break-up of the red-green coalition in Berlin eventually occurred in November 1990 on the occasion of a police operation against squatters in the former East Berlin. Although this chapter deals with the development of factions during the tumultuous first 10 years of the Green Party, the 5 percent barrier is still an important issue today.—Eds.

4. Joschka Fischer, "Identität in Gefahr!" in Thomas Kluge, ed., *Grüne Politik* (Frankfurt am Main: Fischer, 1984), 34.

5. *Frankfurter Rundschau,* March 6, 1989.

6. Werner Hülsberg, "The Greens at the Crossroads," *New Left Review,* no. 152 (July–August 1985) 27.

7. See the "Mothers' Manifesto" in Chapter 14 in this volume.

8. Thomas Ebermann and Rainer Trampert, *Die Zukunft der Grünen: Ein realistisches Konzept für eine radikale Partei* (Hamburg: Konkret Literatur, 1984).

9. Ibid. 280.

10. Ibid. 277.

11. Printed in *grüner basis-dienst,* no. 1 (1984) 10.

12. "Ökolibertäre Grüne, Einigkeit und Grün und Freiheit: Gründungserklärung," *grüner basis-dienst,* no. 3 (1984) 31.

13. For a critique of the eco-libertarians see Wolfgang Kraushaar, "Die neue Leutseligkeit," in Helmut Dubiel, ed., *Populismus und Aufklärung* (Frankfurt am Main: Suhrkamp, 1986) 278–315.

14. Rudolf Bahro, "Pfeiler am anderen Ufer: Beiträge zur Politik der Grünen von Hagen bis Karlsruhe," Special issue of the journal *Befreiung* (Berlin, 1984) 65.

15. Jutta Ditfurth, "Radikal und phantasievoll gesellschaftliche Gegenmacht organisieren: Skizzen einer radikalökologischen Position," in *Grüne Politik,* Kluge, 57–69.

16. Jutta Ditfurth, "Der radikale Weg verspricht Erfolg: Für Bündnisse mit den sozialen Bewegungen," Wolfram Bickerich, ed. *SPD und Grüne: Das neue Bündnis?* (Hamburg: Rowohlt, 1985), 250–74.

17. Ebermann and Trampert, *Zukunft der Grünen, 271.*

18. See Wolfgang Ehmke, Joschka Fischer, Jo Müller, et al. "Verantwortung und Aufgabe der Grünen," *grüner basis-dienst,* no. 1 (1985) 15.

19. Joschka Fischer, *Der Umbau der Industriegesellschaft: Plädoyer wider die herrschende Umweltlüge* (Frankfurt am Main: Eichborn, 1989) 59–61.

20. "Mit rot-grün die Brüche im herrschenden Konsens vertiefen," statement of the Left Forum at the Greens' federal party congress in Duisburg, introduced at the nationwide meeting on February 19, 1989, p. 4.

21. Ludger Vollmer, "Gegen Realo, gegen Fundamentalo, für eine starke Zentralo-Fraktion: Versuch, einem Dilemma zu entrinnen," *grüner basis-dienst,* no. 4 (1985) 39.

22. Quotations from *Das Einfache, das schwer zu machen ist: Unabhängige Texte zur Krise der Grünen* (Bonn, December 12, 1987).

23. Bundesgeschäftsstelle Die Grünen, "Die Krisen-Klausur im 'Pantheon': Protokoll der gemeinsamen Sitzung des Bundeshauptausschusses der Grünen mit VertreterInnen der Landesvorstände und den Abgeordneten der Grünen im Bundestag am 12. Dezember 1987 in Bonn" (Bonn, March 1988) 35.

24. *Urabstimmung* was originally the trade-union term for a strike ballot. The Greens use it in the sense of a basic vote regarding fundamental party issues.—Eds.

25. Cf. Thomas Ebermann and Rainer Trampert, "Yuppie ayeah," *Konkret*, no. 7 (1988).

26. Antje Vollmer in an interview with the members' magazine of the Greens' state organization in Hesse, *Stichwort Grün*, no. 1 (1988) 10.

27. "Cabinet-wing" refers to those Green Party officials who had entered government positions.—Eds.

28. "Langweilige Bekenntnisse zu einer illusionslosen Bestandsaufnahme" (June 1988).

29. Christian Schmidt, "Realo gegen Fundi," *MOZ* (Vienna, April 1988) 42–43.

30. Statement of the federal executive committee regarding the Report of Inquiry into Financial Matters, delivered at the meeting of the *Bundeshauptausschu* β on October 15–16, 1988.

31. The *Bundeshauptausschuß* is the Green Party's enlarged federal executive committee, designed for grassroots representation on the national level and used in the 1980s as an instrument of Fundi strategy.—Eds.

32. Cf. *Stuttgarter Zeitung*, February 6, 1989.

33. Ludger Vollmer in a discussion with Hubert Kleinert, in *Deutsche Volkszeitung/Die Tat*, no. 10 (March 3, 1988).

34. Cf. Tatjana Botzat et al., *Ein deutscher Herbst: Zustände, Dokumente, Berichte, Kommentare* (Frankfurt am Main: Neue Kritik, 1978); Margit Mayer, "The German Fall of 1977," *New German Critique*, no. 13 (Winter 1978).

35. Cf. Hubert Kleinert, "Was ist der Grünen Identität? Annäherungen an einen problematischen Begriff," in Erwin Jurtschitsch, Alexander Rudnick, and Friede Otto Wolff, eds., *Grünes und alternatives Jahrbuch 1986/87: Strategien der Grünen und ökologische Krise* (Berlin: VAS, 1986) 21–41.

36. For the fundamentalist critique of the "women's version of *Realpolitik*," see Regula Bott, "Mehr Staat oder mehr Bewegung?" die *tageszeitung*, February 5, 1987.

37. For the women's movement see Sybille Plogstedt, "Was ist seit 1968 erreicht? Bilanz nach 15 Jahren," *Erziehung und Wissenschaft* (1983) 7–8; for the differentiation within individual movements, see Dieter Rucht, "Themes, Logics and Arenas of Social Movements," in B. Klandermans et al., eds. *From Structure to Action: Comparing Social Movements across Cultures* (Greenwich, Conn. JAI, 1988) 305–28. For the "demise" see Karl-Werner Brand, Detlef Büsser, and Dieter Rucht. *Aufbruch in eine andere Gesellschaft: Neue soziale Bewegungen in der Bundesrepublik* (Frankfurt am Main: Campus, 1986).

38. See Alberto A. Melucci et al., *Altri Codici* (Bologna: Il Mulino, 1984).

39. Cf. Detlef Murphy, "Politischer Protest und strukturelle Korruption: Die Grünen und die staatliche Parteienfinanzierung," in G. Wewer, ed., *Parteienfinanzierung und politischer Wettbewerb: Rechtsnormen—Realanalysen—Reformvorschläge* (Opladen: Westdeutscher Verlag, 1990).

40. See, for example, Matthias Horx, *Das Ende der Alternativen oder die verlorene Unschuld der Radikalität: Ein Rechenschaftsbericht* (Munich/Vienna: Hanser, 1985).

41. With differing valuations Otto Schily, *Vom Zustand der Republik* (Berlin: Wagenbach, 1986); Johannes Agnoli, "Zwanzig Jahre danach: Die Transformation der Demokratie," *Prokla*, no. 62 (1986) 7–40.

42. Ralf Fücks, "Bricht Grün auf?" *Kommune* 7, no. 2 (February 1989) 13.

43. Cf. Claus Offe, "Konkurrenzpartei und kollektive politische Identität," in Roland Roth, ed., *Parlamentarisches Ritual und politische Alternativen* (Frankfurt am Main: Campus, 1980) 26–42.

ᴏᴠ

# Who Votes Green?

## Sources and Trends of Green Support

LUTZ MEZ

*Green, that was the affirmative color for a new beginning.*
*For staying fresh and not turning into wood.*

Ernst Bloch
*Freiheit und Ordnung* (1969)

In March 1983, having won 2.2 million votes (5.6 percent of the total), the Greens entered the Bundestag with 27 seats. This unique event marked the end not only of the three-party system but of the ritualized voting pattern in the Federal Republic of Germany (FRG) as well. How did this new political situation emerge? Who are the Greens? Who votes Green? What are the relationships among the Green electoral base, voting behavior, and election results? An overview of some important findings from German survey research can provide the answers.

The German "party state" used to be considered an example of encrusted politics par excellence. The Berlin political scientists Johannes Agnoli, for example, criticized it as a "transformation of democracy."[1] Many studies noted the party state's inability to deal with conflicts or the impotence of politics vis-à-vis economically powerful actors. Nevertheless, since the end of the 1960s the political landscape of the FRG has been restructured by a slow process of change that was mainly brought about by thousands of citizen and grassroots initiatives.[2] These new social movements have tilled the land for the "new politics", they have broken down the traditional clichés of left and right and overcome labels like "progressive" and "reactionary."

Only because of these new social movements do the Greens exist. However, the Green Party is not identical with the environmental, the women's, or the peace movement. The social base of the environmental movement in the FRG alone is estimated to be almost 6 million people.[3] About 13 million citizens are adherents of or activists in the initiatives and groups of the new social movements, and this group is virtually identical with the potential electorate of the Greens. (The memberships of the different movements, of course, tend to overlap.) In contrast, the Greens' nearly 40,000 members resemble a cadre party. On one hand, their function is to integrate those new social movements into the parliamentary system of the FRG. On the other hand, the Greens are an anti-party whose history and origin are strongly shaped by the FRG's political system in general and its party system in particular.

Up to the end of the 1960s, the FRG's party system reflected the "cleavage structures" of the 1920s. Factors such as social status and religion strongly determined voters' choices. After 1970 voting behavior began to be less influenced by these traditional status factors, which were gradually complemented by political questions as decisive factors. Up to the end of the 1970s, however, the new issues of ecology, peace, and women's rights were avoided by the established parties and were taken up only by groups campaigning against nuclear power plants, women's organizations, self-help groups in the health area, and the new peace movement. The Greens were not the harbingers of the new political landscape; the new social movements were.[4]

The Bielefeld sociologist Horst-Dieter Rönsch was one of the first to study the changes in voting behavior under this new social situation. He analyzed the conflict revolving around the projected Wyhl nuclear power plant and described a phenomenon he called "Wyhler Wahl-Wanne" (the "Wyhl election crater").[5] As protest against that plant grew, the regional majority of the Christian Democratic Union (CDU) dropped in a pattern resembling a crater. Preconditions for the "crater effect" are: the region affected by the conflict is small; the political fronts in the conflict are clearcut; and the affected population is broadly mobilized. In Rönsch's opinion, however, environmental protest does not lead to typical protest behavior in elections. The Greens' core electorate is located in the urban residential areas of the new middle classes of the service sector. The "M.A.s" (the label used for the young, highly educated population) were the first Green voters, as Rönsch has demonstrated in an analysis of the election results of the Greens' Bunte Listen ("Rainbow Lists") in Northfriesland, Steinburg, Darmstadt, Hameln-Pyrmont, Osnabrück, Bielefeld, and Hamburg.[6]

The relationship between the Green Party's voters and the new social movements is much tighter than the one between other parties and their electorate. In other words, the Green electorate consists overwhelmingly of adherents and members of the new social movements. Two out of three Green voters are active or have been active in those movements. Nine out of 10 Green voters are opposed to nuclear power, while only six out of 10 voters of the German Social Democratic Party (SPD) take this stance. Thus, the Mannheim-based Elections Research Group (Forschungsgruppe Wahlen Mannheim) put forward the thesis that the established parties' inability to take up in parliament controversial debate over nuclear power played a crucial role in the formation of the Greens.[7] In the aftermath of the 1980 Bundestag elections, the political scientists Wilhelm Bürklin noted Green gains far above the average in areas where there were acute environmental conflicts or a combination of environmental conflicts and university milieus.[8] Bürklin later analyzed the empirical dimension of the Greens' electoral potential by using a theoretical model revolving around the following thesis: "New ideologies will lead to a successful restructuring of the party system by the structurally depraved political elite of the third generation when the material prospects for the future of parts of the electorate are decreasing."[9] That is, Bürklin regarded the bad job prospects for highly educated youth as one of the major causes of the formation of the Greens.

Green voters have also been characterized as a "new middle class critical of the system."[10] According to Heinz-Ulrich Brinkmann, most were born after World War II and have a high level of education but unfulfilled expectations with regard to their social status.[11] In contrast, Peter von Oertzen found that the Greens' electoral base is a stable part of the young West German population. If one compares the Green electorate with others in the respective age groups, the Green voters would be practically identical with those groups with regard to their educational level.[12] Oertzen wondered about the development over time of the voting behavior of this part of the electorate and the voting behavior of new generations. A trend, at least, can be deduced from election statistics. The level of mobilization of the Green electoral base (i.e., the relation between the potential and the actual votes for the Greens) has up to 1990 been determined mainly by environmental conflicts and regional peculiarities, such as residential structure (city, countryside, industrial area).[13] The overwhelming majority of Green voters live in university towns and center of the service sector.

The interaction of Green voting behavior and sociodemographic factors like age, gender, level of education, and job situation will now be demonstrated against the background of the West German party and electoral system and the findings of statistical election and survey research.

## The Party and Electoral System of the FRG

The Federal Republic of the 1980s had a voting population (i.e., people above the age of 18) of about 60 million. This breaks down to about 43.2 million potential voters in 1980, about 44.1 million in 1983, and about 45.3 million in 1987. Women make up 53 percent of the electorate, and men 47 percent.

From 1949 to 1961, the number of parties with parliamentary representation dropped quickly. Thus, the political landscape of the FRG developed in a fundamentally different direction than that of the Weimar Republic. The 11 parties active at the beginning of the Federal Republic shrank to three: SPD, CDU/Christian Social Union (CSU), and the Free Democratic Party (FDP). In comparison to other Western countries, the voting pattern in the FRG shows three peculiarities: a high turnout at elections, an extraordinary stability of the constituencies up to the mid-1970s, and the exercise of a tremendous integrative power by the three traditional parties (see Table 4.1).

Parliaments are elected by a system of personalized proportional voting. Half of the parliamentary seats are gained by direct mandates, and the other half by list mandates, elected respectively by the first and second votes. A party obtains parliamentary representation only when it has gained at least 5 percent of the second votes or three direct mandates. This restriction gave

TABLE 4.1: Electoral Participation and Percentage of Second Vote for Traditional Parties in Bundestag Elections, 1949–1987

| | 1949 | 1953 | 1957 | 1961 | 1965 | 1969 | 1972 | 1976 | 1980 | 1983 | 1987 |
|---|---|---|---|---|---|---|---|---|---|---|---|
| Total vote for traditional parties[a] | 72.1 | 83.5 | 89.7 | 94.3 | 96.4 | 94.6 | 99.1 | 99.1 | 98.0 | 93.9 | 90.4 |
| Electoral participation | 78.5 | 86.0 | 87.6 | 87.7 | 86.8 | 86.7 | 91.1 | 90.7 | 88.6 | 89.1 | 84.3 |
| Votes for traditional parties as percentage of total votes cast | 56.6 | 71.8 | 78.6 | 82.7 | 83.7 | 82 | 90.3 | 89.9 | 86.8 | 83.7 | 76.2 |

[a]This figure is the sum of the votes for the SPD, CDU/CSU, and FDP.
*Source:* Statistisches Bundesamt, *Wahl zum 11. Deutschen Bundestag am 25. January 1987, Fachserie 1* (Stuttgart and Mainz: Kohlhammer, 1987).

an advantage to the parties that were already represented in parliament and made it difficult for smaller parties to enter parliament at all.

## The Electoral Potential of the Greens

In mid-1977 the political scientist Rudolf Wildenmann studied the electoral potential of an ecological party in the Federal Republic for the first time.[14] Asked whether they could imagine voting for an ecological party, 25 percent of the West German population answered yes (see Table 4.2). Thus, given a total electorate of about 45 million people, the Green electoral potential could be estimated at more than 10 million. The decrease to 15 percent in 1980 can be explained by the emergence of the Greens as a concrete choice that did not meet all the expectations for an ecological party. With an increasing ecological consciousness, however, the Green electoral potential again increased to more than 25 percent.[15] Since 1982, the Green electoral potential has been stable at around 25 percent or 11 million voters.

In the 1987 Bundestag elections, the Greens obtained 3.1 million second votes, which means that only about one-third of the Green electoral potential actually voted Green. To put it differently: for every mobilized Green voter there are two potential Green voters who have either chosen another party or have not voted at all.

## Green Results in State and Bundestag Elections

From 1977 onward the Greens emerged from sources that had existed side by side before they even eventually joined forces in the party. In general, one can say that the transformation of the citizen initiatives and the anti–nuclear power movement into the Green Party was not launched by

TABLE 4.2: Electoral Potential of an Ecological Party in the FRG[a]

|                  | 1977 | 1978 | 1979 | 1980 | 1982 |
|------------------|------|------|------|------|------|
| Potential voters | 25.1 | 29.0 | 27.0 | 15.0 | 28.0 |

[a]The figures represent the percentage of the population who said they would vote for an ecological party.

*Source:* Rudolph Wildenman, Emnid GmbH & Co. Institut für Marktforschung.

those movements themselves but rather imposed on them by certain political groups and personalities.

Two sources stand out: the "left" Alternative and Rainbow Lists and politicians who had "failed" within their original established parties. The first group was especially decisive in big cities such as Hamburg, Berlin, and Frankfurt with founding core groups from left-communist mini-parties. The second position presented itself as a conservative alternative to the "left anarchists."

In the hot founding period (until the middle of 1979) the various lists and approaches were still very much shaped by the ideological background of the respective factions. "Left" and "conservative" groups existed side by side, with the left faction being slightly stronger than the conservative one but still unable to dominate. The strength of the factions varied from state to state. But the realistic insight that the common denominator was an interest in electoral success confined ideological differences to the background for a while. Given the lack of organization, funds, and time for preparation, the electoral successes of this period were quite impressive.[16] As time went on, more and more activists from the citizen initiatives joined the party, adding a third position. They joined at least partly in order to prevent the exploitation of years of their work by self-appointed representatives.

Since 1977, the Greens have participated in elections on the local and state levels. During the first direct elections for the European parliament in 1979, four West German green lists formed the "Other Political Association—the Greens." They gained almost 900,000 votes, not enough (3.2 percent) to qualify for parliament, but the reimbursement of campaign funds of about 4.5 million DM gave them a good start financially. In the Bremen state elections (October 7, 1979) and those in Baden-Württemberg (March 16, 1980), the Greens passed the 5 percent barrier for the first time. In September 1979, the representatives of the Green, Alternative, and Rainbow Lists agreed on joint participation in the 1980 Bundestag elections. The Party was founded in January 1980.

At the elections for the ninth German Bundestag on October 5, 1980, the Greens gained 732,619 first votes (1.9 percent) and 569,589 second votes (1.5 percent). They obtained even better electoral results in the aftermath of those elections. In Berlin (May 10, 1981), Lower Saxony (March 21, 1982), and Hamburg (June 6, 1982), Greens made it into the state parliament (see Table 4.3). The gap between electoral potential and actual voting behavior began to shrink.

After the Social Democratic/Liberal coalition in Bonn broke up in September 1982, the Greens reached their best results in the Hessian state elections (September 26, 1982)—8 percent. However, they gained only 4.6 percent in Bavaria (October 10, 1982) and thus failed for the first time after

TABLE 4.3: Electoral Results of the Greens, and Rainbow, Alternative Lists for the Bundestag, European Parliament, and State Parliaments

BUNDESTAG AND EUROPEAN PARLIAMENT

| Election | Party | % | Votes in 1,000 | Seats | Total Seats |
|----------|-------|-----|------|-------|------|
| EUR 1979 | GRE | 3.2 | 894 | — | 78 |
| BUN 1980 | GRE | 1.5 | 570 | — | 497 |
| BUN 1983 | GRE | 5.6 | 2,167 | 27 | 498 |
| EUR 1984 | GRE | 8.2 | 2,026 | 7 | 81 |
| BUN 1987 | GRE | 8.3 | 3,126 | 42 | 497 |

STATE PARLIAMENTS

*Baden-Württemberg*

| | | | | | |
|----------|-------|-----|------|-------|------|
| 1980 | GRE | 5.3 | 241 | 6 | 124 |
| 1984 | GRE | 8.0 | 372 | 9 | 126 |
| 1988 | GRE | 7.1 | 383 | 10 | 125 |

*Bavaria*

| | | | | | |
|----------|-------|-----|------|-------|------|
| 1978 | AUD | 1.8 | 211 | — | 204 |
| 1982 | GRE | 4.6 | 559 | — | 204 |
|  | ÖDP | 0.4 | 45 | — | 0 |
| 1986 | GRE | 7.5 | 853 | 15 | 204 |
|  | ÖDP | 0.7 | 77 | — | 0 |

*Berlin*

| | | | | | |
|----------|-------|-----|------|-------|------|
| 1979 | AL | 3.7 | 84 | — | 135 |
| 1981 | AL | 7.2 | 91 | 9 | 132 |
|  | GL | 0.3 | 4 | — | 0 |
| 1985 | AL | 10.6 | 132 | 15 | 144 |

*Bremen*

| | | | | | |
|----------|-------|-----|------|-------|------|
| 1979 | AL | 1.4 | 6 | — | 100 |
|  | GL | 5.1 | 21 | 4 | 0 |
| 1983 | GRE | 5.4 | 22 | 5 | 100 |
|  | GL | 2.4 | 10 | — | 0 |
|  | BAL | 1.4 | 6 | — | 0 |
| 1987 | GRE | 10.2 | 40 | 10 | 101 |

*Hamburg*

| | | | | | |
|----------|-------|-----|------|-------|------|
| 1978 | BL | 3.5 | 33 | — | 120 |
| 6/82 | GAL | 7.7 | 73 | 9 | 120 |

| 12/82 | GAL | 6.8 | 71 | 8 | 120 |
|---|---|---|---|---|---|
| 1986 | GAL | 10.4 | 100 | 13 | 120 |
| 1987 | GAL | 7.0 | 69 | 8 | 120 |
| *Hesse* | | | | | |
| 1978 | GL | 1 1 | 38 | — | 110 |
| | GAZ | 0.9 | 31 | — | 0 |
| 1982 | GRE | 8.0 | 278 | 9 | 110 |
| 1983 | GRE | 5.9 | 200 | 7 | 110 |
| 1987 | GRE | 9.4 | 311 | 10 | 110 |
| *Lower Saxony* | | | | | |
| 1978 | GLU | 3.9 | 158 | — | 155 |
| 1982 | GRE | 6.5 | 273 | 11 | 171 |
| 1986 | GRE | 7.1 | 304 | 11 | 171 |
| *North Rhine–Westphalia* | | | | | |
| 1980 | GRE | 3.0 | 291 | — | 201 |
| 1985 | GRE | 4.6 | 431 | — | 227 |
| *Rhineland-Palatinate* | | | | | |
| 1983 | GRE | 4.5 | 114 | — | 100 |
| 1987 | GRE | 5.9 | 129 | 5 | 100 |
| *Saarland* | | | | | |
| 1980 | GRE | 2.9 | 20 | — | 51 |
| 1985 | GRE | 2.5 | 18 | — | 51 |
| *Schleswig-Holstein* | | | | | |
| 1979 | GL | 2.4 | 38 | — | 73 |
| 1983 | GRE | 3.6 | 59 | — | 74 |
| 1987 | GRE | 3.9 | 60 | — | 74 |
| 1988 | GRE | 2.9 | 45 | — | 74 |

*Key:*

| | |
|---|---|
| AL | Alternative List (Alternative List) |
| AUD | Aktionsgemeinschaft Unabhängiger Deutscher (Action Community of Independent Germans) |
| BAL | Betrieblich-Alternative Liste (Shopfloor-Alternative List) |
| BL | Bunte Liste (Rainbow List) |
| BUN | Bundestag elections |
| EUR | Elections to European parliament |
| GAL | Grün-Alternative Liste (Green-Alternative List) |
| GAZ | Grüne Aktion Zukunft (Green Action Future) |
| GL | Grüne Liste (Green List) |
| GRE | The Greens |
| ÖDP | Ökologisch-Demokratische Partei (Ecological-Democratic Party) |

1980 to exceed the 5 percent barrier. In the new elections for the Hamburg state parliament (December 19, 1982), the Hamburg Green Alternative List (GAL) almost matched its previous showing, but the higher turnout reduced its share to 6.8 percent.

Opinion polls on expected voting behavior in the national elections demonstrated that the Greens had lost ground after the change of government in March 1983. It seemed that victory in the Bundestag elections of that year might elude them (see Table 4.4). On March 6, 1983, however, the Greens passed the 5 percent barrier with about 2.2 million second votes (5.6 percent). They gained 27 Bundestag seats and an enhanced status (*Fraktionsstatus*) with additional rights as a parliamentary group. In the direct elections for the European Parliament, the Greens almost maintained this level and got seven seats. Because of the low voter turnout, their share increased to 8.2 percent.

On the state level, their success remained nearly unbroken as elections for the state parliaments were held in Rhineland-Palatinate (March 6, 1983), Schleswig-Holstein (March 13, 1983), Bremen (September 25, 1983), and Hesse (September 25, 1983) (see Table 4.3). The Greens had their strongest increase in the Baden-Württemberg state elections on March 25, 1984; compared with the previous election, they gained about 50 percent more votes and seats. However, they did not get over the 5 percent barrier in the 1985 state elections in the Saarland and in North Rhine–Westphalia.

That same year (March 10, 1985), the Alternative List for the first time achieved a two-digit result (10.6 percent) in the elections to the Berlin state parliament. According to the Berlin political scientist Horst Schmollinger, this success was due to the city's metropolitan character, its political con-

TABLE 4.4: Percentage of Potential Voters Supporting the Greens[a]

| 1982 | | | | | | | | | | | 1983 | |
|---|---|---|---|---|---|---|---|---|---|---|---|---|
| Aug. | | Sept. | | Oct. | | Nov. | | Dec. | | | Jan. | |
| 7.5 | 9.0 | 8.0 | 9.0 | 5.5 | 6.5 | 3.5 | 6.5 | 6.5 | 5.0 | 6.0 | 5.0 | 5.0 |

[a]Emnid question: "Which party would you vote for if the Bundestag elections were to be held next Sunday?" Figures are the percentage of potential voters who answered: "The Greens."

*Source: Der Spiegel,* February 7, 1983, p. 85.

flicts, and its particular population structure.[17] The size of both the young and the old electorate is above average in Berlin, and the city has a high percentage of unemployed people and immigrants. Berlin can be seen as a model for the effective mobilization of the Green electoral potential.

The development in the territorial states[18] was much slower. In the state elections in Lower Saxony (June 15, 1986), however, the Greens gained in number of votes as well as in percentage. In Bavaria (October 12, 1986), they won more than 850,000 votes (7.5 percent of the total) and 15 seats. On November 9, 1986, the Green-Alternative List (GAL) obtained 10.4 percent of the vote in Hamburg, but fell back to the result of 1982 at the renewed elections of May 17, 1987.

The Bundestag elections on January 25, 1987, were another success for the Greens on the federal level. They gained 3,126,256 second votes (8.3 percent), an increase of more than 40 percent compared with the 1983 Bundestag elections. They now held 42 seats. After the red-green coalition in Hesse broke up in the spring of 1987 because of a conflict over nuclear power, the Greens again made progress in the moved-up state elections that followed (April 5, 1987). They did not, however, achieve a new parliamentary majority with the Social Democrats.

In Rhineland-Palatinate, the Greens finally entered parliament on April 17, 1987. In Bremen (September 13, 1987), the Greens won support from about 40,000 voters and thus achieved over 10 percent in West Germany's third city-state. Yet they did not make it into parliament in Schleswig-Holstein.

By 1987, the Greens were represented in nine out of 11 state parliaments (Lower Saxony, Hesse, Baden-Württemberg, Berlin, Bremen, Hamburg, Bavaria, Rhineland-Palatinate, and North Rhine–Westphalia) as well as in the Bundestag and the European parliament. They had failed to pass the 5 percent barrier only in Schleswig-Holstein and the Saarland (see Table 4.3).

## Social Profile of the Green Base of Support

The social structure of the Green electoral potential can be sketched out according to sociodemographic factors like age, gender, educational level, and employment. To some extent, data on religion, marital status, and trade union membership are also available.

The age structure of the West German electorate is shown in Table 4.5. Compared with other countries, West Germany has a disproportionate number of old people. Of the 45.3 million voters, 55 percent are over 45.

As the representative election statistics for the Bundestag elections show, Green voters are disproportionately younger than the average (see Table 4.6).

TABLE 4.5: Age Structure of the Electorate, 1980–1987 (Percentage of Total)

| Year | Age Group | | | | |
|------|-------|-------|-------|-------|-----|
|      | 18–24 | 25–34 | 35–44 | 45–59 | 60+ |
| 1980 | 12.7  | 16.2  | 19.7  | 25.7  | 25.6 |
| 1983 | 12.6  | 16.8  | 17.6  | 26.3  | 26.6 |
| 1987 | 11.9  | 17.4  | 16.0  | 27.9  | 26.9 |

*Source:* Statistisches Bundesamt, *Wahl zum 11. Deutschen Bundestag am 25. Januar 1987, Fachserie 1* (Stuttgart and Mainz: Kohlhammer, 1987), party electorates according to age and gender.

TABLE 4.6: Age Structure of the Electorate by Party, 1980–1987 (Percentage of Total Vote for Party)

| Party | Year | Age Group | | | | |
|-------|------|-------|-------|-------|-------|-----|
|       |      | 18–24 | 25–34 | 35–44 | 45–59 | 60+ |
| SPD   | 1980 | 14.3  | 15.5  | 18.3  | 25.1  | 24.8 |
|       | 1983 | 12.7  | 17.1  | 16.4  | 26.8  | 27.0 |
|       | 1987 | 11.9  | 17.9  | 15.6  | 28.3  | 26.3 |
| CDU   | 1980 | 9.4   | 12.8  | 20.4  | 27.7  | 29.7 |
|       | 1983 | 10.5  | 14.6  | 18.5  | 27.5  | 29.0 |
|       | 1987 | 9.6   | 13.2  | 15.1  | 29.7  | 32.3 |
| CSU   | 1980 | 11.7  | 15.8  | 19.8  | 26.0  | 26.8 |
|       | 1983 | 11.8  | 16.4  | 18.3  | 26.1  | 27.4 |
|       | 1987 | 10.5  | 15.7  | 15.5  | 28.2  | 30.1 |
| FDP   | 1980 | 13.6  | 20.3  | 24.3  | 24.0  | 17.8 |
|       | 1983 | 10.0  | 15.7  | 22.5  | 28.6  | 23.3 |
|       | 1987 | 11.4  | 15.2  | 19.5  | 31.6  | 22.3 |
| GRE   | 1980 | 43.3  | 27.2  | 12.1  | 11.0  | 6.5 |
|       | 1983 | 33.1  | 34.3  | 14.6  | 11.9  | 6.1 |
|       | 1987 | 23.2  | 38.1  | 16.3  | 13.3  | 6.1 |

*Source:* Statistisches Bundesamt, *Wahl zum 11. Deutschen Bundestag am 25. Januar 1987, Fachserie 1* (Stuttgart and Mainz: Kohlhammer, 1987), electorate of the parties according to age and gender.

More than 80 percent of Green voters are younger than 45 years, whereas the established parties have less than 50 percent in that age group. About 60 percent of the Green voters are younger than 35 years, whereas the proportion of this age group in the established parties is less than 30 percent. In the 1980 Bundestag elections, 43.3 percent of Green voters were under 25. In 1983, one-third of the Green voters came from the age group 18–24, and another third from the 25-34 group. In 1987, the 25–34 group was strongest, with 38.1 percent. Thus, Green voters under 35 are highly overrepresented compared with their percentage in the overall electorate.

Another analysis looks at the parties' share of different age groups (see Table 4.7)—that is, what percentage of a certain age group has voted for a party. Such an analysis demonstrates another difference between green voters and those of the established parties. In the 1987 Bundestag elections, for example, the SPD was supported by four out of 10 voters in each age group. While voters over 60 more often voted for the CDU, every third person opted for the CDU in all other age groups. CSU and FDP (just like the SPD) gained about the same percentage in every age group. In contrast, almost every sixth voter in the age groups 18–24 and 25–34 voted Green, while a clearly lower proportion of Green voters were over 45.

A comparison of the Greens' results in the 1980, 1983, and 1987 Bundestag elections (see Table 4.8) also shows that the mobilization of the Green

TABLE 4.7: Bundestag Vote for the Green Party and Other Parties, 1987 (Percentage of Total Vote by Age Group)

| Party | Age Group | | | | | |
|-------|-------|-------|-------|-------|------|-------|
|       | 18–24 | 25–34 | 35–44 | 45–59 | 60+  | TOTAL |
| SPD    | 38.1 | 39.0 | 37.1 | 38.8 | 37.5 | 38.1 |
| CDU    | 27.5 | 25.9 | 32.2 | 36.5 | 41.4 | 34.2 |
| CSU    | 8.5  | 8.7  | 9.3  | 9.8  | 10.9 | 9.6  |
| FDP    | 8.3  | 7.6  | 10.6 | 9.9  | 7.3  | 8.7  |
| GRE    | 15.5 | 17.4 | 9.6  | 3.8  | 1.8  | 8.0  |
| Others | 2.1  | 1.5  | 1.2  | 1.3  | 1.2  | 1.4  |
| FRG    | 11.9 | 17.4 | 16.0 | 27.9 | 26.9 | 100.0 |

*Source:* Statistisches Bundesamt, *Wahl zum 11. Deutschen Bundestag am 25. Januar 1987, Fachserie 1* (Stuttgart and Mainz: Kohlhammer, 1987), male and female votes according to age.

TABLE 4.8: Bundestag Vote for the Green Party, 1980, 1983, 1987

| | Relative Share (%) | | | Relative Gain (%) | |
|---|---|---|---|---|---|
| AGE GROUP | 1980 | 1983 | 1987 | 83–80 | 87–83 |
| 18–24 | 4.8 | 13.9 | 15.5 | 190 | 10 |
| 25–34 | 2.4 | 10.8 | 17.4 | 350 | 60 |
| 35–44 | 0.9 | 4.4 | 9.6 | 390 | 120 |
| 45–59 | 0.6 | 2.4 | 3.8 | 300 | 60 |
| 60+ | 0.4 | 1.2 | 1.8 | 200 | 50 |
| All groups | 1.4 | 5.3 | 8.0 | 280 | 50 |

*Source:* Statistisches Bundesamt, *Wahl zum 11. Deutschen Bundestag am 25. Januar 1987, Fachserie 1* (Stuttgart and Mainz: Kohlhammer, 1987).

electoral potential differed strongly within the various age groups. The strongest increases are in the age group 35–44, while the youngest group clearly shows less than the average increase. For the 1987 Bundestag elections, there was only a very small increase in the youngest group (10 percent), while Green voters of the middle age group nearly doubled. We have to keep in mind that the Green electoral potential in the youngest group has been nearly exhausted and, at the same time, that this group has the most nonvoters.

The large differences between age cohorts first appeared in Berlin. If we compare the 1981 and 1985 elections to the Berlin state parliament, the Alternative List's share of the under-30 group (25.6 percent) did not increase at all, while the share of the other age groups doubled compared with the previous elections (see Table 4.9). The stagnation in the youngest group can be explained by the low voting rates and the fact that this potential had already been mobilized in the 1981 elections.

Up to the Bundestag elections of 1983, more men than women voted Green across all age groups (see Table 4.10). Since the 1987 Bundestag elections, however, more women than men have voted Green, in the 35–44 and over-60 age groups. The slight increase in terms of male first-time voters (14.2 to 14.5 percent) shows that the Berlin trend of abstention from voting by young men also occurs on the federal level. In the 1987 Bundestag elections, the 74.4 percent turnout of men in the 21–25 group was the lowest since 1961: every fourth voter in this category abstained from voting. This trend was surpassed by women in the same age group (a 71.7 percent

TABLE 4.9: Elections to the Berlin State Parliament: Votes for the Alternative List, 1981, 1985

| | *Relative Share (%)* | | *Relative Gain (%)* |
|---|---|---|---|
| AGE GROUP | 1981 | 1985 | |
| 18–29 | 25.6 | 25.6 | 0 |
| 30–44 | 8.3 | 16.5 | 98.0 |
| 45–59 | 2.0 | 3.7 | 85.0 |
| 60+ | 0.6 | 1.2 | 100.0 |
| All groups | 7.5 | 10.1 | 35.0 |

*Source:* Data come from Christine Piperow and Heinz Ahlbrecht, "Wählerverhalten bei den Wahlen zum Abgeordnetenhaus von Berlin am 10. März 1985 nach Geschlecht und Alter: Ergebnisse der repräsentativen Wahlstatistik," *Landespressedienst,* March 29, 1985.

TABLE 4.10: Green Voters by Age and Gender in the Bundestag Elections, 1980, 1983, 1987 (Percentage of Second Vote)

| *Age Group* | *Male* | | | *Female* | | | *Total* | | |
|---|---|---|---|---|---|---|---|---|---|
| | 1980 | 1983 | 1987 | 1980 | 1983 | 1987 | 1980 | 1983 | 1987 |
| 18–24 | 5.3 | 14.2 | 14.5 | 4.3 | 13.5 | 16.5 | 4.8 | 13.9 | 15.5 |
| 25–34 | 2.6 | 11.5 | 16.9 | 2.4 | 10.1 | 17.9 | 2.4 | 10.8 | 17.4 |
| 35–44 | 0.9 | 4.7 | 9.9 | 0.8 | 4.1 | 9.3 | 0.9 | 4.4 | 9.6 |
| 45–59 | 0.6 | 2.4 | 3.7 | 0.6 | 2.4 | 3.9 | 0.6 | 2.4 | 3.8 |
| 60+ | 0.4 | 1.5 | 2.2 | 0.3 | 1.1 | 1.6 | 0.4 | 1.2 | 1.8 |
| Total | 1.6 | 5.9 | 8.3 | 1.2 | 4.8 | 7.7 | 1.4 | 5.3 | 8.0 |

*Source:* Statistisches Bundesamt, *Wahl zum 11. Deutschen Bundestag am 25. Januar 1987, Fachserie 1* (Stuttgart and Mainz: Kohlhammer, 1987), male and female votes according to age.

turnout) and can also be documented in the 1987 Bundestag elections. Since the number of nonvoters in this age group is higher than the number of Green voters, the relationship between abstention from voting and mobilization of the Green electoral potential should be closely analyzed.

The rates of increase are quite different for male and female Green voters.

On the federal level, the female Green votes in all age groups increased about four times between 1980 and 1983, and more than six times by 1987. The strongest increase for male and female Green voters can be seen in the 25–34 and 35–44 age groups. This trend in the 30–44, 45–59, and above 60 groups had already appeared in Berlin: Green voters in these age groups doubled compared with the previous elections (Table 4.11). The 18–29 group shows a slight decrease in male and a slight increase in female votes, indicating that no further mobilization had taken place in this age group. The reasons can be seen in the high abstention by male voters and the fact that the Green electoral potential is mobilized to a higher degree in Berlin than on the federal level.

Analyzing factors other than age and gender, the political scientist Manfred G. Schmidt has found that five out of 10 Green voters are unmarried (Table 4.12). Their social profile in terms of education varies considerably from

TABLE 4.11. Alternative List Voters by Gender and Age in Elections to the Berlin State Parliament, 1981, 1985 (Percentage of Second Vote)

| Age Group | Male | | Female | | Total | |
|-----------|------|------|--------|------|-------|------|
|           | 1981 | 1985 | 1981   | 1985 | 1981  | 1985 |
| 18–29     | 29.4 | 27.1 | 21.5   | 24.0 | 25.6  | 25.6 |
| 30–44     | 9.4  | 17.6 | 7.2    | 15.4 | 8.3   | 16.5 |
| 45–59     | 2.0  | 3.8  | 2.1    | 3.6  | 2.0   | 3.7  |
| 60+       | 0.8  | 1.5  | 0.6    | 1.1  | 0.6   | 1.2  |
| Total     | 9.9  | 12.3 | 5.6    | 8.4  | 7.5   | 10.1 |

*Source:* Christine Piperow and Heinz Ahlbrecht, "Wählerverhalten bei den Wahlen zum Abgeordnetenhaus von Berlin am 10. März 1985 nach Geschlecht und Alter: Ergebnisse der repräsentativen Wahlstatistik," *Landespressedienst,* March 29, 1985.

TABLE 4.12: Marital Status of the Green Electoral Base (Percentage of Total)

| Single | Married | Divorced | Widowed |
|--------|---------|----------|---------|
| 52     | 41      | 4        | 3       |

*Source:* Manfred G. Schmidt, "Demokratie, Wohlfahrtsstaat und neue soziale Bewegungen," *Aus Politik und Zeitgeschichte,* no. 11 (1984) 3–14.

one study to another. Figures for the low and high educational levels differ by as much as 17 percent. The deviations are negligible only with respect to the "middle" level (Table 4.13). As Table 4.13 shows, 62 percent of the national population falls into the "low" educational category. In contrast, only 25 to 42 percent of potential Green voters are in this category. Whereas 22 percent of the West German population has a middle educational level, the share of Green voters in this category lies between 26 and 32 percent. The Green electoral potential is strongest in the "high" category: whereas 16 percent of the general electorate has reached this level, 31 to 44 percent of the Green voters have.

The prominent Social Democrat and political scientist Peter von Oertzen has pointed out that the change in the social profile of the different age groups has important consequences for the assessment of the Green base.[19] He criti-

TABLE 4.13: Educational Level of the Green Electoral Base and FRG Population, 1983, 1984

| Study | Educational Level (%)[a] | | |
|---|---|---|---|
| | LOW | MIDDLE | HIGH |
| Rönsch 1983 | 25.0 | 31.0 | 39.0 |
| Fogt/Uttitz 1984 | 25.0 | 31.0 | 44.0 |
| Gotto/Veen 1984 | 32.0 | 26.0 | 43.0 |
| Müller-Rommel 1984 | 30.3 | 32.3 | 37.4 |
| Schmidt 1984 | 35.0 | 32.0 | 33.0 |
| FRG 1984 | 62.0 | 22.0 | 16.0 |

[a]*Low* indicates eight years of basic education. *Middle* corresponds to an American high school diploma; *high*, to a bachelor's degree and upward.

*Sources:* FRG 1984 data are compiled from *Statistisches Jahrbuch;* Helmut Fogt and Pavel Uttitz, "Die Wähler der Grünen 1980–1983: Systemkritischer neuer Mittelstand," *Zeitschrift für Parlamentsfragen* 15 (1984) 210–26; Klaus Gotto and Hans-Joachim Veen, eds., *Die Grünen: Partei wider Willen* (Mainz: Hase & Koehler, 1984); Ferdinand Müller-Rommel, "Die Grünen im Lichte von neüesten Ergebnissen der Wahlforschüng," in Thomas Kluge, ed., *Grüne Politik: Der Stand einer Auseinandersetzung* (Frankfurt am Main: Fischer, 1984) 125–41; Horst-Dieter Rönsch, "Die Grünen: Wählerbasis, politische Entwicklung, Programmatik," *Gewerkschaftliche Monatshefte,* no. 2 (1983) 98–111; Manfred G. Schmidt, "Demokratie, Wohlfahrtsstaat und neue soziale Bewegungen," *Aus Politik und Zeitgeschichte,* no. 11 (1984) 3–14.

cizes as misleading any comparison of Green voters or potential voters with average West German data because of the dominance of younger people among the Greens. (Table 4.14). He argues that Green voters—in terms of their education level—are representative of these age groups as a whole, so that the Green electoral base is a stable proportion of the younger West German population.

This suggestion raises the question of how the voting behavior of the Green electoral base will develop over time and how new electoral generations will vote. Since Green voting behavior is also determined by political issues and conflicts, the Greens' future electoral results will still depend strongly on the mobilization potential in the metropolitan and industrial areas.

Various studies demonstrate that more than 50 percent of Green voters are working (see Table 4.15). In this regard, Green voters hardly differ from those of other parties. The Greens get stronger support from the unemployed than the other parties do: between 5 and 13 percent of the unemployed population has voted Green or expressed an intention to do so. However, one has to bear in mind that the unemployment rate in the Federal Republic is highest in the 18–25 age group.

The share of Green voters among housewives is about 16%. Between 22 and 36 percent of students have voted or expressed an intention to vote for the Greens.

Some studies[20] demonstrate that, among the working population, the Greens get most of their votes from skilled workers and civil servants. In his study of the voting behavior of the new middle class, the political scientist Heinz Ulrich Brinkmann[21] came to the conclusion that the Greens got most

TABLE 4.14: Social Profile of the FRG

| Age Group | Educational Level | | |
|---|---|---|---|
| | LOW | MIDDLE | HIGH |
| 18–19 | 34.5 | — | — |
| 20–24 | 40.0 | 30.0 | 30.0 |
| 20–39 | 50.5 | 27.0 | 22.5 |
| 18–39 | 46.5 | 34.5 | 19.0 |
| 65–69 | 75.0 | 17.0 | 8.0 |

Source: Wilhelm Bürklin, Grüne Politik (Opladen: Westdeutscher Verlag, 1984).

TABLE 4.15: Occupational Structure of the FRG and the Green Electoral Base
(Percentage of Total by Study)

| | FRG | FOGT/UTTITZ | GOTTO/VEEN | MÜLLER-ROMMEL | SCHMIDT |
|---|---|---|---|---|---|
| | *1984* | *1984* | *1984* | *1984* | *1984* |
| Employed | | | 44 | 51.0 | 52 |
| Workers | 42 | | 16 | | |
| Skilled | | 14.9 | | | |
| Unskilled | | 1.8 | | | |
| White-collar | | 32.2 | 20 | | |
| Public-service | 46[a] | | 6 | | |
| Self-employed | 12 | | 2 | | |
| Students | | 34.0 | 36 | 21.7 | 22 |
| Unemployed | | 12.8 | 5 | 6.1 | 6 |
| Housewives | | 12.8 | 16 | 11.1 | 10 |
| Pensioners | | 4.3 | | 5.6 | 6 |
| Others | | 1.4 | | 4.5 | 4 |

[a]This category includes public-service and white-collar workers.

*Sources:* FRG 1984 data are compiled from *Statistisches Jahrbuch*; Helmut Fogt and Pavel Uttitz, "Die Wähler der Grünen 1980–1983; Systemkritischer neuer Mittelstand," *Zeitschrift für Parlamentsfragen* 15 (1984) 210–26; Klaus Gotto and Hans-Joachim Veen, eds., *Die Grünen: Partei wider Willen* (Mainz: Hase & Koehler, 1984); Ferdinand Müller-Rommel, "Die Grünen im Lichte von neuesten Ergebnissen der Wahlforschung," in Thomas Kluge, ed., *Grüne Politik: Der Stand einer Auseinandersetzung* (Frankfurt am Main: Fischer, 1984) 125–41; Manfred G. Schmidt, "Demokratie, Wohlfahrtsstaat und neue soziale Bewegungen," *Aus Politik und Zeitgeschichte*, no. 11 (1984) 3–14.

of their votes from white-collar workers and civil servants in 1980 and 1983, but increased their votes from self-employed and blue-collar workers.

Up to now, the religious affiliation of potential Green voters has not been a major topic of research, nor do the representative electoral statistics provide data on this question. However, the studies by Horst-Dieter Rönsch and Manfred G. Schmidt suggest a Protestant majority among the Green electorate (see Table 4.16) and a much larger share of nondenominational voters than is found in other West German parties.

Rönsch and Schmidt came to the conclusion that about one-third of Green voters are trade-unions members while two-thirds are unorganized.

TABLE 4.16: Religious Affiliation of the Green Electoral Base (Percentage by Study)

| STUDY | PROTESTANT | CATHOLIC | OTHERS |
|---|---|---|---|
| Rönsch 1983 | 31 | 23 | 34 |
| Schmidt 1984 | 44 | 34 | 22 |

*Sources:* Horst-Dieter Rönsch, "Die Grünen: Wählerbasis, politische Entwicklung, Programmatik," *Gewerkschaftliche Monatshefte*, no. 2 (1983): 98–111; Manfred G. Schmidt, "Demokratie, Wohlfahrtsstaat und neue soziale Bewegungen," *Aus Politik und Zeitgeschichte*, no. 11 (1984) 3–14.

This level of union membership clearly differentiates the Greens from the CDU and the FDP, 80 percent of whose voters are not organized, and from the SPD, whose voters have traditionally maintained close ties to the trade unions. Highly educated young voters living in a household with a trade-union member tend to support the Greens rather than the SPD.[22]

The crucial question is the connection between the new social movements and Green voters. For this, we have insights from *Eurobarometer*, a poll based on data from the entire European Community. In 1982, people were asked about active membership in or opposition to the environmental movement, the anti–nuclear power movement, and the peace movement. The engagement of the West German population in new social movements and their voting decisions are shown in Table 4.17.

At 62 to 68 percent, Green voters show much higher participation in the new social movements than members of other parties. The 5 to 9 percent of Green voters who see themselves as opponents of the new social movements, may belong to factions opposing "leader personalities" or may oppose the leading strategy of the movement, which quite often is declared as opposition to the movement itself.

Interestingly in 1982, just before the deployment of the new U.S. middle-range cruise missiles—26 percent of the CDU/CSU electorate declared they were peace movement activists. With the partial dissolution of the peace movement, this attitude has changed.

## Conclusion

A close relationship to the new social movements is the major difference between Green voters and the electorates of other parties: two out of three Green voters are or have been activists in these movements. Thus, Green

TABLE 4.17 Engagement in New Social Movements: The Green Electoral Base and
Members of Other Parties 1982 (Percentage of Members Polled)

|  | CDU/CSU | SPD | FDP | GRE |
|---|---|---|---|---|
| Ecology movement |  |  |  |  |
| Activist | 12 | 22 | 21 | 68 |
| Opponent | 50 | 31 | 43 | 7 |
| Antinuclear movement |  |  |  |  |
| Activist | 11 | 24 | 18 | 64 |
| Opponent | 56 | 36 | 51 | 9 |
| Peace movement |  |  |  |  |
| Activist | 26 | 42 | 30 | 62 |
| Opponent | 35 | 21 | 31 | 5 |
| Number polled | 475 | 361 | 67 | 134 |

*Sources:* Ferdinand Müller-Rommel, "Die Grünen im Lichte von neuesten Ergebnissen der
Wahlforschung," in Thomas Kluge, ed., *Grüne Politik: Der Stand einer Auseinandersetzung*
(Frankfurt am Main: Fischer, 1984) 125–41; Nicholas S. J. Watts, "Mobilisierungspotential
und gesellschaftspolitische Bedeutung der neuen sozialen Bewegungen: Ein Vergleich der
Länder der europäischen Gemeinschaft," in Roland Roth and Dieter Rucht, eds., *Neue
soziale Bewegungen in der Bundesrepublik Deutschland* (Bonn: Bundeszentrale für politische
Bildung, 1987) 62–63.

voting behavior is strongly influenced by the new cleavages—ecology, peace,
and women's rights. Two-thirds of Green voters express strong political interests, compared with 24 to 31 percent of other parties' supporters.

With respect to sociodemographic factors, one can say that the number
of Green supporters grows with increasing educational levels. Nationwide,
potential and actual Green voters are concentrated in the 18–34 age group;
there are clearly fewer Green voters over 45. In the younger groups, however, up to 30 percent abstain from voting. This trend of abstention and its
relationship to the mobilization of the Green electoral base calls for further
study.

The most important result with respect to occupational structure is the
similarity between Green voters and those of other parties, apart from the
attraction to the Greens of the unemployed and students influenced by unfulfilled status expectations and bad job prospects.

The choice to vote for the Greens has up to now almost always been motivated by acute ecological conflicts in connection with a certain residential structure. The Greens achieved their best results in the service-based and industrial metropolitan areas. The relationship between educational level, urban residence, and ecological conflict has been most significant as a mobilizing factor in the city-states of Berlin, Hamburg, and Bremen, where even the mobilization of the younger groups has been very high.

Recently, shifts with respect to the gender of Green voters have been observed. While more men than women voted Green in all age groups until 1983, women moved into the majority after 1987. Only among people between 35 and above 60 were there more male than female Green voters. This aggregate picture needs to be differentiated for different regions, however.

## NOTES

1. Johannes Agnoli, *Die Transformation der Demokratie* (Berlin: Voltaire, 1967). Agnoli develops his thesis with direct reference to the Greens in "Zwischen Bewegung und Institution," in Wolfgang Kraushaar, ed., *Was wollen die Grünen im Parlament* (Frankfurt am Main: Neue Kritik, 1982) 120–39.—Eds.

2. See, for example, Karl-Werner Brand, Detlef Büsser, and Dieter Rucht, *Aufbruch in eine andere Gesellschaft: Neue Soziale Bewegungen in der Bundesrepublik* (Frankfurt am Main: Campus, 1986).

3. The social base consists of activists and adherents or potential members; besides that, a movement also has sympathizers.—Eds.

4. Lutz Mez, "Von den Bürgerinitiativen zu den Grünen: Zur Entstehungsgeschichte der 'Wahlalternativen' in der Bundesrepublik Deutschland," in Roland Roth and Dieter Rucht, eds., *Neue soziale Bewegungen in der Bundesrepublik Deutschland* (Frankfurt am Main: Campus, 1987) 263–76.

5. Horst-Dieter Rönsch, "Reaktionen auf staatliches Handeln am Beispiel des Wahlverhaltens," in Otthein Rammstedt, ed., *Bürgerbeteiligung und Bürgerinitiativen: Legitimation und Partizipation in der Demokratie angesichts gesellschaftlicher Konfliktsituationen* (Villingen: Neckar-Verlag 1977) 374–96.

6. Horst-Dieter Rönsch, "Grüne Listen: Vorläufer oder Katalysatoren einer neuen Protestbewegung?" in Rammstedt, *Bürgerbeteiligung und Bügerinitiativen*, 397–434.

7. Cf. Manfred Berger et al., "Regierungswechsel und politische Einstellungen: Eine Analyse der Bundestagswahl 1983." *Zeitschrift für Parlamentsfragen*, 14 (1983) 556–82.

8. Cf. Wilhelm P. Bürklin, "Die Grünen und die 'Neue Politik' Abschied vom Dreiparteiensystem?" *Politische Vierteljahresschrift* 22, (1981) 359–82.

9. Wilhelm P. Bürklin, *Grüne Politik: Ideologische Zyklen, Wähler und Parteiensystem* (Opladen: Westdeutscher Verlag, 1984) 47.

10. For example Helmut Fogt and Pavel Uttitz, "Die Wähler der Grünen 1980–1983: Systemkritischer neuer Mittelstand," *Zeitschrift für Parlamentsfragen* 15 (1984) 216–26.

11. Heinz-Ulrich Brinkmann, "Wahlverhalten der 'neuen Mittelschicht' in der Bundesrepublik Deutschland," *Aus Politik und Zeitgeschichte*, nos. 30/31 (1988) 19–32.

12. Peter von Oertzen, "Zum Verhältnis von 'neuen sozialen Bewegungen' und Arbeiterbewegung: Zur Sozialstruktur des grünen Wählerpotentials," in Gerd-Uwe Boguslawski and Bodo Irrek, eds., *Ohne Utopien kann der Mensch nicht leben: Beiträge zur Gewerkschaftsarbeit: Eine Festschrift für Hermann Kantelhardt* (Göttingen: SOVEC, 1985) 243–61; and Peter von Oertzen, "Zur Sozialstruktur des grünen Wählerpotentials: Einige Überlegungen zum Verhältnis von 'neuen sozialen Bewegungen' und Arbeiterbewegung," *Frankfurter Rundschau,* January 11, 1986, and January 13, 1986.

13. Lutz Mez and Lutz Hildebrandt, "Die Grünen bei der Bundestagswahl 1983: Zur Bedeutung akuter Umweltkonflikte," *WZB-Mitteilungen,* no. 22 (1983) 11–13.

14. The representative opinion poll was carried out in April–May 1977 and April–May 1980 by Rudolf Wildenmann with the cooperation of Wilhelm P. Bürklin, Silke Wollweber, and William E. Wright for the journal *Capital.*

15. Hans Kessel and Wolfgang Tischler, *Umweltbewußtsein: Ökologische Wertvorstellungen in westlichen Industrienationen* (Berlin: edition sigma 1984).

16. Lilian Klotzsch and Richard Stöss, "Die Grünen," in Richard Stöss, ed., *Parteien-Handbuch: Die Parteien der Bundesrepublik Deutschland 1945–1980,* vol. 2 (Opladen: Westdeutscher Verlag, 1984) 1509–98.

17. Horst Schmollinger, "Die Wahl zum Berliner Abgeordnetenhaus vom 10. März 1985: Zunehmende Mobilisierungs- und Integrationsschwäche des Parteiensystems," *Zeitschrift für Parlamentsfragen* 16 (1985) 337–54.

18. West Germany has three city-states (Hamburg, Bremen, and Berlin); the rest are territorial states.—Eds.

19. Cf. von Oertzen, "Zum Verhältnis"; von Oertzen, "Zur Sozialstruktur."

20. Hans-Joachim Veen, "Wer wählt grün? Zum Profil der neuen Linken in der Wohlstandsgesellschaft," *Aus Politik und Zeitgeschichte,* nos. 35/36 (1984) 3–17; and Fogt and Uttitz, "Wähler der Grünen."

21. Brinkmann, "Wahlverhalten der 'neuen Mittelschicht.'"

22. Ibid. 32.

# III

## In Parliament

### Green Principles in Real Politics

*Chapter 5*

ॐ

# What Has Happened to Green Principles in Electoral and Parliamentary Politics?

LILIAN KLOTZSCH, KLAUS KÖNEMANN
JÖRG WISCHERMANN, AND BODO ZEUNER

We wrote this chapter in 1987, basing it on a then-ongoing research project, in the hope of adding some novel insights to widespread debates about the Green Party. What was missing in those debates, especially in the English-language literature, was a critical analysis of the effects of parliamentarianism.

Parliamentarianism drastically transformed the Green Party and the social movements that were its base. We try first to demonstrate here how some of the mechanisms of integration work and second to explain the loss of some of the Green Party's original intentions through the action of parliamentary constraints that worked to prevent a substantial challenge to the political system.

In 1997, now that the Greens have become a well-established party, we still see value in reflecting on their original radical views and the critical assessment of parliamentarianism that the party held a mere 10 years ago. It is more necessary than ever to examine and question how integration and adaptation work within our political system.[1]

## Integration through Participation: Why Is Integration a Problem?

The Greens' participation in elections and parliaments has had consequences for the political system of the Federal Republic of Germany (FRG), for the Green Party itself, and, in part, for the party's active social base, the new social movements.[2] The integration of the Greens and the new social movements into the existing ruling system over the period from 1980 to 1987 meant the loss of much of their original identity: a fundamental alternative to existing politics in both form and substance. In their founding era, most Greens viewed existing politics as subordinating society to the requirements of economic growth and a state apparatus acting in accordance with these requirements. They saw this state enter into more and more areas of life in an increasingly uncontrollable way, but at the same time incapable of preventing ecological catastrophes.

From the vantage point of U.S. political culture, it is probably difficult to understand the problem of integration.[3] Citizen and protest movements have a much longer tradition in the United States, but the majority voting system and the prevailing two-party system make it even harder for such movements to exact innovative pressure by founding a political party with parliamentary representation.

A look at the Party's founding phase, when the first fundamental debates over the benefits and dangers of electoral and parliamentary participation took place, will help clarify the relevance of the problem.

The Green Party evolved in a phase of West German development characterized by a high level of political and economic stability compared with other countries, but also by crisis-induced restructuring: the end of a 30-year period of postwar prosperity, mass unemployment, failure of Keynesian control mechanisms, breakup of the social democratic–corporatist consensus, visible ecological and technological dangers, and tendencies toward a marginalized "two-thirds society—that is, a society that marginalizes its lowest third.

In this phase, the new social movements grew and became increasingly politicized as they came to identify their original single issues as a problem of the whole society. Despite their heterogeneity, the new social movements had in common a basic mood that was critical of power. This is also true for those parts of the movements that came together to establish the Green Party in order to oppose the ruling system on its own terrain, in electoral campaigns and in parliaments.

Clear differences in emphasis existed within the framework of this basic mood, and these soon became relevant within the party. One faction emphasized the ruling systems' ecological output. This faction was concerned strictly with the "substance" of politics, an ecological, nongrowth politics aimed at securing survival in the face of civilian and nuclear threats. Since the ruling apparatus was incapable of solving such problems, other organizational forms of political rule had to be found. The nature of those forms did not matter, as long as they served ecological goals. In this perspective, an eco-dictatorship could not be excluded.

Another faction pinned its hopes on a new world view in which human beings would no longer dominate nature but would regard themselves as a part of the eco-system. This was to some extent a religious or semireligious revival, concerned less with changing state politics and more with fostering a different human consciousness. Thus, this faction too was relatively indifferent to prevailing and future organizational forms of power.[4]

The factions that were soon to prevail in the process of party formation developed their basic criticism of power into a critique of ruling structures. Their credo was that not only wrong ideas and aims in politicians' and citizens' heads are bringing about a life-threatening politics; political, economic, and social structures themselves need to be changed if an alternative politics is to have a chance of success.

For those mainly interested in the political systems' ecological output, it seemed obvious to extend extraparliamentary protest to parliaments in order to open up an additional arena and, by competing with the established parties, extort policy changes. For those who had developed a critique of ruling structures, the problem of parliamentary representation was more complicated. They viewed the new social movements' real political achievement as having simultaneously focused and generalized the single-issue protest movements. Through electoral and parliamentary participation, let alone possible governmental participation, parts of these movements were in danger of mutating to become part of the ruling system; at the very least they risked losing the impetus of a power-transcending political movement and losing touch with the extraparliamentary base. This problem was discussed in detail with respect to the role of future Green and alternative parliamentarians. If they tried to use parliament as a forum for propagating alternative policies, providing the government with stimulating debates covered by the television networks, would they make extraparliamentary protest seem unnecessary and weaken it?

It is therefore no accident that the people who dominated the first phase of party formation—the output-oriented and the "deep ecologists"—had a less developed critique of ruling structures and also fewer reservations about integration into the ruling system. But these groups were only a segment of the new social movements' political potential. When people with more decisive structural critiques began entering the new party, as occurred before 1980, they quickly became the majority because their critique of the ruling structures expressed the political impetus common to divergent movements more authentically than the "pure ecologists" (the "green Greens," as they were labeled in the party's early phase) were able to. The "grassroots-democratic" postulate, one of the Green program's four "pillars," is an expression of this polemic against prevailing structures. It is a misunderstanding to view it merely as a peaceful striving for "grassroots democracy" in the U.S. sense.

What caused the critics of the ruling system to help form a party and thus participate in elections and parliamentary work despite their fundamental misgivings? In our view, there are three reasons. First, many, especially leftists, who had experienced (or promoted) a breakup of oppositional groups into sects after the end of the student movement viewed the new party as an opportunity to end divisions and promote open communication and learning. These processes might even end up transforming their own programmatic positions. The tendency to break up would not be overcome by way of the traditional leftist "standardization," but by respecting, not suppressing, even fundamental political differences, and attempting to use these differences productively for political growth by all involved. Thus the common organization was called "list" and not "party" in several states and in many cities and counties during the party's early phase. "List" had a double meaning. On one hand, it refers to the electoral system, which usually requires a list of candidates; on the other, it expresses an explicit desire for plurality. A list is an external enumeration of elements, which, except for their enumerative relationship, have nothing to do with one another. Substantive, communicative, and political homogenization or integration of a list's elements is a task still to be undertaken; it cannot be viewed as solved, as the term *party* inherently suggests.

Second, the formation of a party or a list automatically meant participation in elections to representative bodies. The dangers of integration into the ruling system were weighed against the possible benefits, and for many the benefits carried more weight. These included the opportunity to intensify extraparliamentary protest by making use of the publicity effect accorded to parliaments; to obtain information available to parliament, as well as legal security and financial backing for social movements' projects; to confront the public with new issues; to influence other parties by competing with them for voters; to propagate Green views, through, for instance, the free television time given to all parties running candidates; and even to influence parliamentary decisions directly with regard to laws or the installation of governments.

Finally, fears of absorption and integration were surmounted through the hope that the new forms of politics developed in the social movements themselves could be transferred (at least partly) to the internal organization of the new electoral and parliamentary party. Respect for minority decisions, keeping meetings open to the public, gender parity, the imperative mandate for elected representatives (and parliamentarians, despite their constitutionally defined freedom to vote in accordance with their individual consciences instead of en bloc as the party dictates), prohibition of an accumulation of mandates and offices by individuals, the transfer of all above-average income gained from political mandates to the party or to movement pools, rejection of the status of professional politician, obligation of parliamentarians to be spokespeople for extraparliamentary initiatives—all these principles were designed to have two effects. First, they were to act as a barrier against the integrative tendencies of the ruling system and any tendency for the Greens to become just like the "established" parties; second, many Greens and alternatives hoped that the practice of these political forms would have an enlightening effect, conveying that anyone can "do" politics, and that politics can be "done" in a fundamentally different way.

The arguments used by these fundamental critics of the ruling system to explain their choice of electoral and parliamentary participation despite their skepticism were actually borne out by the events that followed. This makes it necessary to take a closer look at the Greens' parliamentary strategies or the lack of the same. We then describe the actual effects of Green parliamentarians on the political system and, in particular, on parliaments. Finally, we discuss the repercussions of parliamentary participation for the Greens themselves, and the effectiveness of the prophylactic measures they had taken against integration into the system.

## The Greens, the Political System, and Parliamentary Strategy

The Greens regard their own existence and their electoral success as largely a consequence of the citizenry's increasing disaffection from the state and political parties. In contrast to the established parties, whose attention is focused on maintaining the stability of state action and securing a smoother administrative process, they place themselves absolutely on the side of the citizens and citizen initiatives who criticize immobility, the arrogance of power, and bureaucratization and seek new forms of participation. They call for new guiding principles for political and state activities, which should focus on human beings and their needs, push back the state's interference, and reduce its responsibilities in favor of an extension of self-determined areas. But whether and to what degree one can instrumentalize the state to "recover" areas of freedom, or whether recovery demands action against the state, is a hot debate in the Greens. All in all, the Greens have neither a common and theoretically sound understanding of the state nor a common conception of the state's possibilities and limits.

Is the long-term goal improvement or transcendence of existing representational structures? Do demands for more open participatory structures, decentralization, and elements of direct democracy (such as referenda and plebiscites) aim at supplementing or enlivening centralist and representational structures, or do they aim at providing a real alternative?

Although the Greens do not have many consensual answers to these questions, it is striking that almost all Greens restrict their view to the political realm. In contrast, the traditional leftist parliamentary critique was always aimed at the unresolvable contradiction between the political and economic realms. This critique was based on the idea that the relations of production, and issues of property and rule in the economic realm, unless they are transformed, inherently subordinate and will continue to subordinate politics to the logic of the capitalist system. Such conceptions play only a marginal role (at most) in Green thinking, so that reference to the systemic limits of political and state activities is not really possible for them. The Greens are therefore in danger of overestimating the power of politics and politicians and putting the blame for the deplorable state of affairs solely on the political realm. Given the Greens' largely unclarified relationship to the political system and political institutions of the FRG, the Greens' designation of their own function and role within this system had to remain unclear. Thus, the spokeswoman of the Greens' Bundestag group, Marieluise Beck-Oberdorf, addressed party members shortly after the Greens had entered parliament:

> This question, too, has not yet been decided upon: should we attempt to strengthen parliament vis-à-vis the executive, or, in other words, should we be the "better" parliamentarians, or should we regard parliament as an elitist and antiquated representational body? The answers to such questions will influence the Greens' political style.[5]

Depending on the dominant faction, the Greens' individual *Landesverbände* (state party organizations) respond differently to these questions. The position held for many years in Baden-Württemberg, for instance, was that parliaments, as institutions that have developed historically, should be accepted in principle, and it should now be the Greens' task to push for improvements in areas where parliaments (or, rather, the parties and politicians represented in them) fail. The division of power should be (re)instated; parliaments should be strengthened in relation to governments. Parliaments should (again) become places where the important issues of the future are debated and decided upon after all the arguments have been taken into consideration. This necessitates a new political style, based on dialogue instead of confrontation, and characterized by active tolerance and a desire to understand those with differing views. Basically, parliaments are seen as institutions well-suited for furthering the enforcement of Green demands and conceptions. "Therapy instead of denunciation" was the only significant long-term strategy propagated—a distinctly constructive collaboration that aimed at convincing opponents with good arguments and upholding the status of parliaments.

In Hamburg, the situation was quite different. Here, parliaments were mainly viewed as institutions of the bourgeois democratic state whose function it is to bring about a consensus between the ruled and the ruling, thus continually legimating the prevailing relations of power. In this view, parliaments could not be instruments of the new social movements. The Greens' goal should not be to strengthen the legitimacy of parliaments and political institutions in general; on the contrary, they should act to reduce the loyalty of the ruled to the activities of the state and to a smooth ruling process, and where this loyalty is already diminished, to further and radicalize these tendencies. Parliamentary strategy should conform to these goals by revealing the political opponent's links to vested interests and his resulting inability to solve societal problems in the interests of the majority of the population. This strategic conception makes a special point of driving a wedge between the Social Democratic Party (SPD) and its voters by comparing the SPD's promises with the party's actual behavior and the results of Social Democratic policies.

In most state party organizations and on the federal level, no consensus on long-term strategy existed. This meant that the party's own task was delegated to each individual parliamentarian. Typical was the initial situation in the Greens' Bundestag group:

> Our politics in the Bundestag has been one of living from hand to mouth. It is from hand to mouth because it has been characterized by parliamentary initiatives based more on the activity of individuals than on a strategy formulated and carried by the whole parliamentary group. A systematic and thorough debate on how and with what perspective and strategy we Greens in the Bundestag want to work has hardly taken place.[6]

And after a year of work in the Bundestag, the words were not much different:

> What political profile should the parliamentary group have? Both the party and the parliamentary group have neglected to produce a basic evaluation of the parliamentary system's possibilities and of how the Green parliamentary group should work. Terminology such as *fundamentalism* or *pragmatism* can hardly be used to orient ourselves. . . . But this basic evaluation is necessary because the clarification of structural questions of parliamentary work depends on it. The same applies to the question of which coalition partner we should consider to be a future option and how far-reaching our minimal demands for such a coalition should be.[7]

Especially in the beginning, the demand for debates on strategy mainly derived from the parliamentarians' desire to embed their own parliamentary work (usually conducted under the pressure of short-term projects) in a long-term and overarching concept of societal change. They were seeking a compass to keep them from becoming lost and bogged down in the day-to-day parliamentary routine.

But the Green Party was confronted by other problems just after the Bundestag electoral success in 1983. These problems ranged from erecting their own organizational structures to activities in the extraparliamentary realm (generally viewed as of prime importance), to the immense pressure exerted by the electoral campaign itself. In addition, having experienced the exhaustive discussions and disputes of the Greens' formative phase, they feared a resumption of the strategy debate in which the different viewpoints would clash irreconcilably and internal differences would break open again in full intensity. Instead, after the initial electoral successes gave the Greens a parliamentary presence, there was a tendency to gather experience in that unknown terrain, and to evaluate and assess it quietly at a later point. It was not uncommon for Greens to express the hope that this would provide the basis for a consensual position with regard to parliamentary work and the perspectives, opportunities, and limitations resulting from it.

This wait-and-see attitude changed overnight when the question of Green governmental participation was effectively launched in public by the media. (Other important impulses in this direction came from parliamentary groups and individual parliamentarians.) Taking over responsibility for state actions was now openly propagated as a worthwhile goal from within the ranks of the Greens. Now, in the party's endless internal conflicts, the strategy debate was in danger of being reduced to the question of governmental participation. The parliamentary experience that had been gained turned out not to be very helpful, especially if one takes into account that these experiences themselves were dependent upon divergent initial expectations.

Some saw no use in a *direct* enforcement of their (and the extraparliamentary movements') goals by way of parliamentary majority decisions on the basis of the prevailing structural framework. These Greens ultimately regarded their parliamentary work as a tool for mobilization in the extraparliamentary realm. Other Greens, in contrast, had hopes for direct parliamentary successes. They expected occasionally to achieve the consent of the ruling majority through convincing arguments. A state parliamentarian from Baden-Württemberg recalls his beliefs on entering parliament:

> I expected to push through much more because I thought that bad politics
> evolved from ignorance. That they simply do not know certain things, that

they simply have not heard certain arguments, because it is always the same people sitting there. And now, when new people came in, they would be confronted with new arguments and one could then convince them. . . . And I didn't think that one only introduces motions (that are not passed anyway), but I thought that, if you have good people making the drafts, people from the eco-institutes, for instance, who pen a good substantiation of reasons, then they will be astonished how good we are. And then they will cooperate.[8]

Similarly optimistic expectations were expressed by several Green parliamentarians from Hamburg during the short phase of toleration negotiations in 1982.[9] At that time, the ruling SPD lacked a parliamentary majority for six months. The SPD entered into toleration negotiations with the Greens but then abandoned these and gained an absolute majority in new elections. A parliamentarian recalls his own hopes: "I was one of those who had a feeling somewhere inside that said: maybe something will come of it. . . . This made for an even greater disappointment when I saw through the SPD and realized that they did not really mean it."[10]

All the Green parliamentarians, soon after entering parliament, recognized that the chances of realizing their goals in state politics were extremely thin, but they interpreted these experiences in different ways. The original skeptics saw their position confirmed; the disappointed optimists argued that the negative experiences had occurred in a situation of parliamentary opposition, and wanted to see what a coalition government offered. Waltraud Schoppe, the spokeswoman of the Greens' Bundestag group, warned in 1985: "To become dogmatic here is to restrict our opportunities for development. . . . These reports are describing as impossibilities things that we have not even tried out yet."[11]

It is questionable whether the Greens can use a purely empirical method to come up with an analysis of the systemic limits of parliamentary action and develop a theoretical basis for their political strategy. The next empirical step too—participation in government as a junior partner—initially provides only limited opportunities that seem surmountable by one's own effort, perhaps by attempting to gain a higher percentage of votes.

## The Greens' Effects on Parliament

The effect of the Greens upon a parliament's opinion-making and decision-making system depends upon the party constellation there. In the three states we analyzed most closely, the constellation in 1980–1984 was as follows:

— Baden-Württemberg: Majority rule of the Christian Democratic Union (CDU). The Greens were the fourth-strongest party and in the opposition along with the SPD and the Free Democratic Party (FDP).

— Berlin: Governing coalition of the CDU and FDP. The Greens were the third-strongest party and in the opposition with the SPD.[12]

— Hamburg: Majority rule of the SPD (from June to December 1982 with a parliamentary minority and partial backing by the Greens; thereafter with a parliamentary majority). The Greens were in the opposition with the CDU; the FDP had no representation.

In the Bundestag, the Greens, as the fourth-strongest party, were in the opposition with the SPD against a ruling coalition of CDU/CSU and FDP.[13]

The Greens have both structural-formal and informal effects upon parliaments. The Greens' programmatic demands included structural changes in parliamentary and administrative opinion making and decision making—despite the party's unclear relationship to parliamentarism itself. These demands were echoed in phrases such as "greater transparency of decisions," "participation for those affected," "increased parliamentary control of governments and administrations," and "decentralization of administrative apparatuses." However, such changes were not forthcoming, and were usually not even emphatically pursued by Green parliamentarians.

The CDU, SPD, and FDP parliamentarians we interviewed in Baden-Württemberg, Berlin, and Hamburg all deny that such changes have occurred under the Greens' influence; they even contest the need for those changes. Instead, they assert that reforms aimed at bringing government closer to the people and allowing greater participation to those affected took place *prior* to the Greens' parliamentary debut. Moreover, they consider existing opportunities for control and participation sufficient, even if they have not been used enough. Finally, in the words of the FDP speaker in Baden-Württemberg's state parliament, the state-federal relationship (the infringement upon federalism) is the main problem, not state parliaments' lack of control over state governments.[14]

The Greens acknowledge their inefficacy in this area. As the speaker of the Greens' parliamentary group in Hamburg observed; "They knew how to oppose a transformation of parliamentary structures . . . Parliament does not function any differently now than it did two and a half years ago."[15] The Greens encountered massive opposition every time they attempted to insert plebiscitary elements or even to question or supplement the exclusively representational forms. "They are simply scared," the Hamburg speaker continued, "that we will tear parliament apart with plebiscitary elements—this always activates a kind of Weimar syndrome."[16] This was confirmed by the FDP's Baden-Württemberg speaker, who noted that it would be "a completely different debate" if the Greens were to call into question the representative character of existing democracy.

Below the structural level, the Greens did effect some formal-organizational changes in parliaments, such as the establishment of committees on problems of foreigners and women in Hamburg and Berlin. However, a deterioration of parliamentary control was an unintended side-effect of the Greens' parliamentary presence. In all parliaments, use or manipulation of the rules of procedure kept them out of parliamentary organs concerned with "sensitive" areas of the security apparatus, especially the Office for the Protection of the Constitution and other secret services. Their exclusion from the Bundestag subcommittee responsible for the office's budget was declared constitutional by the Supreme Court in a finding that aroused a lot of public controversy in 1986.

The Greens frequently used the existing legal possibilities for parliamentary control of the government and the administration. To an extent out of proportion with the number of offices they held and more vigorously than the other opposition party, Green parliamentarians initiated interpellations, extraordinary plenary and committee meetings, and the establishment of subcommittees and additional committee hearings in which many affected popular groups took part. They tapped informal sources of information in the administration and—as Hamburg's SPD remarked—proved to be an effective instrument against attempts at suppressing scandals. The other side of the coin was the administration's practice of providing less information to parliamentary committees with Green members, as, for example, happened to the Internal Affairs Committee of Berlin's state parliament. One former FDP parliamentarian from Berlin thus described the Greens' entrance into parliament as having unintentionally caused the loss of "an element of parliamentary competence."

A direct effect of Green parliamentary work was a higher frequency and a greater duration of parliamentary meetings, especially in Berlin and Hamburg. Not all of the established parties' representatives were pleased about the additional workload, but in no state did they react by restricting minority parties' speech time or rights to present motions. Except in "security-related" areas, no restrictions of the rules of procedure occurred. The established parties had learned their lesson from the Bremen events. In Bremen, the smallest state and the first in which a Green list got over the 5 percent barrier (1979) the ruling SPD majority in the state parliament overreacted by applying restrictive practices that put an substantial additional strain on the new Green parliamentarians' work. These practices, however, served only to provide the Greens with further publicity. After these experiences, the established parties changed their strategy to one of accepting the new Green parliamentary colleagues, which prevented new accusations of restrictive practices and exposed the Greens to the normal conditions and requirements of parliamentary work.

In all parliaments, the Greens themselves also largely renounced a strategy of provocative disregard for parliamentary rules, which would have given rise to formal restrictions. Filibustering, occasionally to be seen in the U.S. Congress or Italian parliaments, was not even attempted.

The Greens' *informal* parliamentary effects were more important than the structural-formal changes we have been discussing. The changes pertain to the style and the extent of political communication and confrontation in parliaments. Given the Greens' goal of parliamentary participation, questioning the legitimacy of ruling political forms and substance, how did Green parliamentarians express this fundamental difference of political orientation vis-à-vis the other parties' parliamentarians?

In all three states, the Greens extended the spectrum of topics addressed in parliaments, with regard to environmental politics, energy politics, and civil rights in general, as well as minority rights, women's politics, and the politics of (im)migration and foreigners, especially in Hamburg and Berlin. CDU, SPD, and FDP representatives saw an increase in the degree of controversy in parliamentary debates only in Hamburg and Berlin. The Greens' style in Baden-Württemberg was characterized more by an attempt at "dialogue" (the parliamentary group's programmatic formulation) with other parties. The differences are clearly discernible in the comments on the Greens' style by the heads of the SPD's respective state parliamentary groups:

— Baden-Württemberg: "I noticed no change, neither with regard to style nor with regard to loudness of exchanges, nor in the degree of controversy. . . . They were so nice, really, extremely nice. But so normal!"[17]

— Hamburg: "They can really take things apart. And they're with it. . . . And they are really in the process of becoming quite a threat to us in some areas."[18]

Independent of the degree of controversy in parliamentary debates, the Greens' parliamentary activities everywhere *increased the legitimatory pressure* for other parties. However, this has affected the established parties differently depending on their programmatic affinity or electoral competition. The CDU, whether in power or not, is least affected by the legitimatory pressure emanating from the Greens. The CDU politicians we interviewed felt little pressure from the Greens in their governmental or (in Hamburg) oppositional politics, but they reacted with sensitivity wherever they feared losing their own electoral clientele. The left-liberal wing of the FDP, which existed only in Berlin, occasionally felt rattled by the parliamentary initiatives of the Berlin Alternative List (AL).

The SPD provided a completely different picture. Only in Baden-Württemberg did the SPD politicians we interviewed say that they stood under no additional legitimatory pressure. In this state, under their former state party chairman Erhard Eppler, the SPD had begun intensive debates on new ecological orientations long before the Greens came into existence. More over, the Greens' later input could not contribute anything to the results of those debates.

In Berlin, the formerly governing SPD's proportion of the vote dropped to 33 percent in the 1985 state elections in which the AL obtained 10 percent. Representatives of all SPD wings now felt pressure from the AL to delimit themselves on two sides, to CDU voters and to AL voters. The SPD had problems with "the AL's closer contact to the lively sections of the population, . . . to that which is in the process of formation and especially critical," as one SPD parliamentarian from Berlin put it.[19]

These problems were even more pronounced in Hamburg's governing SPD. According to the head of their parliamentary group, the Greens' parliamentary presence has "increased the pressure to legitimize and change direction" at least with respect to environmental politics and the issue of the "authoritarian state." The Greens caused the debates to be held "under a magnifying glass."

In two areas, however, the Greens had no effect: the internal structure of the other parties (except in the area of more opportunity for women) and the readiness to revise basic political decisions. All those interviewed in each party and in each state declared that the Greens' "grassroots democratic" political forms (for instance, rotation of offices, prohibition on the accumulation of mandates and offices, nonprofessionalization of the party, grassroots links for parliamentarians) were more deterrent than exemplary for their parties. The same individuals insisted that the Greens had hardly any effect upon the internal power relations between the different factions and wings. As for revising guiding principles of state activity—support for nuclear energy and cruise missile deployment, opposition to reduction of the work week—readiness to alter these basic stances grew little, if at all. These statements are, of course, based to a degree on the established parties' wish to legitimate and defend themselves by attributing changes to their own decisions and not to pressure from outside. But their statements point to the fact that political directions change not primarily as a result of the parliamentary activities of a minority party, but mainly as a result of societal movements and changes of consciousness.

We have seen that the strongest effect on the political system emanating from the Greens' electoral and parliamentary participation is the additional legitimatory pressure on the other parties, mainly on the SPD. Another effect diametrically opposes the original intentions of the majority factions of the Greens: namely, the Greens' contribution to the legitimization of the ruling system, especially parliament, by masking the relative powerlessness of parliamentary representatives in the political process.

Two left-liberal politicians from Berlin formulated this problem very clearly. An FDP representative in Berlin's state parliament said:

> The AL, intentionally or unintentionally, eased the relationship of certain social and political groups previously opposing or ignoring parliament to the state legislature itself. . . . And the AL can perhaps do this with these groups easier than other parties can. [By extending the spectrum of political issues] the AL does something that actually has to be regarded as quite a strengthening of parliamentarianism, because all issues are brought into parliament.[20]

A former FDP party leader who later, in 1984, switched to the AL's group in the Berlin state parliament, describes this unintended legitimatory function in greater detail and more critically. Without the AL's parliamentary representation of extraparliamentary groups and interests, "the problems would become a lot worse and reach a point where they would spill over into violent conflicts. This means that the AL in parliament is like lubricating oil, by acting as an early-warning instrument for issues in which the system does not work. . . . This makes it a mechanism for preventing violence. One doesn't have to throw bombs in order to get controversies debated in public." But this changes neither political decisions nor the decision-making mechanisms themselves. "In Berlin, seen as a whole, parliament has not become more important for the political system. It has become important as a basis for articulating other political perspectives, but more as part of the media system than as part of the system of political decision-making." This clear-sighted former FDP leader views the Greens' parliamentary activity, to which he himself contributed, with concern: "There is practically no other party parliamentary group or group of individual parliamentarians that take parliaments as seriously as the Greens do. That is dangerous, as it also affects the perspectives of the party and its base."[21]

### Effects of Parliamentary Participation on the Greens and Their Base

If the Greens' parliamentary presence strengthens parliamentary legitimacy without substantially changing ruling politics, the party's entry into parliament could have the "paradoxical effect of slackening the pressure for change exerted on the political system." If people become disillusioned about both the potential of parliaments to affect developments and the Greens' role as a parliamentary opposition, this could have the effect of an "all-clear" siren, in Martin Jänicke's words.[22]

The Greens were aware of the issue in their early phase and discussed it time and again after their initial experiences in parliaments. They attempted to anticipate some of the structural constraints they would be exposed to and to develop mechanisms to counteract them. What happened?

### THE COMPULSION TOWARD GENERAL COMPETENCE AND COMPROMISE POLITICS

In West German parliamentarianism, all parties represented in parliament are expected to take a position in all policy areas, a de factor obstacle to a single-issue party stance. A second expectation is that a party has the capacity to compromise. For the Greens, both expectations were problematic from the outset.

#### *General Competence*
The Greens, born amid a host of single-issue movements, regarded the inevitable tendency toward political generalization evinced by the processes of party formation and electoral participation with dread and hope. Some regarded it as an opportunity to develop programmatically and transcend particularisms; others thought it would overtax the Greens in the face of their many unclarified basic issues.[23] Clearly, the development of the party program and the breadth of the internal political debates during the initial phase of parliamentary work in no way equipped the Greens to cover all policy areas—from state activities such as foreign and security policy, justice, finance, infrastructure, economics, and social policy to societal politics tailored to particular "problem groups."

Political systems tackle fundamental and overarching societal problems by breaking them down on the basis of a division of labor in line with departmental responsibilities. The division into different policy areas or departments on the governmental level corresponds to the division into different committees with one or more respective policy areas in parliament. Each party's parliamentary group attains proportional representation in these committees. These committees, the FRG's "working parliaments," consider most motions and draft bills in detail. If they are well-argued, individual initiatives of opposition parties have a chance of success, although, in matters of importance, voting behavior runs along the parliamentary group's or coalition's preset line.

Committee positions are filled in one of the first acts of parliamentary business at the beginning of every legislative period. The Greens' parliamentary groups were forced either to name their committee representatives on short notice or symbolically forgo this form of participation. Although the Greens could have taken the occasion to debate whether they should send representatives to *all, selected,* or *no* committees, no such debate on principles took place either in the states or in the Bundestag. The Greens filled all the committee seats they were proportionally conceded, so that personnel decisions were taken pragmatically in accordance with the wishes of individual Green parliamentarians. This initial decision had several important consequences:

— Against the party's original intentions, Green parliamentarians gave up the chance to make a general protest against the system of segmenting political problems in accordance with the existing division of labor.

— The Green parliamentarians committed themselves to establish a political profile in all areas and in all details, even if the party had not yet developed programmatic positions in those areas.

— The relatively arbitrary distribution of committee seats created long-term structures of specialization within the Green parliamentary groups. The political system thus began to transfer its own depoliticized division-of-labor structure to its Green opponents.

The reasons for the Greens' decisions are easy to understand. Their implications were either unseen or underestimated. Moreover, the party regarded parliamentary work as an opportunity to get rid of the "single-issue" stigma by showing the established parties and the public how much they knew. They attained this goal everywhere in their parliamentary work; the Greens proved to be the most diligent parliamentarians in all states and in the Bundestag, and now one rarely hears the other parties complain that the Greens did not have much to say in many political areas.

For the Greens themselves, the decision to pursue a general political competence had two consequences. On one hand, the requirement of political generalization accelerated and intensified the programmatic debate, affecting not only parliamentarians but also electoral campaigns and the party as a whole. On the other hand, the Green parliamentarians had put themselves into an increasingly reactive position. They continuously had to formulate positions on issues presented to them by the government or by the governing parties, often without being able to orient themselves on party decisions or seek backing from interested groups or their own base. They entangled and overtaxed themselves, and never found the time for debates on fundamental political issues and a common parliamentary strategy within their parliamentary group.

Individual Green parliamentarians early on called for making a "concentration upon strategic conflicts" in parliamentary work a political priority. The Berlin political scientist and AL parliamentarian Martin Jänicke went so far as to call for the Greens to practice a "politics of empty chairs" with respect to certain issues and to react satirically to "trivial parliamentary business."[24] This took place only once, when the AL in Berlin argued for the equality of cats and dogs during a parliamentary debate over the dog tax, declared this to be a question of conscience, and initiated a complicated voting process. In day-to-day parliamentary affairs, striving for a symbolic emphasis would have meant consciously forgoing certain areas and overcoming the pressure to participate and demonstrate their own competence and seriousness. The Greens' decision tied up energy that would otherwise have been available to the whole parliamentary group for launching concerted parliamentary initiatives on "strategic" issues and thereby increasing the pressure on the established parties.

Priorities were set, but by individual parliamentarians in their areas of specialization because a well-proportioned and intensive covering of the whole political spectrum would have overtaxed the working capacity of a small parliamentary group. These individual priorities were in part coordinated with the appropriate intra-party specialist groups. Coordinating priorities among several people and several related policy areas turned out to be much more difficult, and it was nearly impossible to coordinate and enforce such priorities among the Green parliamentary group as a whole.

### Compromise Politics

During the Greens' formative phase, social movements were extremely suspicious from the outset of compromise as an institution of parliamentarianism. If *a little* nuclear energy or nuclear armament is enough to endanger the survival of *all* of humanity, if a small interference in the eco-system has unforeseeable consequences, then there is little room for negotiations over slightly more or less of the same. The actual experience of the Green factions critical of power was that "compromises" had hitherto always worked against the socially weak or unorganized "general" interests such as a clean environment. Thus, during this period strong tendencies wanted to limit the function of Green parliamentarians to the demonstration of an uncompromising contrast of Green politics to business as usual.

Such tendencies are hardly relevant today. This is also an effect of parliamentary participation. Rather, all important Green factions agree that selective compromises with other parties cannot be excluded in cases where Green interests are furthered thereby. However, this minimal consensus is of little help in deciding concrete issues. Are one's own interests impaired by package compromises ("logrolling") because the decision to agree to unwanted political measures makes the Greens less credible? Does this exclude coalitions or agreement to budget laws?

Most aspects of this problem did not immediately arise after the Greens' entry into parliament. Because the Greens were in the opposition almost everywhere and not needed for getting together a majority, their ability to compromise was not put to the test. Only in the state of Hesse, and later in Berlin, Lower Saxony and Bremen, did the problem of a durable Green compromise with other parties come up.

Thus, although a requirement for compromise politics did not prima facie exist for an opposition party, the Greens were expected by Green party voters and other parties to demonstrate their ability for compromise; some actually hoped to realize some of their goals through compromise in parliamentary committees. Despite an often intensive effort to cooperate constructively and seriously, these hopes were quickly disappointed everywhere. In the committees, single Green parliamentarians were confronted by a majority of CDU or SPD representatives. Under such conditions, it is difficult to stick with a continual oppositional stance. In such a committee, a Green parliamentarian will act like a teacher in a grading committee who regards grading as detrimental to learning but occasionally accedes to an "F" in order to enforce a "B" in other cases.

Their own extraparliamentary base too, often urged Green parliamentarians to accede to compromises. Especially where initiatives had concrete goals that were not fundamentally opposed by other parties, the Greens were urged to cut back their own demands. A Berlin parliamentarian recounted his experience: "The people from extraparliamentary work . . . as in my policy area, the housing initiatives, came by and said: Hey, agree to this, don't go for maximum demands. We will be happy if this gets passed. And we've already spoken with the SPD. Try to back it. It's really sufficient for us if this or that gets passed, even if it doesn't reflect our maximum demands.[25]

Such pressure became almost irresistible with respect to initiatives and projects seeking public funds. Not infrequently parliamentarians are confronted with an impatient unwillingness to listen when they try to explain the problems that would arise in other areas from a compromise on a certain issue. Green parliamentarians can often defend themselves against such pressure from their clientelistically formed base, but only because they are not a governing party but in the opposition.

Opposition in West Germany, however, reflects the continental European understanding of parliamentarianism, in which criticism of the government is supposed to be "constructive," providing articulate solutions to each problem in case the present opposition becomes the governing majority. This rule applies not only to the main opposition parties but also to small and especially left-of-center opposition parties. The Greens in West Germany, like the SPD, not only have to prove that they have realistic ideas for a different government; they also have to prove that they are willing to drop fundamental demands in favor of a coalition compromise with the SPD—that they are *politikfähig* ("willing and able to do [responsible] politics")—since everybody knows that the Greens can never govern alone but only in a coalition with the SPD.[26]

This perspective pushed the Green parliamentary groups in the three states under consideration here—especially those who sought governmental participation—toward a politics of compromise. They were not concerned with reaching real compromises, they wanted to convey that the Greens, despite everything, were *in general* open to compromise. Symbolic signals with this message could also be sought and sent out by representatives of an opposition party. The Green state parliamentarians in Baden-Württemberg served such symbolic needs when they agreed to the SPD's budget law in 1983. The Greens' state parliamentary speaker concluded: "Although we know that a lot of things we oppose will be built if we pass this budget law . . . we will pass it despite our hesitations and say that humanitarian aspects are more important."[27]

The kind of pressure for compromise the Greens experienced as an opposition party is clear in the Green Bundestag group's report of 1984:

> We want to point out the dilemma in which we find ourselves, wedged between the two poles of maximum demands and reform, using an example from budgetary politics. Seen from the position of maximum demands, we would have to fundamentally reject every draft introduced by the government (and this is valid for an SPD government too).
>
> The mistakes begin with the table of contents if the ecological costs are listed in a separate section: the distinction between environment and economy should be abolished, and so many ecological investments should be demanded that the government wouldn't believe its ears (and neither would we). We would be regarded as totally utopian and scandalously unrealistic.
>
> Instead, we make suggestions with regard to the defense budget, suggestions for a new pension model, relatively modest SOS suggestions [Social and Ecological Emergency Program], which means we show our realism, show what is possible here and now, and restrict ourselves to the prevailing conditions. We do all this even though we reject the budget as a whole because of fundamental principles.
>
> Our difficult task (and this is valid for both the party and its parlia-

mentary group) is the vehement presentation of societal needs—and that is radical—while at the same time entering into compromises if they point to a change of direction. What we must decide upon is what kind of political practice we want to choose.[28]

The coercion to practice compromise politics forces the Greens and their base to consider the workability of their ideas, a consideration that otherwise would not be forthcoming. On the other hand, measured in terms of their point of departure, this pressure puts the Greens in a problematic situation. In order to hold onto voters and gain new ones, they have to demonstrate an ability to compromise that leaves them little time to find their own political identity. If their demands are too radical, they become political pariahs; if they picture themselves as moderate, the SPD will say that it already represents those positions, making the Greens superfluous.

## RESISTANCE TO ADAPTATION

The Greens' internal organizational principles were designed to prevent the integration of the parliamentary groups into conventional politics and their separation from the base, as well as to demonstrate alternative forms of politics. For the last aspect, the principle of gender parity is especially important. The Greens have inserted a quota clause into their party statutes, requiring that membership of all party bodies be at least 50 percent female, even though women do not actually make up half of all members. In many cases, the party went even further. Executive committees with only female representatives (*Feminat*) existed in the Bundestag parliamentary group and in the Berlin AL for one-year periods in 1984 and 1985 respectively. In Hamburg, the Greens presented purely female lists (including the rotation candidates for half-term) for a full legislative period on the occasion of the state elections in 1986 and 1987. Green women's success encouraged women in the larger CDU and the SPD (which decided in 1986 to change its party statute to secure a female representation of at least 40 percent in all party bodies in the long run, and it enlivened the debates on quotas and the advancement of women in the working world as well.

Out of all internal organizational principles designed to prevent careerism and the integration of parliamentarians, rotation and the imperative mandate turned out to be the most salient and hotly disputed. (The measures were installed with regard to the Bundestag parliamentary group by the federal party congress in January 1983.) These two requirements were not legally compelling, because parliamentarians enjoy free electoral mandate, in fact, the effort to bind their parliamentarians to party resolutions and to replace them in the middle of the legislative period caused some to accuse the Greens of being anticonstitutional.[29]

For the realization of their resolutions on rotation and the imperative mandate, the Greens were, of course, dependent upon their parliamentarians' good will. The rotation principle, by forbidding the renomination of parliamentarians for a new legislative period, gave away a tool other parties use to control their parliamentarians—namely, the threat to not renominate them. Nevertheless, Green parliamentarians adhered to the rotation principle without exception in Hamburg and Berlin during the time under consideration here. In Baden-Württemberg the principle was not in operation in 1980–1984. The attempt to introduce it on the occasion of the 1984 elections led to heated internal conflicts. In the Bundestag, the principle had already come under strong fire soon after the 1983 elections. The parliamentarians' criticism was based on the specter of decreasing efficacy as well as tensions between the parliamentarians and their mid-term successors who were already working as assistants to the parliamentary group in Bonn. Most Bonn parliamentarians adhered to the Party resolution and made way for their successors in mid-term. Two parliamentarians who kept their mandates, one of whom even left the Green parliamentary group, were not sanctioned by the party. In 1986 the Greens decided to abolish the mid-term rotation principle both in the Bundestag and in all state parliaments except Hamburg and Berlin.[30]

The principle of imperative mandates is also not valid in all areas of the party, for instance, it did not apply in Baden-Württemberg until 1984. Even if there is a consensus that the Green parliamentarians should strive to keep a close relationship with their base, many strongly disagree that the parliamentarian has to adhere to the will of the base even if it runs against his or her own will. Those defending the imperative mandate regard this close linkage, this unfalsified reflection of the will of the base, and this obligation on the part of the parliamentarian to check important decisions with the base as one of the qualities distinguishing the Greens from other parties. The opponents view the mandate as degrading the parliamentarians to mere order-takers, to puppets or stooges, thus contradicting the Greens' conception of a responsible, autonomous, and free individual. They demand trust instead of control as well as the primacy of individual over collective decisions.

In practice, the principle of imperative mandates played no significant role in day-to-day parliamentary work on the state level, even where it was a formal rule, as in Hamburg and Berlin. No parliamentarian was pushed into the role of an executor of instructions condemned to inactivity without an order from the base. For the daily parliamentary routine, parliamentarians got enough guidance from the consensus laid down in the party program, which still left them more than enough leeway. Where new or potentially controversial questions emerged, the parliamentarians attempted to link up with interested and competent party bodies prior to decisions or initiatives, and in cases of fundamental issues they sought an explicit mandate. Although the party base in Berlin demanded that certain statements be revised, they tolerated abstentions of individual parliamentarians seeking to follow their conscience or personal opinion in such cases. In Hamburg, parliamentarians had no problems at all executing party decisions. In both states, Green parliamentarians complained more about the lack of directives from the base than about a restriction of their activities.

All in all, the imperative mandate, wherever it was accepted as a rule, acted as a precautionary measure and as a regulative principle that encouraged Green parliamentarians to seek closer contact with their party base and active societal groups than is common in other parties.

## THE PARLIAMENTARY GROUPS AS AGENTS OF INTERNAL POWER AND INFLUENCE

In all states and on the federal level, the parliamentary groups developed into the strongest—at least potentially strongest—power centers within the Greens. This poses a dilemma for a party self-conceived as grassroots-democratic and committed to preventing the development of internal hierarchies and power centers. The Greens want their party structures to continue to orient themselves by the developed conceptions of internal democracy: decentralized organizational forms, the autonomy of lower units, and minimal apparatus, bureaucracy, and professionalization. On the other hand, they need an internal counterweight to balance the dominance or even omnipotence of state and Bundestag parliamentary groups.

In contrast to the party, the parliamentary groups have substantial material resources, including a generous financial base and a team of aides with organizational and substantive specialist tasks. Moreover, parliamentarians are usually full-time politicians; the time resources at their disposal are the envy of most Green parliamentary and party representatives, who work as volunteers—that is, without pay. Many state and Bundestag parliamentarians benefit from the information, contacts, access, and qualifications that emanate directly or indirectly from their parliamentary work.

Parliamentarians and their staffs enjoy their most significant advantage over the rest of the party when it comes to the internal workings of the political system, and the specialization of individual parliamentarians. The Green parliamentarians also have more intense contacts than regular party members with the leading politicians of the other parties, who, in contrast to the Greens, almost all have parliamentary mandates. Organizations and lobby groups seek contact with the Green parliamentary groups more often than with the party leaders or other party members. This means that the Greens have opened up opportunities for discourse and points of contact that would not have been forthcoming without their parliamentary representation.

Even more important are the better contacts to the media that the parliamentary groups and individual parliamentarians have. They have a greater media echo and can more easily obtain access to a wider public. Interestingly, the parliamentarians have learned that it is much easier to gain media attention with personalized intraparty conflicts or conflicts within the parliamentary group than with issues of substance.

The potential concentration of power in the parliamentary groups presents the Greens with a double problem: it contradicts the grassroots democratic ideal, and it raises the danger that the part of the party most strongly bound to the constraints of the political system and thus continuously leaning toward a potentially integrative-reformist politics will automatically dominate the development of the whole party, a problem the SPD encountered before 1914.

In this area, however, the Greens' abstract critique of power gets in their way. In 1984, the spokeswoman of the Baden-Württemberg Greens diagnosed a "broken and very mendacious relationship to power." On the outside, there is a consensus: "No power for anybody." But in actual fact many strive for and grasp positions of power, especially in the parliamentary groups. "And when the party executive committees maintain that the party needs more power vis-à-vis the parliamentary group, this is blocked off."[31]

On the federal level, the problem of balancing the parliamentary group's power by way of an internal counterweight was acknowledged, but no solution was found:

> After the establishment of the Bundestag parliamentary group with its 36 full-time politicians and numerous assistants, the federal executive committee arrived at a seemingly hopeless position. The parliamentary group was extremely hard-working, but was tied up with the power apparatus in Bonn. Individuals there were exposed to strong pressures to adapt. If the federal executive committee argued as fundamentalistically as it did, this was for the purpose of creating a counterweight.[32]

In Hamburg and Berlin, the need for a counterweight to the parliamentary group in the form of a more professionalized party executive committee with greater political competence was often discussed, but the attempts to create one were not very successful. That this structural problem did not become more virulent is due—at least in Berlin and Hamburg—to the parliamentary groups' self-limitation. They nearly always avoided using all their potential power; they never, for instance, presented themselves as a closed group in internal political discussions. In Baden-Württemberg in 1980–1984, however, the first parliamentary group's leading figures were less cautious. They attempted to push the party in a reformist direction and favored cooperating with the SPD. This evinced strong opposition from the party base and contributed to the party's failure to renominate any of those parliamentarians for the next state electoral list.

In sum, we can say that the Greens' party organization may be in a position to have its way in individual conflicts with its parliamentarians and prevail in situations where parliamentarians openly attempt to set the direction of Green politics. But on neither the state nor the federal level has it succeeded in developing a permanent internal counterweight to the parliamentary groups and thus decreasing or balancing the parliamentarians' advantage with respect to everyday politics.

## Conclusion: Have the Greens Adapted?

Let us return to the initial question: have the Greens become an established party through their electoral and parliamentary participation? If so, to what extent and what were the causes? What did the Greens lose in this process and what did they gain? What developmental potential results from this situation for the Green Party and for existing and future social movements?

Our investigations have shown that the Greens did not hold their ground as a "new type of party." Rather, in the course of their electoral successes and their parliamentary activity, the Greens became more similar to the established parties. Power and tactical electoral considerations play a pronounced role in their most intense conflict so far, the debate over the question of cooperation with the SPD; their linkage with the extraparliamentary movements (and those movements themselves) became weaker; and "patchwork techniques" prevailed in their parliamentary work and in their electoral program. The fact that no professionalized party apparatus has developed—in view of the professionally working potential power centers that have developed in the parliamentary groups—had a detrimental effect on "grassroots democracy." An internal structural principle designed to prevent the development of Green political careerism and simultaneously to demonstrate alternative political culture—the rotation of mandates—was largely abolished because it actually or purportedly restricted parliamentary efficacy and the Greens' ability to cooperate with other parties.

These losses—measured in terms of initial expectations—must be contrasted with gains the Greens undoubtedly secured: electoral stabilization despite a persistent legitimatory pressure upon the established parties; expansion of the spectrum of issues discussed in parliaments and in the media; further development of the party program, or at least discussions toward that end, especially with regard to social and economic policies; establishment of new contacts and dialogues with social groups and interest organizations such as small farmers, pensioners, and, even, to some extent, the trade unions, which initially maintained a silent distance from the Greens.

The Greens have not lost all their power to symbolize an alternative to prevailing politics. They are still the preferred conversation partner for non-conservative extraparliamentary initiatives and movements, and Green parliamentarians take the role of spokesperson and supporter for these initiatives very seriously, even participating in nonviolent civil disobedience. From the vantage point of internal structure, too, the Greens have put other parties under pressure to imitate their own novel policies, especially with respect to the representation of women.

Nevertheless, in the course of electoral and parliamentary participation, the dynamic of a political force that is a fundamental alternative to prevailing politics and policies has been, if not lost, at least decisively reduced. This dynamic was based on the utopian character of the substance and forms of the politics of the new social movements and the Greens during the 1970s and early 1980s in the FRG. Participants of the ruling system as well as the vast majority of the population saw as utopian—in the sense of unimaginable under the prevailing conditions—getting out of nuclear energy, a societal future without linear economic growth, unilateral disarmament, and equal representation of women in all occupations and leading positions, to recall just a few of the demands of the extraparliamentary movements and the Greens. At the same time, these demands corresponded to the real desires or needs of large groups, desires that went beyond what was possible under the prevailing conditions of power. The new social movements and the Greens must be credited with articulating these demands during the phase of their entry into the party system without being distracted or intimidated by charges that they were dreamers, idiots, or social fiends.

The four demands mentioned above have meanwhile become common issues in the political debate and have been adopted rhetorically by the established parties, especially by the SPD. Not one of these demands has even begun to be realized, but the utopians of 10 years ago are now regarded as serious interlocutors, and some of them (for example, the Greens in Hesse and Berlin) were even coalition partners.

The Greens draw diametrically opposed strategic lessons from this situation. Some call for consciously integrating the party into the political system not only in order to gain respect for their own demands but also, step by step, to gain opportunities for their enforcement and even participate in that enforcement themselves. Thus two spokesman of the "eco-libertarian" faction, Winfried Kretschmann and Thomas Schmid, warned their party not to fall into righteousness and "sectarian" radicalism, especially against the SPD, in the aftermath of the Chernobyl shock of May 1986. In this case "the forces of radical opposition had again effected nothing more than an innovative surge within the spectrum of the established parties. But we want more: to actively play out the strength and imagination existing in the Party. We no longer want to be the ones giving a push; we want to participate in the enforcement."[33]

Those who draw the opposite lesson want to regain their dynamic by stressing radical criticism and new demands that are still considered utopian today, and by reactivating the extraparliamentary movements. An integration toward a co-governing reform party, this faction maintains, would open up few chances for enforcing Green political concepts but would extinguish the Greens' ability to effect innovative surges in the political system.

Our task here is not to decide which faction is right but to analyze to what extent the development toward integrative tendencies has been caused by electoral and parliamentary participation. Our summary thesis is that the above-mentioned development is not in the first place caused by the work and power of Green parliamentarians, but has a lot more to do with the voter orientation of the party as a whole, which presently differs little from that of the established parties. Most of all, it is due to the new social movements' decline since 1983. This decline in activity is in itself only in small part a result of the Greens' presence in parliaments.

For lack of space, our argument in support of this thesis must remain short and speculative here, with four main points.

First, Green state and Bundestag parliamentarians have not uniformly supported tendencies toward integration, toward demonstrating an ability to compromise or a willingness to cooperate with the SPD, or toward abolishing grassroots-democratic rules; a majority of them usually did not support such tendencies at all.[34] Whenever they nevertheless attempted to influence the direction of the party by using their public prestige, they often encountered intense and effective opposition by the Party rank and file, as happened in Baden-Württemberg in 1984. According to the frequently presented model of the development of the SPD between 1891 and 1914, parliamentarians should be agents of reformist integration into the system. But this model has little empirical value in explaining the Green's transformation between 1980 and 1987. Although Green parliamentarians acceded to some of the pressures exacted by the political system in parliament, most of them possessed both an oppositional impetus and a capacity for self-reflection that was too highly developed for them to function as transmitters of these constraints to their own party and movement base.

Second, where such a transmission did take place, it depended more on the mechanisms of electoral participation and the electoral law's 5 percent barrier. After the initial electoral successes, all Green factions oriented themselves more strongly toward the electoral base. Increasing the share of votes was an obvious goal, while a decreasing share of the vote or even a failure to surpass the 5 percent barrier was viewed as a threat to the existence of the Greens as a political force. And while the interests of homosexuals or electorally non-eligible groups such as foreigners were still represented without tactical cuts, the effect upon the electorate became an increasingly important argument in internal political discussions. The programmatic debates also followed the rhythm of state and federal elections, and the need to present the voter with the image of a serious party with a sophisticated program, more than they followed the impulses of the extraparliamentary movements and the substantive discussions of the party base.

This orientation toward elections and the electorate had not been obvious during the Greens' first days as an electoral movement. Electoral participation was often mainly regarded as an opportunity for presenting oneself, and the established parties were criticized for being opportunistic machines for electoral maximization. Although the Greens have not become a "catch-all party," their attempt to convince voters by confronting them with their prejudices and to use election campaigns to activate citizens is increasingly being replaced by a strategy of adapting to the electorate's consciousness. This consciousness may be more harmonious and governmental in West Germany than in other western European countries. The majority of Green voters expect their party to attain its goals primarily by participation in government instead of by oppositional pressure. A strategy of enlightening and provoking their own electoral base (which bears the risk of electoral setbacks) is much more difficult to enforce in the Greens today than it was in 1980.

This brings us to our third point. A multi-party system with coalition governments exerts an arithmetic pressure that can be explosive. Much sooner than they expected, the Greens' parliamentary votes were needed to form a government with the SPD. This situation, independent of the Greens' will, is characterized by difficult alternatives: either to take on co-responsibility for largely unwanted government policies or to be held responsible for the even less desired continuation of conservative rule.

Finally, political activity by the new social movements declined after the peace movement failed to prevent the deployment of U.S. cruise missiles in the Federal Republic in the fall of 1983. We regard this decline as perhaps the decisive reason for the Greens' trend toward integration. The reasons for the decline of the movements themselves—the peace and ecology movements, youth protest, citizen initiatives, the alternative economic project scene, and the women's movement—cannot be analyzed here. But they have to do with economic issues (mass unemployment and cutbacks in social services have pushed postmaterialist values into the background vis-à-vis bread-and-butter questions), with issues of political hegemony (the neoconservative politics of societal division since the first Kohl government in 1982 had its ideological effects; the oppositional SPD could again absorb protests), and with the internal dynamics of political movements and their cycles.

Nevertheless, the decline of direct political pressure by the new social movements does not say much about their long-term effects on political culture. Changed political socialization and behavioral orientations are still at work and the substrate for new politically effective movements in the future has surely grown.

How is this situation related to the Greens' parliamentary presence? The initial fear had been that citizens would regard ecological protest and criticism of power as superfluous as soon as its representatives had parliamentary representation. This has occurred for locally defined citizen initiatives on the communal level, once activists believed their issues were in good hands. But initiatives and other movements regarding themselves as supra-local or political often felt strengthened and encouraged by the Green parliamentarians' activities, even if some of their activists were lost to base work because they went to work in the Greens' parliamentary groups. In the phases of movement decline, the Green Party or Green parliamentarians were confronted with high expectations regarding stabilization of the social movements that were sometimes disappointed. The Green parliamentarians were very conscientious about their role as "spokespeople" for the extraparliamentary initiatives, and they have also attempted to restrain themselves from any kind of usurpatory representational politics. Whether their general legitimation of parliamentary forms of political conflict resolution put a damper on *potential* extraparliamentary protest is a question our empirical observations—and maybe empirical observations per se—cannot answer.

The opposite effect, however, is very clear. The decline of the extraparliamentary movements' political activities had to structurally and functionally endanger the existential basis of a party that had been established with the goal of representing these movements. The Greens depended on a continual influx from and adjustments by their active social base. As soon as this activist base declined or began to view itself as a mere Green clientele, the party lost an important element of its life elixir. Many founders of the party had believed that close contact to the movements' base would counter the temptation of integration; the Greens now experienced pleas from professionalized movement leftovers to undertake compromise politics in order to channel public funds (*Staatsknete*) to their projects. While the Greens initially lived off a continual influx from the movements, they now have to deal with a decline of party activists and even of parliamentary candidates. The danger now is that the Greens, lacking membership, will develop into a party dominated by a professionalized oligarchy rotating between party offices and parliamentary seats.

## NOTES

1. Further publications by our group and individual members delineate the mechanisms of the parliamentary system: see, for example, Lilian Klotzsch et al., "Zwischen Systemopposition und staatstragender Funktion: Die Grünen unter dem Anpassungsdruck parlamentarischer Mechanismen," in Dietrich Herzog and Bernhard Weßels, eds., *Konfliktpotentiale und Konsensstrategien: Beiträge zur politischen Soziologie der Bundesrepublik* (Opladen: Westdeutscher Verlag, 1989) 180–215; Jörg Wischermann, *Anpassung und Gegenwehr: Die Parlamentsbeteiligung der Grün-Alternativen Liste Hamburg und ihre Folgen in der ersten Hälfte der achtziger Jahre* (Frankfurt: Peter Lang, 1992); Bodo Zeuner, "Die Partei der Grünen: Zwischen Bewegung und Staat," in Werner Süß, ed., *Die Bundesrepublik in den achtziger Jahren* (Opladen: Leske & Budrich, 1991) 53–68. Some members have also published an analysis of the relationship between the German Social Democrats and the Greens on the local level: Bodo Zeuner and Jörg Wischermann, *Rot-Grün in den Kommunen: Konfliktpotentiale und Reformperspektiven: Ergebnisse einer Befragung von Kommunalpolitikern* (Opladen: Leske & Budrich, 1995).

2. This was also the topic of a research project funded by the Deutsche Forschungsgemeinschaft (German Society for the Advancement of Scientific Research), in which the authors analyzed the development of the Greens in the states of Baden-Württemberg, Hamburg, and West Berlin between 1980 and 1984. In this chapter, "The Greens" refers to the party carrying the same name as well as the Alternative/Bunte Listen ("Rainbow Lists"). Thus, it includes the Hamburg Green-Alternative List (GAL) and the Berlin Alternative List (AL).

3. Fritjof Capra and Charlene Spretnak, for instance, frequently use Petra Kelly and Rudolf Bahro as chief representatives of the spiritualist-holistic tendencies in the Greens, but they treat as a side-issue Kelly and Bahro's critique of the transition to a conventional and no longer fundamentally alternative party. But it is in no way a side-issue: Bahro left the Party in 1985 not because of a lack of Green spiritually but because he viewed the Greens' *Realpolitik* in the "coalition issue" as an integrative path leading straight into the ruling apparatus, Cf. Fritjof Capra and Charlene Spretnak, *Green Politics* (New York: Dutton, 1984).

4. Capra and Spretnak consider the German Greens an expression of the two above-mentioned factions, with whom they clearly sympathize. However, they miss both factions' basic criticism of power. Ibid.

5. Marieluise Beck-Oberdorf, "Mögliche Perspektiven grüner Programmatik für künftige Parlamentswahlen," *Grüne Blätter* (Die Grünen Baden-Württemberg), no. 22 (June 1983) 7.

6. Ibid. 6.

7. Die Grünen im Bundestag informieren, "Auszüge aus dem Rechenschaftsbericht," *Grünes Bulletin* (Bonn, March 1984), p. 7.

8. Interview held on April 6, 1984.

9. Toleration negotiations: the Greens wanted to support a minority government of the SPD, but not form a red-green coalition.—Eds.

10. Interview held on March 22, 1984.

11. Waltraud Schoppe, "Unsere Initiativen haben das Handeln der Herrschenden gestört: Rechenschaftsbericht der Grünen im Bundestag (Teil II)," *grüner basis-dienst*, no. 1 (1985) 35.

12. The West Berlin AL participated in a coalition government with the SPD in 1989/90.—Eds.

13. The CSU (Christian Social Union) is the Bavarian sister-party of the CDU and traditionally forms a tight coalition with the latter in the Bundestag.—Eds.

The Greens are in the opposition in the state parliaments of Lower Saxony (CDU government; a CDU/FDP coalition since 1986), Bavaria (CSU government), Rhineland-Palatinate (CDU/FDP government), and in the North Rhine-Westphalia (since 1989). In Hesse they were in a coalition with the governing SPD from 1985 to 1987. They are not represented in the state parliaments of Schleswig-Holstein and the Saarland. In 1996, the Greens are represented in 12 of 16 state parliaments, among these all states of the "old" western Federal Republic. They form coalition governments with the SPD in North Rhine–Westphalia, Hesse, Schleswig-Holstein, and Sachsen-Anhalt. In the late 1980s and early 1990s, the Greens also formed red-green coalitions, sometimes including the FDP, in Lower Saxony, West Berlin, Bremen, and Brandenburg.

14. Interview held on July 24, 1984.

15. Interview held on July 4, 1984.

16. The constitution of the Weimar Republic provided for plebiscites and for the direct election of the president *(Reichspräsident)*. An important tradition in German political thought holds these plebiscitary elements of the constitution responsible for the failure of the first German democracy.

17. Interview held on July 23, 1984.

18. Interview held on August 3, 1984.

19. Interview held on September 6, 1984.

20. Interview held on August 27, 1984.

21. Interview held on September 20, 1984.

22. Martin Jänicke, "Parlamentarische Entwarnungseffekte? Zur Ortsbestimmung der Alternativbewegung," in Jörg R. Mettke, ed., *Die Grünen, Regierungspartner von morgen?* (Reinbeck bei Hamburg: Rowohlt 1982) 75.

23. See, for instance, Claus Offe, "Konkurrenzpartei und kollektive politische Identität," in Roland Roth, ed., *Parlamentarisches Ritual und politische Alternativen* (Frankfurt: Campus Verlag, 1980) 38–42 (opportunity); Herbert Kitschelt, "Parlamentarismus und ökologische Opposition," ibid. 97–120 (overtaxing).

24. Jänicke, "Parlamentarische Entwarnungseffekte?" 75–76.

25. Interview held on May 14, 1984.

26. According to polls of the late 1980s, 70 to 90 percent of Green voters wanted the Greens to enter a coalition with the SPD.

27. Plenary protocol 8/59, February 24, 1983, p. 4666.

28. Die Grünen im Bundestag informieren, "Auszüge aus dem Rechenschaftsbericht," 7.

29. In 1984, for instance, the president of the Lower Saxony state parliament refused to

accept the Greens' resignation of mandates for the purpose of rotation. Lower Saxony's state supreme court viewed the rotation principle as anticonstitutional in its 1985 decision but allowed the rotation anyway (cf. Bernd Rebe, "Die erlaubte verfassungswidrige Rotation," *Zeitschrift für Parlamentsfragen,* 4 [1985]: 468–74). Conservative constitutional lawyers demanded (in vain) that the Greens be banned or kept from participating in elections because of their anticonstitutionality. (See Richard Stöss, "Sollen die Grünen verboten werden?" *Politische Vierteljahresschrift* 25 (1984): 4403–24.

30. On this issue, cf. Chapter 7 by Alex Demirović, in this volume.

31. Interview held on July 31, 1984.

32. Wilhelm Knabe, "Einsatz für Ökologie und Menschenrechte, Rechenschaftsbericht des Bundesvorstandes (Teil II)," *grüner basis-dienst,* no. 1 (1985) 31–32.

33. *Der Spiegel,* June 21, 1986, p. 45.

34. This is supported by the results of our interviews as well as, for instance, by those described by Gene Frankland: (see E. Gene Frankland, "The Greens: Parliamentary Challenges and Responses," paper presented to the congress of the American Political Science Association, August–September 1985.

## Chapter 6

ॐ

# Green Feminism in Parliamentary Politics

CLAUDIA PINL

*Well, up to a certain point, it's easy to get something from the Greens: money, a female delegate, an electoral list with equal gender representation. But only if it doesn't touch upon our men's hot spots—namely, takes away their power.*

Regina Michalik
"Ohne uns läuft nichts"
(1985)

"Grassroots-democratic, nonviolent, ecological, social"—the four bases of Green Party politics are also thought to be antipatriarchal. For some feminists, the development of the autonomous women's movement into an alternative social and cultural scene was not enough. After the Green Party was founded, many feminists moved into or toward it. (Formal membership is not a requirement for political activity in the Green Party.)

Feminists viewpoints did not easily gain ground in the party at first, even though it was established as a collection of movements. Conservative attitudes clashed with fundamental feminist convictions over abortion; women's right to self-determination was pitted against the inviolability of life in all its forms.[1] The party finally agreed on a common stance to abolish Paragraph 218 of the civil code—but this position was based on very different viewpoints.[2] Even today, some Green Bundestag parliamentarians reject an abolition of Paragraph 218 without substitution.

The Greens' critique of prevailing political structures, and their advocacy of grassroots democracy and decentralization, facilitated the creation of rules that secure at least formal equality for the 30 percent of Green members who are female. Under the term "parity," the Greens have instituted a 50 percent quota for all party offices and parliamentary mandates, independent of their hierarchical position. Lists for Bundestag, state, and local elections are based on this principle of parity, whereby the first position in a list is nearly always reserved for a woman. The lists for speeches during Green party congresses usually alternate female and male speakers too, a quota system that allows men and women to speak equally instead of favoring those quick enough to call out first. The women's statute (embedded in the party statute) opens up the possibility of having party congress issues relevant to women voted on only by women. The Greens' electoral lists—including the Bundestag list—are open to nonmembers, which means that male or female activists from the grassroots (for instance, from the autonomous women's movement) can stand for nomination. On the federal and state levels of the party organization, the Greens have established women's affairs offices.

## Feminist Beginnings in Bonn

Many of the formalities described above, though more or less commonplace today, were not yet established in the Green Party when the Greens first entered the Bundestag with 10 women (out of a total of 28 Green parliamentary representatives) in March 1983. These representatives soon forced the Honorable House to deal with heretofore unheard-of issues. In the counterstatement to the chancellor's inaugural speech, Waltraud Schoppe demanded the abolition of Paragraph 218 and urged the chancellor to declare publicly that forms of love-making existed that could be extremely pleasurable while at the same time excluding pregnancy—but one could only speak on issues that one understood at least a little . . . (Third Session, May 5, 1983, see Chapter 13). During the initial public appearances of female Green parliamentarians, many Union men—members of the male-dominated conservative parties, the Christian Democratic Union (CDU) and its Bavarian sister-party, the Christian Social Union (CSU)—reacted in a mob-like and vulgar way. The Greens' demand to establish a women's committee in the Bundestag was turned down. In late 1983, the Green parliamentary group decided to take the women's issue out of its party's parliamentary working group "Work and Social Affairs" and to establish an independent working group, "Women's Politics," although there was and is no equivalent Bundestag committee. The final push to establish such a working group came from the so-called Hecker scandal.

In the summer of 1983, the Green parliamentarian Klaus Hecker sexually harassed several women co-workers. Instead of passing over these events in shame and silence, as happens in thousands of workplaces all the time, the harassed women went on the offensive, publicized Hecker's behavior, and called for him to resign his seat. The Green parliamentary group commissioned research on sexual harassment in the workplace and encouraged public discussion of this problem. Hecker resigned.

Beginning the women's working group AK 6 (*Arbeitskreis* 6) was not easy. It was difficult to obtain funds and staff (two people were initially provided) from the Greens' parliamentary group itself, and work got off to a slow start. The parliamentarians interested in women's issues invested only a small portion of their working energy in the AK 6 because they simultaneously had to take care of their "regular" working groups, corresponding to the respective Bundestag committees.

In 1985 the mid-term parliamentary successor Birgit Arkenstette described the working group's problems like this:

> We from the working group Women's Politics are the lowest on the totem pole. There are, for instance, two people whose work focuses on the politics of immigrants. In reality, that is men's politics. And everything that can be supplemented from a women's-politics point of view is given to our working group: "Why don't *you* do this!" That's what happens in all areas.[3]

Nevertheless, the working group had already made parliamentary history by that time because after an especially frustrating evening meeting, it had given birth to the idea of the Feminat, the all-women executive committee.[4] After weeks of tiring disputes in the parliamentary group, which the old executive committee led by Joschka Fischer, Otto Schily, and Petra Kelly was not able to control, six women took power: Waltraud Schoppe, Antje Vollmer, and Annemarie Borgmann as speakers of the parliamentary group, and Christa Nickels, Erika Hickel, and Heidemarie Dann as parliamentary secretaries. Things quieted down, and some journalists speculated about a "housewife-ification" of politics and teased that the new executive committee would function as "rubble women" and "social workers."[5]

Members of the AK 6 complained that even with a female executive committee, no feminist concept of parliamentary work existed. Nevertheless, the mere existence of the female executive committee probably did more to propagate Green women's policies than all parliamentary initiatives taken together. The public had to acknowledge not only that the Greens made demands in the area of women's issues, but that women stood, spoke, and acted in the front line—women who were bold, women who said what they thought, women who did not fit the traditional image of Bonn politicians of both sexes, pale through years of adaptation. For Nickels and the other women, politics was even fun:

> In the Council of Elders, a certain degree of dignity seems to be a must. If you just look at the noble room and the dignified atmosphere! We are served food each time. I find this amusing too. I often had conflicts or disputes with Barzel. . . . And he often tried to give me lessons, for instance with respect to the rules of procedure, in which Ms. Renger always made a point of supporting him. I think she doesn't like me either. She is always on her best behavior. Sometimes even I wish I could keep my mouth shut. But I'm so impulsive. To argue with Barzel a little was fun. Although Barzel always tries hard to keep cool, I once succeeded in upsetting him so much that he called his (male) whip "*Ms.* Schäuble."[6]

## Parliament: A Platform for the Women's Struggle?

In a conversation in late 1984, four Green women, Hickel, Schoppe, Gaby Potthast, and the Hesse state parliamentarian Marita Haibach sketched their parliamentary goals. What counts, said Bundestag member Potthast, is to make visible the invisible, namely women and their problems, and to use parliament as a platform for the women's struggle. Hickel sought to accelerate the slow change of consciousness in society with respect to patriarchal oppression by using the parliament as a forum and thereby reaching the public more effectively. She found that quite a few components of the patriarchal parliamentary apparatus had already been made to feel very uncertain. It is important that the Green women in Bonn remain incalculable, since calculability is a part of the system and part of patriarchal logic, which (Potthast said) women need to break. Schoppe formulated the goal of recasting feminist demands into parliamentary initiatives, acknowledging that this would entail losing some of the radicalism of the women's movement.[7]

Whether that radicalism can be transferred to the level of party, parliament, or even government (Hesse had a governing coalition of the Greens and the Social Democratic Party, SPD, in 1986–87) is what feminist critics inside and outside the Party question. People accused the Green women parliamentarians of having a naive conception of the state when they spoke of it as a neutral machine that could be used for lobbying women's issues. What they overlooked was the state's inherently repressive function. In the critics' view, participating in government for only small benefits, as the Green

women did in Hesse, paved the way for an integration of the women's movement into the patriarchal system.[8]

The criticism coming from the Green women holding jobs or offices in
the party or parliament was less fundamental: the women's movement had
neglected to make use of the Green Party in the way the *Graue Panther*
("Gray Panthers") had. The latter had made a "spokesperson contract" with
the Bundestag Greens in which the Greens had committed themselves to
carry the unfiltered demands of the alternative old people's organization to
the public and to represent their interests in parliament. The female executive committee could perhaps be a test run for the "real coup" that is, an executive committee of six feminists with a developed concept of women's politics that would necessarily differ from male politics, as Regina Michalik
suggested.[9]

## The Heroines Are Tired

Six years later, the old ideas regarding feminist parliamentary work appear touching in their naive optimism. The initial drive is lost, the green and
gray political patriarchy no longer feels challenged, and people have returned
to the old agenda. From time to time, old stories are revived—such as the
time when the female Green parliamentarian Jutta Oesterle-Schwerin debated with the president of the Bundestag, Philipp Jenninger, about
whether including the words "lesbians" and "gays" in the plenary protocol
would damage the dignity of the High House. But the process of adaptation has also left its traces on Green parliamentarians. They—both male and
female—try to function in their environment, they do not question parliamentary rules and procedures, they like to go into parliamentary committee
meetings well prepared, and they now have a high regard for law experts.

The Green women used to criticize the political "un-culture" of the
other parties and their own "politicos," like Otto Schily and Joschka
Fischer—their careerism, competitiveness, publicity seeking, and constant
attention to the media. That un-culture, however, has affected female Green
parliamentarians too. Teamwork is hardly possible anymore in the AK 6, especially since the substantive consensus shared by the first generation has
been lost. Radical affirmative action, especially in the area of wage labor, and
the abolition of the gendered division of labor are no longer core beliefs
among Green women in the Bundestag.

On the surface, much has changed for the better: the parliamentary
group's quota level is overfilled with 24 female parliamentarians; with its
three female researchers and a specialist, the working group stands on a firm

organizational basis for the first time (additionally, there are numerous female staff members from parliamentarians' personal offices); and an annual budget of around 100,000 DM is available. But advocates of women's politics are a minority within the Green parliamentary group; at present, only four parliamentarians participate more or less regularly in the working group. Even worse, there is no consensus among them. Feminist demands are less likely to obtain a majority in the parliamentary group than in the 10th legislative period (1983–1987). The persistence with which the majority of the Green parliamentary group pushed for a reduction of the minimum penalty for rape is an indication of the changing position with respect to feminist issues. When the bill concerning the abolition of the prohibition of abortion (Paragraph 218) was introduced in early March 1988 (it was the first one drafted by the working group Women's Politics in this legislative period), it was almost a surprise that the Green parliamentary group let it pass without complaint.

## "Mothers" against Feminists

With the publication of the "Müttermanifest" ("Mothers' Manifesto") in March 1987 (if not before), the Green women no longer had a common emancipatory strategy. The manifesto calls for an "idea of emancipation that integrates the contents of traditional women's work (i.e., caring for people, acting on behalf of social relations, questioning so-called 'objective constraints' (*Sachzwänge*)."[10] It criticizes the women's politics practiced by the Greens up to then for having one-sidedly emphasized participation in the workforce and for favoring the childless, independent, and skilled woman (and her adaptation to the men's world) with the anti-discrimination law and the demand for quotas. The manifesto attacks the "ghetto of nonmothers" and the "aquarium of career women."

Three prominent Green women—Nickels, Vollmer, and Schoppe—swung over to this viewpoint. Schoppe had just recently (in the fall of 1985) proclaimed to the participants in the Greens' first federal women's congress, "Patriarchy has to fall." Now she proclaimed the era of "post-feminism," or at least a "new feminism." In this "new feminism," the abolition of gender violence has been superseded by "gender reconciliation," the "admission of mutual oppression," and a "dialogue" with "men, who feel insecure and who also suffer."[11]

The relationship between the sexes and the question of the origin of violence and oppression were heatedly discussed in the party and in the Bundestag group for years. The new spark was the issue of the penalty for rape.

## The Dispute over the Minimum Penalty for Rape

In the 10th legislative period, the Greens introduced a draft bill entitled "Anti-Discrimination Law" (ADG) into the Bundestag. Drawn up by the Bundestag working group Women's Politics and the Green Party's Federal Working Group on Women, the ADG was the Green Bundestag group's first big hit with respect to women's politics. The goal was to package the women's movement's most important demands: women's claim to half of everything, the abolition of the abortion prohibition, and sanctions against male violence. Existing laws were analyzed to ascertain how they discriminated against women or suppressed them. Men in the Green Party and Bundestag group did not all agree with the bill even then. The quota system, abolishing Paragraph 218, broadening the definition of a criminal offence in the case of rape, giving prostitutes the status of "normal" workers (later temporarily dropped), and other provocations strewn in among the bill's paragraphs evoked a storm of indignation. Nevertheless, a majority of the parliamentary group passed the draft bill in September 1986.

The ADG draft proposed to delete three provisions of the existing penal code that were especially damaging to women: the provision concerning the "less severe case," which serves to make rape look like a petty offense in court; the physically defined criterion for "violence," whereby a woman is most credible in court if she has been beaten almost to death; and the term "extramarital intercourse," which stamps wives as persons with lesser rights.

Just before these and related parts of the ADG were to be introduced into the Bundestag again in November 1987, the parliamentary group decided, after barely half an hour of debate, to decrease the minimum penalty for rape from two years (as in the existing law) to one. The argument brought forward (usually by men) was an arithmetic formula: if the elements of a criminal offense are to be extended and the one-year penalty for the "less severe case" is deleted, then the minimum sentence should be decreased for balance.

More interesting in this context were the women's arguments for decreasing the minimum penalty. Nickels warned of reacting to patriarchal violence with patriarchal means, such as "feelings of vengeance" and the "sledgehammer of jail." Schoppe was initially concerned with the "potential for reconciliation" (for instance, between husband and wife), which would no longer be possible if the husband had to be put behind bars for rape (a penalty of two years usually means that no parole is possible), even if the wife wanted to save the marriage: "A one-year minimum penalty better corresponds to the life-reality of women," she told the meeting of the parliamentary group on November 3, 1987.

Even after the controversial draft bill was withdrawn from the Bundestag because of strong protest from the Party grassroots, battered women's groups, and others, the dispute over punishment continued. Only after two party congresses had demanded that the Bundestag group reintroduce the draft bill in its original form (with a two-year minimum penalty) did this occur in the fall of 1989. The discussion no longer focused on the abolition of societal relations in which men dominate and exploit women, humiliate them, and use their bodies. Instead, the focus was on "dialogue" with "men who feel insecure and who also suffer." In Schoppe's words: "I want a new communication and understanding between the sexes. There is no reconciliation of contradictions *within one* sex without the reconciliation with the other." Without a "strategy of moving the sexes closer together," the relations of violence will not be changed.[12]

How far gender relations can be improved through dialogue remains in question. That issue, like the existence of a specific female lifestyle, inevitably following from "gender difference," remained hotly contested within the Greens' Bundestag group.

## "Zigzag": A New Emancipatory Concept

Female Realo politicians like Schoppe, Birgit Laubach, and Gisela Wülffing do not explain different male and female social roles in terms of biological differences, but they do not question the patriarchal roots of gender roles. On the contrary, they give these "differences" a positive value. There are "different viewpoints of men and women . . . on the basis of which life courses with different desires are formulated. To acknowledge these differences without viewing them as unequal per se and without straining ourselves to the point of deformation could be the basis for a new gender dialogue."[13]

"An active transformation of society requires not only the breakup of the historically grown gendered division of labor but also the self-confident acknowledgment and acceptance of female life courses that run in zigzags rather than pursuing one occupational goal in a straightforward fashion."[14] Is this the new emancipatory concept—a happy affirmation of the "zigzagged" patchwork of the female life course, without asking where this zigzaggedness comes from, whether women can actually choose their life plan freely and in a self-determined way? This does not seem to be the case in a society that does not even grant women the right to their own bodies, not to speak of their comparative material impoverishment and marginalization on the labor market. The "politics of diversity" represented by

Schoppe and her co-workers has direct consequences for the women's politics of the Greens' Bundestag group. Other problems arise with regard to the question of "compatibility of working and living with children."

## "Compatibility" of Employment and Parenthood

More than the debate on punishment for rapists, the discussion of the "compatibility" of motherhood and paid employment focuses on a central issue of feminist analysis, namely, the gendered division of labor, its relationship to the patriarchal system of domination, and its concrete expression in the everyday life of women and men.

For the majority of the Greens' Bundestag group—women as well as men—the question of "compatibility" is essentially one of how *women* can cope. The life plans of men remain excluded; their "private sphere" does not become "political," and neither does their lifelong orientation to job and career, or their remoteness from everyday human relations, including responsibility for the elderly, the weak, and children.

In November 1987, the majority of the Greens' Bundestag group changed a provision of their draft bill on working hours. The original draft called for a three-year parental leave scheme coupled with wage compensation, but linked to a rule requiring an *equal split* of the leave time between mother and father; otherwise half of the time benefit would be lost. This was a cautious attempt on the part of the former parliamentary group to exert motivational pressure on men to accept their share of responsibility for children and the work involved in raising them. The argument against it, as expressed at a meeting of the Green parliamentary group on November 3, 1987, was that the "gendered, hierarchical division of labor" could not be abolished in this way, "coercively at the expense of women and children." Moreover, this division was said to be a case of "cultural conditioning" over centuries, and one could not simply transfer the struggle against it into families by legal-coercive means.

Here we see patriarchy's material basis and the basis of violence against women, the gendered division of labor, played down into a "question of culture." Or it is reinterpreted as a question of "gendered *hierarchical* division of labor," assuming there could be such a thing as a gendered division of labor that is not hierarchical.

In the meantime, a compromise paper on "compatibility" was drawn up and negotiated by the parliamentarians Marieluise Beck-Oberdorf and Jutta Oesterle-Schwerin and then passed by the majority of the parliamentary group. The paper suggests a scheme of reduced parental working time with wage compensation, or, for the unemployed, a payment for rearing children (*Erziehungsgeld*). Parents or guardians with one or more children under the age of three can also have themselves completely released from work. For a child or children between four and 12, a claim to a subsidized reduction of working hours should exist "for male and/or female parents or guardians." This model allows for two persons to be released from work for two hours a day each, or for one person to be released on a half-day basis; the parent can return to a full-time position at any time. How the parents decide to divide their working time—whether, for instance, both will reduce their workday by two hours, whether only the mother will take a half-day job, or whether one parent will leave his/her job completely in the first two years of the child's life—is "up to them," in Beck-Oberdorf's words.

This model leaves the responsibility for children with the woman, as there is nothing that would force men to live out their fatherhood socially. Men can take advantage of the opportunity to reduce work—without financial cost—but they are not forced to do so. That means that, in nearly all cases, they will act in accordance with their company's (and/or their own) interests in a continuous and lifelong "availability for the labor market." Thus, an opportunity is forgone to break up the normal male's working biography and to integrate men into relations of everyday life, part of which is caring for the elderly, for the needy, or for children.

## What Has Been Achieved

The work of Green women in parliament has undoubtedly exerted pressure on the other political parties and their parliamentary groups. Meanwhile, all parties are attempting, to varying degrees, to give women's issues greater consideration and women more opportunities. In 1988, the SPD was debating the quota issue more intensely than the Greens. Without the Greens' parliamentary impulses, which themselves emanated from the women's movement, I cannot imagine a CDU party congress on women's issues (the first took place in 1985), or a Rita Süssmuth, federal minister of women's and family affairs until 1988. The federal government coalition of the CDU/Free Democratic Party (FDP), has proposed a bill penalizing rape in marriage. A majority of Bundestag parliamentarians of all party affiliations have spoken out in favor of using a gender-neutral wording in future laws.

The societal climate has improved. Demands concerning women's issues no longer face immediate rejection. The actual distribution of power between men and women in the Federal Republic has, however, hardly changed. While female politicians, especially Social Democrats, work their way through the boggy patriarchal swamp toward goals once set by Green feminists—even if with less radical demands—the latter are in a state of uneasy hesitation. In 1990, the time of writing, except for a short SPD-Green governing coalition in Hesse, another one of 18 months duration in Berlin, and several local red-green coalitions, Green programs were never enforced and Green demands never tested in practice. This fact has led many to doubt whether the path taken was correct.

Within the Green Party and its Bundestag group, women's politics has increasingly become merely a tactical issue in the struggle between different factions. While the radical feminists have found an (insecure) haven under the wings of the party left and/or the "Fundis" (fundamentalists), "post-feminism" has become the ideology of the other two Party factions, the "Realos" (*Realpolitik* politicians) and the "Grüner Aufbruch" ("Green Awakening"). Many male and female Realos regard de-radicalized demands and a greater adaptation to trends of the times as a recipe for success. The liberal "yuppie" has become their new political focus of attention, and "postfeminism" and gender reconciliation are seen as the new path of women's politics. The majority of the Green Bundestag group are on this path, while radical-feminist demands more often find majorities in Green party congresses.

The "grassroots"—in this case the autonomous women's movement—no longer provides many impulses. Expectations have waned, and demands from the autonomous sphere reach the Green parliamentarians less and less often. This has surely contributed to the dissolution of a uniform Green position with respect to women's politics. The first generation of female Green parliamentarians declared its intention to secure, financially and organizationally, the open spaces the women's movement had successfully fought for. This promise could be kept only selectively in red-green local coalition governments, not taking into account the short experiments in Hesse and Berlin. But the so-called objective political constraints (*Sachzwänge*) are not the only forces working against these demands. The uneasiness of large parts of the women's movement about coming into contact with the "system" sometimes serves as a brake on parliamentary energy.

The Women's Politics working group, for example, attempted to draft a concept for uniform federal financing for shelters for battered women. Representatives of the autonomous women's centers cooperated closely in this effort, but a majority feared that a federal financing scheme (initially by way of a foundation) would lead to bureaucratic hurdles and controls. First attempts to re-establish contacts with the autonomous women's initiatives in the 1987–1990 legislative period have failed.

Recent debates on establishing foundations close to the Greens effected a renewed interest on the part of the autonomous women's groups. "Enough was enough in all due modesty" when Green and autonomous feminists demanded all of the available funds (up to 50 million DM annually) for use in their model of a women's foundation. In the meantime, they accepted a compromise solution whereby the funds are divided among three foundation models, one of which is the "Women's *Anstiftung*."[15] As the biggest part of the funds made available to the political foundations is earmarked for international issues, the foundations could give new impetus to the international women's politics of the Greens, an area that had an extremely low profile for a long time.[16]

The women's politics of the Greens stands at a crossroads. If the majority of Greens take the postfeminist path, which unhistorically celebrates gender differences as part of the "plurality of life," welcomes the supposed openness of women's life plans as a new freedom, and prematurely supports gender reconciliation, many, especially many men, may applaud this turn. But it is increasingly difficult to find a difference between Green concepts of women's politics and those of the FDP and the CDU. The radical feminism endorsed by a minority in the Greens' Bundestag group and an (insecure) majority in the party thus urgently requires new impulses and renewed support from the women's movement.

## NOTES

1. Paragraph 218 of the West German Federal Civil Code limits a woman's right to an abortion to cases of medical or physical emergency."—Eds.

2. Christa Nickels stated: "As a Christian and as a member of the Greens I am against abortion. . . . Nevertheless, I am for the abolition of Paragraph 218 because rigorous laws against abortion do not prevent abortion. . . . Paragraph 218 is especially unfair to women." *Grüner Frauenexpress,* March 1988.

3. Brigitte Jäger and Claudia Pinl, *Zwischen Rotation und Routine: Die Grünen im Bundestag* (Cologne: Kiepenhauer und Witsch, 1985) 3.

4. Anne Klein and Regina Michalik, "Frauenvorstand—feministischer Coup oder nur ein Vorstand ohne Männer?" *Beiträge zur feministischen Theorie und Praxis* (Cologne), no. 13 (1985) 128.

5. Cf. Cora Stephan, "Hausfrauisierung in der Politik?" in Susan Heenen, ed., *Frauenstrategien* (Frankfurt am Main: Suhrkamp, 1984). After World War II the "rubble women" cleared away the masses of bomb rubble from German cities.

6. Christa Nickels, "Ich habe gelernt, mit Anstand auf die Nase zu fallen," in Jäger and Pinl, *Zwischen Rotation und Routine,* 172–73. Rainer Barzel was president of the Bundestag until deposed because of his involvement in the "Flick" bribery scandal. Annemarie Renger was one of the vice-presidents of the Bundestag.—Eds.

7. Barbara Böttger, Anne Lütkes, and Carola Möller, "Grüne Parlamentarierinnen— Macht für Frauen?" *Beiträge zur feministischen Theorie und Praxis,* no. 13 (1985) 131–44.

8. Verena Krieger, "Radikale Gleichstellungsforderungen, Systemgrenzen und feministische Politik in den Grünen," in Die Grünen., *Lebensmodelle für Frauen: Reader zur Zweiten Grünen Bundesfrauenkonferenz,* November 28–29, 1987, pp. 63–66.

9. Klein and Michalik, "Frauenvorstand," 130.

10. "Müttermanifest: Leben mit Kindern—Mütter werden laut," pamphlet, March 1987 (see Chapter 14).

11. Waltraud Schoppe and Gisela Wülffing, "Grüne Frauenpolitik," in "Sein oder Nichtsein: Entwurf für ein Manifest grüner Realpolitik," manuscript (Summer 1988) 11.

12. Waltraud Schoppe, *tageszeitung,* June 9, 1988 (italics in the original).

13. Schoppe and Wülffing, "Grüne Frauenpolitik," 6.

14. Hubert Kleinert, Charlotte Garbe, and Waltraud Schoppe, "Von der Mühsal grüner Reformpolitik," mimeographed (Bonn, 1988) 2–3.

15. *Anstiftung* ("instigation") is an ironical extension of the term Stiftung ("foundation").—Trans.

16. In 1986, Women's Politics attempted to document the relationship between the world economy, the suppression of women, and global ecological destruction by organizing a congress entitled "Women and Ecology." Cf. Die Grünen im Bundestag/AK Frauenpolitik, *Frauen und Ökologie: Gegen den Machbarkeitswahn* (Cologne: Kölner Volksblatt, 1987).

*Chapter 7*

❧

# Grassroots Democracy
## Contradictions and Implications

ALEX DEMIROVIĆ

T he Green Party claims to be a new type of party. Its grassroots-democratic approach is supposed to open up the possibility of a "politics from below," a "politics with the people instead of one that moves above their heads."[1] This new type of party seeks to encourage people to become more active and political. Its grassroots-democratic nature sets the Greens apart from the established parties of the Federal Republic, whose model of representational politics they criticize and reject.

As a party, an organization competing for votes, developing programs, competing with other parties, sending representatives into parliament, and so on, the Greens in parliament and in public life fight so "that the people should decide for themselves in ever-increasing measure."[2] In other words, they fight for their fundamental goal of grassroots democracy with the means of party representation, although the means of parliamentary representation by parties threatens grassroots democracy. The contradiction is clear.

The Greens have always been aware of this dilemma, but party activists long entertained the hope that the strong ties to the new social movements would, if not solve the contradiction, then at least keep it suspended. They tried "to function as a party and a movement," as Phil Hill of the U.S. Greens put it, in order to keep the balance. For a time, the party was thus seen as the spokesperson for the movements or as their parliamentary representative—that is, as a movement party, whereas the movements were seen as the relatively stable social base and inexhaustible resource on which the Greens' politics, should and could directly rely.[3]

Meanwhile, the apparent decline of the protest movements especially in West Germany seems to have made obsolete the effort to achieve a balance between movement and party and between decisions of the grassroots and politics from above. The necessity of political professionalization appears to be generally acknowledged, and the debate over grassroots democracy appears outdated. A hard core of professional politicians, cutting across the different tendencies, consider parliamentary cooperation, legislative initiatives, predictability, and the ability to enter coalitions—in short, the imperatives of the political apparatus—as the essence of political culture and (because of their supposed rationality) as an inescapable reality. Television spots for the 1990 federal election proclaimed the Greens to be social, ecological, and civil. Grassroots democracy as a topic was dropped, and activities aimed at developing and implementing democratic goals and decision-making processes moved to the background—even if the Greens welcomed the institution of "round tables" as a democratic achievement of the citizens' movement of the former German Democratic Republic (GDR).[4]

This tendency to accept the dominant political forms—the professionalization of Green politics—has aroused strong opposition among those who criticize pragmatic parliamentary politics and call for a return to radical opposition. The loss of perspective and the conformism to *Realpolitik* in the party caused many Greens to turn to more radical forms of noninstitutional politics. Some important figures of the left have left the party to organize a "Radical Left." Others became members of the successor of the Socialist Unity Party (SED), the Party of Democratic Socialism (PDS), where they can work for an ecological socialism.[5] This development raises problems, since it keeps the political options of the now united German left in the same cycle of abstract and sterile contradictions—namely, the strict rejection of parliament versus its uncritical acceptance. Caught in this decades-old contradiction, the German left and the Greens cannot further the project of democratic self-government and popular self-determination.

In this chapter I argue that the Greens' dilemma with respect to democracy emanates at least partly from their adherence to a political theory related to the New Left's parliamentary critique of the 1960s and 1970s. This tradition has provided the basis for various suggestions with respect to grassroots democracy and its practice in the party and programmatically in society. Negative experiences with grassroots democracy eventually led the Greens to propose problematic solutions for these theoretical contradictions. These suggestions tend to move the party away from the project of democratizing the asymmetrical societal processes of political interest articulation in the Federal Republic—at least insofar as this process might be influenced by the Greens.

## The Critique of Parliamentarianism

At the core of the political theory of West Germany's new social movements in the 1960s and 1970s was the critique of the distinction between the political-statist sphere on the one hand and the societal and private sphere on the other. This distinction leads to a configuration in which individuals, social groups, and classes follow their respective particular and conflicting interests, and an institution of compromise develops and decides on the public good. The state seems to be or desires to be this institution independent of competing particular interests and incorporating the public good, while the various social interests, as mere particular interests, are accorded a lower status. Representative parliamentary democracy can be seen as a compromise between the perfect incorporation of individuals' interests and the impossibility of giving due consideration to and coordinating all these territorially scattered interests. The compromise consists in aggregating the different interests programmatically in a party through certain common standards and thereby enforcing them and inserting them into the political process.

The critique of parliamentarianism takes up several aspects of this generalization of interests. First, it objects to the distinction between state and society, since it splits individuals' interests into general social ones and private ones, thereby denying any kind of general dimension to individuals' interests as such. Second, the critique asks whether the state and political parties can legitimately claim to represent the general interest. The argument here is that the state will give priority to capital and powerful interest groups; in a society based on private property, it would be a delusion to believe in the equal weight of every citizen's voice and vote. Rather, the private appropriation and concentration of social resources almost fully determine the premises upon which the state's decisions and actions rest. The fabric of economy and society, and the web of infrastructure, investments, jobs, and taxes, are so dense that the voter's voice can hardly penetrate it.

Moreover, parties tend to make themselves independent of the people they represent. In particular, the necessity of competing with other parties and increasing the share of votes has led to increasingly amorphous and inflated party programs. The parties lose touch with the interests of the population and become opportunistic machines for maximizing votes. Generalization furthers the ability of party leaders and the executive heads of governing parties to push through their own interests. Parties are more likely to be cut off from those whom they supposedly represent because political parties in the Federal Republic have a constitutionally defined task not only of aggregating and representing the will of the population but also of taking part in the "formation of the population's political opinion"[5]—from above, so to speak.

The critique of the ideology of parliamentarianism, one can conclude, aims at the state's role of pursuing the particular interests of certain social groups, usually capitalist interests. The political institutions responsible for guaranteeing a democratic mediation between state and society follow the logic of those interests and the state's claim of representing the public good and thereby strengthen the subordination of social interests under the statist-administrative imperative. Yet, at the same time—and this is their contribution to the reproduction of domination—may mobilize loyalty in society for government decisions and the procedures of decision making by creating the impression that the population is actually participating in the state's decisions. Thus, they help legitimize state decision-making processes, with the result that such decisions appear to be general decisions, while the interests of the population can only claim to be particular ones.

According to this critique, the state claims (without foundation) to represent the public good with the aim of incorporating the population into the legitimation processes without actually granting it participation in its decisions, delegitimizing social protest in the process. In contrast, the social movements—organized so that people's participation in the decision-making process is linked directly to participation in carrying out those decisions, thus rendering obsolete the mechanism of representation—appear to incorporate truly general social goals. They do try, precisely with particular orientations, to save and to defend collective goods such as nature, animals, health, and so on, goods that are endangered by industry and the state in collaboration with political parties and interest groups on the grounds of short-term gains. "Thus, one could speak of a particularism of causes and situations, yet not one of goals. And it would only seem to be a paradox that the most general struggles, those most representative for the totality of emancipatory interests, in fact take place locally."[7]

In Claus Offe's formulation, one of the self-evident truths of the German left and the new social movements becomes tangible. If the social movements as such incorporate a general interest, we must ask how they define their position with respect to the official state representation of the general good. Will they attempt to create a kind of antipower, or will they coordinate their claims of representing the general interest with those of the state?

Two consequences follow from the argument that the state actually represents only particular interests. In the first and radical case, the state's claim is merely a pretense that has to be systematically criticized and destroyed in order to free the population from its loyalty to the state. In the second case, an opposition movement will demand the realization of the goals proclaimed by the constitution, and will point out that it represents the population's general interests, which the political elites are excluding from the process of political interest articulation. Therefore, the latter have to be forced to act in line with the constitution. The Greens vacillate from one extreme of this ideological critique to the other without finding a theoretical or political solution to the dilemma emanating from the fact that the bourgeois state actually does represent real general interests to a certain extent. It would lead us too far a field to discuss the empirical evidence here.[8] The important point is, rather, that the Greens acknowledge this problem by at least tactically understanding the state as a medium for the self-coordination of the social movements. It was, for example, a familiar argument in the early 1980s that the social movements should use the "party of a new type" to exploit the resources of the state for their own goals. The organization of a party and its participation in parliament would help the social movements to publicize their goals, transcend the local limits of their initiatives, improve their working conditions, and mobilize support from citizens not directly involved in specific conflicts, thereby assuring activists that their issues really represent the general interest.[9] However, using state resources to coordinate themselves and reassure themselves of their general representativeness, they imply that the state embodies a greater or at least a more powerful claim to rationality to which they subordinate themselves, and to which they add new standards of rationality: "It is an irony that the alternative movements have to remind the state of its own logic of survival."[10] Neither the rationality claim of the state nor the structural weakness of the social movements have been publicly discussed either by the latter or by the Greens. One can, however, come across the legitimate argument that the Greens as a parliamentary party are a consequence of the weakness of the new social movements, which have not succeeded in coordinating their own goals with those of other (passive) groups in society.[11] Therefore, one can conclude that the goals of the new social movements have in fact not been general in an "exemplary way" but were always interests that had to be coordinated and articulated with other interests.

With the founding of the Green Party and the dynamic of political action created by this process, the weakness of the abstract critique of parliamentarianism outlined above became apparent. As a parliamentary party, the Greens could no longer credibly claim that the movements directly represented the public good. But a political theory was missing that would have allowed the activists to balance grassroots mechanisms of articulating interests and parliamentary representation. Although a critical acknowledgment of the state's claim of generality had become impossible, the conceptual alternative was reduced to the goal of realizing the "real" constitution. The grassroots-democratic elements so central to the party's construction were gradually crushed by this constellation and by the dynamics of official politics. Grassroots democracy on the level of society as a whole as well as within the party remained an abstract programmatic claim that was never (or only tactically) concretized. This has been noted by a Tübingen member of the Greens: "The term 'grassroots democracy' was coined as a term for political struggle, as a declaration of war on that dominant prattle that misuses the term "democracy" at every opportunity . . . and tries to 'democratically legitimize' bureaucratic rule. We have only rarely defined in precise terms what 'grassroots democracy' is supposed to mean. We took it as a sweeping negation of the dominant and perverted form of democracy."[12]

## Grassroots Democracy: Program and Practice

Bodo Zeuner argues that the concept of grassroots democracy actually links two different models of politics. The model of council democracy acknowledges the necessity of representation and delegation but at the same time subordinates the delegates to the grassroots to prevent them from becoming cut off from it.[13] The de-centralized and autonomous model aims at the decentralization of decision-making institutions in order to support and strengthen the decision-making power of grassroots units. Following this argument, I first present the dimension of grassroots democracy within the party and then its societal dimension.

### INTERNAL DEMOCRACY

The concept of grassroots democracy within the Greens was limited right from the start by tactical considerations, as Joseph Huber has pointed out.[14] He quotes an article published in 1978 in which Max Winkler argues that the (still to be founded) Green Party would be successful and prevent the centralist abuse of power "only with the support and feedback of grassroots democracy."

"For the time being that was it," Huber continues. "Nevertheless, it demonstrated clearly that this approach did not imply a politics defined or carried out by some grassroots constituency. Rather, it envisioned a politics carried out by Greens who themselves did not belong to this grassroots, but a politics that was then to be fed back to the grassroots in order to achieve their support.[15]

Thus, grassroots democracy is an *internal* concept, one that merely encourages the Party to realize, quickly and attentively, the motives and goals of the grassroots—that is, the ecological and other protest movements—thereby pursuing its own political interests more effectively. This means that the Greens are not a movement party; they are neither the movements' *Spielbein* (kicking leg) in parliament nor their spokespersons. Rather, according to their own concept of political democracy, they are structurally a part of the political system, which (thanks to the Greens and grassroots democracy) has acquired a higher level of sensitivity to the social problems arising out of the post–World War II growth cycle, and which can demonstrate its capacity to learn.[16]

With this concept of grassroots democracy—strictly limited by organizational and tactical considerations—a broad participation in the politics of the Greens depends to a large extent on what exactly is meant by the grassroots, since the Party's attention is activated, interests are defined and selected, engagement mobilized, and participation channeled according to that definition. Huber distinguishes three kinds of grassroots: members (active and passive members of the Green Party), movements (the new social movements committed to peace, the environment, and women's liberation), and voters, permanent and spontaneous. In order to attend adequately to these different groups, one would have to distinguish clearly between them and even develop different processes for their respective participation. Such processes have not been developed. Mixing all three different concepts of grassroots has had various consequences. Measured in terms of the Greens' programmatic goals, these consequences have to be assessed as counterproductive, since they have all strengthened the party apparatus, the parliamentary groups, and informal power structures.

There are several reasons for this development. First of all, the grassroots exerts no control, since it barely exists. As in the established parties, only about 10 percent of all party members are active participants. Furthermore, the party's surprisingly fast successes have led to a situation in which the number of mandates and positions to be filled by far exceeds the number of active members willing to take on these responsibilities. As a result of this gap in personnel recruitment, Green parliamentarians and party officials are mostly debating among themselves. Besides, the grassroots does not really want to hear, in any detail, about the problems Green parliamentarians are confronted with. Thus, Green parliamentarians are forced to solve problems in their daily routine by their own standards. The grassroots sees itself as just that, and it wants to deliberate only on its own problems, not on parliamentary matters:

> The members of parliament are given up to "parliamentarization," while the organizational grassroots insisting on the primacy of the extraparlia-

mentary "leg"—resists being absorbed by the parliamentary problems that the members of parliament communicate to them. . . . Thus, a natural division of labor arises in which parliamentarians are responsible for their parliamentary work alone, while the grassroots is free to deal with the really important political matters—programmatic issues, those of general political opinion making, or extraparliamentary actions.[17]

In a complementary development, parliamentarians have also come to define themselves as a grassroots group in their own right, pursuing their interests within the party just as other party bodies or party congresses do. The Greens' group in the Hesse state parliament offered a case in point when it became a homogeneous group with an internal solidarity and denied "outsiders"—in this case the party congress as its body of democratic control—insight into its internal matters. Thus, the clashes of interest within the parliamentary group as well as between it and the party rank and file are not resolved by formalized processes but are dealt with, instead, on an informal basis.[18]

This situation engenders serious conflicts over the prerogatives of different party agencies. It is not clear, for example, which party body has the right to pass a resolution and demand loyalty from party members and functionaries. Is the parliamentarian's decision guided by the executive committee, the parliamentary group, or the resolutions of the party congress? The lack of a clear distinction between party and parliamentary group provides party bodies, which define themselves as an incorporation of the decisions taken by the grassroots, with an opportunity to intervene in the affairs of the parliamentary group according to their own interests. On the other hand, a parliamentary group, can exploit its greater access to information and to the media by interpreting and thus determining the politics of the Greens. Finally, even nonelected party employees can exert a tremendous amount of informal power just because they are around permanently. In fact, vagueness about different levels and bodies does not lead to more democratization but, instead, to a growing confusion about competencies. The federal party congress, the highest party body, does not function as a real counterweight in this situation, since party resolutions are only rarely taken by voting from the rank and file upward.

In principle, grassroots democracy is a democracy of participation. Because of the very loose interpretation of this principle in the party's early phase, no limits or quotas were formulated for the decision-making process during party congresses, with the result that quite often a chance majority made decisions. "The people who want to come, come, and those who are there take part in the discussion and the voting—without any responsibility for the consequences and therefore mostly without consequences."[19] The formally open and unbureaucratic local meetings were supposed to safeguard the interests of the grassroots. However, they usually led to broad and arduous discussions over rules of procedure, with some participants convinced that formal rules could be agreed upon, and others exploiting such debates to produce decisions at a time when favorable majorities seemed likely. As a result of this experience, the party congresses on the federal and state levels are now no longer open to nonmembers, and only delegates can vote.

The vagueness of party rules and the Greens' political uncertainties about their parliamentary work also affected the institutional precautions that were designed to guarantee grassroots democracy within the party and install a systematic link between the party's political leaders and its rank and file.

The first, *imperative mandate,* was supposed to bind parliamentarians to party resolutions—that is, prevent their departure from party goals by subjecting them to direct control through party members. Actually, it reduced them to functioning as technocratic "messengers" and made them inflexible with respect to changing political situations. On top of that, the controlling rank and file was not clearly defined, so that the party apparatus increasingly tended to become the controlling institution and to gain informal power, all in the name of the grassroots.

Second, the *principle of rotation* was supposed to prevent the corruption of parliamentarians and counteract the tendency to develop a political elite following its own professional interests. It aimed to prevent depoliticization and safeguard a high level of direct participation of nonmembers in the Greens' party politics. Some of the *Realpolitiker* criticized rotation for failing to take into account the personality fixation of the public and the media. But the crucial point of criticism was that it prevented the development of a personal and relevant continuity in Green politics. This problem was only exacerbated by the shortage of experienced and competent parliamentary successors.[20] In contrast, others argued that the idea that parliamentarians need to be highly skilled, highly qualified experts is wrong and runs counter to grassroots-democratic assumptions about governance: anybody can do it![21] Rotation did not, after all, prevent the development of an informal political elite—especially of opinion leaders immune to formal procedures anyway. On the contrary, it actually supported the trend toward a small caste of politicians who rotated among party or parliamentary functions, the so-called "optical rotation."[22] The gap between this oligarchy of politicians and the grassroots was not overcome but in fact broadened by rotation.

The level of rotation among Green parliamentarians is still quite high (after the 1990 federal elections, about 75 percent of Green parliamentarians left office). But the procedure is relatively lose and is implemented in different ways. In particular, it is no longer practiced during legislative periods.

The third mechanism, *separation of mandate and office,* aimed at preventing both the accumulation of political functions by one person and a monopoly of power. But the scarcity of active party members resulted in the election of increasingly inexperienced individuals into important political positions. These fast political climbers often "became puppets for power-conscious" Machiavellians who influenced decisions without taking a prominent stance themselves.[23] This development also had implications for the prerogative position of different party bodies. The strict functional separation between parliamentary groups and party bodies not only led to information gaps on both sides but also nurtured the parliamentarians' independence (because of their competence and their connection to the media) and weakened the party's executive committees. Since the party executives' tasks are mostly executed by volunteers who are not as well informed on topical issues as the parliamentarians, the gap between the committees and the political process widens. But the major problem is that the committees are totally incapable of controlling the parliamentary groups or even influencing their policies.

Despite everyone's hopes, the major institutions of grassroots democracy, the imperative mandate, rotation, the separation of mandate and office, volunteerism, openness to nonmembers, the protection of minorities, and the principle of consensus, have been recognized as partly responsible for the obscurity of decision-making structures, the impossibility of members' and nonmembers' participation, and difficulties encountered in recruiting members. Moreover, they are now considered to have created the conditions for the development of an informal power clique and a multifunctional elite of politicians. Often these party mechanisms are nullified according to the imperatives of *raison d'état* and party, but even more regularly they are exploited as instruments in the struggle between different tendencies within the party. And this probably explains why the principle of grassroots democracy is not given up. It was remarkable how often criticism of the evolution of informal power groups was mouthed by those seeking to strengthen their own formal power positions. This is how the informal character of the Greens' decision-making processes led to a "jungle war of self-appointed 'grassroots groups' following the principle of 'all against all' on all levels," as Roland Schaeffer concludes.[24]

In any case, no basic consensus to stabilize or even expand internal party democracy has been achieved. The failure to draft procedures for grassroots-democratic politics, as well as negative experiences with the practice of grassroots-democratic mechanisms in the party, justifies understanding "grassroots democracy" less as an unproblematic political recipe than as an "experimental rule"[25] whose validity and practice depend on the political will of the participating actors. However, making grassroots democracy dependent on individuals' political will and on their moral responsibility with respect to the Greens' basic principles was bound to lead to the end of any kind of experiment with grassroots-democratic principles.[26] In fact, keeping grassroots democracy open to further experiments would have meant making it dependent on the factors that had led people to question it in the first place. A conceptional clarification and (even more) time would have been necessary—and time was exactly the resource that was unavailable in the type of political process the Greens had entered. All critics of grassroots democracy agreed that only those with ample time at their disposal were able to practice it and actually take part in as many political activities and party meetings as possible.

Observers as well as participants agree that only clearly spelled out formal and consistent processes would make a truly grassroots-democratic procedure possible. This requirement stands in contrast to the vagueness of the prevailing concept of grassroots democracy, with its informal and personalistic power structures. Suggestions for reform include concentrating on some issues instead of feeling responsible for all; regularizing interest articulation to reduce the time-consuming procedure of controlling delegates by different categories of grassroots groups; overcoming the informal norm that participation and decision making should depend on the extent of personal effort and activity; self-limitation of all party committees by statute and the spelling out of their competencies; flexibility in applying the principle of separation of mandate and office; and professionalization, especially of party positions, in order to give them more political weight.[27]

These suggestions for reform have hardly ever been discussed by the Greens. When they did discuss them, grassroots-democratic processes were not clarified. Rather, such suggestions were drawn into the internal struggle between Fundis and Realos and were mostly interpreted in terms of the demand to professionalize Green politics. Professionalization became quite prominent as a solution to the problem of time because it could draw on established political mechanisms, and thus on existing instruments of political time-management. In the aftermath of the December 1990 federal elections, in which the Greens failed to pass the 5 percent threshold to get into the Bundestag, representatives of the Realo group blamed the party's grassroots-democratic principles for this failure. They suggested changing the party statutes to require the installation of an executive committee. In order to connect the party and the parliamentary group more closely, the Realos also suggested allowing individuals to hold a parliamentary mandate and a party position simultaneously. Finally, they proposed redesigning the party's representation in public in order to concentrate on personalities with high name-recognition—which meant abandoning the principle of rotation. While not all these changes have been made, there can be no doubt that they will occur during one of the next party congresses.[28]

An alternative to the strategy of professionalization and the acceptance of the criteria spelled out by official politics would be linked to the goal of societal decentralization. Time is a scarce resource in the political decision-making process only because of the nature of political decisions, which require the necessary social decisions to be clustered in a few political institutions. These are themselves structurally overloaded with this responsibility.[29] It would be more consistent with the Greens' programmatic goal to react to the pressure toward politicization by allowing society to reappropriate social decisions and thereby decrease the amount of decision making by political, social, and statist bodies. This could mean supporting a development that shrinks the necessity for social decisions, or it could mean supporting the social grassroots in making their own decisions and coordinating their interests and goals in nonstate forms. In this context, some recent projects of the Greens should be mentioned, such as ecological forums for the social control of new technologies (mainly biotechnology), the climate-alliance between European cities and the Amazon peoples, and institutionalized debates between urban and rural areas on the social regulation of ecological contradictions (in waste disposal, water supply, etc.) between the city and its environs. Whether such projects can meet the Greens' claims about democratization and socialization of politics, as some of their protagonists believe and hope, remains to be seen.

## GRASSROOTS DEMOCRACY AND THE NEW SOCIAL MOVEMENTS

Citizen initiatives and the new social movements have been and still are a point of reference for grassroots-democratic strategies. It is a common assumption that because the statist-administrative decision-making processes did not pay enough attention to the interests of different groups of citizens and the political representative system was either closed or considered to be closed to them, the citizens affected by specific problems produced by the state bureaucracy had to organize and defend themselves against large-scale projects such as the construction of nuclear power plants and highways, against environmental destruction and pollution, against the overdevelopment of the countryside and the destruction of urban areas. In attending to the interests of these "affected" groups, the Greens frequently have the expectation that being "affected" will directly support the development on an ecological perspective and the realization of an ecological logic in the political system and society at large. Simple demands for reform will eventually turn into the logic of an ecological society, if pursued consistently enough.[30] Thus, the concept of grassroots democracy is linked to the idea that immediate engagement would politicize the affected citizenry and drive them beyond their direct concern to an ecologically acceptable form of self-reliant societal organization. This process is understood to be inevitable, since the issues fundamentally affect the life interests of every individual. But what happens to the concept of grassroots democracy if the self-politicization of the population does not occur as expected or the linear translation from individual into general life interests proves to be an illusion?

I demonstrate above that the inner dynamic of the concept of grassroots democracy within the party has led to a gap between party politics and parliamentary politics on the one hand and the grassroots initiatives on the other, as well as to a professionalization of Green politicians. Thus, the Green Party can no longer directly claim to speak for the movements and citizen initiatives; increasingly, it has become a party competing with other parties for votes in order to realize certain political goals. The goal of grassroots democracy in society has turned into a tactical phenomenon by which the Greens seek to gain an advantage in competition with other parties. In this sense, grassroots democracy has to be pursued at least programmatically because "without this qualitative distinction"—from the established parties—". . .fewer and fewer people will see convincing reasons to vote Green." The social content of grassroots democracy, too, is defined mainly from the vantage point of the political system. The Greens expect ecological issues to permeate the political system if the principle of grassroots democracy as a supplement and a corrective to parliamentary mechanisms is realized:

> On all levels of public life, those affected need to have an opportunity to stop projects initiated by parliamentary bodies, to correct the latter's decisions, and to decide on political guidelines themselves (by initiatives or referenda) when it becomes clear that these bodies are not acting in accordance with the public will and the public good. . . . Without the realization of the grassroots-democratic principle, we will not be able to realistically enact the desired fundamental transformation into a society that acts in accordance with nature and human beings.[32]

Accordingly, the Greens no longer really see themselves as spokespersons for the grassroots movements—which is only consistent. Rather, they generally consider the latter as potential voters who have to be won over with plausible political concepts. And one of these concepts is grassroots democracy, which is supposed to help open up the political system for ecological problems—that is, to transform it according to ecological necessities and support the success of the "life and survival movements."[33] But since the Hagen party congress in 1985, when the Greens approved a motion to back the *Aktion Volksentscheid* (action for a referendum), they consider grassroots democracy a mere *supplement* to the interest-articulation process organized by parliament and political parties. The petition for a referendum and the referendum itself are thus considered to be part of the political system. The Greens view this supplement as directly corresponding to Article 20, Paragraph 2 of the Basic Law, which states: "All state authority derives from the people. It is exercised by the people in elections *and* ballots and through certain legislative, executive, and judicial bodies" (emphasis added). But, as if to increase the confusion about the concept of grassroots democracy, the referendum as planned in the *Bundesabstimmungsgesetz* (law on federal referenda, ballots, and elections) is supposed to be regulated according to grassroots-democratic principles; that is, in contrast to the practice in other countries, such as Switzerland, the population "is supposed to speak and decide directly."[34]

Whether a referendum is the instrument that can make this happen can be disputed, since the same arguments can be raised against this form of democratic participation that are raised against the mechanism of parliamentary interest articulation. According to these arguments, the referendum limits the concept of grassroots democracy to a mere appendix of the parliamentary procedure and does nothing to support the autonomy and self-government of the population.[35] Four main arguments support this objection: (1) it seems all too easy for organizations and parties to launch a referendum using front men or women; (2) objective, single-issue decisions cannot be taken for granted because the government can threaten to resign and thus reintegrate the issue into the general complex of its politics; (3) despite laws regulating access to the media, the information phase is likely to resemble an advertising campaign for a new laundry detergent; (4) finally, conservative majorities are very likely to be successful in referenda, and the initiators' goal may thus be missed. In fact, it is a dilemma of left and Green politics in the Federal Republic that the very parliamentary decision-making processes they criticize offer protection against reactionary mass mobilizations.[36] Democratic left and Green forces must ask whether it pays to implement a political mechanism that might just solidify the prevailing conservative majorities. Referendum supporters maintain that "unlike the other parties, the Greens are not afraid of the people,"[37] but Tilman Evers considers this naive and evasive. He regards the assumption that "when it comes to survival, everybody is an expert"[38] as outright wrong. Evers criticizes the

*Aktion Volksentscheid* for posing a populist contradiction between the people and those "up there," presuming, a priori, a democratic attitude on the part of the citizens, with an abstract reference to their life interests, but without defining what specifically makes this process democratic.

Evers concludes that referenda will fail to achieve their main purpose—namely, to initiate a democratic learning process by mobilizing the citizenry—because they transform the fundamental and substantial goals of democracy as expressed in the social movements and the grassroots initiatives into the quantitative bureaucratic mechanism of majority rule. Direct initiatives are suppressed once they become the object of the Yes-No logic of the voting process. Their demands will also be delegitimized as soon as the ballot has turned them down. This is exactly the aspect emphasized by conservatives: "If I had the means of a referendum I could tell every citizen initiative to go out and get enough votes to be heard in a legal way . . . we could thus install a pressure valve to neutralize minorities with excessive demands."[39] The procedure itself and the limitation of participation to a simplified Yes-No vote undermine the specific achievement of the citizen initiatives movement, which was to further political experience, engagement, and the competence of the activists. The routine of the referendum procedure, which leads to a short-term hypermobilization and afterward to exhaustion, will in time inspire indifference.

As a representative of the *Aktion Volksentscheid,* Herbert Schliffka has criticized Evers for counterposing quantitative and qualitative principles of democracy. He points out that majority decisions as such are a qualitative characteristic of democratic processes insofar as they are fundamentally characterized by the ability to reverse majorities and their decisions.[40] Emerging conservative majorities must be conceded the right to revision too. Evers' desire for a procedural guarantee against conservative majorities is essentially undemocratic. This also holds true for Evers' fear that referenda would endanger existing laws by, for example, re-establishing the death penalty or abolishing the right to political asylum. In this view, Evers wants to secure more democratic and liberal legislation by accepting a fundamental limitation of democracy on the constitutional level.

Schliffka's argument, however, does not precisely address Evers' objections, because Evers started out from the constitutional-theoretical provision to introduce referenda and merely wanted to point out some of the negative effects to be expected. Furthermore, he sought to show that a referendum could also be used as an instrument to aggressively prevent participation."[41] This insight is obscured by the identification of grassroots democracy with the referendum issue.

This debate demonstrates quite clearly the difficulties the left faction in the Greens has in accepting the citizenry as the direct democratic sovereign. Even if suspicion of the people as sovereign is justified in the light of the historical experience of a legal takeover by the National Socialists, it leads to an elitist and paternalist understanding of democracy. This contradiction not only characterized the status quo in the Federal Republic before unification, but influenced the political perception of the process of unification as well. Many among the left and the Greens rejected the pro-unification plebiscite of the GDR's citizenry because they considered the people in the east creatures of a dictatorship who would only strengthen the authoritarian tendencies in the western part of the Federal Republic. At the same time, the debate about new constitutional rights to direct democratic participation gained momentum and defined the concept of grassroots democracy in a new sense that went beyond the claim for referendum. In the GDR, the process of democratization required a new constitution. Members of the East German citizen initiative movements not only participated in the decision-making process by means of their "round tables" but also demanded the future establishment of "round tables" as a constitutional institution. This demand was in accordance with political reality and, at the same time, went beyond the model of the referendum.

Discussions of this kind increased interest in democratizing the constitution of the unified Federal Republic. The Basic Law's requirement that the German people provide themselves with a new constitution after unification led to a novel discussion and opened up an opportunity to establish procedures of direct participation. Drafts for a new all-German constitution were put forward by the working group New Constitution for the GDR under the auspices of the Round Table, the Committee for a Democratic Federation of German *Länder,* the Social Democratic Party (SPD), Women for a New Constitution, the Frankfurt Women's Manifesto, and other women's initiatives. All these drafts echo the demand for direct participation of citizens and citizen initiative movements in state decisions. Organizations and citizen initiative movements attending to public tasks were to be put under the special protection of the constitution, with direct access to parliaments and to administrative information. These demands suddenly radicalized the concept of grassroots democracy, pushing it beyond the merely technical process of a referendum.

## The Retreat from Grassroots Democracy

Despite these recent developments, one can say that grassroots democracy is only vaguely defined in the political conception of the Greens and remains little more than a catchword. Despite (or maybe even because of) the actors' best grassroots-democratic intentions and attitudes, the nature of their democratic aims has never been precisely defined. This situation indirectly supported internal struggles insofar as grassroots democracy could be used in certain situations to sabotage formal bodies and control mechanisms. "Grassroots democracy was thus transformed into a mere tactical instrument in elections. Any discussion that goes beyond the declaration of moral intentions remains oriented to the established parliamentary procedures, which are simply defined as grassroots-democratic. All the way into the so-called fundamentalist wing, the assumption prevails that parliaments have only become democratized through the Greens' presence in them. Grassroots democracy is understood as nothing more than a supplement to statist decision making.

One reason for this assumption is to be found in the political model of grassroots democracy itself, which is seen as a linear politicization of the affected citizenry and the resulting participation of the population in politics. Grassroots democracy is supposed to transform the citizen into a universal politician, a person continuously interested and active in all political areas. Thus, the core problem of democratization is reduced to the question of how the citizenry can be politicized and led from passivity to activity. In the light of such models of politicization, however, the decentralization of political power and the emancipation of social time from the pressure of political decisions play only a marginal role.[42]

Professionalization is also considered a solution to the problem of extensive politicization and its inherent demand for full-time participation. It is well observed that one of the fundamental contradictions of capitalist societies, the division of society into a private and a public sphere, cannot be overcome by the good will of individuals. A comprehensive engagement of individuals who are concerned, competent, and capable of making decisions in all policy areas equally well cannot be expected. The Greens' organizational structure, however, actually started from the assumption of a full-time participant who would take part in all bodies and in all decision-making processes because all political decisions would concern him or her at some point, thanks to overcomplex unintentional effects. Furthermore, the informal character of the Greens' decision-making processes increased the amount of time required, because insight into and participation in decision making was guaranteed only in the case of permanent presence:

> Doesn't this form of permanent participation of the grassroots and continual feedback to parliamentarians presuppose an amount of time and working capacity that can be summoned up only by people with a lot of free time or at least a high degree of flexibility in their jobs, thus excluding, for example, full-time wage workers or women with a double work load?[43]

Since the *raison d'état* and that of the party were already dominating the Greens' concept of grassroots democracy, it is not surprising to note a growing tendency within the Greens actually to view professionalization itself as their task. Only professional politicians can be expected to handle political power with responsibility.[44]

In this view, the problem of political power and the monopolization of societal decision-making competence by the state—a monopoly that leads to a specific rationality and a reduction of the resource time for the actors within it—is either ignored or, even worse, defended. But another argument borrowed from the liberal tradition points in the same direction and links the defense of professionalization with the libertarian critique of politics.[45] The consequence of this eco-liberal position (numerically weak in the Green Party but nevertheless quite influential) is the abandonment of every effort to generalize the forms of direct democracy. According to this view, the citizen's opposition to the state is founded on an unwillingness to take on the burden of political activity and a wish to delegate this task to an elected representative. Representation offers relief from permanent political demands and has the effect of limiting the political on the level of society. Representation and delegation "are helpful means to limit the expansive tendencies of the political, to relieve people of certain tasks and create a complex societal body, whose reproduction is thus guaranteed and whose further development thus made possible."[46]

As legitimate as the goal of criticizing politics seems to be, the aim should be its socialization rather than the concentration of decisions among professional politicians. It is hardly plausible to assume that a greater professionalization of the Green Party will limit or weaken its politics. At most, it will lead to more passivity and limit the political competence of nonpoliticians. In the functionally differentiated society that Thomas Schmid has in mind, the well-known and widely discussed problem is that subsystems have unintended side-effects that can prove to be catastrophic for all. But, most importantly, one of the subsystems—the political-administrative one—usually takes on the task of making decisions legitimate and obligatory. The idea that professionalization of Green politics will solve the problem is thus a utopian dream of Green politicians—a dream that, in the end, is identical with the status quo of the traditional parliamentary parties. In a strange historical dialectic, the Greens considered parliamentarianism as the highest form of democracy long before conservatives—after the fall of the Berlin Wall and the disintegration of the post-Stalinist societies—began speaking of the final victory of capitalism and the end of history.

Seeking relief in professional politics has its counterpart in overcomplexity. Relief from politics in the sense of a strengthening and concentration of politics actually means that individuals are thrown back by their own political elite to a level from which they had tried to emancipate themselves through engagement in citizen initiatives and social movements. Individual and collective control over everyday life in a capitalist society does not get strengthened in this way. Instead, this collective control again and to an even higher degree becomes dependent upon societal coincidence. Nontransparency and dependency will once again force individuals into a mentality of competitiveness and cleverness, which teaches them always to seek advantages (now extended to include ecological aspects) because the individual conditions for life and survival are not in their own hands. All the social time saved (and then some) is lost again in competing and tackling the consequences of overcomplexity in daily life.

The Greens' experiences with grassroots democracy have been interpreted according to psychological development models or as a political learning process of gaining experience and growing more mature, of leaving behind the illusionary eggshells of youthful radicalism (see, for example, Chapter 8 in this volume, by Claus Offe). Even if the postadolescent cleverness of many grown-ups is not very impressive, one could regard as a positive outcome of this process the insight that neither social groups nor institutions, neither the grassroots nor the state, can claim to represent the general interest.

Unfortunately, this insight is only rarely made the starting point for further reflection. Instead of confronting the existence of various social interests, their contradictions, and the problem of their democratic coordination in order to discuss the resulting strategic dilemmas for the Greens, they often try to solve problems by an illusionary simplification (such as accepting the state's claim to a power monopoly, which contradicts the Greens' programmatic claim of nonviolence). Political parties—apparently including the Greens—often hope to solve social problems by ignoring them. A realist politics would not be *Realpolitik* but instead would take into account a variety of factors: the real if limited common will (*volonté general*) of the state and its learning capacity, the plurality and ever-changing nature of interests, the differential participation of social actors in societal decisions, as well as the need for societal coordination and societal decisions—and all this with the long-term goal of making politics obsolete as an independent sphere of social common will and reintegrating decisions into social processes.

## NOTES

1. Die Grünen, *Bundestagswahlprogramm 1987: Farbe bekennen,* mimeograph (Bonn) 7.
2. Ibid.
3. In this connection, compare the warnings of Helmut Wiesenthal, "Grün-Rational," in

Gabriel Falkenberg and Heiner Kersting, eds., *Eingriffe im Diesseits* (Essen: Klartext, 1985) 1–41. "Green Rational," a shortened version in English, can be found in Chapter 12 in this volume.—Eds.

4. "Round tables" were established, on both the local and the national level, to allow for the participation of the citizens' movement of 1989–1990 in the transitional government of the GDR.—Eds.

5. The German Socialist Unity Party (Sozialistische Einheitspartei Deutschlands, SED), was the ruling party in East Germany. After reunification it changed its name to the Party of Democratic Socialism (Partei des Demokratischen Sozialismus, PDS)—Eds.

6. Article 21 of the Basic Law. The West German Constitution was initially called "Basic Law" because of its temporary status in a divided Germany.—Eds.

7. Claus Offe, "Konkurrenzpartei und kollektive politische Identität," in Roland Roth, ed, *Parlamentarisches Ritual und politische Alternativen* (Frankfurt: Campus, 1980) 38.

8. This problem is an issue in the debate on bourgeois hegemony. See, for example, Christine Büci-Glücksmann and Göran Therborn, *Der sozialdemokratische Staat* (Hamburg: VSA, 1982); Adam Przeworski, *Capitalism and Social Democracy* (Cambridge: Cambridge University Press, 1985).—Eds.

9. Offe, "Konkurrenzpartei," 39–40; Martin Jänicke, "Parlamentarische Entwarnungs-effekte? Zur Ortsbestimmung der Alternativbewegung," in Jörg R. Mettke, ed., *Die Grünen: Regierungspartner von morgen?* (Hamburg: Rowohlt, 1982) 73–74.

10. Jänicke, "Parlamentarische Entwarnungseffekte," 78.

11. Cf. Otto Kallscheuer, ed., *Die Grünen—Letzte Wahl? Vorgaben in Sachen Zukunfts-bewältigung* (Berlin: Rotbuch, 1986), 17.

12. Cf. Joseph Huber, "Basisdemokratie und Parlamentarismus," in Wolfgang Kraus-haar, ed., *Was wollen die Grünen in Parlament?* (Frankfurt: Neue Kritik, 1983) 70–71; see also Roland Schaeffer, "Basisdemokratie, oder: wenn der Löwenzahn nicht wachsen will, müssen wir eben Kopfsalat essen," *Kursbuch,* no. 74 (1983) 91–92.

13. Bodo Zeuner, "Aktuelle Anmerkungen zum Postulat der 'Basisdemokratie' bei den Grünen/Alternativen," *Prokla,* no. 51 (1983) 106–7.

14. Huber, "Basisdemokratie und Parlamentarismus," 68.

15. Ibid.

16. See, for example, Wolfgang Ismayr, "Die Grünen im Bundestag: Parlamentarisierung und Basisanbindung," *Zeitschrift für Parlamentsfragen,* no. 3 (1987) 299–321.

17. Zeuner, "Aktuelle Anmerkungen," 116.

18. Cf. Schaeffer, "Basisdemokratie," 82.

19. Huber, "Basisdemokratie und Parlamentarismus," 77.

20. Cf. Norbert Kostede, "Paternoster: Die Folgen des Rotationsprinzips," *Kursbuch,* no. 74 (1983) 98; Helmut Fogt, "Basisdemokratie oder Herrschaft der Aktivisten? Zum Poli-tikverständnis der Grünen," *Politische Vierteljahresschrift,* no. 1 (1984) 108.

21. Jänicke, "Parlamentarische Entwarnungseffekte," 77; Bodo Zeuner, "Wo kommen die Maßstäbe her?—Eine Replik zum Beitrag von Fogt," *Politische Vierteljahresschrift,* no. 1 (1984) 118.

22. Cf. Kostede, "Paternoster," 102; Schaeffer, "Basisdemokratie," 85.

23. Schaeffer, "Basisdemokratie," 86.

24. Ibid. 90.

25. Huber, "Basisdemokratie und Parlamentarismus."

26. Bodo Zeuner, "Parlamentarisierung der Grünen," *Prokla,* no. 61 (1985) 13.

27. Zeuner, "Aktuelle Anmerkungen," 116–17; Schaeffer, "Basisdemokratie," 90–91.

28. Meanwhile, this expectation has been borne out. Alliance 90/ The Greens concen-

trate the presentation of their politics even more on persons with high name-recognition. And they are very successful with this strategy. Thus, the Realpolitician Rezzo Schlauch, gaining 39 percent of the vote in local elections in Stuttgart in the fall of 1996, was able to displace the candidate of the SPD as number two. The delegates at the party congress in Suhl in December enthusiastically celebrated Schlauch for this achievement. The delegates saw in it the success of a politics that increasingly targets voters in the center of the political spectrum, and that considers the political goals of the 1980s and forms of grassroots democracy merely as an impediment on the path to acquiring governing power.

29. See in detail John Burnheim, *Is Democracy Possible?* (Berkeley: University of California Press, 1985).

30. Walter Oswalt, "Die politische Logik der Sonnenblume," in Kraushaar, *Was wollen die Grünen,* 94.

31. "Arbeitsmappe Volksentscheid," mimeograph (first edition, 1985) 1.

32. Ibid.

33. "Manifest für direkte Demokratie. Für eine Ergänzung der parlamentarisch-repräsentativen Demokratie." (Resolution of the Greens' Federal Party Congress), December 13–15, 1985, p. 1.

34. Ibid.

35. Tilman Evers, "Quantitative oder substantielle Demokratie?" *Kommune,* no. 9 (1986) 41–48.

36. Ulrich Rödel, "Die Grünen und das Prinzip der Basisdemokratie," in Wolf Schäfer, ed., *Neue Soziale Bewegungen: Konservativer Aufbruch in buntem Gewand?* (Frankfurt: Fischer, 1983) 101–6.

37. *Arbeitsmappe Volksentscheid,* 2.

38. Ibid. 10–11; Evers, "Quantitative," 47.

39. Professor Doehrung, quoted in Evers, "Quantitative," 43.

40. Herbert Schliffka, "Die Demokratie verwirklichen," *Kommune,* no. 2 (1987) 62.

41. Evers, "Quantitative," 43.

42. One of the few attempts to define more precisely the concept of decentralization in a highly developed industrial society is to be found in Claus Offe, "Die Utopie der Null-Option: Modernität und Modernisierung als politische Gütekriterien," in Peter Koslowski et al., eds., *Moderne oder Postmoderne* (Weinheim: VCH Verlagsgesellschaft, 1986) 143–72. See also the English version: "The Utopia of the Zero-Solution," *Praxis International* 7 (April 1987).

43. Zeuner, "Aktuelle Anmerkungen," 112.

44. Cf. Schaeffer, "Basisdemokratie," 92; Kostede, "Paternoster"; and, critically, Alex Demirović, "Intellektuellenfeindlichkeit und gesellschaftliche Arbeitsteilung," *Kommune,* no. 5 (1988) 82–84.

45. Cf. Alex Demirović, "Ecological Crisis and the Future of Democracy," *Capitalism, Nature, Socialism,* no. 2 (1989) 40–61.

46. Thomas Schmid, "Aufforderung zum Tanz: Über die Auf- und Abwertung von Parlamenten, die Balance zwischen Engagement und Privatheit sowie die Möglichkeiten der Demokratie," *Freibeuter,* no. 28 (1986) 96.

# IV

## Positions in the Debate

### How to Resolve the Paradox

## Chapter 8

# From Youth to Maturity
## The Challenge of Party Politics

CLAUS OFFE

S ince its inception, the Green Party has continually been confronted with the question of whether this novel phenomenon—novel in terms of social structure, organization, and ideology—would be only transitory and exceptional or, instead, would become a lasting element of the political system in the Federal Republic of Germany (FRG). Answers to this question are extremely undependable, in part because political science and the sociology of political parties do not possess sufficient prognostic capacity for predicting lasting tendencies of stability and transition within the party system. The best we can do is to deduce the endurance of the "Green factor" in the party system from the territorial spread of the Green phenomenon, now that Green parties exist in nearly all Western European countries. Such predictions, moreover, need to be handled with care, as they frequently originate from interested parties. The seeping of such predictions into public political opinion can have very real consequences for the fate of the Green Party. The danger is especially great when a party is "new" and "small" (i.e., subject to the 5 percent barrier) and "electoral" (as opposed to a member party), all factors applicable to the Greens, who need to avoid circles of self-fulfilling (positive or negative) prophecies. The Greens are highly dependent upon how other parties depict their future. The spectrum of such biased interpretations reaches from conservative and constitutionally reactionary efforts to redefine the party concept underlying the Basic Law in a way that would set the Greens outside the constitution, or at least question their status as a party, to various shades of Social Democratic opinion, uncertain whether they should wish the Greens a quick

A German version of this chapter, entitled "Zwischen Bewegung und Partei: Die Grünen in der politischen Adoleszenzkrise," appears in Otto Kallscheuer, ed., *Die Grünen—Letzte Wahl? Vorgaben in Sachen Zukunftsbewältigung* (Berlin: Rotbuch Verlag, 1986). Used by permission of Rotbuch Verlag.

death, a gradual reformation, or, even better, a role as a "kingmaker" and a more or less welcome partner in governmental responsibility.

Do the Greens have a future? This question will be resolved on different levels: (1) long-term shifts in the social structure of the electorate; (2) strategic framing policies and prediction tactics on the part of rival parties or the mass media that depict and comment upon such rivalries; (3) quickly fluctuating issues and problems; and (4) the Green Party's own policies and program.

It is important to see the relatively small role the Green Party plays in the determination of its own future, its successes and its defeats. It is only a slight exaggeration to say that even if the Greens did everything wrong, their continued existence would not necessarily be endangered if concomitantly beneficial outside conditions apply on levels 1 to 3. Conversely, under unfavorable outside conditions, even a display of extreme strategic rationality would not necessarily imply the Greens' stability or growth. This said, it is still altogether unclear whether the Green Party, due to its lack of organizational form, its programmatic vagueness, and its character as a cartel of different factions held together only by the 5% clause, can even be described as an actor capable of such strategic options.

The Greens are far more object than subject of the developments determining their own future. They are not backed by any *Weltgeist,* and no big coalition partner takes them by the hand. But this is no excuse for the kind of political-strategic frivolities and carelessness that were rampant during the Hanover party congress in May 1986. A disappointing electoral result followed, despite unusually favorable outside conditions, including Chernobyl and heavy losses by the Christian Democratic Union (CDU).

My primary thesis in this chapter is that the Greens have *one* central problem of strategic rationality, which is reflected in all their internal debates and conflicts. If left unresolved through negligence, this problem will, in the absence of miracles, push the party into political oblivion.

The Greens are currently in a developmental dilemma. They can afford neither to "remain as they are" nor "to become like a normal party" without completely breaking with their identity. Assuming otherwise constant conditions, only the successful management of that dilemma can secure continuity and growth. Maybe it is not too dangerous to use the psychological metaphor of the "adolescent crisis" to describe this transition. In the transition from youth to adulthood, we say that change is necessary in order to stay "oneself," that the forms a child uses to handle life situations normally and successfully no longer suffice. The path toward future adulthood is not clearly marked but needs to be explored and defined for oneself. What this situation requires is a reflective, self-conscious, and actively changing position with regard to one's *forms of interaction* with the environment—not, in the main, a position with regard to the environment itself. One is floating between original situation and goal. It is clear that the practices and orientations useful in the original situation are no longer needed, while it is never very clear how to define and reach the goal.

New political groups like the Greens, in their transition from a "politics of protest and movement" to a "party politics," experience the peculiar pressure to act against that which they are accustomed to and thereby save their own identity and secure their developmental opportunities. In this chapter I use a four-phase model to show the typical difficulties and "developmental disorders" but also the strategies for coping with these during the transition process. The first phase consists of the Greens' origin in a politics of protest and movement. In the second phase, it becomes manifest that the linear continuation and spread of this initially very successful type of political action is becoming counterproductive and self-destructive. In a third phase, ambivalent strategies of self-rationalization and institutionalization emerge with results that can be regarded and accepted as "successful" and consistent only if, in a fourth phase, it turns out that we are looking not at a destruction of identity, but at a retaining and "suspension" of the original situation.

This phase model is not to be seen as a periodization schema with which one could order the past development of the West German Greens into time segments and transition points. Such an attempt would invariably fail, because the development of the various organizational levels, within the various regional bodies and fields of activity, took place with very different rhythms. The phase model employed here is merely designed to elucidate a sequence of dilemmas and decision-making problems with which specifically a Green Party is confronted. In an extreme case, such as a debate during a party congress, members may run through this sequence in a matter of hours. At the other extreme, resolution can require many years or even remain incomplete. What is of interest here is merely the inner inevitability with which problems of decision making evolve in a certain sequence, whatever the speed of that evolution is.

## The Phase of Movement Politics

The Greens (and similar parties in other European countries) emerged in the second half of the 1970s from a sociopolitical constellation that can be characterized by three elements: new problems, new actors, and the incompetence of existing political parties and organizations. The new problems, to which the mass media helped to direct attention, included the dramatic increase in ecological perils with respect to soil, water, and air; the large-scale industrial use of nuclear energy, accelerated by the state; and, with a certain temporal shift, the entry into a new phase of east-west conflict.

December 1979 brought on a combination of events that have to be regarded as a symbolic break, at least for postwar Germany. At its Berlin Congress, the Social Democratic Party (SPD) supported NATO's "twin track" decision on missile deployment, initiated by Chancellor Helmut Schmidt. Not much later, Rudi Dutschke died from the late sequelae of the assassination attempt on him in 1968, just after he began participating in the founding activities of the Green Party.[1] The Soviet Union's Red Army entered Afghanistan. The context of this founding phase of the Green Party also included the theoretical and political demise of Peking/Moscow-oriented political Marxism in western Europe, the brief life of "Eurocommunism," with its autonomous western European doctrines and parties, and the deteriorating situation of the labor market following the oil-price shock of late 1973.

Joining this objective constellation of tensions and problems of a world-economic, ecological, theoretical-political, and military nature were new groups of actors, new political motives, and new forms of action. Willy Brandt had succeeded by his spectacular success at the polls in September 1969 in electorally integrating the urban middle class and young voters mobilized by the student movement and the Vietnam protest movement.

Helmut Schmidt, his successor as of 1974, had little chance for a comparable integratory achievement. Quite the opposite: a wide protest movement had already emerged in the early 1970s against *Berufsverbote*,[2] occupational bans initiated by the Social Democratic administration. A deep distrust of the arrogance and the hypertrophy of the state's enforcement of internal political power was bequeathed to the FRG by the state's handling of political terrorism, climaxing in the fall of 1977.

Aside from the protest motives provoked by the state, of more long-term relevance was the development of noninstitutional forms of political interest in the citizen initiatives movement, the spread of political feminism and a general mobilization of women, and the political reorientations that were soon to be labeled the "postmaterialist value change." Socio-structurally the new political motives of state criticism, anti-institutionalism, participation and critique of "affluence and security" had their basis in the social strata and social categories whose quantitative growth is characteristic of the "postindustrial" capitalist phase: namely, the middle-class service sector, students and schoolchildren, and other groups whose interests and conflict potentials are not primarily defined by the confrontation between labor and capital.

The second half of the 1970s also witnessed a manifest incompetence in grasping these problems as well as an insufficient responsiveness on the part of the established political parties. The German party system was incapable of acknowledging and attending to the above-mentioned problems and their interpretations by the new social movements, let alone heeding their demands.

Together, the new problems, actors, and motives and the rigid political parties produced an undertow of political innovation whose result was the establishment of green party organizations, initially on the state level, and later (January 1980) on the federal level. These founding conditions influenced the newly established party's peculiarities of political style and political organization.

In the early phase, the Green Party declared its intention to act as an electoral and (where successful) a parliamentary amplifier and extended arm of social movements. The demands were hardly complex and took a short-term perspective; presented in a radical phraseology, they concentrated on a few political fields: energy, environment, peace, and (later and increasingly) women's issues. They called for either an end to state intervention and state initiatives ("Stop the nuclear energy program!") or, conversely, for an aggressive deployment of coercive state power (e.g., demands for bans) or state funds to further certain group interests, technologies, and economic forms. This logic of radical single-issue demands or calls for immediate action echoes the social movements and corresponds exactly to the organizational form in which movement politics takes place. This form is characterized by a strong distrust of professionalization and the material and immaterial interests that the occupants of party offices or mandates might develop.

In this initial phase of the Green Party, the principle of rotation as well as an extensive "grassroots" transparency in the process of interest articulation were expected to insulate against the domination of such interests. Everybody who was present and interested could take part in the deliberations of party bodies and their votes. Formal party membership was not a precondition for running for office. In this way, the party's parliamentary work was often accompanied, intensified, and underpinned by extraparliamentary activities and calculated, often subculturally tinted, breaches of parliamentary rules and conventions. This was, to a high degree, a movement/protest politics, focused on the present and current thematic cycles. Its success depended upon a wide coverage by a media interested in novelty and scandal, while the Green Party itself made excessive use of expressive and subcultural styles based on an ethics of convictions. Formal party organization played an accordingly small role. It restricted itself to satisfying the minimal standards of legal regulation and hardly had to fulfill any recognized or substantial function, neither internally vis-à-vis the members, nor externally vis-à-vis the electorate, media, and other political parties.

This phase was concerned with manageable, intuitively convincing, and extremely moralized "problem solving." The conceptional and argumentative preparation, explication, and distribution of these solutions did not require a party organization or a continually active administrative staff. In sum, the phase of the Greens' founding and initial electoral successes on the state and federal levels can be described as one in which favorable circumstances had to be politically evaluated and, as yet, no reason existed for a clear structural differentiation between the party and its social movement environment or between the party and the media-sensitized public.

## The Phase of the Exhaustion of Movement Politics

The Green Party's spectacular initial successes show how high the political "surplus" emanating from unconventional, spontaneous, anti-institutional, moralizing, and issue-oriented political forms can be, at least for a while. For internal and external reasons, however, the productivity of this source of surplus, handled and exploited so skillfully by the Green Party's activists, is rapidly decreasing. Political practices that were a precondition for success in the initial phase now become stumbling blocks, and, worse, inspire processes of internal and external disintegration.

Early on, people inside and outside the party feared that the successes achieved through movement politics could very well be the seed for later defeats, because the successes would induce the activists to draw the wrong conclusion and commit themselves to practices that would, in the long run, be self-destructive. The rotation principle, for example, was soon, at least tacitly, acknowledged to put a systematic premium on incompetence and deter "political talents." More importantly, the recipe for electoral successes, combining but not integrating packages of radical single issues, proved to be of limited suitability.

A series of disappointing electoral results proved the naiveté of a strategy limited to picking up topical demands (usually in the abolish, stop, close down, and prohibit category) from the street as if they were lying there in some kind of natural state, and carrying these demands into parliaments and to the media. On the one hand, they apparently soon lost the support of potential voters who had been mobilized by the social movements, voters suspicious of parliamentary "politics of representation" and fearful that their pure moral-political motives would be instrumentalized by a parliamenta- rized Green Party politics but also deradicalized and pragmatized by com- promise. This was especially true of peace and women's groups.

On the other hand, voters who accepted *some* of the demands on the Greens' electoral platform but could not accept others proved immune to the Green invitation. A person supporting radical energy and environmen- tal demands might or might not favor total legalization of abortion, de- pending on how far away he or she is from the Greens' subcultural base among the metropolitan, young, relatively well-educated, Protestant or nonreligious middle-class individuals of the service sector.

The failure to depart from the mode of movement politics and enter into more complex political forms backfires on the party in this second phase, causing self-destructive frictions that emerge in its relationship to compet- ing political parties. Much sooner than most Green activists expected, these parties caught up on the learning curve and occupied the Greens' thematic spectrum. They thus managed at least to suggest to large parts of the elec- torate that they were as engaged as the Greens in the political arenas of peace, women, and the environment but additionally had a much larger competence with regard to solving these problems. The dangerous anti- institutional arrogance that led Green politicians and parliamentarians to speak of all the other parties as "old parties" surely provoked the latter to get together in a kind of negative coalition and accuse the Greens of com- pletely lacking "the ability to undertake politics" (*Politikfähigkeit*), as the head of the SPD's Bundestag group, H. J. Vogel, put it.

The model of the negative coalition was used by the Greens with con- siderable initial but soon diminishing success. The claim to be "not right, not left, but in front" has become a slogan that is neither theoretically nor practically tenable, a pure frivolity. The refusal to undertake a theoretical self-definition leads to an incapacity for strategy, since this slogan is seriously intended to make redundant a differential evaluation of coalition perspec- tives with other political forces. A person who regards all cats as gray will have enormous problems in a situation requiring him or her to choose, or even only to differentiate, between two cats. A person who merrily relies on having arrived in a "postideological" era where only life and survival are at stake, may achieve tactical successes by focusing on the most pressing tasks, thereby gain time by circumventing tedious debates about principles, and in this way even attract comrades-in-arms from very different political-cultural camps. But this short-term gain is obtained at the expense of a long-term strategic disadvantage: the differentiating criteria indispensable for a long- term and fundamental project of social and political change are neglected or even put under a taboo.

The Greens' initial tactical successes, based on an extreme conception of an ideologically neutralized mass party transcending traditional left-right categories, were quite deceptive. For the neglect of political-theoretical work exacted a double price, external and internal. In the party's relationship to potential voters and sympathizers, the reservoir of arguments and evidence supplied by normative political theories or "ideologies" (and *only* by them) dries out. These are the arguments that can persuade people that political action can overcome the tension between public interest and individual interest, between collective goods and individual goods, and that these poles or extremes can be reconciled.

However ideologically vapid our two "mass parties," the SPD and the CDU, may seem, they clearly have at their disposal political-theoretical formulas that are, perhaps, inadequate, but that they can use to work out this fundamental argumentative burden. Not, however, the Greens, who in this instance are more like a mirror image of a laissez-faire Free Democratic Party (FDP). While the FDP, in view of its decreasing clientele, limits itself to canonizing the human urge to get rich and leaves the decision about the consequences for the public or collective good up to individual "free will," the Greens' discourse of catastrophe operates exactly the other way around. Using radical gestures, phrases, and unexamined borrowings from ultraleftist theories, this discourse conjures up the demands of the public good and our responsibilities toward nature, the Third World, and future generations. However, it does so without—at least during this second phase—being able to indicate what interests and material circumstances should make the individual addressees of such moralizing messages feel compelled to make the requested sacrifices and to favor the desired investments in the public good.

Common to both liberal-economic and Green positions, otherwise diametrically opposed, is their dodging of argumentative mediation and organizational modeling of the difficult relationship between public and individual interests. Instead, they place themselves on one side or the other. In this way, the putative tactical benefits arising from the principle of dodging the fundamental political-theoretical dispute caused the Greens' advances to the electorate to rebound, because that electorate, not surprisingly, feels in large part morally overtaxed. In addition, dodging has nurtured an intraparty discourse that, despite the Greens' relatively intellectual regular electorate, is characterized by extreme anti-intellectualism and open reservations against forms of political articulation and debate that are emotionally neutral and conceptually disciplined.

A second problem emanating from the Greens' tactical renunciation of a theoretical self-definition shows up in this second phase in internal disputes. Here, the scene is not characterized by peacefully coexisting groups with different ideological orientations and contextual origins. Rather, it is characterized by an open antagonism between two blocks that label themselves "Fundamentalist" and "Realpolitiker," an antagonism that is not resolvable by any majority decision, resolution, intellectual authority, or intraparty court ruling. Taken by themselves, each of these large camps is a cartel of currents and moral-political value orientations that can be distinguished as libertarian, council communist, radical democratic, ecological, feminist, and antimodernist or romantic.

This mélange of diverging conceptions and positions is held together neither by a set of common basic convictions nor by a generally recognized compromise-making procedure. The only integrating forces that can be made out are the common support of slogan-like (and often hard to operationalize) core demands as well as a general agreement upon rules of gender and faction-based proportionality with regard to the political personnel in the party's organs and parliamentary groups. As further institutionalized mechanisms for agreement are lacking, there is a constant danger that the different levels of communication within the party will become separated from one another and spin loose. Different statements are made in party congresses, parliamentary groups, and press interviews, providing the competing party factions and parts of the mass media with a welcome opportunity to discredit the Greens as a political formation eaten up by internal contradictions, lacking political profile, and, in general, highly untrustworthy.

This criticism is certainly valid in the sense that, given the strong divergence of positions represented within the Party, one can hardly imagine that the Greens' members would have voluntarily sought and retained membership in one and the same party if it had not been for the compelling argument of electoral politics: the 5 percent barrier that no grouping can dispense with the rival factions. In this phase of their development, the Greens thus look like an artifact of the 5 percent threshold because their cohesion is based on an externally exacted requirement for cooperation. This may well be ruinous for the Greens' political survival in the long run; it is also paradoxical, inasmuch as the barrier was designed to prevent the emergence of new and supposedly destabilizing forces within the West German party system.

## The Phase of Self-Rationalization

In the second phase, forms of politics and organization that had proved to be successful in the initial phase acted as a dramatic impediment to Green politics. In a third phase, promisingly, this fact is beginning to be taken to heart and constructively dealt with. The decisive questions in this phase will be if, for whom, and how soon the party can achieve those Munchhausen effects by which it would pull itself out of the swamp by its own bootstraps.

Initial efforts toward such organizational and political self-rationalization are always precarious. Here we see the Social Democrats' big revisionism debate of 1899–1916 re-enacted by an amateur theater group, with the Fundamentalists and Realos in the historical costumes of the social revolutionaries and the revisionists/opportunists. This re-enactment could be taken seriously if it included a theoretically presentable counterpart to Karl Kautsky's conception of 1891. Kautsky envisioned the breakdown of capitalism and the equally inevitable emergence of socialism; a modern counterpart would be a contemporary theory of revolutionary transformation in the western European industrial societies. But as such a theory does not exist, the fundamentalist attack on efforts toward political-organizational self-rationalization merely serves as a rhetorical barrage; their gunmen would run low on ammunition in any serious confrontation. Hopes for a continuing and successful process of self-rationalization are based partly on this structural argumentative weakness on the part of the Fundamentalists.

If I am correct, advances have been made in at least three areas: in party organization, in economic and social policy, and in the definition of the Greens' position on the constitution and the state's monopoly of force. I see two lines of development leading toward a common logic of such processes of evolution and rationalization. First, the switch from a style of politics that is naively and expressively obsessed with the immediate "solution of problems" to a more complex style of politics that at least methodologically does not shy away from also considering the "problems of solutions." This style of politics will also offer solutions to such problems, solutions—so to speak—of a second degree.

Second, the Greens seem increasingly to acknowledge the "dialectic of the increase of power," which consists in the recognition that, beyond a certain and usually rather low threshold, one's opportunities for power and transformation can no longer be furthered by an emphatic mobilization and exhaustion of all of one's resources but, paradoxically, only by self-containment and self-limitation.

These two principles have initially borne fruit in the area of organizational self-rationalization. The discovery that the rotation principle and "grassroots democracy" harbor problems or are even phony solutions, and that one can make headway in certain not untypical situations of political action only if one abides by the rules of professionalism, procedural discipline, and division of labor, was such an overwhelming and primary political experience that its fruits were able to ripen even in the deep shadows cast by anti-institutional and identity-democratic rhetoric.

A well-known experience with "grassroots-democratic" arrangements, but one that must be recognized over and over, boils down to the fact that such arrangements only seem to create conditions favorable to egalitarianism and innovation—and seem this way only to the well-intentioned originators; in reality, the playing ground is being surrendered to the political cliques of activist minorities. Even gender proportionality, attractive as it may be for other tactical and strategic reasons, can in practice lead to a situation where a minimal level of political competence and professionalism is actually underbidden because sometimes, in part as a result of the gendered division of labor and discrimination in society at large, not enough "qualified" (male or female) candidates are available, inevitably making those nominated exclusively on the basis of proportionality more dependent upon instructions and perhaps even patronizing directives from "professionals."

Further processes of rationalization and steps toward transcending "grassroots-democratic" practices of proportionality, rotation, and decentralization will depend upon the Greens' success in correcting the enormous imbalance between a large electorate and a small party membership by extending membership significantly over the presently existing limits of lifestyle and age.

Even more important is the rationalization process taking place, at least in small steps and in influential projects, in the area of Green economic and social programs. Here, too, we can observe an increasing willingness to take into consideration the evident followup problems inherent in demands for a partial "shutdown" and ecological "disarmament" of industrial society's structures. They increasingly acknowledge that workers may exhibit legitimate and tenacious interests, which can well lead to the failure of large-scale ecological reform and restructuring programs. Thus, the Greens increasingly see the need to consider the "problems of solutions" in this area too, and to develop strategies, make suggestions, and design programs to accompany and make acceptable those moral demands which go hand in hand with an ecological renewal of industrial society.

Examples of such policy patterns can be found in programmatic conceptions developed by green parties worldwide with regard to agriculture, reduction of labor time, shifting social policy toward tax-financed basic income, furthering the cooperative system and alternative economy, debureaucratization of social services, and other areas. Self-restrictions and self-commitments, including under certain conditions drastic limitations of one's own political options, are connected to such strategies of solution in the sense that labor union and Social Democratic (and perhaps even petit-bourgeois commercial and agrarian?) milieus must be targeted as potential partners for joint action, or even for coalition, on the assumption that they can be won over to cooperate in such long-term and complex political strategies. Of course, this has important consequences for the party's organizational principles, as such partners need to be nurtured, cared for, and strengthened in their desire to cooperate. At the very least, it means they cannot be confronted with policy changes passed in hastily convened party congresses every six months.

Such political models, which are designed for mid-term and long-term perspectives, take into account objective problem constellations and the need for cooperation, and are temporally, substantively, and socially integrated, will succeed only if the Greens manage to silence the doubts about their relationship to the legal and constitutional order and the state's monopoly of force. This is presumably not a merely tactical and pragmatic issue, but is of fundamental importance. The grassroots political ideal carried along from the "movement phase," where the grassroots not only bindingly *decides* on policies but also ("decentrally") *implements* those policies, proves to be less and less realistic or even desirable.

It also has become evident that the emphatic desire for a "reappropriation of politics by society," with the concomitant calling into question of the state's monopoly of power and of politics, is a short-circuited and insufficiently intelligent recipe. There are many reasons for this, and those reasons have left marks in the Green Party, even if they do not show in party congresses and other festive occasions characterized by a self-indulgent radicalism. One reason is that ambitious programs of socioecological reform, of "restructuring" industrial society, cannot very well do without that resource which modern societies have invented and developed for the purpose of organizing themselves—namely, state power.

Beyond the points of practicality that demand acknowledgment and strategic application of the state's monopoly of force, points of political legitimacy speak for this, especially when one takes into account the *real* tendencies toward an "appropriation of politics by society"—semiprivatization, corporate contracting-out, and the structural vulnerability of public politics to corruption and coercion, for instance, in the FRG. In view of such rapidly spreading phenomena, one can conclude that the idea of a democratically controlled state monopoly of power is progressive, since it counteracts reactionary tendencies of "destatification" and deregulation.

Be that as it may, one must be skeptical of positions seeking to limit and abolish state competence when one considers the forces, motives, and resources that society would have at its disposal as soon as it wanted to control itself "directly" without the mediation of state power. Here, we should certainly not dramatize the significance of a willingness to use violence that is hardly "radical" but rather is politically wayward and hopeless, that has internally and externally become aestheticized and abstract in purpose, that societies such as ours apparently breed and that poses itself against the state. But we also should not ignore it, which we would do if we interpreted it solely as an artifact and a consequence of the breaches of the public peace on the part of the *police.*

Rather more important is that notion of Oscar Wilde's that is presently going the rounds: Wilde objected to socialism because it just took up too many free evenings. This is a complaint that Green political planners, with their enthusiasm for "decentralized self-government" and its concomitant plethora of organs, committees, liaison offices, and councils, have all too easily brushed aside in the past.

### The Phase of Self-Rationalization versus "Identity"?

We can easily predict that rationalization processes of the kind current in the third phase, to the extent that they are developed at all, will be accompanied by an increasing suspicion that things are moving toward a regressive normalization leading away from the original intentions of radical change. In this context, the history of the SPD is regularly employed as a warning and deterrent example, and this provides those who fundamentally oppose processes of political rationalization with their favorite rationale.

This argument, however, could very well be used in the opposite manner: in a political history and culture in which the failure of Social Democratic politics and reform concepts has become as clear as it has in Germany, one can presuppose a certain degree of immunity to developments leading to, in the end, a mere "social-democratization" of the Greens. In more general terms, mistrust of institutions and skepticism about any claims for the basic reasonableness of political forms as such are sufficiently rooted particularly in Germany to justify the assumption that the above-mentioned political-organizational rationalization processes will not overshoot the mark of a rationally controlled increase in power and strategic capability.

These assessments will not necessarily silence critics who believe that the (seeming) gains of self-rationalization must invariably be paid for by a loss of identity. I do, however, regard all these misgivings about formalistic, legalistic, and in the end opportunistic deformations of prevailing politics as providing a strong guarantee, but not the only one, that the fear of a "social-democratization" of the Greens can be ignored. For the model of a revolutionary, institutionally unchanneled, and "historically necessary" politics of social change is not the only one that is obsolete today. So is its counter-part—namely, the political model of the bureaucratized mass party, of the unconditional loyalty to the state and constitution, of gradualism in politi-cal reforms, and of political action focused only on growth and security. To the extent that this is true, a self-rationalization process on the part of the Greens that comes close to being indistinguishable from the Social Demo-cratic archetype is not very likely subjectively, nor does it promise to be very successful objectively.

I base this thesis on three lines of thought that I shall briefly sketch be-low. Their common denominator consists in the claim that the three forms of rationality with which nineteenth- and twentieth-century societal mod-ernization processes have been enacted and legitimized—namely, scientific technology, capitalist economic calculation, and legal regulation—have been discredited as incomplete, unreliable, and potentially unreasonable, at least to the extent that no one today will base a claim on the reasonableness of potential action *exclusively* on these criteria. It is precisely the *critique* of the unreliability of criteria of rationality based on technology, capital, and the state (or on the natural sciences, conventional economic theory, and law) that underlies the Greens' political motives and projects. Their identity is based on the easily illustrated suspicion that a politics reduced to legal forms, to the grammar of dictates, prohibitions, and material incentives, while si-multaneously neglecting the "implicit meaning" of the constitutional state, of democracy, and of the welfare state, will either operate ineffectively or lead to totally illegitimate results.

Legally bound state power and bureaucratic intervention are indispens-able instruments of social change, but at the same time they are increasingly inadequate instruments. Gender conflicts in the family, at work, and in pol-itics show how little conventional instruments of rational political action can contribute to their resolution, and that especially instructive example is not the only one. All political problems of reform and regulation touching upon the sphere of lifestyle, having to do with consumption, pedagogical styles, discriminatory relations, gender conflicts, associative action, appropriation of cultural traditions, and other forms of behavior, by definition lie outside the range of those instruments of behavioral coordination that politics, in the form of law, material incentives, and scientifically authorized truths, has at its disposal.

Neither the resolution of gender conflicts nor that of international rela-tions, not even the enforcement of a sensible pattern of energy consump-tion, is a task that can be effectively tackled using these limited instruments. The "suspended" repertoire of movement politics remains indispensable to cover this "gap" in traditional forms of political intervention. In much the same way, the real and potential dangers involved in the "peaceful" and un-peaceful use of nuclear energy show that natural sciences and technology provide indispensable but also highly inadequate instruments and criteria for securing minimal standards of societal reason. Of course, the same goes for the quality criteria of state capitalist or socialist managed economic growth.

From this widespread and well-founded critique of modernization and of the quality criteria it is based on, I would draw the conclusion that the Greens and the sociopolitical strata that support them exhibit neither the subjective preconditions nor the objective conditions (i.e., dangers) for a successful renaissance of such "modernist" measures of progress. (Even the SPD is struggling to distance itself from such measures.) In my view, this means that the Greens could subject themselves to those political-organizational rationalization processes upon whose success their political future will be based with even greater determination and self-confidence. And they could do so without neurotically fearing a "loss of identity."

## NOTES

1. Dutschke was the most prominent figure in the West German New Left during the 1960s, and a supporter, just before he died in 1979, of the newly forming Greens.—Eds.

2. In 1972 the SPD-led federal government passed laws barring from the civil service any members of political parties opposed to the "basic democratic order" of the FRG, particularly the neo-Nazi National Democratic Party (NPD) and the East German–oriented German Communist Party (DKP).—Eds.

## Chapter 9

%

# A Party Is Not a Movement
# and Vice Versa

JOACHIM HIRSCH

The West German Greens like to invoke the legend that they are the party or even the "extended arm" of the new social movements. This legend does not gain truthfulness through its cultivation in social-science analysis. The diffuse concoction of groups, initiatives, and milieus summed up by the abstract term "social movements" was hardly able to undertake a strategic act like founding a party. In fact, the Greens emerged and became successful only because new social movements and new lines of conflict had brought about a constellation of political forces that permitted such phenomena.

Founding the Green Party was the achievement of a rather diffuse group consisting of disappointed adherents of the established parties, remnants of the dogmatic sects that evolved in the wake of the student movement, activists frustrated by arduous grassroots work, nature conservationists, and, last but not least, members of the "undogmatic" left who had failed in establishing a left-socialist party. The crucial background for these developments is the crisis that hit both the Social Democratic Party (SPD) and the "Model Germany"[1] it administered in the second half of the 1970s.

A comprehensive explanation for the establishment and development of the Greens, including their complicated relationship to the new social movements, would require a precise analysis of West German economic, social, and political developments and their nineteenth-century precursors. "Model Germany," the political-economic structure that made West Germany an extremely strong, competitive, and—at first glance—democratically stable country, had two prerequisites. It had a highly organized structure of capitalist companies, which had even been strengthened by National Socialism and had survived it relatively unscathed, regulated by finance capital and tightly enmeshed with the state. Second, its weakened working class had not recovered from defeat and breakup under Fascism because its scope of action was very limited under the conditions of the Cold War and the western allies' interventions. Both factors laid the basis for a capitalist reorganization characterized by high growth rates (the German *Wirtschaftswunder*)[2] and an accelerated "modernization" of social structures and conditions of life. Here is rooted the "antimodernist" tendency so characteristic of the new social movements of the 1970s.

On this socioeconomic base, a political system developed that was characterized by "people's parties,"[3] which were bureaucratically, governmentally, and programmatically focused on the social status quo as well as an extremely powerful corporatist structure. This structure was held together especially by the SPD, which, after the ban of the politically no longer relevant German Communist Party during the Cold War, could finally develop into a capitalist reform party. Its particular achievement consisted of the inclusion of labor unions in the corporatist regulatory matrix that bound together relevant sections of big capital, the state bureaucracy, political parties, and the interest organizations of wage labor. The basis for this uncodified "social contract" was the unrestrained economic growth that simultaneously provided the necessary margin for redistributive measures by the welfare state. This successfully installed "growth cartel" was a central pillar of the West German variant of "Fordist" postwar capitalism.

The crisis of Model Germany began in the mid-1970s for several reasons. Under the conditions of the global economic crisis, the "socially acceptable," regulated process of capital accumulation had evidently reached its limits, (indicated by stagnation, growing unemployment, and the state's financial crisis.) At the same time, new protest movements were voicing a radical critique of the values, ways of life, and political forms embedded in Model Germany. In this way, the new social movements are a product of Fordist postwar capitalism. Their central theme became the struggle against the destruction of nature induced by "technological" capitalism; against the effects of progressing rationalization of the labor process, insufficiently compensated by welfare-state regulation and consumerism; against the "unpolitical privatism" of the postwar era; against bureaucratic control and regimentation. The new women's movement is also in large part a result of the Fordist Model Germany's process of societal modernization, responding to increasing female labor-market participation and the breakdown of traditional family structures.

The surprising force with which the new social movements of the 1970s developed was due to a failure on the part of a political apparatus characterized by corporatist nepotism and statist consolidation, especially labor unions and political parties. That apparatus, unable to address these new interests and values, increasingly reacted with political marginalization and criminalization. In comparable western European countries, a radical leftist, socialist, or communist opposition party could act as a "contact" for the new social movements and carry the new interests and conflicts into the political apparatus; in Germany, such a party was lacking.

The new social movements' extreme "anti-institutional" character, their strong detachment from established political institutions and forms, as well as their "grassroots orientation," which valued autonomous self-organization, mass mobilization, and direct action, were not, however, a result of this political constellation alone, they were in part a legacy of the student movement's critique of parliamentarianism and the state. Hence, the formation of a *party* referring to these movements with their alternative milieus was not an inevitable development. The conditions under which party formation became possible and successful lie in the changes in the political system of Model Germany and in the development of the movements themselves. The crisis of the Fordist Model Germany manifested itself above all as a crisis of the SPD, which, as the governing party, guaranteed a socially acceptable strategy of capital accumulation. Under conditions of economic crisis, it became harder to maintain a reformist capitalist modernization policy, and the SPD-led government itself began to enact a strategy of sociopolitical cutbacks and financial austerity.

Disappointed reform expectations led to growing contradictions between the government and the party as well as increasing electoral losses. In addition, the new social movements, though they did not much influence governmental policy, increasingly mobilized intraparty conflicts, which eventually led to a quasi division of the SPD, especially with regard to nuclear and defense policies.

At the same time, the ecological movement's politics of mass mobilization seemed to have led to a dead end. Though the original dimension of the West German nuclear program had been successfully cut back, a complete termination of the nuclear industry could not be brought about. The strategy of mass demonstrations and site occupations ran aground in the face of the state's apparatus of physical coercion and the unity of the ruling political institutions. Finally, the so-called German Autumn of 1977 played an important role. Under the guise of antiterrorism, a heretofore unimaginable orgy of state security took place, accompanied by curbs on the right to demonstrate, the dismantling of constitutional guarantees, clandestine operations, and criminalization of oppositional movements. In view of these developments toward perfecting the authoritarian "security state," the extrainstitutional movements' chances for success seemed to fade away.

The crisis of the SPD and the perceived failure of radical extrainstitutional movements' politics had a twofold consequence: a weakening of Social Democratic reformism (causing many activists and followers to turn their backs on the SPD) and a political deradicalization of social movements. From the outset, these movements had possessed a wider social base and had been politically and ideologically more heterogeneous than the student movement from which they had inherited their theoretically grounded cultural-revolutionary motives as well as their critique of the state and of capitalism. The pressure exerted by economic and political developments weakened such traditions and furthered people's readiness to adjust to the prevailing conditions.

Institutional blockage and the failure of existing strategic concepts had created a gap in the West German political system. The Greens filled it. For the first time in West German history, a party situated to the left of the established "people's parties" had a chance of getting over the electoral law's 5 percent barrier and entering parliament. This opportunity was successfully seized by a small group of activists.

The emergence of the Greens has at the very least transformed the party landscape and politics in West Germany. As a protest party, and independent of the details of their rather diffuse program, the Greens were initially able to base themselves in the movement milieus, and they gave the latters' values and goals effective media coverage. They loosened up some of the long-established nepotist power networks and effected more transparency in the public sphere of politics. Last but not least, their existence as an electoral competitor forced the established parties to make certain programmatic and even some political adjustments.

Whether the Greens have been able to effect much more than that in "real-political" terms is difficult to say. Whether they provided the new social movements with greater margins of influence or actually weakened those movements remains controversial. Without doubt, their emergence has furthered the tendency toward a retraditionalization of political orientations and behavior and has absorbed a lot of energy and (wo)manpower in unproductive organizational disputes. Out of their very own self-interest, their leaders had to strengthen the belief that power derives primarily from parliamentary majorities and that electoral results are in themselves decisive for setting the political course. In short, they contributed to bending attempts at political self-organization, at direct action, and at autonomous interest articulation *against* the ruling institutional system back onto the tracks of traditional state reformism and representational politics. And they contributed to the trend slowly replacing the critique of bourgeois democracy (which was still forceful in the student movement) by a rather naive belief in it.

On the other hand, the Greens were not able to completely absorb what still existed of the social movements and radical protest, either organizationally or politically. In time, the skepticism about the Greens held by many movement activists from the outset became even more pronounced, and the number of party members remained extremely small in comparison to the number of movement activists. It is clear, however, that the Greens' politically integrative and neutralizing effect had an impact only to the extent that social movements had already begun to disintegrate and weaken and the radical political impetus of alternative milieus had slackened.

By the end of the 1980s, the Greens had been gripped by a serious crisis that goes deeper than the severe internal conflicts that have shaped them all along. The external reasons for this crisis are a series of electoral failures and parliamentary fiascoes, a common phenomenon for political parties. The dream of continued electoral growth and a position as the decisive "third force" alongside the SPD and the conservatives is—for the time being— over. After the good times of the initial years, the charm of novelty has faded and the attractiveness of the so-called anti-party party has given way to daily routine.

The Greens are on the path toward becoming a normal party just like the others, and the hotly disputed formulas of many of their party congresses—"grassroots democracy," "rotation of parliamentary mandates," or "imperative mandates"—are hardly heard anymore. Even the shock exacted by the Chernobyl incident benefited the SPD more than the Greens, and the attempt to form a governing coalition in Hesse with that party failed very quickly because of political irreconcilabilities.

Prospects for governmental participation, especially on the federal level, have dropped to zero for the time being, as the SPD has taken up an increasingly negative attitude.[4] That the latter prefers to remain in the opposition rather than form a coalition with the Greens is also an expression of the existing economic and political power relations. A coalition with the Greens would not only lock the SPD into a direct confrontation with decisive economic power groups but would, moreover, divide its own electoral base. Thus many high-flying hopes were dashed, and internal conflicts escalated within the Greens. The controversies between "fundamentalists," bent on a strict oppositional politics and seeking to tie the party to the social movements, and "Realos," preferring pragmatic reformist policies and cooperation with the SPD, have turned into open battle. The party is divided, occupied mainly with itself, and largely incapacitated in political terms. Both sides are now in danger of succumbing to hardened abstract dogmas that ignore the existing social conditions of a possible Green politics.

The crisis of Fordist capitalism is one of the most important causes for the emergence of the new social movements and the Greens, as well as the promising attempts at "post-Fordist" economic and social reorganization. These attempts have left clear marks in West Germany's social structure, marks that reach all the way into the movement milieus. Model Germany has armed itself for a new high-tech export offensive and is drastically transforming production and work processes with the aid of new information and communication technologies. Far-reaching social upheavals have resulted: mass unemployment and a growing number of people working in peripheral, insecure, and fluctuating jobs. The industrial workforce is decreasing, while the weight of the relatively privileged and well-paid social stratum consisting of white-collar workers in the so-called new service sector is growing. The increasing heterogeneity and flexibility of working conditions has weakened labor unions and made visible the social division between a relatively stable "core" and a marginalized "periphery." This has also had the effect of breaking up the social base of alternative milieus and movements while the expanding disparity in material living standards has strengthened the tendency toward political-ideological differentiation.

Within the movements, a paradoxical mixture has existed all along of collective solidarity and privatist self-assertion, critique of consumerism and "lust for luxury," feminism and the new familial idyll, fascination for high technology and nature conservation, Social Darwinism and pacifism, theoretical enlightenment and pseudo-religiosity, the critique of capitalism and the nurturing of alternative small businesses, as well as careerist and dropout mentalities. The inconsistencies are now becoming more clear-cut and more divisive. Many experiments with alternative forms of life and politics, political-social "networks" and "counterpublic spheres," have petered out; new lifestyles are commercialized and normalized; and elements of the former "counterculture" are integrated into the ruling mainstream culture. This is, of course, not only a consequence of changes in the social structure but is also related to the fact that the student movement's theoretically based critique of capitalism and its cultural-revolutionary verve have faded. This, again, is partly a consequence of the social broadening of the movements during the 1970s and, last but not least, of a generational change that has permitted new social conflicts and experiences as well as changed political socialization processes to become effective. At any rate, we can no longer speak of a social movement that is somewhat unified with respect to social conceptions and political goals. The so-called new social movements or their remnants have long been a politically and ideologically heterogeneous concoction of currents, groups, milieus, and scenes. As a party without a political tradition and identity, the Greens were hardly in a position to counteract this development. Instead, one can say that they even reproduced this development within their own party.

While an important political point of reference for the Greens has re-
ceded with the demise of the protest movements and their "countersocietal"
milieus, they have at the same time been affected by the changes taking place
in the party system in general, changes they helped to further. In the context of these social restructuring processes, the traditional political camps
and cleavages have partly disintegrated, in no small degree thanks to the crisis of the SPD and unionism. The big "people's parties" had to suffer the erosion of an electorate they had long regarded as secure, as electoral behavior
became more incalculable and the "regular electorate" smaller and smaller.
They attempted to address these problems with considerable organizational
reforms as well as new electoral and "target-group-oriented" public-
relations strategies, designed to discursively bring together very different social milieus, interests, and value structures.

These reforms took up, reformulated and processed many of the protest
movements' issues and motives in their own way. The first to benefit politically from these developments were the liberal-conservative parties, which,
for instance, could pick up the thread of the alternatives' critique of the bureaucratic welfare state or their "small is beautiful" ideology and even develop their own liberal-conservative conceptions with regard to the issues of
"ecology" or "women." In any case, they managed to integrate several of
the new social movements' critiques of society and of technology into a concept of capitalist modernization based on the market economy, high technology, and the "new femininity," and all of this, of course, "ecologically."

In this way, the crisis of the SPD and the political-ideological development within the alternative and protest milieus have contributed to the consolidation of conservative ideological hegemony. The SPD had to try to
counteract the migration of much of its electorate to the Greens through
programmatic renewal and was also somewhat successful in taking over
"green" topics. Thus, the gap in the party system that the Greens had for a
while filled became smaller. For some of their clientele, the established parties have gained renewed electoral attraction—to the extent that people still
vote at all. (This, too, is an important trend.)

The intraparty trench war between fundamentalists and Realos, is increasingly taking place in a vacuum. While the Fundis' supposed "foothold"
(the new social movements) is breaking away, the Realos' concept of social-
ecological reform, to the extent that it has ever been tangible, is losing its
peculiarity. The social conditions in West Germany seem to be developing
in the direction of a "post-Fordist" individualization, heterogenization, and
division of society that will not prevent recurrent conflicts but will make the
continued existence or new formation of comprehensive social movements
unlikely. And the established "people's parties," which were afflicted by cri-

sis themselves during this transformation, are in the process of successfully adapting to these new conditions.

Thus, the question is whether the Greens are more than a mere final or "daughter" product of a movement cycle now coming to its end, a phenomenon of a political transition phase in the aftermath of the big crisis of the 1970s. In this case, they could be regarded as a mere vehicle for the party system's adaptation to changed sociopolitical conditions without a long-term perspective of their own. Speaking in favor of this view is the fact that the social and political constellation in which the Greens developed and enjoyed their initial successes has changed fundamentally and will not recur in this form. Speaking against it, on the other hand, is the clearly discernible electoral erosion afflicting the big "people's parties," whose losses consistently go to the small parties. One reason for this is the obvious inadequacy of both traditional conservative and social democratic political concepts for solving the contemporary social problems of adapting "post-Fordist" capitalism to the new international conditions of capital valorization and competition. This has led to far-reaching strategic disputes within the big parties, especially, of course, in the governing Christian Democratic Union/ Christian Social Union (CDU/CSU). On the other hand, "post-Fordist" capitalism's tendencies toward social individualization, heterogenization, and division seem to produce a fluctuation of political orientations that can be advantageously exploited by smaller parties, especially under the conditions of the prevailing representational voting system, which excludes only splinter parties. The era of big political blocs and calculable cleavages seems to be fading in favor of a political complexity that confronts party strategists with considerable problems.

In a political constellation that offers a pure protest party only an increasingly slim margin, the Greens will have to develop a convincing and consistent program that sets them apart from the other parties but at the same time opens up a plausible perspective for a "reformist" transformation of society. However, the Greens are having a hard time doing precisely this. This difficulty showed up in a somewhat dramatic form when the Greens attempted to formulate an economic program, which ended up in a chaotic mixture of "grassroots" and authoritarian or state-bureaucratic recipes. This brought to light a new truth: the habitual controversies between fundamentalists and Realos are not confined to questions of parliamentary tactics but conceal fundamental differences in the analysis of social relations and in goals.

The Greens are, as already mentioned, historically a conglomerate of widely differing political currents and groupings that are still mainly held together by the common desire to jump the 5 percent barrier. Their character

as a "left" party is more a result of the political system's specific constellation of forces (the above-mentioned "gap") than of a consistent political
profile of their own. The Greens still consist of a diffuse mixture of conservative, liberal, radical-democratic, and socialist currents of widely differing
provenance that is increasingly difficult to keep glued together merely by the
color green. Whether they can actually become an ecological-radical-
democratic-socialist party (for which there is in fact a "need" in West Germany and for which there is perhaps also a sufficient political base) thus
seems somewhat questionable. Such a development would probably involve
disputes and divisions threatening the political survival of the party.

A different line of development is, however, clearly emerging. Increasingly prevalent is a strategy of tactical vote maximization in electoral competition by means of the discursive "target-group approach," patterned after the other parties' practices. The Greens' diffuse appearance and their
many currents and factions, their freedom from the burden of political traditions, and their lack of interconnection with social interest groups (such
as organized labor) could predestine them for such a course. And the Greens
seem actually to have the stuff to become a really "postmodern" party that,
without a clear political conception of society, maximizes votes tactically by
finding niches in heterogeneous electoral milieus neglected by other parties
and flexibly adapting to these. At any rate, the intensity of the recent debate
over possibilities of tapping new electoral pools is noteworthy.

This interest is not astonishing, given the decline of the milieus and
movements from which the party initially gained its support. And it is also
hardly surprising that the new electoral "target groups" are sought in exactly
those "unattached middle classes" of the service sector in which the other
parties are also concentrating their efforts. From the outset the Greens (as
well as the social base of the "new social movements") were in fact a
"middle-class party" with respect to both members and voters. And in the
face of the rather dramatic changes that are taking place among these middle classes, not only sociologically but, even more, politically, an alternative
yuppie party might have a chance, too: more unconventional, less narrow-
minded than the all in all rather traditional and petit-bourgeois FDP, modern, innovative, liberal, and, of course, ecological.

An ideological current within the Greens is ready for this development.
While it is hardly visible in internal disputes, it is all the more effective ideologically and politically: the so-called eco-libertarians, with their attach-
ment to free-market economics, innovative small businesses, individualism,
consumptive hedonism, and individual freedom, and their corresponding
distaste for the welfare state, bureaucracy, and "collectivism." Although
hardly visible in public political debates, this current possesses quite an in-

tellectual potential outside the party and clearly has an increasing influence on the latter's programmatic development. Fitting such a trend is a certain unconventionality. A relaxed way of dealing with social and political taboos can be maintained, as well as a positive relationship to all kinds of cultural and political movements that remain important as trend-setters and innovative stimulants for such a party.

Tolerance and flexibility have their limits, however, as became obvious, for example, in the rather curious debates on acknowledging the so-called state monopoly of force, characterized more by party tactics than by theoretical-political considerations. Such debates show that a tendency to distance themselves from militant forms of action and radical sections of the protest movements is gaining the upper hand within the Greens. The more "normal" and the more bound to parliamentary work the party became, the more it tended to enhance the divisions within the various movement scenes. Nevertheless, this too will not occur without enormous internal conflicts, and the path toward an alternative yuppie party would entail a risk of division and failure as much as any other path would.

Party and social movement? As the recent history of the Federal Republic has shown, these phenomena follow rather different conditional constellations and logics, and they embody forms of politics that are in the end irreconcilable. Their relationship must, therefore, remain contradictory and conflictual. It is not impossible that such a conflict contains a force that is productive and can support processes of social emancipation. But this requires participating actors to have a clear picture of the prerequisites and implications of their actions. The emergence and development of the West German Greens was accompanied by many political illusions, illusions pertaining to the nature of the existing state and the conditions of parliamentary politics, to socioeconomic dynamics, and, last but not least, to the objective implications of a party-based politics characterized by structural constraints that are not easily overcome even with a lot of good will.

Whether the West German Greens have a political future is presently an open question. Their political survival will require a fundamental transformation of the party that will involve enormous intraparty conflicts, and it remains very uncertain that they can weather such a transformation process without sinking back into the irrelevancy of a splinter party. It would be good if they succeeded in upholding the protest movements' initial social-revolutionary and cultural-revolutionary approaches within the political system. Without the propellant that radical movements provide, however, the party will find itself without much room to maneuver in the direction of a politics of social transformation.

NOTES

1. "Model Germany" refers to the state-directed and corporatist modernization policies and political vision of the ruling SPD during the 1970s. See Andrei Markovits, ed., *The Political Economy of West Germany: Modell Deutschland* (New York: Praeger, 1982). This vision sought a tight accord between government, trade unions, and capital, which tended to exclude the concerns and issues of the new social movements emerging during the 1970s.—Eds.

2. The West German *Wirtschaftswunder* ("economic miracle") refers to the era of growth in the 1950s and 1960s.—Trans.

3. The "people's" or "catch-all" parties, the successful Social and Christian Democratic parties, managed to overcome individual class and religious boundaries to build a large but pluralistic federal base.—Eds.

4. This assessment has proven to be too negative. In 1996 the Greens participated in four state governments. The argument still holds for the federal level and some states, however. See n. 13 to Chapter 5.

# V

# Beyond Germany

## Chapter 10

❦

# Green Politics in Europe
# and the United States

### JOHN ELY

### Shades of Green in Europe

The West German Greens were neither the first ecology or green party to be formed in Europe nor the one that seemed at first most likely to succeed. Yet the entrance of their first delegation into the German parliament in March 1983 instantly made them the premiere example of the "new politics" in party form. It also made them the standard of measurement for subsequent green parties.

A number of reasons account for the first successes in Germany. A high level of industrialization in a relatively small area means that ecological problems tend to affect everyone. Where Sellafield, Love Canal, or Lake Erie were the focus of regional concern (albeit with national and international publicity), the Rhine literally flows throughout Germany. Second, Germany has a weak tradition of citizen democracy and interest pluralism, allowing little recognized space for local citizen initiatives to express their opposition. The popular and ecological groups emerging during the 1970s found themselves locked out by an impermeable governing bloc of party, business, and labor interests pushing a social democratic modernization program.[1] In contrast to France, Italy, and England, where a Eurocommunist presence tended to absorb traditional leftist claims around housing and social policy, women's issues, rights for minorities, and Third World issues,[2] in West Germany leftists and new social movements had no established party to turn to. They found that they had to work together with ecological groups to create "alternative" conceptions of social policy and to create an access to the state.

Finally, West Germany's limited sovereignty in the North Atlantic Treaty Organization, the absence of its own nuclear deterrence, the presence of large numbers of foreign troops, and its position as a likely battlefield for any possible European war meant that the German peace movement enjoyed a much greater public resonance than its counterparts elsewhere in Europe. This strong peace movement forged links with the ecology movement. For example, West Germany's largest and most active environmental federation, the Federation of Citizen Initiatives for Environmental Protection (BBU), also became the umbrella organization of the peace movement.[3]

The West German Greens' successes had a striking effect on other European green developments. Soon after the entry of the German Greens into the Bundestag, the British Ecology Party launched a revamped and politically broadened program called a "Politics for Life," with the sunflower as its new symbol.[4] Subsequently it changed its name to the "Greens." During the 1970s the West Germans had learned innovative policy ideas such as the rotation of parliamentary delegates from the Italian Radical Party; after 1983 the Italians sought to emulate the Greens.[5] The success of the West German Greens in the 1984 Euro-Parliament elections (8.2 percent in comparison to the 5.6 percent in the 1983 national elections) gave them seven seats, three more than the total for all the rest of the European green parties that put up candidates, including parties from Belgium, Luxembourg, France, the Netherlands, the United Kingdom, and Ireland. A Dutch green group that followed the West German model of a broad coalition including the New Left, peace groups and unorthodox communists was also successful.[6] A more purist, "green-green" focus on environmental issues, such as that taken by the French Greens, failed decisively in the 1984 elections.[7]

This split between an approach integrating New Left elements with close ties to the new social movements and a purely environmental outlook critical of leftist perspectives has characterized the Green parties in Europe since their emergence.[8] The former perspective develops a broad spectrum of alternative positions, including Third World issues and rights for minorities, gays, and lesbians, and emphasizes democratic structures in the party. Green-green perspectives, on the other hand, avoid an antiestablishment profile and emphasize "genuine ecology issues that do not bring them deeply into policy conflict with the established parties over social welfare state and foreign policy."[9]

After the 1984 Euro-Parliament elections, the West German Greens participated in the organization of various New Left, local, and left-socialist parties along with green parties to form a "Rainbow" group in the European parliament. The rainbow came to signify this New Left–influenced alternative approach. The Rainbow Faction was formed in conjunction with the Green Alternative European Link (GRAEL), a federation of green-alternative parties in Europe and their left-radical fellow travelers. During the five-year electoral period, the Rainbow Faction and GRAEL opposed nuclear power and weapons, European Community–sponsored support of agro-industry at the expense of family farms, and the antidemocratic organizational structure that allowed EC politics to facilitate large-scale industrial expansion.[10]

The June 1989 elections for the European parliament registered the growth of the Greens and the decline of the Communists. Communist seats dropped from 48 to 41, while the number of Rainbow seats doubled from 20 to 42. The most spectacular and unexpected success was that of the British Greens, who leapt from half a percentage point in the 1985 national elections to 14.5 percent (2.4 million votes) in the June 1989 European parliament elections, though none of this translated into seats because of the traditional first-past-the-post British election system.[11] The German Greens scored only modest gains and lost their position as the largest faction, gaining only one new seat with 8.4 percent of the vote. In France, after success in the 1989 municipal elections, Les Verts made a spectacular breakthrough after a long silence.[12] With 10.6 percent, and particular strength in Alsace (18.7 percent), they became the third-strongest party representing the French in Strasbourg, while the French Communists continued their dive by dropping three seats.

The left-oriented "Rainbow Greens" in Italy logged 2.4 percent and two seats, while the more green-green "Smiling Sun" Green Lists counted 3.8 percent and three delegates. The New Left Proletarian Democracy also gained a seat, giving the Italian faction a total of six seats. However, the Italian situation emphasized (as did the momentous changes in Eastern European Communist parties since the European elections) the ambiguity of the Communist Bloc. More than half of the 41 Communist seats are accounted for by the Italian Communists (22 seats, down five from the prior elections), who have since changed their name to the Party of the Democratic Left (PDS). They have become a kind of red-green formation, with their political sympathies split equally between old-school Communists, New Left green tendencies, and the largest faction, which looks toward the German Social Democrats as a model.

Greens registered modest gains in Luxembourg, the Netherlands, and Belgium as well. In Belgium, they were the party with the most gains, Agalev drawing 12.3 percent in the Flemish area, and Ecolo 16.1 in the Wallonian. For Greece, too, a sub-headline a Papandreou's defeat was the success of the Green-Alternative Coalition. With just 1.3 percent, they were 3,000 votes short of a seat (the vote was also split with a smaller group, the "Ecological Renaissance"). The Portuguese Green, Maria Santos, campaigned on the fourth spot in an electoral coalition with the Portuguese Communists, and won her seat. In Spain, the Green List's one percent did not win it any seats, largely because of the "front" campaign of a so-called Humanist Sect, which copied Green symbols, sunflower and all, and took one percent of the vote with them.

This grouping of 30 deputies in the European parliament has constituted the green core of a Rainbow Bloc, which in the legislative period from 1984 to 1989 included several regional lists approximating a green political profile. The Danish Greens, for example, were part of an anti–European Community Coalition that logged 20 percent of the vote and won four seats. And beyond them, some 12 other regionalists could be added to the Rainbow Bloc. The post-1989 Rainbow spectrum consisted of Greens and green-related Members of Parliament (MPs) elected on 12 different lists from seven countries: Portugal, Spain, France, Germany, Italy, Belgium, and the Netherlands.[13]

At the end of the 1980s, Greens had, in one form or another, factions in the national parliaments of Sweden, Finland, West Germany, the Netherlands, Belgium, Luxembourg, Austria, Switzerland, Italy, Portugal, Malta, Ireland, Greece, East Germany, and Lithuania. The left-socialist parties in Norway and Denmark and the Women's Party in Iceland function with the profile of green parties. At the fifth Congress of the European Greens, GRAEL grew to include Die Grüne Alternative (Austria), Ecolo (Wallonia), Agalev (Flanders), Comhaontas Glas (Ireland), Les Verts (France), Die Greng Alternative (Luxembourg), Parti Ecologiste Suisse (Switzerland), Die Grünen (West Germany), De Gronne (Denmark), Vihrea Liito (Finland), Federazione delle Liste Verde (Italy), De Groenen (the Netherlands), Os Verdes (Portugal), Miljopartiet De Grona (Sweden), and the Green Party (United Kingdom). Representatives from newly formed Green parties in Lithuania, Latvia, and Estonia were present as well.[14]

This Rainbow-Alternative unity was, however, broken shortly after the election results. The purist Greens were spearheaded by the Alsatian Anton Waechter from France, who brandished the slogan "Nothing further left than the Germans." They sought to exclude New Left and ex-Maoist elements. Waechter was successful in keeping out the Danes, the Dutch Green-Alternative Accord (composed of the unorthodox Dutch Communists and Pacifist Socialists), and the Rainbow Green list from Italy. The core faction was thus cut down to 23, against the opposition of the German Greens and those parties mentioned above. The original Rainbow symbol was changed to the pure green Sunflower to denote this change.[15]

The purist "moss green" tendency is purest in France, where it has been strong ever since the French ecologists split over the issue in 1978.[16] The other major green parties have a more mixed profile. Both Flemish groups are opposed to association with left parties, but differ in other ways. *Agalev*

("Living Differently") has a strong Christian background inspired by the Jesuit thinker Luc Versteylen and no particular socialist orientation, while the Wallonian Ecolo has strong anarchist tendencies stemming from the libertarian socialism of the Belgian Friends of the Earth and anarchists in the antinuclear movement.[17] Italy's Green Federation, united in its refusal to form a national party and sharing a federalist and radical democratic outlook,[18] is split between the more purist Smiling Sun Greens led by the environmentalist Gianfranco Amendola and the Rainbow Federation (including groupings from the New Left Proletarian Democracy and the Radical Party).[19] Sara Parkin, International Liaison Secretary of the British Green Party, strongly opposed the West German Greens' desire to maintain a "rainbow" tie to older leftist parties, but credited much of the success of her own party to its upholding of unilateral disarmament demands at a time when the Labor Party was backpeddling.[20] Jonathan Porritt, Friends of the Earth director and another important figure in the British Greens, saw a system-confronting "dark" green outlook as an important counterweight to a "light" green outlook that could lead to cooptation by Labor and leftists, who "aren't serious about ecology." Porritt, however, did not shy away from social conceptions of the economy, though these have a more guild socialist or communitarian focus.[21]

Among the smaller European green parties, there has been widespread resentment of the German Green media stars, but the desire to "break the hegemony" of the German model has deeper roots, too. Waechter, for example, a leading representative of this "purist green" sentiment, focuses on bird preservation rather than nuclear power, and accuses the West German Greens of being dominated by the "extreme left" and too focused on the Third World and the anti–nuclear power movement.[22] He seeks to achieve a pure environmental politics by downplaying the left's agenda. The Amendola group in Italy, the majority of the British Greens (especially people associated with Parkin), and sectors of the Dutch and Belgian Greens all seem to be influenced by Wachter's approach.

This purist tendency challenges the coalitionary, inclusive, and social-justice orientation of European green politics at precisely the point when the radical right has demonstrated success with xenophobic politics and the changes in eastern Europe have weakened socialist platforms. Particular political circumstances encourage, even vindicate, the green-green strategy, especially in France, but also in Italy and England. Hence, in France, where the Greens have grown in membership from 1,000 to some 4,600 since their local and European electoral successes in the early summer of 1989, the argument that a left-green outlook is the only one broad enough to be successful has not yet been proved.

The results of the 1989 European parliament elections indicated that social democratic/green coalitions are emerging as the left profile in the major nations of the EC. If the European elections were repeated in England, the Greens would replace the Liberal–Social Democratic coalition as the third force in England. Though difficulties in the party and obstacles posed by the British electoral system make this unlikely, the underlying potential for "environmental" votes is evident.[23] Both Italian and French Greens struggle to define themselves independently of "friendly" Socialist transformist discourse. In Italy, even though the Communist Party (PCI) is moving toward a red-green axis, the more dynamic, middle-class Italian Socialists may pose bigger problems to the Greens. The Socialist Environmental guru Giorgio Ruffolo has been cultivating a perspective upsetting the Italian Greens; his propaganda approach in the journal *MicroMega* demonstrates the potential of a "transformist" effect in Italy, where mainstream politics quickly takes up claims and issues of more radical parties.[24] A comparable pattern was observable in France, where the Greens have drawn votes from the New Left splinter parties, left-liberal groupings, and the Socialists, but *not* particularly from the Communists.

Thus, the general framework found first in Germany holds for Europe as a whole: the parties all have "a general left-wing egalitarian disposition."[25] The major Green parties are organized in characteristically federalistic and democratic form regardless of their particular profile.[26] Where socialist parties or the traditional left seek to avoid decline by realigning on a red-green axis, there have been attempts to create rhetorical distance from socialist perspectives. But even here, when confronted with the actual mechanisms of growth in capitalist societies, the Greens' basic "antigrowth" perspective has translated into proposals to regulate capital according to nonmarket (that is, ecological and social) criteria not unlike socialist proposals for regulating the economy. Despite the antileftist rhetoric of prominent figures such as Parkin and Waechter in the British and French Greens respectively, both parties' programs call for versions of a guaranteed minimum income.[27]

This tension between a right (purist) and a left perspective throughout Europe is unlike the split generated by the issue of governmental coalitions that has characterized the West German Greens. Against the "Fundi" (fundamentalist) position, the "Realos" would engage in governing coalitions with mainstream political parties. But among other European parties, purist Greens tend to act more like "realists." For example, the influence of the left among the Dutch Greens means that they have been strong in supporting antiracist movements;[28] the French Greens supported the SOS-Racism movement against the National Front, while remaining "discreet in their active participation."[29] Similarly, those parties emerging from less successful antinuclear movements, as in France, achieved electoral success only by developing a mainstream profile and distancing themselves from this movement.[30] In general, the green parties with a moderate "purist" outlook (such as those in Great Britain, France, Belgium, and Italy) did not emerge from a background of strong and widespread civic and grassroots movements, as was the case in West Germany.[31]

Pressure to attract voters also strengthened the realists within the German Greens and led them to distance themselves from a purely movement rhetoric.[32] In spite of this pragmatism, responsible for the Realos' focus on ecology as a means of distinguishing the Green profile from Social Democracy,[33] the German Greens never gave in to red-baiting and thus managed to maintain a broader political base to generate their identity.

The immediate results of a common European market will be deleterious for both labor and ecologists. The unified market will weaken the hand of the strongest trade unions and the most secure social welfare states, those in the industrially most advanced nations (which also have the strongest green parties). Environmental legislation has been and will continue to be enacted on a "least common denominator" basis, in which one country's higher environmental standards are reduced to the lower standards of the others. This "protective community for polluters" has given the EC nations significantly worse environmental standards overall than comparable western European nations that are not members. Only one percent of the annual EC budget goes to environmental protection. Meanwhile, the political changes in eastern Europe have revealed an ecological crisis in that part of Europe.

Hardly any tolerance and acceptability levels have been established, and only since 1987 has there been any environmental legislation at all in the EC. Even such minor eco-protectionist laws as the ones prohibiting preservatives in German beer, or dried eggs in Italian pasta, have been repealed. Greens have protested against the advantage that the new common market will give to agro-industrial interests at the expense of small, and especially organic, farmers. But with the exception of the Danes and the Austrians, none of the Green formations have explicitly opposed European unification per se.

At the same time, the emergence of a clear Social Democratic/Green/Communist majority in the European parliament is liable to increase the pressure for a stronger "social charter" and initiate demands for an "ecological charter." The green parties' successes in the European Parliament may be a fortunate irony of history. Because of them, the Greens active on the European level have tended to take a more universalist attitude that runs counter to antistatist and decentralist tendencies in the domestic parties.

## From *Grün* to Green:
## Problems of Translation in the United States

The Greens in the United States owe their birth to the international wave of publicity caused by the West German Greens' successes after 1983. The U.S. group began as an initiative of individuals formed by the co-author of a "new age" interpretation of the West German movement, Charlene Spretnak, along with David Haenke from the North American Bioregional Congress, Mark Satin, editor of *New Options* and author of *New Age Politics,* and Harry Boyte. Boyte helped give the initiative a civic republican twist by calling it the Committees of Correspondence (COC), after the founding committees of the American Revolutionary era that ultimately organized the Continental Congress. At first the U.S. Greens were a particular American shade of "moss green," characterized by spiritualist and "new age" elements, a "deep" ecology, emphasis on consensus decision making, and a critique of traditional versions of a left perspective.

The COC, which was to become the basis of an American Green Party, did not establish itself at the high point of either environmental or antinuclear movement intensity, much less at a point at which extraelectoral activism had reached evident *limits*. The year the Committees were founded, 1984, was a relatively low point in the ebb and flow of the alternative movements. Further, the U.S. environmental movement itself was never identified closely with opposition to nuclear power. The environmental movement had reached its peak in the early 1970s, when the aftermath of the first Earth Day coincided with a series of oil shocks and led to the first major legislative reforms: the National Environmental Protection Act, the Clean Air and Water Acts, speed limit reforms, the founding of the Environmental Protection Agency.[34] The peak of the antinuclear movement occurred in 1977–80, when campaigns around Seabrook, Three Mile Island (Harrisburg), Shoreham, and Diablo Canyon galvanized opponents *after* a noticeable decline in environmentalism in the United States.[35]

The direct-democratic, civil-disobedience orientation of the anti–nuclear power movement did coincide with a deepening of ecology in the United States. This was evident in the emergence of "transformative" ecological voices like those expressed in the magazines *Co-Evolution Quarterly, Rain,* and *New Roots,* in the publication of books like Ernest Callenbach's *Ecotopia* (1976), in the rise of the "new age" perspective and the alternative technology movement (represented by New Alchemy and the Farralones Institute), and in eco-anarchist projects like Murray Bookchin's Institute for Social Ecology.

These radical elements, while innovative and influential internationally, remained almost completely detached from the first major attempt to campaign for office on the issue of ecology: namely, Barry Commoner's Citizens' Party. Although its platform was similar to European green party platforms, the Citizens' Party showed little interest in radical ecology or ties with movement organizations like the New England Clamshell Alliance or the Northern California Abalone Alliance; and it had no ties to the left (which in both social democratic and Marxist-Leninist sectarian form ignored ecology). Because of increasing popular concern over nuclear power after the Three Mile Island incident, the Citizens' Party decided to put all its chips on one presidential campaign, but the effort yielded less than a fourth of the million votes for which the party had hoped. Thus, the Citizens' Party was a stepchild more properly of the first environmental movement than of the more radical anti–nuclear power movement.

This disjunction between the environmental and antinuclear movements and the split between these movements and the Citizens' Party project help to account for the belated and relatively weak appearance of a Green Party in the United States.[36] The various grouplets that formed the original COC constitute only a fraction of the large movement spectrum that in Germany led to the formation of the Greens. There, a broad range of social movements channeled diverse political viewpoints and issues into the Green Party, including politics pertaining to industrial policy, trade unions, inner-city housing, and the rights of marginalized groups like urban youth, gays, lesbians, immigrants, and political refugees. In contrast, the U.S. greens, drawing a spiritual and "new age" emphasis from the party's founders, have been identified with a narrower ecological focus, a perception that is only slowly changing.[37]

Underlying these differences between the U.S. and the German Greens are different political structures and their impacts on social movements. Americans do not use the word "state" outside the fields of sociology and political science influenced by Weber and Marx. What Europeans call the "state," Americans call the "government"; and what Europeans call the "government," Americans call the "administration." The American usage denotes the extremely pliable, relatively *ad hoc* nature of the administrative apparatus, a flexibility that also pertains to the legislative sphere. The nonproportional ("winner-take-all") electoral system goes hand in hand with weak political parties and strong individual legislators. Politicians are less beholden to their party's national committees than to their local districts—that is, to all kinds of newly developing and frequently changing interests. In Europe, the requirement of ideological consistency and party unity for electoral success, and party discipline exerted from above, tend to hold in check the independent forays of individual parliamentary representatives. Likewise, a

U.S. president has more executive flexibility vis-à-vis his own party and the legislature than a prime minister in a parliamentary system or the German chancellor; this has played an important role in environmental enactment and "spin" control via executive fiat.

Social restructuring processes and their impact on social movements also vary significantly between the two countries. New middle-class claims challenging business interests with quality-of-life and no-growth demands are voiced in both nations, but the interface is different. The Federal Republic has generated the most ideologically united, anticapitalist, and antistatist environmental movement, but the actual effect of this movement on state policy and industrial development has been less noticeable. The quiet, more pragmatic style prevalent in the U.S. movement, with the door-to-door canvassing of citizen action groups and the lobbying of mainstream environmentalist groups, has provided a greater challenge (at least in the short term).

Thanks to the success of this challenge, environmental regulations have added significantly to the costs of capital in the United States, posing a serious problem for the capital goods sector of the U.S. economy throughout the 1970s and 1980s.[38] In Germany, such a threat is less evident despite development of movement-financed litigation based on stringent regulatory legislation. Actual standards for environmental impacts and air, water, and soil quality and regulations such as the one requiring catalytic converters lag far behind those developed in the United States. The political parties in power have kept nuclear power afloat despite tremendous civic opposition to some facilities. In the United States, in contrast, one local referendum sponsored by the anti-nuclear movement has stopped at least one and maybe both nuclear power station projects in Seabrook, New Hampshire, bankrupting a statewide power company in the process.[39] Endless cost overruns and state executive orders that cannot be superseded by the federal government (such as Governor Mario Cuomo's orders regarding the evacuation plans for the area around the Shoreham Plant on Long Island) have tipped the scales against the U.S. civilian nuclear power industry. In Germany, the industry grew virtually unchecked until the late 1980s, protected by federal veto of potentially interfering local and state interests and by an impenetrable web of corporatist interests involving the state, parties, and unions. Indeed, this protection approached criminal conspiracy at the end of the 1980s at the reprocessing plant in Hanau, Hesse.[40]

In the United States, single-interest groups and coalitions are not merely capable of pushing through new laws, or enforcing regulatory standards through litigation, but indeed can take on entire agencies of government, or resort to them, depending on the agencies' political stance.[41] The groups behind these activities thus are much more "effective" than the German "citizen initiatives," but are also thoroughly managerial and market-oriented. Door-to-door canvasing and large-scale computer-directed mailings, as important a form of citizen action for the Public Interest Research Groups (PIRGs) and the Sierra Club as for the Jehovah's Witnesses and the Moral Majority, are hardly known in the FRG. Furthermore, commercialization of alternative forms has taken a more rapid path in the United States, unchecked by an anticapitalist ethos.[42]

Thus, in the United States, the weak state and a highly modern, commodified "civil society" pose long-term problems for green, as opposed to environmentalist, politics. The U.S. system of interest-group pluralism can place strong legal constraints on capital but does not encourage conceptualizing an alternative to it. It is conducive to solving first-order problems—catalytic converters or abolition of dangerous contaminants such as DDT or heavy metals—and setting and enforcing stricter standards of environmental health. But ecological rebuilding, requiring a general social project, politically developed institutional power, and a supportive constituency, is more difficult.[43] The same institutional characteristics that helped force nuclear power on West German citizens—state-protected and steered industrial policy—also keep the West German recyclying program running smoothly, while the United States paper carefully collected by conscientious citizens is thrown by the ton into landfills because the country does not have the industries to make use of it.

The Greens in Germany have been able to confront such complex new developments in a more organized fashion. They never carried out a fundamental ideological debate, however, or sought a shared definition of the term "ecology."[44] Avoiding struggles over the definition of "ecology" and "nature" has helped the German Greens skirt debilitating debates over versions of ecological *doctrine,* and above all the competing "social" and "deep" versions.

The U.S. perspective tends to be dominated by a "world view"–oriented ecology. Early in its development, for example, the New York City chapter of the COC was split between advocates of a "left green" perspective similar to Murray Bookchin's and "bioregionalists" such as the followers of Kirkpatric Sale. The bioregionalists advocated relocation of the urban poor to areas like the Catskill Mountains, where they would not be such an "insult to the eco-system." Eventually such antihuman viewpoints become more moderate, though they have infected currents oriented around deep ecology and bioregionalism.[45] Bookchin's social ecology and "libertarian muncipalism," on the other hand, underscore the strength within the Greens of both a doctrinal conception of ecology and a civic republican discourse of "communities." He defends a militantly libertarian doctrine of anarchist communism, advocating radical decentralism and sovereignty at the societal level alone, and opposing reform and electoral measures that seek to change the state from within.[46] But since the American Greens are marginalized from a larger discourse of the left (dominated in the United States by social democrats and orthodox Marxists immune to the ecological problematic), there has been little discussion of a green project in the American left.[47] There, the left Greens remain a small (libertarian) segment of the whole spectrum of left opinions that in Germany went into the Greens.

The cause of this limited role may be found in the peculiar communitarian heritage of American democracy. American "green politics" is based on this political tradition, entwining interest-group pluralism with civic republicanism. In U.S. history, "interest groups" and their power in politics are not merely beholden to liberal and procedural "norms," but are part and parcel of its "communitarian" tradition of associations. The development of new social movements there reflects this tradition. During their peak decade, the 1970s, interest in the "town meeting," "ward democracy," and the power of citizen movements had a widespread renaissance.[48] As Boyte observed, the development of the "freeze" movement in western Massachusetts resulted largely from the mobilization of these town meetings as locus of decision making, or at least, opinion making.[49]

One important element of civic republicanism, consensus decision making, harks back to the Quaker tradition. Small-scale "affinity groups" in New England's antinuclear movement developed consensus decision making as their basic organizational form. (The more widespread, interest-group-pluralist form of American "environmentalism" exhibits a more conventional political profile.) Consensus serves, as it was originally intended to serve by the Quakers, as a conservative force. In the COC, it gives precedence to the elites who organized the Committees of Correspondence, and to their organizational ethos and "values."[50] Howard Hawkins, an American Green activist and an initiator of the Left Green Network, has argued that consensus serves largely to maintain the interests of minorities, since it permits them to override the policy decisions of significant majorities in the organization (up to 70 percent).[51] Complaints of "burn-out" and lost activists and members are evidence of the low level of political effectiveness produced by disagreements over the applicability of the consensus principle.[52]

Roots in the libertarian and more radical wings of the ecology and antinuclear movements and a background of civic republicanism enrich the American Greens, establishing a firm egalitarianism in the groups forming the Committees of Correspondence. Circular meeting forms, the focus on consensus as a mode of decision making, and the probably unique custom of almost exclusively using first names, even on broadsides and in newsletters and publications, are evidence of this radical form of democracy. Problems develop most often because of a lack of politics in the Green groupings, as when, for example, the Greens in California went about founding a third party in the traditional fashion with little evident reflection about the limitations of a third-party approach in the U.S. context. The "inside/outside" strategy of the Democratic Socialists of America (DSA), who support left-leaning Democrats where they are likely to be elected and independent or third-party candidates where these show some hope, might be a more productive course. Hostility toward left-socialist and social democratic traditions hinders the Greens from learning this lesson—one built from years, even decades, of considering how to begin anew within the constraints of the American political system.

Such hostility is understandable, given the contempt with which socialists have for years regarded the Greens. This attitude, in turn, reflects the historical frustration of the rump of the American socialist and social democratic left about the failure of its own project—a social democratic welfare state. Socialists have failed to see the environmental movement as a significant barrier to capital accumulation. Meanwhile, the environmentalists' discourse of a special American tradition of "civic republicanism" and opposition to "socialism" is always implicitly, and many times explicitly, a *nationalist* one. Seeing America's "exceptional" path as justifying a different approach for politics there, the environmentalists insist on the inapplicability of any other experience of politics to "our conditions."

## NOTES

1. See Joachim Hirsch, "A Party Is Not a Movement and Vice Versa," Chapter 9 in this volume.

2. Jane Jensen, "From *Baba Cool* to *Vote Utile*: The Trajectory of the French *Verts*," *French Politics and Society* 7, no. 4 (1989) 1–15, notes that the French Greens have been most successful in those areas where the Communists are weak (p. 6).

3. In France, in contrast, national pride in the *force de frappe* was connected with a popular focus on the economic success of the state-directed nuclear power industry and a lack of concern for nuclear hazards. The *Rainbow Warrior* incident was more properly a "scandal" than an occasion for movement outrage and mobilization. The scandal was not the deed, but the French government's failure to carry it out "successfully" and without the details being leaked to the world. Similarly, after the Chernobyl disaster, one noted that in the West German areas of Baden, on the border with France, all the livestock and children were carefully sheltered in barn and house, while across the border in Alsace the cows continued to graze and the children to play outside.

4. Ecology Party, *Politics for Life* (London: Ecology Party, 1983).

5. See respectively Alexander Langer, "Politik als Ware: Warum es in Italien keine grüne, wohl aber eine Radikale Partei gibt," *Freibeuter,* no. 15 (1983); Alexander Langer, "Grüne ohne Partei," *Freibeuter,* no. 37 (1988).

6. Wolfgang Rüdig, "The Greens in Europe: Ecological Parties and the European Election of 1984," *Parliamentary Affairs* 38, no. 1 (1985) 65.

7. For general discussion of the Greens' development throughout Europe prior to the 1984 Euro-Parliament elections, see Rüdig, "Greens in Europe"; Ferdinand Müller-Rommel, ed., *New Politics in Western Europe: The Rise and Success of Green Parties and Alternative Lists* (Boulder: Westview Press, 1989); Michael Franken and Walter Ohler, eds., *Natürlich Europa: 1992—Chance für die Natur?* (Cologne: Volksblatt Verlag, 1988); Dick Richardson and Chris Rootes, eds., *The Green Challenge: The Development of Green Parties in Europe* (London: Routledge, (1995); and Wolfgang Rüdig, ed., *Green Politics One* (Edinburgh: Edinburgh University Press, 1990).

8. Ferdinand Müller-Rommel, "Ecology Parties in Western Europe," *West European Politics* 5, no. 1 (1982) 72–73; Rüdig, "Greens in Europe" 70–71; Ferdinand Müller-Rommel, "The Greens in Western Europe: Similar but Different," *International Political Science Review* (1985) 483.

9. Müller-Rommel, "Greens in Western Europe," 491.

10. Dietrich-Jörn Weder, "Schutzgemeinschaft für Umweltverschmutzer," in Franken and Ohler, *Natürlich Europa: 1992,* 165. GRAEL regarded networking between European movements and those elsewhere (above all solidarity with the Third World) as its "second major task." It also organized an international congress of prostitutes in October 1986, called for international control of the world market above and beyond canceling Third World debts, opposed the expansion of a European security policy based on nuclear deterrence, and called for the mobilization of all the new social movements to hinder the project of turning a united Europe into a new "superpower." See Margret Krannich, "Feministische Politik in GRAEL," *Straßburg Times,* no. 3 (September 1988); "Grüne im Europa-Parlament ziehen positive Zwischenbilanz," *grüner basis-dienst,* no. 7 (1985); Rainbow Faction, "Südostasien: Wenn Zusammenarbeit EG-ASEAN, dann nur unter Wahrung der Menschenrechte," (Regenbogenfraktion im EB, 1988); Frieder Otto Wolf, "Building the 'Common House of Europe' from Below," in *Green Peace Policy,* GRAEL Paper no. 13 (January 1988).

11. Polls by the *Independent* shortly after the elections suggested as much as a 45 percent voter potential for the British Greens.

12. John Ely, "Green Grows in France, Finally," *Alternatives* 16, no. 3 (1989).

13. Greens have had success in non-EC countries as well. In the Swedish national elections of November 1988, the Greens attained more than 20 MPs with 5.5 percent, the first time in 70 years that a new party made the jump into the Rikstag. Greens have also had success in Switzerland, not only in local elections, but also as part of the coalition along with left and pacifist groups that collected 110,000 signatures for a referendum calling for the abolition of the Swiss Army. Though only some 25 percent of the population voted for abolition in November 1989, the "susceptibility of youth to the arguments and slogans of the Greens, which played an important role in the antiarmy initiative, alarmed politicians": Konrad Mrusek, "Eine Schweiz ohne Armee? Die Angst vor einer Umweltkrise ist größer als die Furcht vor einem Krieg," *Frankfurter Allgemeine Zeitung,* November 23, 1989.

14. Jürgen Maier, "The Green Parties in Western Europe—A Brief History, Their Successes and Their Current Problems," in *Mezhdunarodnaya (Zhinzn/International Affairs* (Moscow), December 1989; Georg Blume, "Wird der Regenbogen einfarbig," *die tageszeitung,* April 10, 1989; Jürgen Peter Esders, "Überall die grünen Nasen hineinstecken," *Das Parlament,* nos. 24–25 (June 1989).

15. Thomas Scheuer, "Vom Regenbogen zur Sonnenblume," *die tageszeitung,* June 27, 1989, p. 4.

16. Gregory Starkey, "French Ecologists Split," *New Ecologist*, no. 1 (January–February 1978); Jeff Bridgeford, "The Ecologist Movement and the French General Elections," *Parliamentary Affairs* 31, no. 3 (1978); Rüdig, "Greens in Europe," 61–64.

17. Rüdig, "Greens in Europe," 63–64.

18. Langer, "Grüne ohne Partei."

19. Gerhard Fritz, "Aufbruchstimmung im Schrebergarten", *Kommune*, no. 1 (1989) 37–40.

20. Sara Parkin, "I Love You Green," *Resurgence*, no. 136 (1990) 4–5.

21. Jonathan Porritt, *The Coming of the Greens* (London: Fontana, 1988).

22. Thomas Scheuer, "Tanz unterm Regenbogen," *die tageszeitung*, April 10, 1989.

23. See Horst Lohrer, "Green Party in Großbritannien: Nach dem Wachstum—neue Herausforderungen," *Kommune*, October 1989, pp. 23–24.

24. Giorgio Ruffolo, "Ambientalisti, amici miei," *MicroMega*, no. 4 (September–October 1989); Roberto Biorcio and Giovanni Lodi, eds., *La sfida verde: Il movimento ecologista in Italia* (Padua: Liviana, 1988). On "transformism" in general, see Antonio Gramsci, *Selections from His Prison Notebooks* (London: International Publishers, 1980) 58–59, 128–29.

25. Ferdinand Müller-Rommel, "Green Parties and Alternative Lists under Cross-National Perspective," in Müller-Rommel, *New Politics*, 8.

26. Some parties with a more purist green profile (such as the French, Belgian, and, to some extent, Italian examples) have more federal structures and weaker executives than the German Greens. However, in those countries where the parties focus on the environment and electoral strategies, individual figures function more as charismatic party leaders (e.g., Parkin in Britain, Waechter in France, and Amendola in Italy) than is the case in countries with a leftist tradition in green party formation.

27. The British Greens' "Politics for Life" program (*Politics for Life*, 10–11) explicitly calls for reducing the "distinction between paid and unpaid labor," shortening the working day, sharp controls on large and multinational corporations, and "wholesale redistribution of work," though it still has a largely Proudhonian vision of a local, entrepreneurial, managed, artisan economy. The French Greens have been influenced by the "work-sharing" proposals combined with demands for reduction of the working day advocated by Andre Gorz in *Farewell to the Working Class* (Boston: South End, 1982); they also tap into the syndicalist tradition of self-management or "autogestion" with their own concept of "ecogestion": Brendan Prendiville, "Les Verts," in Müller-Rommel, *New Politics*, 93–94.,

28. Thomas Scheuer, "Tanz auf dem Regenbogen: Der GRAEL im Europaparlament," in Franken, *Natürlich Europa: 1992*, 188.

29. Prendiville, "Les Verts," 191.

30. George Blume, "Frankreich: Auf der Suche nach einer umweltpolitischen Moral," in Franken, *Natürlich Europa: 1992*, 26–27.

31. Ibid.; Rolf Paasch, "Großbritannien: Grüner Seiltanz im Thatcherismus," ibid., 92–93; Werner Raith, "Bella Italia und das ökologische Gewissen," ibid., 108; and Peter Vanhoutte and Jos Bertrand, "Belgien: Unabhängigkeit tut not," ibid., 148.

32. See Helmut Wiesenthal, "Green Rational," in Chapter 12 in this volume.

33. See, e.g., Joschka Fischer, *Der Umbau der Industriegesellschaft* (Frankfurt: Eichborn, 1989). The West German Realos have an explicitly left pedigree and moved "right" to occupy this realist political space. Their approach to the problem of ecology is more structural than the French: rather than focusing on preservation of species and environmental protection, they focus on global warming as a central mode of pushing the ecological crisis in the direction of "rebuilding" society as a whole.

34. Samuel P. Hays, "From Conservation to Environment: Environmental Politics in the United States since World War II," *Environmental Review* 6, no. 2 (1982) 24–29; Laura Lake,

"The Environmental Mandate: Activists and the Electorate," *Political Science Quarterly* 98 (1983) 218; Richard Andrews, "Class Politics or Environmental Reform: Environmentalism and American Political Institutions," *National Resources Journal,* 20 (1980) 324.

35. Lester Milbraith, *Environmentalists: Vanguard for a New Society* (Albany: SUNY Press, 1984) 121.

36. Otherwise, the history of social movements leading to the development of green parties has been rather similar in the two countries. In both, the New Left arose during the 1960s; and the U.S. and German New Lefts broke down almost within months of each other in 1969–70. The collapse produced a similar assortment of Marxist-Leninist sects and fragments of scattered libertarian groupings and initiatives. It also catalyzed the second wave of feminism in both countries, which arose as a revolt against the sexist practices of the New Left. U.S. movements led the way in discovering and implementing new organizational forms and action repertoires (sit-ins, consciousness-raising groups, affinity groups); but by the end of the 1970s, this role had shifted to the Federal Republic. Later strategies of the U.S. antinuclear movement were directly influenced by the larger West German movement.

37. Cf. Peter Borrelli, "Environmentalism at a Crossroads," in *Crossroads: Environmental Priorities for the Future* (Washington: Island Press, 1988) 21; Robert Gottlieb, *Forcing the Spring: The Transformation of the American Environmental Movement* (Washington, D.C.: Island Press, 1993).

38. On the environmental movement as a limit to capital, see Roger C. Cramton and Barry B. Boyer, "Citizen Suits in the Environmental Field: Peril or Promise," *Ecology Law Quarterly* 2, no. 3 (1972); Martin Belsky, "Environmental Law in the 1980s: Shifting Back the Burden of Proof," *Ecology Law Quarterly* 12, no. 1 (1984) 1–88; James O'Connor and Daniel Faber, "The Struggle for Nature: Environmental Crisis and the Crisis of Environmentalism in the United States," *Capitalism, Nature, Socialism,* no. 2 (Summer 1989) 12–39.

39. The referendum prohibited the state power company from charging customers to pay for a new nuclear power station. Cf. Henry Bedford, *Seabrook Station: Citizen Politics and Nuclear Power* (Amherst: University of Massachusetts Press, 1990). See also Lee Daniels, "Bankruptcy File by Leading Utility in Seabrook Plant," *New York Times,* January 29, 1988; Timothy Aeppel, "Seabrook-driven Bankruptcy: An Omen for Nuclear Industry?" *Christian Science Monitor,* February 1, 1988.

40. Horst Bieber et al., "Atom-Korruption im Weltmaßstab," *Die Zeit,* January 29, 1988. In the United States, this phenomenon is evident only in nuclear weapons production, which is kept largely secret and immune to the "interest-group pluralism" of normal American politics.

41. Richard P. Gale, "Social Movements and the State: The Environmental Movement, Counter Movement and Government Agencies," *Sociological Perspectives* 29 (April 1986) 202–40; Laura Lake, *Environmental Regulation: The Political Effects of Implementation* (New York: Praeger, 1982).

42. For example, a green-alternative magazine like the Frankfurt *Pflasterstrand* took 15 years to evolve from a libertarian "Sponti" scene weekly to a yuppified organ of Green *Realpolitik* (before finally going bottom up).

43. A project of social rebuilding and ecological Keynesianism is part of the German Greens' policy platform. Cf. Dieter Suhr, "Pläydoyer für eine neue Geldordnung. Eine keynesianische Alternative zum Keynesianismus," in Projektgruppe Grüner Morgentau, *Perspektiven ökologischer Wirtschaftspolitik* (Frankfurt am Main: Campus, 1986) 431–61; Frank Beckenbach et al., eds., *Grüne Wirtschaftspolitik* (Cologne: Kiepenheuer und Witsch, 1985); Fischer, *Umbau der Industriegesellschaft.*

44. The terms "bioregionalism" and "deep ecology" do not exist in the German language

or within the politics of the German Greens. U.S. advocates and critics often, incorrectly, project their own categories. For example, Barry Commoner characterizes the German "fundamentalists" as those advocating "basic ecological principles," among them "advocacy of a social structure based on 'unity with nature'" and a "spiritual devotion to harmonious relations between people and nations": see "The Environment," in Borrelli, *Crossroads*, 165.

45. See "Social Ecology versus 'Deep' Ecology," *Green Perspectives*, nos. 4–5 (Summer 1987) and "Which Way for the US Greens," *New Politics* 2, no. 2 (Winter 1989). For examples of a continued presence of Malthusian thought in the environmental movement, see Dick Russell, "The Monkeywrenchers," in Borrelli, *Crossroads*, 32, and Peter Borrelli, "the Ecophilosophers," ibid., 81–83.

46. See Murray Bookchin, *The Ecology of Freedom* (Palo Alto: Cheshire, 1982), and *The Rise of Urbanization and the Decline of Citizenship* (San Francisco: Sierra Club, 1987).

47. In the minor journals of the left, little has appeared on the German Greens. *Socialist Review* printed one in-depth article on the West German elections of 1983, but portrayed it mistakenly as an article on the Greens: Andrei Markovits, "West Germany's Political Future: The 1983 Bundestag Elections," *Socialist Review* 13, no. 4 (July–August 1983) 67–98. *Telos* has never printed an article on the Greens, though it continues to print articles on the SPD. *Dissent* printed one article by Jean Cohen and Andrew Arato, "The German Green Party: A Movement Between Fundamentalism and Modernism," vol. 31, no. 3 (Summer 1984) 327–32. Only the small-circulation *New Political Science*, the anarchist *Our Generation*, and the relatively new publications *New Politics* and *Zeta* have discussed the Greens or encouraged debates about their politics.

48. Note the appearance of the journal *democracy* (edited by Sheldon Wolin, one of the premier left-wing advocates of "civic republicanism"), excitement over town meetings in the peace movement, and much talk of the "new populism," all of which accompanied the rise of the new social movements in the 1970s.

49. Harry Boyte, "The Formation of the New Peace Movement," *Social Policy* 13, no. 1 (1982) 4–8.

50. A similar phenomenon was observable in struggles within the Clamshell Alliance, where consensus also strengthened the interests of the more moderate elites by freezing the collective rationality of general assemblies and newer, more radical groups in the organization.

51. Howard Hawkins, "Minority Rule Expels New England Green Alliance from the Interregional Committee [of the COC]," *Green Action*, May 1990.

52. Traditional leftists have reproached the moderate or green-style greens in the United States for being politically undeveloped and incoherent—a reproach the moderates sorely resent: cf. Charlene Spretnak and Danny Moses, "A Consideration of COC History," *Greener Times*, Spring 1989. Their proposals for an economic program do, however, lend themselves to such reproach, as when they attack their own misguided notion of socialism but yet call for the "de-monetization" of "human life": David Haenke, "Bio-Regional Economics," *Green Letter*, Winter 1989, pp. 7–8. "Bioregionalists" like Sale and Haenke argue that we ought to ignore political boundaries and focus on ecological-natural ones, but they also advocate "decentralization of the economy." How these borders are to be conceived in order to decentralize, to "regulate" interregional "commerce," or to control the "multinational" corporations remains in the dark; see Spretnak and Moses, "Consideration"; "Economics," in *Evolving Green COC Program, Green Letter*, Spring 1990, 49–50; and Haenke, "Bio-Regional Economics."

# VI

## Documents

# Chapter 11

ॐ

# Founding Documents

## Program of the Lower Saxony Party of Environmental Protection (1977)

The Lower Saxony Party of Environmental Protection is dedicated to the most important task of the present: protecting life by protecting the environment.

Its sphere of action is presently restricted to Lower Saxony, as decisions concerning environmental protection are mainly taken on a state level and Lower Saxony is designated as a future location for environmentally hazardous industries (nuclear program, industrialization plan for the seaboard).

A large section of the population has become aware of the relationship between the consumption of raw materials and energy and the destruction of the environment. Nevertheless, when goals clash with environmental protection, conflicts are still resolved in favor of the primacy of economic growth.

This situation has to be changed. . . . Natural diversity and the natural wealth of nature and landscape are indispensable conditions of a humane environment that cannot be replaced by any kind of technology.

Citizens alarmed by the increasingly far-reaching destruction of the natural environment have thus joined up to form the Lower Saxony Party of Environmental Protection in order to exert political influence on the state parliament and state bureaucracy and attain the following goals:

1. Proper and extensive enforcement of the existing laws and regulations enacted in the interests of environmental protection.

2. Prohibition of the authorization to erect and run nuclear power plants, uranium and nuclear waste reprocessing plants, and interim or final disposal sites for nuclear waste.

3. Termination of the intolerable pollution of rivers and lakes with hazardous materials. Programs to return rivers and lakes to their natural state and increased funds for the construction of sewage purification plants so that our rivers can again become the life-sustaining veins of the landscape.

4. Special protection for and increased preservation of forests. Maintenance and development of a rich population of free-roaming animals and wild plants. Effective measures against further extinction of individual animal and plant populations.

5. Maintaining livable neighborhoods within cities. Allowing sufficient opportunities for rest and relaxation by providing sports facilities, gardens, green areas, and natural waterways. Protection of historic buildings and historic places. Avoiding urban forms of construction in rural areas.

6. Abandoning the construction of expensive mammoth bureaucracies distant from the people. . . . The reform of local government is to be subjected to an unsparing scrutiny; here, broad changes are to be made possible through public referenda.

## Hesse Green List: Electoral Initiative for Environmental Protection and Democracy (1977)

### 1. ECOLOGY

The Hesse Green List (GLH) advocates a society in which ecological principles are given precedence over so-called "objective economic constraints." Human beings are both a part and a partner of nature and not its master. This precludes any kind of exploitative and destructive economic activity. Environmental questions are questions of life and have precedence over all kinds of economic and profit motives. This means:

—Shutting down all nuclear power plants in West Germany and elsewhere!

—Scrapping all ABC weapons[1] in West Germany and elsewhere!

—Abandoning the West German government's nuclear program, and

—Opposing the destruction of our cities and countryside.

### 2. DEMOCRACY

The GLH considers environmental protection and democracy to be inseparable. We view human rights as being not merely basic rights guaranteed on paper, but rights that have to be fought for daily all over the world. People who support the death penalty do not belong in the GLH. We fight against the dismantling of democratic rights, against every form of political discrimination and oppression: Occupational bans, union decisions about membership irreconcilability, ideological spying, wiretapping, spying by the Office for the Defense of the Constitution and the BGS, spreading self-censorship by the media, discrimination against attorneys, the Law on Banning Contact with Prisoners, police-raid laws, the unified federal police law, repressive police actions, etc.:[2] all these phenomena have supported developments showing strong tendencies toward an authoritarian security state.

We believe that the struggle against these developments must be comprehensive and not selective. This means especially that we are concerned here with the defense of democratic rights and of the right to self-determination of everybody, without discriminating against certain positions, organizations, or groups.

We advocate the freedom and self-realization of all individuals: children and the elderly, gays and lesbians, the handicapped and the sick, foreigners and other minorities!

### 3. WOMEN

A precondition of the contemporary form of domination is the oppression of women by men. Therefore, the GLH supports every initiative seeking the emancipation of women and regards the women's movement's right to autonomy as a necessary condition for this struggle. To counter the particular oppression of women by society, in the family, on the job, and in politics, the GLH demands women's self-determination over their bodies. . . . The women within the GLH are not willing to support an electoral coalition where forces calling for a new housewife ideology have a prominent influence. We call upon the delegates of the GLH to act in accordance with the majority of the electorate by nominating an appropriately large proportion of female candidates.

### 4. SOCIAL SECTOR

The struggle for humane living and working conditions is part of our program. We support the demands voiced on shopfloors and in unions. We also support the social demands voiced by those without work. But we do not support demands directed against our environmental or living conditions, such as, for instance, demands by union functionaries for the construction of nuclear power plants. . . . We advocate the enforcement of the unrestricted right of conscientious objection and demand the abolition of the hearing for establishing the status of conscientious objectors.

### 5. HOW WE SEE OURSELVES AND HOW WE SEE PARLIAMENTARIANISM

The members of the GLH come from different backgrounds: from citizen and grassroots initiatives, especially in the environmental protection and antinuclear areas, but also from different political organizations. We are open to all individuals seeking to contribute to our electoral initiative on the condition that they share the basic principles that we jointly formulated and represent these outside the organization. The GLH has not taken any decisions on irreconcilability of membership. It is open to all, regardless of *Weltanschauung* or political organization, as long as people are actively engaged in environmental protection and democracy. We reject any kind of cooperation with fascists. We do not have any illusions regarding the role of parliamentary elections. Effective representation of our interests and goals on the parliamentary level will be possible only in a rudimentary way, if at all. According to our concept of politics, our political activity will emphasize central and decentralized grassroots and extra-parliamentary efforts.

We will use "electoral campaigns" as an instrument for:

—Revealing the extent of environmental destruction and destruction of life as well as the dismantling of democratic rights,

—Sharpening the awareness of such politics, and

—Extending both the base and the margin of action of the protest movement.

We will use parliament as a public platform. We will not participate in any kind of coalition.

GLH meetings, especially meetings of the delegates, committee meetings, and negotiations on all levels, especially on the parliamentary level, are—without exception—always open to the public. GLH state parliamentarians are required to surrender most of their emoluments, the exact sum to be determined collectively, together with the parliamentarian, on the basis of individual need (family, etc.). The process of nomination of GLH candidates requires nominees to be working in some kind of a grassroots initiative and to continue to do so after the election. We do not tolerate free riders or careerists. Potential state parliamentarians have to account for their parliamentary work to this initiative and are bound by the decisions of the grassroots.

A central tenet of our understanding of democracy is the autonomy of groups and regions. . . . However, the principles contained in this document are the binding basis for the GLH's activities.

### Green Basic Program: Draft by the Action Third Way/Free International University (1980)

( . . . )

## I. PRINCIPLES OF AN ALTERNATIVE ECONOMIC POLICY: SOLIDARITY VERSUS COMPETITION —PROTECTION OF LIFE VERSUS DESTRUCTION OF LIFE

What is the task of economic life once conditions have been set right? Only the satisfaction of everyone's needs for a humane existence. Is this still utopian? No, because we have long been able to attain this for all peoples of the world. The unavoidable prerequisite is, however, that we terminate the gigantic waste inherent in the western and eastern mode of production. Today, political realism can only mean that the capitalist and state-communist economic modes must be replaced by a reasonable alternative based on frugal and equitable exchange with the materials and forces of nature, a resolute eradication of social privileges, and the realization of a technology on a humane scale.

Because the world's raw materials are unevenly distributed and the technical means of production are unevenly developed, the realization of a worldwide economic order based on solidarity is the only way to prevent barbaric distribution wars. Armed confrontations that involve the danger of annihilating humanity—and especially the nuclear devastation of Central Europe—are increasingly likely if we do not get rid of what is blocking a healthy development today: private ownership in the area of production and economic activity directed to profit maximization act to prevent this solidarity-based alternative as much as state-bureaucratic planning does.

The draft bills of a Green economic policy will therefore be directed toward freeing the sphere of production from these constraints, which are also responsible for unfettered and disproportionate growth, in order to enable production to be directed toward consumer needs and ecological necessities. Everything else is a senseless waste of skills, raw materials, and energies. . . .

Within the framework of a self-administrative order encompassing the whole economy we need:

—Organs for joint consultations among colleagues, in which all aspects required for the fulfillment of tasks in the respective area of work are discussed freely (i.e., independent of profit constraints and bureaucratic regulations);

—Organs for democratic negotiations in which, using knowledge gained in the consultative organs, those affected by a problem decide upon legal regulations. Those affected can then act freely on the basis of these regulations. Examples of such organs could include meetings of a work department or all the employees of a company, a citizens' meeting, plebiscite, or parliament. This lays the basis for

—Organs of solidarity-based action—that is, for associations of those working in a specific area of production to fulfill their tasks according to consumer needs.

These three functional systems of consultation, decision making, and execution constitute the new basic structure of the sphere of societal work. Not only the production and service sectors will be designed in accordance with these systems, but also the political and cultural spheres of the social organism. . . .

The self-administration alternative the Greens propose does not subject economic activity to any constraint. Rather, it creates conditions allowing for the development (from decentralized decision-making processes) of whatever people regard as healthy and in accordance with their needs. . . .

Economic enterprises—freed from the pressures of profit interests and plan-fulfillment—can then engage in an unconstrained free competition of ideas and performance directed by those goals which derive from the ecological turn and from the transition to consumption-oriented economic activity. This enhances, for example,

—The utilization of recyclable natural products,

—The recycling of raw materials from old products,

—The tendency to abandon materials and processes that negatively affect the ecological balance and endanger human life and health,

—The trend toward the protection of nature and the landscape,

—The production of consumer goods that are durable and easy to repair,

—Research into and development of alternative techniques of energy production that enable us to completely dispense with life-destructive technologies such as nuclear energy, and

—The trend toward the decentralization of production, which also includes savings in energy and transportation.

If we design our economic and working world in this direction in the future, this will be to the benefit of humanity as well as all other forms of life. It serves the earth and all we have the duty to protect. . . .


II. *Principles of an Alternative Financial and Tax Policy:*
Democratization versus Monopolization of Financial Assets

Of central importance for the wrong path the industrial nations have taken is the power connected to financial transactions under capitalist conditions. Democracy is undermined by financial interests and is farcical as long as we hold on to the present financial regime. This regime not only allows but furthers the conditions of domination and exploitation under which humanity and the kingdoms of nature have to suffer.

The financial regime is integrated into the structures of the capitalist

"Sie verschandelt unsere politische Landschaft." ("It is ruining our political landscape.") This poster plays on the alternative Green political style and the "ruin" caused by unchecked industrial expansion. This poster and the two that follow (all from the 1983 election campaign) illustrate both the sense of irony and the seriousness prevalent in the early election campaign.

"Demokratie braucht Luft zum Atmen." ("Democracy needs air in order to breathe.") This poster depicts an elderly woman surrounded by policemen in riot gear—a common scene at demonstrations against nuclear power stations.

"Übel. Auch wenn Sie das kleinere Übel wählen—Sie wählen den Weg in den Atomstaat." ("Even if you vote for the lesser evil—you're voting your way into the nuclear state.")

"Ein bewaffneter Friede ist die Ruhe vor dem Sturm. Entrüstet Euch." ("An armed peace is the quiet before the storm. Disarm yourself.") This poster was used at the high point of the peace movement in 1983–84. "Entrüstet Euch," a slogan of the peace movement, actually has two meanings: "Disarm yourself" and "Get out-

"Viele sind arbeitslos. Andere müssen zuviel arbeiten. Es gibt sinnvolle Arbeit für alle." ("Many are unemployed. Others must work too much. There is meaningful work for all.") Campaign poster for the June 1984 European Parliament elections.

"CDU. Legal. Illegal. Scheißegal. Mittlerweile auf alles gefaßt. Die Grünen." This 1987 federal elections poster is directed against the ruling Christian Democratic Union. It roughly translates as: "CDU. Legal. Illegal. Who gives a shit. Meanwhile this applies to everything. The Greens." The word play is based on the meaning of *egal*—"all the same."

"Grüne Regie rungsverantwortung." ("The Greens direct responsible government.") Alfred Hitchock holds up an announcement for a campaign event in this poster from the Hesse elections, where the Greens were part of a red-green coalition government. The Frankfurt Greens were publicizing a panel discussion held in January 1987. Fischer was minister for the environment; Haibach was secretary for women's affairs in the coalition government.

Poster advertising the fictitious film "River of No Return." This poster appeared after a 1988 fire at the Basel chemical firm Sandoz, which dumped immense amounts of chemicals into the Rhine. The chemical firms Ciba-Geigy, BASF, and Hoechst AG used the occasion to cover the dumping of their own chemicals. The banner at the bottom reads: "The Greens are canceling this film."

economy in a way that precludes democratic control. This means that decisions about the what, how, and where of production(-work) are presently made exclusively by those in whose hands financial assets are concentrated. But it is clearly an absurdity that the direction of societal development should be determined by financial power and not by people's insights into what is required on the basis of humanity's and nature's living conditions. This means that production occurs only when assets are available. And for what purpose? For the increase of financial assets, of influence, and of power, which is again tied to the disposition of money. And, as a universal mechanism of exchange, money entitles its owners to indiscriminately appropriate human labor, nature, production sites, and consumer values.

The indiscriminate character of the present function of money is an anachronism that leads to the increasing destruction of all other orders. . . .

It is completely unreasonable to let money in its exchange function gain influence in the sphere of work. This must lead to functional disruptions in the whole social organism, as, in the area of production, the exchange function of money involves domination, degradation of human beings, and abuse of nature. Instead of social justice, the principle of interest and of profit always entails the power of ownership and the competition of capital. Instead of a solidarity-based cooperation for meaningful human goals, we get alienated work and the wage relationship, which turns work into a commodity. . . .

The Green alternative starts out from the insight that financial processes have, within production, an exclusively nonprofit, public function. This would mean that

—Human labor is no longer purchased; what is bought is the realization of the human right to a humane income based on principles of social justice, and this amounts to a victory over the inhumane wage relationship.

—Real estate and the means of production can no longer be purchased; the services that businesses produce for one another are financed by the prices of consumer goods without thereby legitimating a right to ownership. The sites of production exist for the consumers, and are managed on a trust basis by the workers. This amounts to a victory over the power of ownership.

—There is no longer any reason to neglect the laws of natural life, since benefits no longer arise when the income resulting from production no longer invests businesses with private rights. . . . This amounts to a victory over the profit principle.

How can we make the financial system function healthily without suffering from cyclical disturbances (as in state-communist systems) or from unfettered cancerous growth (as in capitalism)? . . .

The Green alternative leads to this important social goal by the simple measure of obliging economic enterprises to repay the loans provided to them for production. As this affects all business enterprises, it necessitates the forwarding of surpluses built into prices to agencies that undertake tasks such as teaching, environmental protection, etc.—that is, that provide public services for free on the basis of democratic agreements. This prevents imbalances between the development of consumption and production. Only when this state of affairs has been attained can we speak of a dynamic "balanced economy" whose currency is stable. Under such conditions of financial policy, inflationary tendencies (price increases) can arise only in relation to supranational markets ("imported inflation"). . . .

### III. *Principles of an Alternative Social Policy:* Security of Existence versus Handouts and Charity

The redesign of economic, financial, and tax policies allows for a new regulation of basic rights regarding income and work and is the basis of the Greens' social policy.

Income must be viewed as an elementary human right that is a precondition for everything else. Our production possibilities are sufficiently advanced today to allow this basic right to be fulfilled. This is all the more true since only about a third of our total present level of production is required to fulfill our needs. Two-thirds of all expended services, raw materials, and energy are unnecessary—advertising, waste, planned attrition, and financial burdens in the form of interest and compound interest. And if we take into account the fact that already today every person in the Federal Republic of Germany receives at least a minimum income (e.g., welfare benefits, unemployment benefits, motherhood pay, children's benefits, social security etc.) independent of his or her work performance, then it is not utopian to demand, as a guiding principle for legal improvements, a guaranteed basic income for all people in all life phases, independent of work performance, to provide sufficient food, clothing, housing, training, and care for old age and sickness.

A basic income is a precondition for the realization of a second fundamental right: the right to a self-determined contribution to the economic life of the overall economic organism. This puts an end to the degrading state of affairs where people have to sell themselves for wages without being able to address the purpose of their lives. . . .

### IV. *Principles of an Alternative Cultural Policy:* Freedom versus Determination by Others

Of importance with regard to all cultural activities—education, school, science, art, religion, occupational training, and the whole information sector—is the unrestricted development of all impulses emanating from the intellectual and spiritual perspectives of human beings.

This becomes possible when we consider that financial institutions of course have the obligation to provide producers of cultural services (such as schools) with the income and investment funds necessary to fulfill their requirements, without, however, thereby exerting an influence on those institutions, as is the case today because of the state's tax policy. In this way, cultural institutions can avail themselves of the right to develop such self-management structures as befit their individual tasks. . . .

### V. *Principles of an Alternative Policy of the State:* Shrinking the State versus Statification of Society

Because the fundamental transformations described above will remove the causes of nearly all existing ecological, economic, cultural, and social damage, state activity will be reduced to upholding public order, managing public matters, executing democratic laws, and securing compliance with those laws. In general, the state will have to be dismantled as much as possible in favor of the self-determined activities of economic and cultural initiatives. Two basic measures can serve to move developments in the right direction:

—Extension of basic human rights with regard to the existing economic, social, cultural, and ecological state of affairs

—Reduction of state competence and clear definition of the limits of the state: that is, less instead of more state activity

Both measures are inherently connected to one another. Whoever speaks only of destatification without simultaneously demanding extensive democratic rights in the economic and cultural realms reveals that he [*sic:*] is only interested in surrendering people fully to the economic forces. The Greens do not want that.

### VI. *Principles of a Parliamentary Alternative:* Grassroots Democracy versus Formal Democracy

It is necessary now to strengthen the Greens so that the consequences of this new political direction—a third way transcending capitalism and "real existing socialism"—can be discussed and then realized in detail within parliaments, from the Bundestag and the state parliaments to city councils and municipalities. This debate will inject new intellectual and spiritual life into parliaments. But this is not enough. Because crucial questions concerning the shaping of our future lives, perhaps the only chance of survival, are at stake, as many citizens as possible should take part actively and intensely in this debate. . . .

NOTES

1. "ABC" stands for "atomic, biological, and chemical."—Eds.

2. The *Berufsverbot,* a law passed at the end of the 1960s, excluded members of the German Communist Party from the civil service, which in the Federal Republic includes teachers in the public schools and the police. Nor could union members belong to any Communist organization. *Bundesgrenzschutz* (BGS) refers to the Federal Border Police.—Eds.

## Chapter 12

# Position Papers of the Main Factions within the Green Party

### Eco-Socialists: "Ecological Crisis and Social Transformation—12 Theses"

1. Humanity is presently destroying the natural foundations for its life.

2. This destruction obviously has to do with the laws inherent in capitalism (the need for growth, accumulation, scrupulous attention to profit, competition). This (capitalism) has to be overcome.

3. Real existing socialism proves that one way of overcoming capitalism, the abandonment of private ownership of the means of production, does not solve the crisis of external nature.

4. The necessary preservation of the conditions of human life in nature requires drastic changes in production and in the consumption habits of a majority of people in the industrial metropoles.

5. The emancipation of Third World peoples—its specific form must be chosen by them, and their provision with food, clothing, housing, and a humane life must be secured— also does not merely touch upon international capital but requires a different model of consumption in the industrial metropoles, at least at present.

6. The destruction of nature and the situation in the Third World require future societies to develop practices of conscious renunciation and departure from cherished habits in order to permit humane life elsewhere, dispose of accrued damage (garbage dumps), and prevent potentially and incalculably destructive emanations from the production process.

7. This renunciation is not a general one. An egalitarian society that equitably redistributes the wealth held by a minority, that reduces or abandons the production of useless goods (armaments) as well as the "services" (insurance industry) and repressive functions (state apparatus) inherent in this system, and that does not dispense with the production of goods and services just because the rate of profit is not right, that does not destroy use values because they cannot be marketed profitably, could more than offset whatever the capitalist system produces in terms of poverty, social dislocation, and overtaxing of human labor.

223

8. A relationship with nature and with one's own body and psyche that is considerate and anticipates the future can develop only if the threat of complete material impoverishment does not overpower everything else.

9. However, it is important to realize that today's wants and needs belong to today's societal system (and its precursor). They can be criticized and changed. Radical needs that are something other than a copy of the ruling class's conditions of life and consumption and that, among other things, aim at human creativity, community, enjoyment of nature, etc., are already important motives for rebellion against this system.

10. The system of needs is strongly (but not exclusively) shaped by the position of individuals in the production process. Only if the destruction of human health and creativity here can be stopped, if creative work can be reinstated as much as possible, will a gradual reappropriation of truly human needs become possible. This is the only path enabling a society to appropriate "ecological reason" without despotic and dictatorial state measures against the people.

11. Following from this perspective is the rejection of "productivity" as the ultimate purpose of societal production. Where people stand in the production process (and the effects upon external nature) is of crucial importance. This rejection is more possible today than ever because humanity's ability to reproduce its basis of life in a productive relationship with nature has increased immensely. This has also led to an increase in the objective freedom to revise the relationship between work and life without merely distributing scarcity.

12. The concept of "free time"—the shortened working day— is as ill-suited as the present concept of productivity to be the sole or determining measure of societal wealth.

### Radical Ecologists: "Radical and Full of Fantasy"

Jutta Ditfurth and Manfred Zieran from Frankfurt were the two best-known figures of the small but influential (at least until 1988) "radical ecologist" tendency (other early fundamentalists, like Rudolf Bahro, quit or became professional Green MPs, like Petra Kelly). Since the radical ecologists have played a major role in the party but have neither written "manifestos" nor developed theoretical positions addressing the nation's course, it is no coincidence that Ditfurth's sketch focuses largely on the local or civic realm as the place where Green politics is possible,

"Radical and Full of Fantasy" is from Jutta Ditfurth, ed., *Radikalökologische Politik* (Frankfurt: Karo-Druck, 1984).

criticizing political engagement in larger arenas. Zieran was involved in the Hessian Greens' first statements (see Chapter 11). He and Ditfurth made names for themselves as members of the Frankfurt city council.[1]

When it comes to the relationship to parliamentarianism and representative democracy, the Greens are divided into two fundamentally different and exclusive camps.

Those seeking to undertake a so-called *Realpolitik*, believe it is time for the Greens to come to terms with the fact that they are a totally normal party. The Greens should develop into a "proper parliamentary party." . . . All those who can imagine a path between reformism and armed militancy, as we radical ecologists do, and who follow such a path (for instance, in the Frankfurt city council), are vigorously attacked.

The classic reformist path involves giving up on any kind of fundamental change in the ecological and social system that would oppose the logic of capital. It is nothing less than the abandonment of the concrete utopia of a humane life free of exploitation and misery and based on a respectful partnership with the natural environment. . . .

The situation in Hesse in the winter and spring of 1983/84 shows how the reformist path exhausts itself and ultimately becomes ineffective. Even the possibility of short-term electoral gain by affirming the quotidian consciousness of existing voters should not obscure the bleak prospects for such a politics in the long term . . . We wield a lever of social counterforce when we help to organize social pressure in the direction of utopia, even in small steps of real reform. The reformists voluntarily give up this lever.

The reformists do not question the state's monopoly of force but aspire to redistribute it. But since when is force better if exerted by the Greens? Instead of four monopolists of force, we will have five.

The logical result of this kind of politics is the need to pacify social movements, as we can already see with regard to the movement against the extension of the Frankfurt airport and the blockades of the Pershing II missile site in Frankfurt-Hausen. The "new doers" perceive the pressure from the street not as an invigorating dynamic strengthening the Greens' negotiating position, but as a practical obstacle to their reformist strategies.

. . . A necessary precondition of Green reformism is an image of the Greens as stable and predictable coalition partners. Predictability takes the place of the Greens' strength of unpredictability, the principle of surprise in politics. Once taken, this path becomes narrower and narrower with respect to forms of action and political efficacy. The engagement with the undemocratic mechanisms of representative democracy and the present form of parliamentarianism leads to the abandonment of all possibilities of changing this system for the better.

One of the most central barriers to fundamental change is the principle of the party-state in representative democracy. A feature of this system is the principle of representation, the practical *and* conscious delegation of one's own interests to representatives in party apparatuses. The filters built into party hierarchies usually lead to a complete deformation of the delegated interests, which are nevertheless still considered to be represented.

. . . In parliament, delegates must commit themselves to the general good and to a balance between opposing interests. Although balancing the interests of capital and labor is not possible, this mediatory mechanism is employed to bring into "harmony" the interests of different social groups. Legitimate (ecological or social) interests are thereby watered down. In a capitalist system this mediation of interests, which is the ideological basis of the *Volksparteien* (people's parties), always works to the detriment of socially weak groups and the environment. . . .

It is characteristic of this party-state that the large *Volksparteien*, the Social Democratic Party (SPD) and the Christian Democratic Union (CDV), have developed a shared concept for insulating themselves against oppositional movements and groups critical of the system. On the basis of a largely comparable ideology, they settle differences in a manner supportive of the state and are no longer in a position to react to challenges from the extra-parliamentary opposition with anything but repression. Social Democracy's outstanding feature has always been a habit of breaking the back of strong social movements in a regular historical rhythm. Harsh repression of social groups in opposition to the SPD's power interests is followed—if the movement remains strong—by a phase in which movement people and ideas capable of being integrated are absorbed while the others are socially marginalized. In the end the battleship has been carefully overhauled, but, despite the Green reformists' hopes—there is no real transformation of the party; rather, the renovation guarantees its continued existence on the same basis as before. The fact that parts of the movements and of the Greens believe (again and again) in such a substantial transformation *is* what makes the Social Democratic absorption principle so unbelievably effective. Two contemporary cases in point are the lesser-evil ideology and the orientation of Green reformists and left-wing Social Democrats toward coalitions between the Greens and the SPD. Such coalitions, without quality and substance, merely oppose the "turnaround" in Bonn.[2]

The extensive similarity of the characters of the two big parties . . . has given us a kind of modern oligarchy in West Germany. In elections, what happens is that interchangeable groups within one ruling block merely swap places. Historical experience (see the instructive example of Social Democracy) shows that striving to participate in government has always led to the abandonment of the social interests of the party rank and file as well as the party's social base such as the labor movement. . . .

Bourgeoisification, centralization, and a concentration of authority and power characterize the SPD and increasingly also the reformist wing of the Greens, as evidenced, for instance, in internal debates on rotation, connection to the grassroots, and professionalization. An adaptation in parliaments is the goal, and then the adaptation of executive committees and other Green organs to the parliamentarians' working structures. Instead of entering the institutions in order to transform them, the motto now is: enter the Greens and transform them in accordance with the institutions to which we have adapted ourselves.

When Joschka Fischer claims that the radical ecologists in Hesse persistently filled important positions with mediocre individuals in order to maintain their influence, this seems ridiculous at first glance. But such statements are important. This one not only reveals a lot about Fischer's projections of power and about his relationship to other people; even more importantly, it shows that one element of Green culture is totally alien to him and the other reformists: that we have to consciously seek to qualify as many people as possible outside and inside the Greens through learning processes, instead of allowing those who are already qualified to accrue more and more power. . . .

A positive political perspective must take a path that is delimited on two sides. On the one side we have the delimitation of the extraparliamentary forms of action: the illusion that society can be transformed by using force against people. On the other side, there is the intraparliamentary delimitation of taking part in and adapting to the system of representative parliamentarianism and its executive. . . . We have to make transparent the decision-making structures and mode of functioning within parliaments and between parliaments, the administration, and industry. Raising people's consciousness about the contradiction between the SPDCDUFDP's (programmatic) appearance and their concrete parliamentary practice is also helpful in organizing societal pressure from outside, which itself may lead to progressive reforms in parliaments. . . . Every reform measure and every agreement with parliamentary groups must fulfill one basic condition: it must not stand in the way of the concrete utopia, it should neither ideologically nor materially obstruct Green paths. And this is precisely where the negotiations in Hesse have failed.

In terms of practical parliamentary work, this demands that we avail ourselves of any opportunity to shift decision-making competence down from the centralist level to the level of those concerned: from the federal to the state level, from state to municipal, within cities to neighborhoods and blocks and in rural areas into villages. Elements of direct democracy such as plebiscites, citizen initiatives, etc., must be furthered; bureaucracy—and not the social net—must be dismantled.

Internal Green structures must reflect these goals. We need to remain open to experiments and, despite continual blows by the bourgeois media, attempt to anchor grassroots democratic structures within a party and counteract the development of aloof functionary cliques by integrating many people.

## Realos: "Green Rational"

Helmut Wiesenthal was teaching at the University of Bielefeld when this essay was written. He is one of the few social scientists directly involved in the Green Party. Part of a group of intellectual "realists" from the University of Bielefeld including Claus Offe, Norbert Kostede, and Johannes Berger, Wiesenthal has emerged as a key party strategist, especially regarding social policy, despite less than spectacular success at achieving national prominence as a politician.

This essay, "Green Rational," published originally in *Kommune* (no. 4, 1984), republished elsewhere, and widely distributed, produced an important critique of the "Fundis'" reliance on social movements for their conception of politics, and served perhaps more than any other contribution to define and argue for a realist perspective. Though that perspective emerged simultaneously with fundamentalist positions, it is presented after them in this volume. The critical survey of those positions offered in this essay is in some sense an indicator of the manner in which *Realpolitik* in the Greens emerged not programmatically but rather from the fluid interaction between the programmatic left of the Greens and the existing constraints of the political system. Recognition of those constraints is required, in the realists' view, for any effective implementation of Green political demands.[3]

The essay is here rendered in an extremely abridged version. For a full-length representation of Wiesenthal's position, the English-speaking reader may consult his *Realism in Green Politics* (Manchester: Manchester University Press, 1993).

## I. WHAT IS THE DEBATE ON STRATEGY ALL ABOUT?

. . . The strategy debate in the Greens is dominated by several undoubtedly important topics triggered by circumstances: conditions for tolerating a minority government, the state's monopoly of force, programmatic radicalism, the ability to form coalitions, governmental participation, and other issues. But the surprisingly high level of conflict can only be explained by the fundamental nature of the questions that are simultaneously addressed. How do we get closer to a fundamental transformation of society? Or, in more concrete terms, what activities of the Greens (or the social movements) are correct, wrong, or ineffective as they move toward an ecological, demilitarized society with a low level of domination? For another: what is the institutional character of a "better" society? How are we to conceive of this society: as a council-democratic socialism, as a vast patchwork of small towns, as a market economy constrained by eco-socialism, or as a continuation of the existing state of affairs with more perfect technological means?

Although these fundamental questions are, of course, related to one another, they do not all have the same significance. The question of the "how" of political practice inevitably occupies everyone who has to make a decision (e.g., toleration at what cost?). The question of "where to," however, becomes relevant only when political engagement is underpinned by a *Weltanschauung* (because one then, of course, "knows" that no brand of socialism or only socialism will solve our problems). It is not hard to grasp why the "big" issues of "how" and "where to" cannot simply be discussed, resolved, decided upon, and put aside.

There is probably another reason the "how" question is so hotly disputed. Whoever believes he or she has a "right" answer has to feel doubly uncertain. For one thing each line of reasoning holds great uncertainties that can be used to justify an opposite position by others. For another, historical experience holds lots of disappointments but hardly any valid rules for practitioners of radical transformation strategies. Even if the Greens outwardly are still holding on to the clearly inadequate strategic model of "dismay"—information—discernment—political activity—societal transformation," it is not easy to escape self-doubt. This is one of the reasons why people tend to dogmatize strategic questions and answers.

The following thoughts should be seen as a contribution to the debate and should not be construed as a proposal for new dogmas. Their point of departure is doubts about the still-widespread idea that the desired transformations can be attained through the path of gradually "gaining the majority," and only through this path (II). Instead, I will propose an "alternative" framework for strategic analysis that seems to correspond better with social conditions and conflicts than the "gaining the majority" model or the recourse to Leninist party concepts (III). On the basis of the conceptual model of a multiple conflict structure, I will formulate several consequences for the Greens' political strategy.

## II. Radical Change by Gaining the Majority?

On one point all of the tendencies within the Greens are in agreement: the most important goal is not the improvement of the existing state of affairs but a "fundamental transformation in this society" (Trampert), either in the form of a "certain degree of dismantling of the industrial system" (Kretschmann), or along the lines of a "social turnaround moving away from the industrial system" (Bahro).[4] At any rate, it is a question of "a new model of societal development not only transcending capitalism but transcending industrialism itself, whose basic tenets, however, are as yet largely unclear."[5]

But we are dealing with a mobilization dilemma: We are winning either weakly motivated support "in relatively large numbers" or a largely utopian, emotional potential that is small in number. "Active majorities" are very difficult to achieve. This means that we have to analyze the inner logic of the presently dominant "radicalization strategies."

### Radicalism as a Program?

What are the success criteria of fundamental opposition? Not an increasing proportion of the vote! That would force the fundamentalists into a situation where they either participate in a toleration or coalition setting or get held responsible for a Big Coalition government of the great evil. So, although it contradicts the goal of gaining political influence, Petra Kelly is completely consistent in terms of a radical self-conception when she declares: "Yes, I am sometimes scared that the Greens will suddenly get 13 percent and become a power-seeking party. We should rather stay at 6 or 7 and remain uncompromising in our basic demands."[6]

A fundamental parliamentary opposition can thus consider only its failures to be a success, because these at least pay off ideologically:[7] The "impermeability of the system" confirms its danger and corroborates the necessity for fundamental changes.

### Radicalism through Failures?

Because electoral gains are not a criterion for success, the fundamentalist opposition banks on a kind of "learning by disappointment." When the voters recognize that the radical opposition can not realize its goals in parliament—this being the thesis of the Hamburg Green Alternative List (GAL) politicians—they will themselves become politically active as a social movement outside parliament.

Parliamentary participation is here understood as an amplifier for the mobilization of real extraparliamentary forces. For this to succeed, however, at least three preconditions would have to be fulfilled: first, the voters (as rationally calculating protorevolutionaries) must be convinced that not even a growing proportion of the vote (and not even the majority of parliamentary seats) would bring a real increase of power. Second, they must actually strive for the same political goals as the political organization pursuing this strategy. These two conditions have not existed at any time in the history of the workers' movement (and never occurred simultaneously at all), and it is highly unlikely that ecological conflict contains enough dynamite to mobilize and unify people. Third, at least the active base of the organization has to have a split consciousness: it has to decide upon programs, undertake election campaigns, and persuade all potential voters to give their vote—so that it can afterward confirm its belief that efforts of this type are useless. This perspective of "self-frustration" is not a strategy but a "recipe for failure," as is well-known from the workers' movement; its only "sure" effect is to turn party functionaires into asocial cynics.

### Radicalism through Change of Identity?

Rudolf Bahro's strategy is also characterized by a desire to radicalize both analysis and program, but more in a cultural than in a political sense. The clearly defined goal of establishing autonomous and self-supporting communities as a definite advantage over all other goals circulating in the green-alternative spectrum. It is already elaborated with sufficient precision to allow everyone to assess the personal costs that a radical break with the evils of industrial society will require.

Success is measured in terms of an ongoing cultural and value change, in the course of which at least the subjective barrier to "exiting" becomes easier to overcome.

The strategy of focusing on the self-transformation of individuals implies a heavy sacrifice of internal democracy and openness of organization. Why? People who seriously decide to become" someone else" will—in their own interest—seek to protect themselves from changes endangering that very decision; in other words, they will reach for mechanisms of self-bondage to prevent changes of preference. The obvious mechanism (and the one commonly adopted by sectlike groups to prevent "relapses") is one of prophylactic self-incapacitation, which works like this: of his or her own free will, the individual agrees not to be taken seriously if he/she should one day suddenly again advocate *A* instead of *B*. . . .

All the dilemmas sketched here can be summarized in a theory of the impossibility of radical majorities. It assumes that the desire for comprehensive institutional change must include the willingness of those who seek the change to transform themselves so that they "fit" the changed social institutions. This double willingness for change does not emerge simply in response to the persuasive power of rational arguments. Rather, it presupposes certain world-views and orientations. These would have to be (*a*) collectively shared from the outset, *(b)* removed from (dissociating) daily conflicts, and *(c)* more or less free from verifiable claims of fact. However, social reality contradicts these premises, since it produces orientations that (*a*) are predominantly differentiated on a subjective basis, (*b*) are related to daily problems, and (*c*) can be revised on the basis of experience. Unfortunately, the majority of radical convictions tend to seal themselves off from one another (instead of fusing and expanding). Even if the role of radical consciousness within phases of historical restructuring cannot be easily ascertained, the contemporary obstacles standing in the way of radicalism are—in the face of irreversible social differentiation—evident.

### III. Politics within a New Conflictual Logic

The new social movements and the Greens who, as a party, are based on the movements, are confronted with a different type of conflict than earlier movements and party organizations experienced. Since the mid-1970s, a second conflictual axis has developed that does not overlap with the traditional left–right axis but cuts across it.[8] The whole green-alternative movement is confronted with two lines of conflict at the same time: the left–right conflict over the distribution of material life conditions and political power; and all those left-wingers and right-wingers who seek to address distributional questions as formal and quantitative rather than material and qualitative.

### Second Strategy Dilemma

Because of the high degree of complexity of the "system of industrial society" (whose fracture points are not determined by "simple" causal relationships), intentional social change has to struggle with enormous and largely unknown problems with respect to the relationship between goals and means. The challenging movement receives systematically distorted, often definitively wrong, "learning incentives." There is no certain and known relationship between the suitability and efficacy of political actions on the one hand and the intensity of the opponent's defense or repression "responses" on the other. Therefore, even a slight tendency toward wishful thinking or dogmatism is enough to cause the movement to strike at the hardest parts of the system with the best of intentions, where it will certainly fail because of the system's complexity or because of the unmatchable superiority of state power.

*Multiple Conflicts: Multiplicity, Uncertainty, "Part"-incipators*

It seems to be true that capitalist industrial society, despite its enormous conflict potential, has become too complex to produce a real breakdown (as was anticipated for simpler societal systems of the nineteenth century), and we can instead observe "the permanence of a whole array of sectoral crises and societal disintegration processes" (Hirsch).[9] The problem therefore poses itself in an especially crass way: how can a dynamic of societal change emerge from the heterogeneity, complexity, and unevenness of the "new" conflicts?

The answer to this question will come to light only when we discard some plausible but nevertheless no longer valid background assumptions and accept the complexity of present conditions. We have to abandon the concept of cumulative learning, because it is not the case that individuals become more "conscious" with each action (or, in simpler terms, with each Bundestag election) until they finally realize that "the system itself," the "conditions of ownership," or a different root cause of all "evil" has to be addressed.

Contrary to this idea of a cumulatively growing radical consciousness, it appears to be urgently necessary to think through the new conflictual logic with respect to the status or the role of the social actors. The new and necessary perspective would have to start from the assessment based on experience and theory that both the multiplicity and the case-by-case particularity of conflicts do not produce actors who are identical and "unified" with regard to all conflicts and all conflictual themes. Instead (this is the central thesis of this section) we have a situation in which there is a very widespread willingness to act, but the actions are focused on very small parts of the whole transformation process.

In more concrete terms, the heterogeneity of living situations (that includes the varying social and cognitive "proximity" to conflict themes) and the diversity of social ties, constraints, and value orientations, have certain effects. For example: many participants in the peace movement do not (yet?) engage themselves in the ecology movement; many participants in the ecology movement do not (and will not?) support feminist demands; the desire to stop further construction of nuclear plants or of automobile infrastructure does not coincide with "radical" goals such as exclusive use of solar energy or the abandonment of all forms of individual motor vehicles; a 70-year-old, after years of hesitancy, participates "only" in an initiative for the census boycott while continuing to adhere to the opinion that schoolchildren need to be taught better manners; and, finally, individual political activity is, for many reasons, subject to strong fluctuations in the life cycle instead of (as the cumulative thesis assumes) increasing steadily in concurrence with the pressure exerted by objective problems or with requirements for political action. All of these deviations from the ideal type of political action, however, are not exceptions. Rather, they are examplary for normal participation in social conflicts.

### Complex Transformations

From the activists' vantage point, social change that is effected by multiple conflicts is unsteady and merely particular. From case to case, different individuals act out the conflicts. What secures unity and continuity in the sense of "development" are, for one thing, the few general principles and value orientations that everyone shares and, for another, the institutional changes that are brought about—that is, the results of, rather than the preconditions for, successful individual conflicts.

Simplified, one could imagine a gradual process in which certain preferences transform the circumstances in which those preferences originated and upon which they are based. Within the new circumstances, new preferences develop, which may lead to transforming those circumstances (e.g., in other areas of action), once they are successfully processed politically.

If we accord to particularist conflicts the same status as motors of social change that revolutionary organizational efforts once demanded, then we can circumvent the dangerous trap of incredibility mentioned above. It simply does not make sense when people warn of imminent catastrophes but reject interventions into their development process with the argument that this would not alter "anything" and would "only" gain time.

### Securing Existence and Autonomy of Action

While enhancing options in general can probably be seen as the most important success criterion of many and various conflicts, it is nearly impossible to identify the substantive fracture points of future conflicts in advance. At best, we can make a few preliminary assumptions about the present situation. One topic seems to be gaining importance: the issue of income distribution or access to income. This theme is of great relevance because the central distributive mechanism—the "labor market"—leaves a large and increasing number of people unaccounted for, and fails to meet their claims for autonomous opportunities.

Every chance at securing an "alternative" existence outside the conditions of bribery that the labor market offers us, favoring the economically and politically powerful, is important. I do not have the space here to weigh the concrete alternatives against one another (transfer incomes, drastic redistribution of work, self-help initiatives and neighborhood projects, production cooperatives, etc.), but even a cursory glance at potential criteria for their usefulness reveals what the decisive measures could be. Instead of a vision of a complete "exit" (which is only understood within the alternative culture anyway), we need options for "normalos": opportunities to "survive" materially in communication with others and without losing self-respect, if the plant shuts down, if the job gets to be too much, or if they want to swap the breadwinning role with their partner. Generally: we need such options if and when the possibilities for collective opposition have been exhausted without success or have not even taken hold, but individual retreat would remain politically without consequences.

The multifaceted "second net" does not have to be so large as to carry "everyone" simultaneously. The desired effect is to be able to announce opposition in the system more effectively because one is either less dependent on the system's services or has the option to choose between alternative modes of existence, and this effect requires much less than that. (This "much less," however, would amount to a social revolution compared with the present situation.)

### Beyond Economism: A Second Value Dimension

The conflict on the level of values and the importance of new, unconventional (or, from a conservative perspective, ambitious) orientations must not be underestimated. The new orientations as well as new "material" options have a strategic significance: in specific conflicts, they allow individuals to evaluate the disadvantages and costs resulting from participation, not merely in economic terms, but as an investment in the fulfillment of "qualitative needs"; furthermore, they allow people to choose "indirect strategies" in accordance with their goals. The idea is quite simple: losses of a material-economic nature (e.g., the time and money costs of political activities) have to show up on a second "scale" as gains if one does not want to bank exclusively on irrational behavior.

For a better understanding of this idea, it helps to remember the strategic deficiency of a purely materialist doctrine, which considers reference to subjective values as an "idealist" deviation from the goal of resource gains. But seen exclusively from a perspective of economic rationality, the material costs of collective action must of necessity appear as a "step backward." Thus, in the face of the usual uncertainty of success, they often prove to be too high.[10] In this sense, ecological-emancipative values and qualitative claims to an autonomous way of life are perhaps the most valuable capital the new social movements have. It would be unwise to waste this capital, for instance, in opportunistic attempts at widening support by subordinating such claims to the undoubtedly legitimate desires for economic improvements. Even the unions are now becoming increasingly dependent on motives of this kind in order to secure a minimum of influence upon working conditions. The fact that the demand to "work differently" has kept and even increased its attractiveness despite unemployment and a shrinking security of existence makes the further development of conflict along the value dimension appear quite hopeful.

## IV. THE ROLE OF THE PARTY IN ANONYMOUS SOCIAL CHANGE

Seeing social change as a series of particular and uneven conflicts with changing, nonradical actors is rather different from the prevailing ways of conceiving the relationship between movements and party. Nevertheless, it is clear that social conflicts are not organized administratively; rather, seen in retrospect, they appear to "happen." Aside from giving organizational support during the initial phases and "ratifying" positive results in parliament, a party like the Greens will above all need to relate in a productive way to conflicts as they occur, in order to encourage extraparliamentary movements and speed up the dynamic of social change.

At the same time, the suggested projection of multiple single-issue conflicts into one main project—attaining a realm of action for the realization of ecological-emancipative values—has many preconditions. Achieving continuity, accumulating and securing experiences, and defending the social claims voiced in the conflicts against attempts to distort them undoubtedly require a political organization that is active beside and between the conflicts. Only under an oversimplified formula such as "the citizen initiatives are parliamentarizing themselves" was it possible to see the Greens as an appendix, an organizational branch of the initiatives' politics. Meanwhile, the differences between the movement form and party form are much clearer, and it has become apparent that the party encounters problems of a particular kind as it competes for member loyalties and votes.

### Principles

A productive relationship with autonomous conflicts means strengthening those aspects that further the envisaged transformation and criticizing those which threaten to stop or to deflect it.

The core of Green political goals, the unrenounceable substance of all "new" demands in terms of political forms and contents, can be reduced to two postulates: preservation and emancipation.

The *preservation postulate*[11] is common to all demands that are labeled "ecological", but it refers to quite different "objects," In the (one) extreme case of threats that are experienced in an ethical-aesthetic manner, it refers to the threat to all nature from industrialization and civilization. In the other extreme case the issue is the stability of industrial society and of civilization (i.e., finite resources in their role as raw materials). There are two paradoxical aspects to this dimension of preservation. One lies in the peculiar reversal of the problem perspective at the two extremes: at one pole, society appears as the cause of threats; at the other, society itself is threatened. The second paradox is that apparently, rational political goals can only be formulated in the center field but not at the extremes.

The *emancipatory postulate* does not refer to general social categories or even "class," but seems to refer to margins of action claimed by individuals. Both normative and structural constraints on autonomy of action are at issue, and this is why "one-dimensional" problem-solving options (making structural improvements without changing discriminatory norms or changing the norms without eliminating structural discrimination) are regularly criticized as inadequate and tend to be "underestimated" (as prerequisites for further progress). The movement for women's emancipation so far seems to have been the most important agent of a rigorous emancipatory postulate.

To identify preservation and emancipation as the "highest" principles implies acknowledging the different character of the other principles that guide alternative-political business, a character that is more instrumental than goal-related. This is surely the case for the principle of "grassroots democracy" as well as the Greens' socialist heritage. Both grassroots democratic procedures and the vision of socialist institutions originate from a (historical) ideological context that has little to do with the claims emerging in today's conflicts. This is why difficulties repeatedly emerge when someone appeals to "tradition," with respect to ecological and emancipatory priorities. Such difficulties cannot easily be resolved by subsuming the new goal-oriented values under old and merely instrumental principles.

It is also difficult but important to avoid the trap of an unreflective "leftist" self-conception. Aside from the programmatically diffuse eco-libertarians, the Greens are leftist both in their self-conception and in their position in social conflicts as long as they invariably evaluate political alternatives according to two genuinely "left" issues: domination and distribution. Curbing or controlling domination and equalizing distribution (favoring disadvantaged social groups) are seen as unrenounceable (secondary) goals.

In fact, however, what "left" is supposed to mean in terms of the preservation and emancipation postulates is rather underdetermined. Not infrequently, the industrial mode of production is identified as that which is to be preserved. Sometimes the preservation postulate is subordinated to certain principles of social order, such as elimination of all markets or nationalization as a precondition of ecological production.

The underdetermination of a more "left" position shows us how necessary a precise positioning of the Greens in the "new" and "old" conflicts has become. To create continuity between particular conflicts, to highlight the goal common to *all* the movements, and to establish a basis for attacking the old ties of loyalty, the Greens need a new and clear principle of progress—one that cannot be misunderstood or mistaken for the socialist tradition.

### Adversaries

In conflicts with more powerful adversaries, direct attacks promise nothing but defeats. Only if industrial society is viewed not as a mere structure for distributing power but as a precarious balance of several conditions of existence that cannot easily be fulfilled but are "problematic" and "contradictory" in themselves, only on the basis of this second perspective, can "weak" parts of the system be identified as suitable targets for intervention.

The deficiencies (the "ungovernabilities") of the established institutions have to be used politically: their surplus of internal problems (including contradictory goals, a low level of integration, and social conflicts of interest), and their relative inability to shape or control social conditions according to their "needs." To cleverly take advantage of such potential options implies that the direction of the adaptive reactions that will become necessary will have to be "co-determined." The movements can refer bureaucracies, party apparatuses, and other organizations to the "escape routes" that are intentionally or unintentionally being offered to them by the incalculable "turbulences" around them: boycott actions, the delegitimization of "normal" political practice, blockage of specific functions. This will make it possible to get closer to goals that are unattainable through direct attacks: the broadening of individual and collective possibilities for action.

Furthermore, we should not overlook the fact that despite the enormous resource and power discrepancies in highly differentiated societies, there are fewer adversaries than people usually assume. There is a high threshold of defense against change, and there are plenty of repressive and ideological mechanisms to marginalize "people seeking to change the system," but the participants in particular conflicts of the new social movements are not confronting a state that is integrated and acting intentionally and without contradictions, nor is "capital" a protagonist with uniform plans and united action. Diverging interests, uneven perception of problems, a personal association with a conflict in one case, a spatial association in another—all these features of real or virtual disintegration suggest that we should discard the notion of real homogenization of societal conditions that is so widespread in the Marxist tradition."[12]

Thus, it is nonsensical to urge individuals to ignore their far-reaching dependence on state-organized income maintenance with mobilization goals such as an unspecified "opposition to the state." Instead, it would seem more appropriate to help the social movements to a more differentiated picture of the conflict field and to combine a tactic of dividing and isolating the other side with an ability to form flexible coalitions with forces outside one's own camp.

Anyone looking for a social location that might serve as a "fracture point of the system" cannot look past the potential dynamite of unsatisfied social needs in "structurally problematic" areas of society. Even if people's existing preferences do not "fit" the overall program of societal transformation, only here will we find the "material" for structural changes upon which new and perhaps more far-reaching preferences can develop.

## V. FINAL COMMENTS

The perspective suggested here and the strategy following from it contradict several conventional strategies of reform and revolution. And many political activists cling to the idea of an impending (because necessary) revolution as passionately as to the goal of an ecological and emancipated society. But how important are realistic and nonutopian strategies? Is it not conceivable that a little self-deception about what is feasible and an extravagant radicalism are—true—irrational, but perhaps also necessary for success?

Counterarguments do exist. One is that the theory whose political-practical realization required such immunizing claims has meanwhile revealed some structural defects (not only a lack of adaptation to reality but also a lack of internal consistency). I would also like to stress another counter argument: We cannot find just the right degree of falsehood of orientations to guide intentional and determined action. But if there is no "expedient" falsehood of thinking; all we can do is search for logical consistency and the closest possible proximity to reality, and attempt to avoid the trap of (self-) deception.

How high is the risk of orienting ourselves with a strategy that may be false? Will we miss opportunities that will never again arise if we focus on the multiple and complex conflicts with changing and nonradical participants, instead of attempting to convince people of the necessity of "the" revolution? The answer is not difficult: the approaches suggested here do not destroy options, even that of revolution, if it exists. Rather, they aim at the optimal "use" of really existing possibilities. If these possibilities include developing a revolution (however this is defined), then this will come to the force precisely through this strategy. It is especially in this regard that a politics of broadening opportunities for action and orientation seems to be superior to a radicalization campaign even if it is carried out in a rhetorically clever way.

Are we really restricted to thinking what is politically feasible? Or will that unnecessarily keep us within the limits of the system? All of the observations made above answer these very questions. There are no paths toward changing this society except the ones found within this society. What is politically feasible is not something definitive, fixed for all time; the scope of possibilities expands or shrinks with and through political action. But the reverse is also true: there are political impossibilities, logically impossible things that one can think and talk about but not have or do. Not to be realized in this sense is the desire for a quick and radical transformation (revolution), because the prerequisites for a hoped-for social change (and thus also for the revolution) are lacking. Here, we are dealing with the recurring confusion of two meanings of "necessity": is change necessary (in the sense of inevitable) because its preconditions are present, because they are already "inherent in the system"? Or is something declared a necessity precisely because this is not the case, because the desire has no basis in reality? The second variant is closely connected with the mythical hope of revolution.

The futile effort to discover the preconditions of political action in its potential results is called "attentism"; it is nothing but the hope for something unknown that would relieve us of the annoying task of "doing politics" with real people, with actual dreams and (partly contradictory) demands. However difficult that may be (and how to deal with these difficulties has not been the topic here), it is the only way of taking one's own goals seriously.

The more pressing radical social change may seem, the less we can ignore its preconditions. This essay is basically arguing that we should respect the real starting points of the path leading to a different logic of societal development: multiple, particular conflicts; changing, never "holistically radical" actors; and, especially, a normative level of politics in which new and goal-related values are embedded. With that grounding we can avoid the trap of economism and take the step from subjective will to collective action with greater ease. All this is not the "nonessential" that distracts from the goal of a "basic transformation." Rather, it is the starting point and the first section of the path. We will have to walk this path in order to find out how far it leads.

## Eco-Libertarians: Founding Statement—"Unity, Green, Liberty"

The "eco-libertarians" formed as a political current in the Greens in February 1984. The original endorsers of the position included Winfried Kretschmann, Gisela Erler, Ernst Hoplitschek, and Thomas Schmid. Though they have never formed a significant voting bloc in the party, their influence has been remarkable, particularly via the media. For example, this statement was printed in *Kommune*, the *Frankfurter Rundschau*, and *die tageszeitung*.

The position paper here presented in an abridged form is interesting from a North American perspective. The critique of socialism, the demand for decentralization, the "civic-republican" language of individualism, self-sufficiency, and antistatism, as well as a social sense of ecology embedded in a conception of natural matrix, reminds Americans of ecologists such as Lewis Mumford, Murray Bookchin, Harry Boyte, and Karl Hess.[13] Yet the claim of an opening to conservative political interests in West Germany such as those represented by the Christian and Free Democrats (and their market economies) implies a weak or nonexistent understanding of the way in which the logic of capital itself corrodes the very kinds of decentralized, democratic communities that they advocate. In this sense, while their language is that of "civic republicanism" and radical ecology, their ultimate politics are those of "libertarians" in the North American, not European, sense of this word—support for free markets and opposition to state interference—except that their acceptance of parliamentary democracy as democracy makes them more "liberal" then "libertarian." Ironically, this is in sharp contrast to those Americans mentioned above, whose critique of capitalism makes them much more "libertarian" in the European sense of the term (i.e., democratic communalism), a relatively rare position in North American discourse.

The title of this essay in German ("Einigkeit und Grün und Freiheit") echoes the national anthem's "Einigkeit und Recht und Freiheit."

## 1.

What is meant by ecological politics? Since all the traditional parties are busy integrating the ecological impulse and since ecology is in danger of becoming just one topic among many within the Green Party, some clarification is necessary.

Political ecology is not merely an addition to traditional politics; it does not merely add a new element. Rather, it is based on a radical critique of unfettered industrialism and its history. Unlike the socialists, we do not believe that a better society can be a beneficiary and heir of industrial history, and that all that is required is the transformation of industrial society's political constitution. We completely reject the idea that the forces of production need only to be freed from the constraints of the relations of production for a better society to fall into humanity's lap. We consider private control over the means of production to be a secondary problem. Socialist doctrine has contributed partial insights, but today it no longer contributes to solutions—on the contrary, it has become part of the problem.

The ecological project, however, is historically new and unique. For the first time, a politics is advocated that departs from the self-confidence of the "doers." It was natural in the past 500 years to "do" everything that could possibly be "done"—every invented tool has been utilized, every technical innovation has been mass-produced, and every weapon has been wielded. Ecological politics wants to break with this: it refuses to add another instrument to the arsenal of the "doable." Less feasibility, less state, less promises, less utilization of the technically possible, etc.: all this has never happened, and this idea requires a completely new politics. It has to acknowledge the rights of animate as well as inanimate nature; it seeks a relationship between humans and animals that is based on respect.

We are not, however, advocating the kind of radical survival strategy that transfers findings of a natural science–type ecology to human society. It is impossible to describe human societies in terms of biological cycles, and it would be nonsensical to view the mechanisms of evolution and selection as regulators for human societies. Human society is irrevocably characterized by the fact that it has left the continuum of natural evolution. Human society is not nature but always culture. The industrialist destruction and degeneration of the world was a cultural achievement (though a negative one); and turning away from it will be a cultural feat too.

Ecological politics does not call for moralizing punitive expeditions, but is concerned with diversity and a society in which the happiness of self-confident and responsible individuals has a place. In no way does it fundamentally object to technology, especially as some of the newest technologies offer themselves to decentralized applications; an alternative economy might be able to use them to jump out of the societal niches it currently resides in.

Ecological politics aims at diversity and wealth, but it departs from the dependency mentality evinced by the social movements of the last 100 years. Industrial society, welfare state, and expansion are not compatible with ecology. The large and perpetually available basket of commodities is tied to exploitation; ecological politics would throw out a lot of those commodities, assuming that human needs can be criticized and changed. In social politics it does not advocate a welfare philosophy. Although the social problem is a very real one, it must be regarded as a consequence of industrialism and thus a secondary problem. Industrialism has destroyed old ties and securities without creating new ones; it has robbed individuals of their abilities and skills; it has centralized and created dependencies; it has narrowed activities into wage labor; etc.

Traditional social policy seeks to compensate for this industrial damage using means provided by this growth society. Instead, we need to reverse the statification of the social. Ecological politics attacks the state's (and thus also the social worker's) monopoly on welfare and social security. It wants to return a maximum of competence to the people themselves. As people again rely upon themselves, help one another, and take their affairs into their own hands, the need for the state will shrink. The number of social workers, welfare laws, and welfare institutions is more of a negative than a positive indicator of true welfare. Ecological politics advocates further personal responsibility.

We clearly see that this goal is also propagated by the political right and those organizations to which it has close contacts. But they mean something completely different; they mean the brutal right of the strongest; they want a society in which unfortunate individuals are ignored. Ecological politics has nothing to do with such a Manchester philosophy: rather, it takes as self-evident the right of individuals to have their basic needs met and to be able to develop according to their potential. Of course, society has the obligation to prevent want and destitution. Ecological politics does this by strengthening those forces that support self-help.

In seeking to redesign the welfare state ecologically, we cannot proceed from the Social Democratic fetish of social security, because we would then never escape the expansive logic of a welfare state that tends to undermine self-reliance. We have to set the priorities differently: self-help should be placed in the foreground, and the remaining cases of hardship are the responsibility of the community. Ecological politics aims at forms of social security other than those of the welfare state.

## 2.

An ecological politics is possible only as a libertarian politics. This sounds self-evident, but it is not.

We think it is totally wrong for those who want to carry out ecological politics to think of themselves as standing outside the destructive context. Every single person carries responsibility for society *as it is*—not only governments, corporations, and those groups of people whom we don't like. Therefore, a politics seeking to change the present bad situation has to be based on dialogue. The socialists are convinced that power has to be taken before anything can really change. However, all historical experience has shown that this path is not a libertarian one but is characterized by centralism and a fixation on the state.

The decision to participate in parliamentarianism makes sense only if one thereby tries to reform existing conditions. For us, this decision is also based on the insight that the other paths that have been taken—revolution, civil war, avant-garde coup d'état—are undemocratic and lead to authoritarian or even terrorist conditions that, once established, are not easily changed. For us, the decision for parliamentarianism also entails the rejection of an avant-garde politics supposedly legitimated by some kind of objective class interest or the interest of the masses. With the decision for parliamentarianism, we have also decided to take the democratic path (with all of its consequences); that this society is only formally democratic is another issue.

No other party seriously advocates decentralization, destatification, self-help, and a break with industrialism. Our strength lies in the fact that an increasingly large number of people actually support these ideas. With this pledge in our pocket, we can confidently and without fear enter into negotiations (and not only with the Social Democrats: in our view, such a junior role with regard to the SPD as a matter of principle is wrong). There is a reason for the Greens' fear of Social Democracy's deadly embrace, because if you enter into negotiations equipped with a basic socialist agenda, it could quickly become unclear what distinguishes you from the Social Democrats.

We do not believe that *Realpolitik* has to betray the big goal. Without a long-term perspective it has no chance, but neither can it attain the goal on the first attempt. But this is not desirable anyway. A democratic transformation of society is possible only by way of compromise. We are afraid that some of the opponents of *Realpolitik* have not yet grasped this. The point is to stop the "big machine"; but we have to give ourselves the time necessary for the slow path of democratic change. Thank God no messiah can force the break with industrialism.

## Grüner Aufbruch '88/Green Awakening '88: "A Manifesto"

*Aufbruch*, a word with a long tradition in German social movements and politics, has many meanings: "breakup," "departure," "revolution," and "awakening" (to political consciousness). It is the name chosen by a group of Greens who formed in 1987–1988 to overcome the split between fundamentalists and realists who had calcified into two entrenched wings. The Aufbruch movement was a direct, aggressive political intervention in the party, complete with its own manifesto. We publish here an abridged version of the text, which was written in 1988 by Antje Vollmer, Marieluise Beck-Oberdorf, Lukas Beckmann, Ralf Fücks, Christa Nickels, Thea Bock, and others.

## I. Crisis—A Future without a Lobby

The Greens are in a crisis. This crisis is not like the others. The first attraction between society and the Greens is over. Surprisingly splendid electoral success, dramatic environmental catastrophes, or a short term moratorium in the struggle between the different currents will not "save" us this time.

This crisis confronts us with a choice:

—The Greens can abandon an essential part of their goals and ideals and thereby transform the inevitable disappointment into cynicism and resignation. They would thereby adapt to the mainstream of existing parties and uncouple themselves from the fundamental problems in this society. They can then devote their remaining energy to the continued existence of the party system and securing their own power.

—Or, the Greens and their friends can recognize the crisis as an opportunity for a new awakening on the basis of reality, a new awakening into society. The Greens' present difficulties are *not* the result of the necessary or healthy disillusionment of a young party after its phase of confrontation with social praxis; rather, they result from a dangerous withdrawal from social problems and from a destruction of hopes for the future. These hopes pertain to the core of the founding consensus and the whole Green project.

In the face of a possible failure of the Green project, one "way out of the crisis" is pointed out to us with particular emphasis: the *Realpolitik* path of *normalization*. This path expresses more than the traditional substance of pragmatic *Realpolitik*. It reduces the Green project to a traditional parliamentary "ecological reform politics" that is understood primarily in terms of future governmental participation. The Greens are to become the kind of party that the label of a "green FDP" (Fischer) fits pretty well. This would entail the abandonment of the original Green project to become a "party of a new kind."

We do not want to call this "Green normalization" a betrayal. But it is a fact that much of what was special about Green politics in the last several yeas has proved to be weak in practice and susceptible to the old left-radical ideas. It is also a fact that those Greens who work in a pragmatic-political way consider this way out a pragmatic consequence that should finally be drawn from the party's experiences.

Nevertheless, the path of "Green normalization" fatally misses the potential historical significance of the party. A Green politics without symbolic and utopian moments would be impoverished. It could never ward off the Social Democratic embrace.

II. A Balance Sheet on Green Interventions into Social
Processes: Looking Back without Anger

The Greens have fulfilled a part of their task over the last nine years. Our main task in this period has been to get the right present-day questions onto the political agenda: the question of peace, the apocalyptic environmental situation, the crisis of patriarchy, the emancipation of society from state bureaucrats, the critique of the traditional parties, the question of democracy, the rights of minorities, the critique of industrialism, the problem of technical progress, the redistribution of labor, nature's inherent right to exist, decentralism and cultural autonomy, and new forms of work and of life.

We have successfully intervened in the political and cultural processes of this country in many ways:

1. As a messenger bringing word of dangers: our analyses have been accepted, and our predictions have often come true in a terrible way. We have thus contributed to a widespread new sensitivity in society and in politics, but this sensitivity is not sufficient and is rarely translated into a different practice.

2. As a breaker of taboos on heretofore concealed or marginalized issues (violence against women, the Nazi past, the ungovernability of industrial production, discrimination against minorities). But at some point all taboos have been broken, and the breaking of taboos becomes rather dull.

3. As a "laboratory for new ideas," as impulse-giver for alternative developments (women's parity, all female executives (*Feminat*), a grassroots-democratic challenge to parliaments, ecologically responsible agriculture, the Gray Panthers). This phase is over, in part because many experiments have failed.

4. As advocates of a holistic approach in our critique of the political parties. The formulation of the four pillars of the Greens (ecological—grassroots democratic—social—nonviolent) defined the demands exacted by the activities of individual social movements in accordance with the interests of the other pillars: ecological interests had to reflect social and grassroots-democratic demands, etc.

III. Reasons for a New Awakening: Recognizing a Limit Means
Overcoming It

Every beginning must come to an end. Nine years of party experience is a time span that requires us to take stock of past developments.

*The Conditions—They Are Not Like That (Brecht)*[14]

With regard to the Greens' future-oriented program, social conditions in the Federal Republic have proved to be more tenuous and simultaneously more flexible than we had thought.[15] Thus, the Greens' power and powerlessness to transform social practice are—among other things—also an expression of society's readiness for change, which is not as big as we would like.

### The Other Parties—Some Progress Might Be a Crawling Backward (Wolf Biermann)

The other parties have proven more eager to learn and more flexible in taking up our analyses, positions, and forms of politics than we initially assumed. They added just enough practical substance to their discursive takeover of Green issues to allow a minimum of actual change, and create a maximum effect in publicity.

### Parliamentarianism—Powerlessness on the Rhine[16]

In contrast to our largely successful function as a leader in public opinion, parliamentarianism showed us the limits of our actual power and our concrete practical failure on a daily basis. Especially in the parliaments, the practical routine of the other parties and power-administering apparatuses commanded our respect. After green, rainbow, and alternative lists entered parliaments, the next limit we faced was that of a pure politics of opposition. So we started tolerating and cooperating, which then turned out to be limiting our power in new ways. The step into governing coalitions and into a ministry was to lead us closer to the center of power. But we soon were to learn that government, too, has powerless zones, especially on the state level. The logical next step is taking really important ministries on the federal level. But we predict renewed disappointment. The search for an Archimedean point of power is in vain. The base of the power networks, of which parliament and government are but a part, lies in society—and in the executive offices of the big corporations.

### The State—or Trying to Ride the Tiger

Even if it sounds banal, viewing the state as a contradictory form of domination is the starting point for any meaningful debate on the state. This contradictory form has also been mirrored in the Greens' factional debate over the state. On the one hand, the state was conceived as a hostile "system" of which we should have no part. This view was nurtured mainly by the trauma of Fascism.

As a critical counterreaction to this view, we can observe a tendency to view the state and its agencies merely as a neutral instrument for the enforcement of political interests, as a service and a "welfare state" for all, in which only the quality of its "servants" (i.e., the ministers) determines the direction this organizational instrument of the polity takes.

Neither conception of the state is consistent with our practical experiences. We cannot expect more from intervening in state politics than such a path can offer. Where this makes sense, Green politics has to seek state influence, but mostly it should direct itself to the transformation of people's consciousness—that is, emancipating people from being administered by the state.

## IV. THE CRUX OF ALL QUESTIONS: WHERE IS SOCIETAL REALITY MOVING?

### Democracy Dies Unobtrusively

The present political situation is characterized by an objective tendency toward de-democratization in all classical fields of politics. This de-democratization does not mean that traditional democratic civil rights are being dismantled. We can observe no tendencies toward the abandonment of parliamentary or representative democracy. By de-democratization we mean the tendency to produce an objective development of reality that can no longer be changed by the subjective factor—namely, people and their political intervention. A politics that produces situations that can be redressed neither now nor in the future is fundamentally undemocratic even if it does not dismantle the formal criteria of democracy (e.g., the division of power, parliamentarianism, the representation of interests, freedom of organization, etc.).

### Democratic Awakenings

In the GDR [East Germany], in Hungary, and in Czechoslovakia, civil rights movements are demanding greater democratic freedoms. Even in the Soviet Union, within the context of the reforms Gorbachev has initiated, people are demanding a fundamental democratization of the state and the party and are thereby setting free an exciting process of societal debate.

We are convinced that the Greens have a historic task to fulfill here. By renewing the Green Party in a radical-democratic way, we could provide a model for the further democratization of West German society. While the other parties are still smothering any opposition to authoritarian leadership styles, we can express people's growing criticism of the party system, a system that views the state as its "private property."

### Economics and Ecology

Intervention in the labor process is the crucial issue in any kind of ecological and democratic politics. An ecologically conscious economic mode requires confronting sectoral economic decisions on the "what" and the "how" with their consequences for nature and society. Private ownership must be subjected to shop-floor and societal controls; business activity must be guided by ecological and social criteria.

Given this dimension of necessary changes, the recently fashionable talk of "ecological capitalism" as a guiding principle for Green economic policy is more than annoying, since it blurs the fundamental difference between ecological politics and the prevailing mode of production.

## V. Awakening—Where To?

### Opposition: Powerlessness Until the End of the Century?

A politics that defines itself primarily by its desire to maneuver the Green Party into a position where it can participate in a governing coalition, or one that defines itself by the opposite desire, is passé—it is sterile and boring.

Our task consists in redesigning the new awakening of the Greens *into society* on the basis of the difficulties inherent in the oppositional role.

The old and beloved political models of waiting for better times by viewing ourselves as a government standing in the wings (Realos) or as a revolution in retirement (eco-socialists) will hardly suffice to bring about the urgently needed Green social offensive.

### The Art of Turning a Popular Majority into a Political Majority

There are majorities other than those in the Bonn parliament—for instance, people who want to abandon nuclear energy. But so far, this has led to a departure of those opposing nuclear energy from politics, rather than a departure from nuclear politics. The opposition does not seem to be able to implement majoritarian demands.

In other areas, majorities could be produced in the foreseeable future—whenever the state's continual incompetence destroys its legitimacy, such as with respect to agriculture, women's issues, and unemployment.

It is important to differentiate between situations in which majorities can already be attained, situations in which they still have to be created, and situations in which the hidden must be brought to light. The instruments for getting together possible majorities on the basis of our oppositional role will be especially decisive for the further success of the Green Party.

## VI. Demands and Perspectives: Awakening in Concrete Terms

### Party Reform

In the Green Party, the time has come for a change of attitude rather than a change of statutes. Nevertheless, we definitely believe that it is time for a thorough reform of the Green Party. We are especially concerned with an open debate about the tendencies toward bureaucratization in the Greens and the loss of internal democracy. We seek a fundamental improvement of the rights to participation and decision making of the grassroots:

—The practical application of the *Urabstimmung* (partywide ballot)[17] provided for in the statute on important questions affecting the Green Party. This will extend grassroots democracy and counteract the tendency to have mere representation.

—The introduction of a right to take political initiatives. With this right a minority of *Kreisverbände* (county party organizations) or members can bring ideas and motions to the attention of executive committees or parliamentary groups. These grassroots initiatives can force executive committees and parliamentary groups to provide, by a certain deadline, a statement on issues that the rank and file deem especially important. At present, we have a growing gap between the federal organs of the party, with their direct access to the media, and the groups working locally, whose members can only sit and take note of what the Federal Executive Committee and the Bundestag group serve up;

—Extension of the rank and file's right to ask questions and to gain access to information, as well as the introduction of a right to inspect records and files for country party organizations. This would be analogous to the Greens' Bundestag draft bill.

—A sober debate about the positive and negative aspects of the principle of half-term parliamentary rotation.

—Bringing to light the problems caused by "transverse rotation" (*Querrotation*)—rotation from executive committees into parliaments, to staff positions and back again. It supports the emergence of an (elitist) party oligarchy and the tendency toward professionalization among Green politicians.

—Not abandoning the principle of separation of office and mandate. Those seeking to remove the last formal barrier against the growing oligopolization of the top tier of the party will meet our determined opposition. A democratization of the party through plebiscites, a resuscitation of intraparty life, and an end to the blockage effected by the factional dispute are hardly possible—and our attempts in this direction are hardly credible—if the accumulation of power in the party's upper echelons goes further.

### Conservatism: Productive Discourse Instead of Ignoring It

We support an assertive debate with conservative positions. This includes both the "value-conservative" variant that prevails more in traditional environmental protection organizations or in rural areas than in the CDU/Christian Social Union, and its modernist variant as represented by CDU strategists like Manfred Späth or Kurt Biedenkopf.

We should not repeat the classic mistake of the left and disregard the emancipatory force of people with conservative values who are critical of "progress." Such a force inheres, for example, in skepticism about the blessings of consumer society, in having roots in independent and regional cultures, in the rejection of state centralism, and in religiously motivated rejection of technical manipulation of life.

### Plebiscites: Changing Majorities in Parliament

As an opposition party seeking to swim against the main current (which continues to be necessary, also in the interest of minorities), we must stay within the main current of societal discourse and argument with real-existing people. The elite consciousness of both the classical left and the SPD usually contradicts this position. We advocate all instruments of grassroots—democratic intervention in political decisions: plebiscites and referenda, a right to inspect records, a right by organizations to initiate joint legal proceedings (*Verbandsklage*) against all public authorities and decisions, the democratization of the state bureaucracy, etc.

### Nonviolence Does Not Mean Submission to the State

The Greens support a politics of civil disobedience and nonviolent opposition and oppose a politics of militarizing social conflicts. The confusion of political radicalism and violent militancy is a double trap: it furthers tendencies toward a "strong state," and employing these inhuman measures will reflect on the goals and character of the political movement itself.

For us, nonviolence is a concept of civil struggle and social change and should not be misunderstood as a way of submitting to the state or shunning conflict. Strikes, blockades, and sit-ins are a legitimate repertoire from the tradition of nonviolent opposition.

### An International Union of Ecology and Human Rights

The Green movement is, by definition, international: the ecological effects of human interference with the natural balance transcend national borders. The Chernobyl catastrophe and the loss of the North Sea's ecological balance have again demonstrated the ecological unity of the world. One of the Greens' main tasks is therefore to make people aware of global environmental relationships and to push for the transformation of production and consumption locally: "Think globally—act locally." Reference to these international relationships should not become an excuse for doing nothing, but it obliges us to act in solidarity.

NOTES

1. For a record of this experience, see Die Grünen im Römer, *Was machen die Grünen im Parlament: Haushaltsdokumentation 1983 der Grünen im Römer* (Frankfurt am Main: Karo-Druck, 1983).—Eds.

2. That is, the conservative turnaround.—Eds.

3. For a representative Realo position paper from an earlier date, see Joschka Fischer, "Für einen grünen Radikalreformismus," in Wolfgang Kraushaar, ed., *Was sollen die Grünen im Parlament?* (Frankfurt am Main: Verlag Neue Kritik, 1983) 35–46.

4. Rainer Trampert, speech during the Greens' Sixth Federal Congress on November 18–20, 1983, *grüner basis-dienst,* no. 112 (1983) 11; Winfried Kretschmann, interview with *Moderne Zeiten (MOZ),* no. 11 (1983): 26; Rudolf Bahro, according to the protocol of "Grüne Perspektiven," a forum of debate organized by the political magazines *Kommune, links,* and *Moderne Zeiten* on October 15, 1983, p. 6.

5. Achim Bergmann, Gisela Erler, Wolf-Dieter Hasenclever, Ulrich Hausmann, Ernst Hoplitschek, Gerald Hübner, Hajo von Kracht, Winfried Kretschmann, Rudolf Leineweber, Boje Maaßen, Dieter Marcello, Thomas Schmid, and Josef Schwab, "Wider die Lust am Untergang," *Frankfurter Rundschau,* no. 268, November 18, 1983, p. 11.

6. Petra Kelly, interview with *Der Spiegel,* June 14, 1982, p. 53.

7. Norbert Seitz, "Historische Anmerkungen zum Sinn einer parlamentarisch repräsentierten Fundamentalopposition," in Kraushaar, *Was sollen Die Grünen?* 113–19. On the self-conception of the SPD before World War I as a "fundamental opposition" and representative of the "socialist question," see Cora Stephan, "'Grundsätzlich fundamental dagegen': Basis oder Demokratie?" in Matthias Horx, Albert Sellner, and Cora Stephan, eds., *Infrarot: Wider die Utopie des totalen Lebens* (Berlin: Rotbuch, 1983) 35–58.

8. Cf. Ronald Inglehart, *The Silent Revolution* (Princeton: Princeton University Press, 1977); Kai Hildebrandt and Russell Dalton, "Die neue Politik," *Politische Vierteljahresschrift,* no. 18 (1977) 230–56.

9. Joachim Hirsch, "Alternativbewegung—eine politische Alternative?" in Roland Roth ed., *Parlamentarisches Ritual und politische Alternativen* (Frankfurt am Main and New York: Campus 1980) 137.

10. Cf. Adam Przeworski, "Material Interests, Class Compromise, and the Transition to Socialism," *Politics and Society,* no. 2 (1980) 125–53.

11. See in detail Claus Offe, "Griff nach der Notbremse", in Kraushaar, *Was sollen die Grünen?*

12. Cf. Claus Offe, "Konkurrenzpartei und kollektive politische Identität," in Roth, *Parlamentarisches Ritual,* 37, 85–92.

13. See, e.g., Lewis Mumford, *The City in History* (New York: Harcourt Brace, 1964); Murray Bookchin, *The Ecology of Freedom* (Palo Alto: Cheshire, 1982) and *Urbanization and the Decline of Citizenship* (San Francisco: Sierra Club Books, 1987); Harry Boyte, *The Backyard Revolution* (Philadelphia: Temple University Press, 1980); Karl Hess, *Community Technology (New York: Harper and Row, 1979).*

14. This is a quotation from Brecht's *Threepenny Opera.*—Eds.

15. The introduction to this section draws its language directly from Ernst Bloch's philosophy of process and openness, "venturing beyond."—Eds.

16. "On the Rhine"—that is, in Bonn.—Eds.

17. *Urabstimmung,* "plebiscite," refers to the demand that key decisions for the Greens (and, above all, a definition of its general political program and strategy) ought to be decided by the entire membership of the party in a general plebiscite. The Aufbruch group meant to use it as a means to overcome the divisive Realo-Fundi conflict.—Eds.

## Chapter 13

# New Themes in Old Parliaments
## Parliamentary Speeches and Party Statements

**Waltraud Schoppe: "Women, Abortion, and Marital Rape"**

Waltraud Schoppe in the debate in the German Bundestag on the Revision of the Abortion Law (Paragraph 218), Fifth sitting, May 5, 1983.

President Dr. Barzel: Ms. Schoppe, you may take the floor.

Frau Schoppe (Greens): Ladies and gentlemen, dear friends, I would like to make a brief statement about what happened yesterday evening. Yesterday evening, certain members of parliament displayed a very unqualified coarseness. You will have to work on yourselves, gentlemen, so that the dignity of this High House is not completely ruined.

*(Applause from the Greens, laughter and shouts from the Christian Democratic Union/Christian Social Union [CDU/CSU])*

The debate on Paragraph 218 has again come to the fore. This paragraph, which allows women to terminate a pregnancy under certain conditions, has not been able to reduce the suffering incurred by such an abortion. This paragraph has humiliated women who are in distress and exposed them to the caprice of male experts. Women with low economic status, women who, for example, already have three children but not enough money and are thus not in a position to support a fourth child, . . . at least had the possibility of having an abortion under the cost-reimbursement scheme. . . .

If, as is being envisioned, the cost of abortions undertaken for social reasons is no longer to be carried by the health insurance system, this will make Paragraph 218 much worse and will cement social inequalities.

*(Applause from the Greens and the Social Democratic Party [SPD])*

. . . An abortion puts women into a very difficult position and is not a kind of contraceptive measure.

*(Applause from the Greens. Dr. Herta Däubler-Gmelin, SPD: Very true!)*

Still, there are situations in which women see an abortion as the only way out. The current dismantling of the welfare state will lead to an increase of such predicaments. It doesn't do any good to propagate a pretentious program for the protection of unborn life if a large part of those already alive today are not adequately supported.

The best way to protect the unborn is by defending the living.

*(Applause from the Greens and from some SPD members)*

We live in a society where conditions of life are standardized—standardized fashions, standardized housing, standardized opinions, and even standardized ethics. This has led to a situation where people lie down at night and, before falling asleep, undertake a standardized exercise in which the man usually performs a reckless penetration,

*(Shout from the CDU/CSU: What is that?)*

reckless, because most men do not take contraceptive measures.

*(Shout from the CDU/CSU: How do you know about that?)*

Men participate equally in bringing about a pregnancy. But they dodge their responsibility. In the case of an abortion, only women are penalized by the law. Only later do men again enter into the picture as moral guardians by passing penal laws, by condemning abortion from the pulpit, or, as doctors, by either helping or humiliating women, depending on their moral and political convictions.

*(Applause from the Greens and from some SPD members)*

Pregnancy ends with birth. And here is where the responsibility of caring for a person begins that will last for 18 or 20 years.

*(Shout from the CDU/CSU: That means living and growing!)*

Nowadays, the probability of divorce is between 25 and 30 percent. In the aftermath of a separation, the children usually remain with the mother. But even if the marriage stays intact, child care is provided by women because of the gendered division of labor. This entails sacrificing many other desires and options, such as, for example, a job or career of her own, further education, free time, or political work. In this way, the biological capacity to give birth is still a social destiny for women.

*(Shout from the CDU/CSU: This must be changed!)*

The suppression of women will only stop when the gendered division of labor is abolished.

*(Applause from the Greens and from some SPD members)*

A majority of the Greens, and I belong to this majority, support the demand of the women's movement for a complete abandonment of Paragraph 218.

*(Applause from the Greens)*

If a woman becomes pregnant unintentionally, she alone must be able to decide whether she wants a child or not. As abortion is a question of moral conviction and depends upon the personal life situation, it cannot be an object of legal prosecution.

*(Applause from the Greens—Gerster [CDU/CSU], (Mainz): What is your position on euthanasia?)*

Even if abortion is legalized, an ethical conflict and a moral question have to be resolved.

Our thoroughly patriarchal society is in crisis. In times of crisis, patriarchs give up their benevolence and consign the oppressed to their proper place. The ideological upgrading of the nuclear family is a subliminal tactic to push women back into the family. The new divorce law aims at keeping them there. At home, they are to do housework and raise children, both tasks that do not require qualifications, that are useful, and that remain unpaid. Women's life is again reduced to the three C's: children, cooking, cable television.

*(Applause from the Greens and from some SPD members—Laughter from the CDU/CSU and the Free Democratic Party [FDP])*

Jobs are scarce, and if women are unemployed, the only guarantor for their economic and social security lies in marriage. Women thus exchange autonomy for dependence on men, whose interests and wishes they have to subordinate themselves to. This is what Mr. Kohl—he is not present—means when he extols the family. Back into the family, that is the patriarchal-reactionary strategy to overcome unemployment.

This is not about denouncing those who attempt with great effort to find a bit of happiness in marriage. But the prerequisite for this is a partnership characterized by equality, where both can participate in meaningful work, in politics, and in child care.

*(Applause from the Greens—Bohl (CDU/CSU): Everyone can arrange this as they please!)*

In a society where people are exploited, where politics takes a calculated risk with regard to wars, and where deterrence means the ability to destroy people, violence as a means of settling conflicts has become part of the repertoire for even the closest personal relationships.

*(Shout from the CDU/CSU: You have to disarm rhetorically!)*

We reject with outrage and disgust a politics that supports and furthers such conditions.

*(Applause from the Greens—Shouts from the CDU/CSU)*

In a society flooded by consumer goods, we demand economic security for all women, independent of their support in marriage. We demand an adequate pension especially for women, even if they have not done wage labor because there was no wage labor available for them.

*(Applause from the Greens)*

We demand the prosecution of marital rape. We demand from you to finally grasp that women, too, have a right to self-determination and a right to control their own bodies and lives. We demand from all of you to stop the everyday sexism here in parliament.

*(Applause from the Greens and from SPD-members—Laughter and shouts from the CDU/CSU and from the FDP—Shouts from the CDU/CSU: The love parliament!—Bastian-Kelly!—More shouts and sustained laughter)*

I can see that my remarks hit home.

*(Applause from the Greens and from SPD-members—More shouts from the CDU/CSU)*

By marginalizing women away from work, politics, and culture, society deprives itself of creativity. We, Mr. Chancellor, regard your policy of renewal with horror. We demand measures enabling women to decide for themselves how they want to live.

*(Shout from the CDU/CSU: How much longer will you take?)*

This also entails a woman's decision for or against a child.

At present, children are harassed and tormented, and sexuality becomes an act of domination, resulting often in pregnancy.

Instead of pressuring women by intensifying Paragraph 218, we should take a moment to think about how contraception might be promoted. It would be a real turnaround, for instance, if a chancellor would stand up here and point out to people that there are forms of love making that are extremely pleasurable while at the same time excluding the risk of pregnancy.

*(Laughter from the CDU/CSU and from the FDP)*

But one can only speak on issues that one understands a little.

*(Applause from the Greens and from some SPD-members—Laughter from the CDU/CSU and from the FDP—Shouts from the CDU/CSU)*

Seriously, I would never want to talk to the chancellor about that.

*(Laughter from the CDU/CSU—Seiters [CDU/CSU]: Spell out what you mean!)*

Because he who destroys the environment with his policies and initiates inhuman practices has forsaken the chance to be included in a debate about sensuality.

*(Applause from the Greens and from some SPD members—Laughter and shouts from the CDU/CSU)*


## Joschka Fischer: "Our Minister for Justice and the Case of a Dead Refugee"

Speech in the German Bundestag on September 8, 1983.

Fischer (Greens): Madam President! Ladies and gentlemen! Forty-three years ago, on September 27, 1940, the philosopher and German Jew Walter Benjamin committed suicide at the Spanish–French border. Benjamin, one of the greatest thinkers of the Frankfurt School, poisoned himself because he feared being extradited to Hitler's Gestapo. He feared torture, maiming, and an excruciating death in a concentration camp more than he feared suicide. After his death, his companions, all of them political refugees from Nazi Germany, were allowed to stay in Spain. They were not extradited. It is important to note that this took place in Fascist Spain, one year after the end of the civil war.

On August 30 of this year, the political emigrant and asylum-seeker Kemal Altun threw himself out of the sixth-floor window of the Administrative Court in Berlin. His death is the latest incident in a sad development initiated years ago under the Social-Liberal government: the undermining of the right to political asylum and its transformation into a right to refuse political asylum.

*(Shout from the CDU/CSU: That's outrageous!)*

The authors of the West German Basic Law, these fathers of our liberal constitution who are all too often invoked in celebratory speeches, had good and often personal reasons to write a passage on the right to asylum that upholds human dignity. They still had vivid memories of the misery, the terror, and the torment of the political refugees from Nazi Germany, and some members of this House still have those memories. Willy Brandt would never have had a chance of becoming chancellor if he had been treated according to the same regulations that are in place today with respect to political refugees in the Federal Republic of Germany.[1]

Rightly, back in 1949 the German founders felt the obligation of survivors. Should others have to suffer a similar fate, this republic was to offer them shelter and protection. This was self-evident for the fathers of our constitution. Now, in 1983, applications for political asylum are also ending in suicide in this country. They end in the desperate acts of political refugees who prefer suicide to being deported to murderous military dictatorships and their torturers. Kemal Altun's ordeal in jails and courts, and the way he was used by the political interests of West German democracy, the 13-month-long ordeal of an "asylum-seeker," shows in an exemplary way what has become of this sense of obligation, of this country, and of this democracy.

*(Applause from the Greens—Shout from the CDU/CSU: Thanks to you Greens!)*

... Kemal Altun came to West Berlin in 1981 after the military coup in Turkey and applied for political asylum there in September. On the basis of the so-called close cooperation between German and Turkish police and secret police services, this application was sent to Ankara by the Federal Office of Criminal Investigation as a routine inquiry. The Turkish military promptly issued an arrest warrant as well as a request for extradition, accusing Kemal Altun of having instigated the murder of the former Turkish minister of customs and monopolies, Gün Sazak. This arrest warrant was issued two years after the incident and only after the Federal Office of Criminal Investigation's inquiry was launched. Kemal Altun was then held in extradition arrest in West Berlin.

Kemal Altun would have faced the death penalty in Turkey on the basis of this first request for extradition on a charge of having instigated a murder. An extradition would therefore only be possible with further guarantees. The Turkish military therefore presented the German authorities with a second request for extradition. Herein, however, the contents, dates, and file references had been changed. Now, the charge was aiding the perpetrator of an offense, as Altun had supposedly hidden weapons and people connected to the assassination, an accusation Kemal Altun denied as he had the first one.

Nevertheless, on December 16, 1982, the Fourth Senate of the Berlin Superior Court of Justice declared the extradition to be legal, without ever having heard Altun himself. Moreover, the Berlin Superior Court of Justice did not take into consideration a Turkish court's verdict against several defendants in the Gün Sazak murder case, which had been declared shortly thereafter. In the Turkish case, testimonies that had heretofore incriminated Altun had been reassessed as statements of evasive defense by the other defendants. The same verdict described the Sazak case as—I would like to quote this—"militant attempt to change or abolish the constitution of the Turkish Republic." This is a classical political crime and in itself sufficient reason to foreclose extradition.

The federal government, however, acted quite differently. It acceded to the extradition request on February 21, 1983. Only two days later, in a similar case involving a Turkish political emigrant, the Federal Constitutional Court ruled that, "on the basis of recent experiences, the general guarantee of particularity according to Article 14 of the European Convention on Extradition is not in itself [sufficient] to preclude the danger of political persecution in extradition cases with Turkey. Therefore, an additional case-by-case examination is necessary."

In Kemal Altun's case, such an examination was undertaken neither by the Berlin Superior Court of Justice nor by the federal government. The minister for justice's telling letter of June 21, 1983, to which I will come back later, basically quotes from the Turkish police and drumhead court-martial records.

Let me read some more from the successful appeal to the Federal Constitutional Court in a similar case. This will make clear the extent of the brazen circumvention of the constitution and of the Constitutional Court. And it will enable us to recognize that the ministers for justice and for the interior breached the constitution. This was, as I said, about two days after the federal government's decision:

> Apparently in the past Turkish authorities have attempted, on the basis of the extradition procedure, to get hold of political opponents by using manipulated criminal accusations. . . . If misleading manipulations should be detected with regard to the accusations, the protection of the principle of particularity can hardly be considered as sufficient. In any case, the principle would fail in an extradition for the purpose of executing a politically manipulated verdict. This would have to be viewed as a political persecution, because the persecutee would be jailed on the grounds of an unjustified sentence. Even conditions of imprisonment in accordance with the regulations would not change the fact of political persecution.

The Federal Constitutional Court refers to Amnesty International, whose appeals to the federal government in the Altun case went unheard, speaks of the torture practiced under the Turkish military regime, points out that the federal government does not have adequate information on the human rights situation in Turkey, and mentions various resolutions by the European parliament from 1981 to 1983 on the issue of torture in Turkey and on the necessity of a moratorium on extraditions of political persecutees. Finally, the Court also refers to the still-pending charge of human rights violations by the Turkish government filed in Strasbourg by Denmark, France, the Netherlands, Norway, and Sweden.

So the facts were well known. Everyone who wants to know knows what has happened in the Turkey of the generals since September 1980: 21,000 political prisoners are in the dungeons; a poem is punished with several years imprisonment; the use of the Kurdish language is forbidden; prisoners are tortured to death, are executed, or simply disappear.

However, on July 21, 1983, the minister for justice was still of the opinion that—quote—"there is no reasonable basis for fearing that Kemal Altun might be subjected to inhuman treatment after his extradition." But it was common knowledge—and the federal government and especially the minister of justice had to know—what the politically persecuted were in for in Turkey. Definitely after the successful appeal to the Federal Constitutional Court by Ibrahim Sen in February 1983, Kemal Altun should have been dismissed from extradition arrest as a free man.

All the appeals and petitions by human rights organizations, by the United Nations High Commissioner on Refugees, by labor unions, and by numerous personalities and politicians went unheard. The minister for justice did not want to take notice, did not want to acknowledge anything, because he obviously had a different aim. In contrast to Article 16, Section 2, of the Basic Law, which accords everyone the right to asylum, and in contrast to the Federal Constitutional Court's concrete interpretation of this article with regard to the Turkish regime, the minister's aim was to maintain the good relations with the generals in the area of security. The constitution was to be circumvented, and it was circumvented; and a decisive article on human rights was thereby annulled.

This, Mr. Engelhard,[2] is what we normally call a breach of the constitution, a cold breach of the constitution, undertaken by a liberal minister for justice and supported by a determined helper, of whom I will speak shortly. We consider this minister for justice to be intolerable!

Questioned about his reaction to Altun's suicide in an interview, Mr. Engelhard said: "I am deeply touched. His death is especially tragic because we undertook everything humanly possible." But let us listen to that minister for justice one month earlier, in his letter of July 21, 1983:

> We have to assume that the division will dismiss the legal action initiated by the federal commissioner. Because of the fundamental nature of the issue, the latter has already announced his intention of filing an appeal. The decision to wait for the conclusion of the asylum procedure would, however, practically make it impossible to execute the extradition. [In that case], the execution of the extradition would no longer be secured.

*(Hear! Hear! from the SPD)*

Quick action is called for.

*(Hoffmann [SPD]: He did everything humanly possible!)*

In other words, Mr. Engelhard, this means: we have to hurry up with the deportation before Altun is accorded the status of a political refugee.

*(Applause from the Greens and from the SPD)*

. . . So everything humanly possible was done, Mr. Minister for Justice? We believe everything humanly possible was done to deliver Altun to his executioners or push him into suicide; for honesty's sake, you should have added this.

Now let us speak of the minister for justice's determined supporter in the cabinet. Let us speak of the minister for the interior, Mr. Zimmermann, who has made the expulsion of Turkish people living in the Federal Republic, and especially those that are apolitical, a matter close to his heart.

*(Shouts from the CDU/CSU: That's an insult!—Incredible! —Dr. Waigel*

*(CDU/CSU): What you are saying is vile!—Boos and more shouts from the CDU/CSU)*

For Zimmermann, the minister for justice was still too hesitant. The constitution, human rights, and humanitarianism no longer exist in his deliberations.

*(Shouts from the CDU/CSU)*

On the very day of his return from Turkey—he could not even wait 24 hours—he penned a letter addressed to the minister for justice in which he personally complained that—again I quote: "contrary to Undersecretary of State Dr. Kinkel's announcement that the Altun case would be presented in the cabinet with the aim of acceding to the extradition request, the issue was not on the agenda of the cabinet meeting on July 20"—Mr. Zimmermann, July 20 was the anniversary of the assassination attempt on Hitler! The Minister for the Interior continues—I quote:

*(Loud shouts from the CDU/CSU: That's enough!)*

"In the interest of upholding our relationship of close police cooperation . . .

*(Prolonged shouts from the CDU/CSU)*

The fact that you do not want to hear this is obvious. But you will nevertheless have to listen to me.

Vice-President Renger: One moment! Ladies and gentlemen, this is a very difficult topic. I ask you to allow the speaker to continue, as everyone here has the opportunity to present his or her statements.

*(Schily [Greens]: What was that about shouting down people this morning, Mr. Chancellor? Who actually shouts down whom?)*

Fischer: The Minister for the Interior continues:

> In the interest of upholding our relationship of close police cooperation with Turkey, but also in the interest of upholding the credibility of extradition procedures with Turkey, I ask you to declare the authorizing decision dated February 21, 1983, to be enforced so that the extradition can be executed without delay.

*(Shame! Shame!—from the Greens)*

What kind of a deal, Mr. Zimmermann, did you actually agree to in Ankara? Was it a tradeoff to extradite Turkish dissidents from the Federal Republic against a Turkish assurance to abandon its stance against the impending principle of free movement according to the EC Association Agreement?

. . . Kemal Altun was held in extradition arrest for 13 months. Day and night, he had to reckon with his extradition. He knew the generals in Ankara wanted him. He knew of their powerful friends in the federal government. He knew of this country's NATO interests, and he experienced the policy of bureaucratic expulsion of Turkish citizens living in Germany.

Kemal Altun was scared. I would like to quote part of a letter from his nephew to make clear to you what Altun was scared of. I quote:

> Shortly after dusk . . . they came to take me back into a room, where they tied my hands and feet to a pole . . . and hung me from the ceiling. Then they continued with the interrogation. They wanted me to tell them everything I knew about my Uncle Kemal, about my father—my father was, as you know, a member of parliament before the military coup d'état—and about my friends. Despite my begging and pleading, they attached electric wires to my hands and this time also to my genitals.

This gruesome account goes on for a long time.

But let me add something pertaining directly to Mr. Zimmermann. He enjoys the reputation of being the tough guy in the federal government. But he is particularly tough with regard to those 1.7 million Turks living in the Federal Republic, who possess no political rights and whose human rights, guaranteed by our constitution, are increasingly undermined.

*(Shouts from the CDU/CSU: Incredible!—Dr. Althammer [CDU/CSU]: But these are Turkish citizens!)*

The Turks cannot vote here. It is really easy to gain distinction as a tough guy by harassing them, even if this, as in the Altun case, entails deaths.

Mr. Zimmermann, I find your behavior toward these people politically disastrous and, in a very personal sense, morally depraved.

*(Applause from the Greens—Boos from the CDU/CSU—Shout from the CDU/CSU: Who is really depraved (corrupt) here?—Further loud shouting from the CDU/CSU)*

Vice-president Renger: Ladies and gentlemen, please let the speaker continue. We have further members wishing to speak.

*(Continual shouting from the CDU/CSU)*

—Ladies and gentlemen, that is my decision.

*(Shout from the CDU/CSU: Where are we?)*

Fischer: In the German parliament, that's all! And people still have the right to speak out on such issues in this High House.

*(Continual loud shouting from the CDU/CSU)*

—You will have to allow me to point out to you your responsibilities, gentlemen from the CDU/CSU, you can bet on that.

*(Applause from the Greens—Continued shouts from the CDU/CSU)*

That's enough: it's unbearable that in the face of political persecution in Turkey, the constitution and human rights continue to be trampled on by the very ministers that are responsible for upholding the same;—

*(Applause from the Greens—Continual shouting from the CDU/CSU: You disgusting rowdy!)*

—it's unbearable that we continue to deny fundamental civil and human rights to people lacking political rights and that we force them to leave through coercive bureaucratic measures. For good reasons, I rarely use this word, but today, Mr. Zimmermann, I have to tell you that, as a German, and as your compatriot, I am ashamed of your policies, which—while not covered by the constitution—are likely backed by a majority of Germans sitting at their local hangouts.

Kemal Altun's death must not be in vain. We do not demand much. All we want is that the constitution and human rights be respected. We therefore ask you to carry the two motions for dismissal today.

Finally, I would like to say a personal word to the chancellor: Mr. Chancellor, in the end, you decide upon whether political dissidents are extradited to Turkey or not . . . I ask you, yes, I appeal to you, to prevent further extraditions to Turkey. You owe this to your official oath, your Christian belief, and also to humanity. Thank you.

### Benny Härlin: "A Voice for Freedom"—Using 'Europarliamentary Immunity' for Networking Self-Help Initiatives

Benny Härlin worked for the left radical daily *die tageszeitung* and as the press secretary for the Self-Help Network, a group funded by regular private contributors to assist self-managed "alternative projects."

But Härlin is best known as the one-time chief editor of the periodical *radikal*. This magazine was the mouthpiece of the militant left, the revolutionary cells, the Red Army Faction, the Autonomen, those who cut down power lines and participated in militant demonstrations. Under Paragraph 129a, the "terrorist conspiracy" law, Härlin and a co-worker, Michael Klöckner, were tried and convicted of "publicizing in support of a terrorist association" and given prison sentences. The Greens freed them by electing both to the European parliament in June 1984. Below is Härlin's campaign statement.

Imagine that you have been nominated by the Greens as their candidate for the European parliament: "Who me? But why? What am I supposed to do there? That's silly!" is what you would probably say.

You see, in principle, that's how I felt too. That Michael Klöckner and

I are on the list of Green candidates for the European parliament is a result of German rule of law and Green spontaneity.

Only a few days prior to the Greens' nomination party congress in Karlsruhe on March 3–4, 1984, both of us had been sentenced to 28 months of detention by the Berlin Superior Court of Justice for supposedly having undertaken "propaganda for a terrorist group" (Paragraph 129a) and instigating criminal offenses. Because we were editors of the periodical *radikal,* the authorities arbitrarily sentenced us for reprinting letters claiming responsibility for actions by the "Revolutionary Cells."

The attorney general views us as the "public relations managers of terrorism and the forces of chaos in Berlin." The press, unions, and the associations of journalists and of authors, however, consider this verdict to be a scandal as well as a serious threat to both freedom of expression and freedom of information. . . .

By nominating us as their candidates for the European parliament, the Green Party has given us a shield of Euro-parliamentary immunity—if this is what the voters want. Then the only way the authorities can get hold of us is by applying for and justifying the suspension of our immunity.

I have lived and worked in the by now famous alternative scene in Berlin for 10 years. I co-founded a print collective and gained initial experience there with both "new technology" and a new form of work organization— namely, self-management.

Then I worked as a local editor for the *tageszeitung* while simultaneously squatting in a vacant building owned by the "Neue Heimat." We are now in the third year of defending this house against the company's renewal mania and its disgraceful business practices. We are not only attempting to live on the basis of self-management, but are also trying to develop a new living context that can perhaps best be labeled "clanism."

Finally, I was intensely involved from the outset, in the Self-Help Network and presently earn a living as their press secretary.

"Everyone wants to engage in satisfying activities. But our system threatens many people with unemployment and occupational bans. Fear and apathy spread, whereas optimistic impulses are what we need. Let's do something about it!"

This was the first paragraph of the Network's founding appeal. Since then, the Network has supported more than three hundred alternative projects, self-help groups, citizen initiatives, and political campaigns financially and organizationally. Wherever people attempt to take things into their own hands, wherever they begin to develop practical alternatives instead of merely formulating demands and delegating these to some representatives (even if they are Green representatives), our organization helps out.

Meanwhile, there are 34 Networks in the Federal Republic of Germany, Switzerland, Austria, Belgium, and Australia. And, incidentally, I have never really understood why *all* Greens have not become Network members.

In the European parliament, as well as in the broader context of the Euro-bureaucracy, I will try to represent the interests of self-managed businesses, self-help groups, and initiatives, to build up a network of contacts, and to carry information and experience across regional and national borders.

This seems to be a worthwhile task because small grassroots-democratic groups and projects are often prone to pay for their local orientation with a provincialism that is not what the slogan "A Europe of the Regions" is supposed to mean.

. . . Self-help initiatives and alternative companies cannot abolish capitalism, nor do they want to. But they can offer examples of how things can be done differently and show that bosses are superfluous; that work and income can be distributed *more* equitably; that, using imagination and self-confidence, everyone can organize and undertake a lot more on their own initiative than professional disempowerers would like to have us believe; that, in all areas of life, democracy starts at the bottom, but also that it takes time and energy; that working less can be a precondition for getting more done; that competition and addiction to power, to work, and to possessions are outdated; . . . and that women are usually superior in such contexts to men. This list could go on and on.

The question of what all this has to do with Europe confuses me a little, as long as I associate "Europe" mainly with a colorful map of seemingly absurd and partially threatening supraorganizations or with a tangle of lofty ideals and ideological fragments about national identity, the West, folklore, international understanding, etc.

But if I imagine that, with our support, workers who have occupied their plants can meet and communicate, or that collectives and cooperatives can get in touch with one another and gain information on useful European Community (EC) programs and institutions, then this, even if it is not revolutionary, is useful and promising. . . .

Last but not least, I plan to continue practicing my profession. From the perspective of a "bloody layman," I would like to describe my experiences in Brussels and Strasbourg in simple words and publish these in the form of articles and reports. Because this obscure structure and its unintelligible European Currency Units quota terminology are commonly viewed as hard to describe, even harder to grasp, and impossible to change. Maybe that is not true? You will hear from me.

NOTES

1. Willy Brandt enjoyed political asylum in Norway in the 1930s, when he had to flee from the Nazis because of his membership in a socialist youth organization.

2. Hans A. Engelhard was minister for justice in the Conservative-Liberal coalition at the time, and a member of the FDP.—Eds.

# Chapter 14

# Programmatic Texts and Resolutions

## The Umbau Program: The Transformation of Industrial Society— Steps toward Overcoming Unemployment, Poverty, and Environmental Destruction (1986)

*Umbau,* the "rebuilding" or "reconstruction" of industrial society, is the word the Greens introduced into German politics to designate their second, more detailed economic program, accepted in final form at the Nuremberg congress in September 1986. The first program, *Purpose in Work—Solidarity in Life,*[1] passed in Sindelfingen in 1983, was never renounced, however, and the Umbau program is meant to be an addition to that document, with short-term measures complementing the long-term utopian Sindelfingen program. Though several introductions from varying political directions were proposed, the program itself is predominantly the work of four individuals representing a mixture of political tendencies in the party: two Realos, Hubert Kleinert and Jo Müller, an eco-socialist, Eckhard Stratmann, and Hans Veheyen, committed to working out a compromise between the other camps.

The program is presented below in a drastically shortened form, which emphasizes elements relevant to an English-speaking audience, or areas, such as social or industrial policy, that the other documents in this collection do not deal with. The shortening has frequently obscured the overall structure of the text. Originally, each of the policy sections was divided into four portions: a "sketch of the problems," "concepts of the old parties," "alternative concepts," and "instruments of rebuilding." In contrast to earlier Green positions, the Umbau program's focus on the state as the predominant means of "rebuilding" is striking. This focus was criticized from both a left-radical and an eco-libertarian position.[2] Particularly because it did not consider possible market strategies for ecological transformation, the Umbau program failed to address the issue of "ecological taxes," which the Social democrats subsequently introduced in their "Progress 90" program, generated for the 1990 federal elections. By 1996, the so-called "eco-tax" had become the center of the Greens' program for reforming industrial society, and its provisions for taxing energy are rather more drastic than the SPD's motion.[3]

PREFACE

The following text is not the Greens' economic or basic program, but a program for immediate action against the three big challenges of our time: mass unemployment, poverty, and environmental destruction. This program seeks to point out the margins for political action on the federal level. It is directed against the alleged "objective constraints" behind which established politics entrenches itself. It shows paths that could be taken if the necessary political will existed.


PREAMBLE

*Conceptualizing and Enforcing the Umbau Program*

The present Umbau program suggests practical steps toward transcending unemployment, poverty, and environmental destruction in a coherent context. It takes up demands formulated by manifold social movements—the labor movement, the women's movement, the antinuclear protest movement, the environmental and consumer movements, etc.—and can only be implemented through a collaboration between the Greens and these movements.

With this Umbau program, the Greens present a concrete and realizable utopia. It is a utopia because the transformation of the economy is a long-term issue and the necessary changes are fundamental and radical. But it is realizable if a sufficiently strong political will exists. We have spelled out the instruments required for these changes, taken into account the financial effects, have computed the costs and savings incurred by the restructuring, or, where this was not possible, made estimates on the basis of solid calculations, and have thus proved the financial feasibility of the program.

This demonstration is important because it seeks to forestall the frequent and popular criticism that our suggestions cannot be realized because of objective constraints or tight finances. We know that reality will not evolve according to a Green script. Even to launch this program would trigger a powerful reaction from business: we know the threatening gestures already. But this is no reason for us to become resigned or submissive. On the contrary, it is a reason to inform and politically educate the population, whose willingness and whose strong pressure are crucial for actually realizing this Umbau program. The same goes for such changes as drastic reductions in working hours: this would not be possible without labor union action against capital. The duration and political results of such actions are, of course, not calculable. Therefore every financial calculation, but also every calculation of expected labor-market effects, will remain a mere model calculation.

The Umbau program comprises a plethora of state measures initiating and enforcing its provisions. It would be politically wrong to conclude from this that the state, and especially the federal state and its budget policies, are at the heart of the Umbau concept. Support for an ecological transformation can only be roused if it is clear that it does not entail a loss of job security and income for the majority of low- and medium-income groups. But even if this support exists, transformation will be opposed by capital (e.g., the chemical and automobile industries) and will fail without political pressure from people, unions, citizen initiatives, environmental and consumer organizations, and the critical media. This is why many of the proposed state measures are directed at enhancing the population's opportunities for action and enforcing their democratic rights. These include giving individual citizens the right to inspect files and records, extending the democratic rights of workers within companies, expanding union rights through a ban on lockouts, and strengthening the competence of local governments and their control over their finances. Many instruments of state intervention included in our program therefore do not actually serve to strengthen the state; they aim at decentralizing power and strengthening citizen initiatives and social movements against the powerful interest organizations prevailing today.[4]

## I. SECURING THE NATURAL BASIS OF LIFE

### The Air We Breathe

It cannot be the goal of Green environmental policy to implement new threshold values for the pollution of natural systems. Threshold values are an instrument for managing scarcity that the Greens' clean air policy has to engage with as long as the real goal, the drastic reduction of environmental interventions, has not yet been achieved.

—The program for measuring emissions must be expanded to evaluate the effects of polluted air on human health, nature, and the environment.

—Threshold values should not be established on the basis of median spatial values (i.e., for one or more square kilometers); with respect to short-term values, the highest values should no longer be omitted.

—The smog-alarm values currently used have to be at least halved. With special emphasis on endangered groups, the population is to be informed every day (and if necessary warned) about air quality in an understandable manner (radio, television).

*The Water We Drink*

On the basis of old water rights, industry still gets drinking-quality water for next to nothing and uses it for purposes where recycled water would suffice. Water works usually grant large-scale users special terms, although a progressive rate aimed at reducing water use is needed. Groundwater is also seriously impaired by lignite surface mining and by hard-coal underground mining, as well as by sealed surfaces, regulation of rivers, and canalization of streams.

*Alternative Concepts*

The Greens' policy on water is based on the natural water cycle, into which human use must integrate itself harmoniously. Rain and snow must be allowed to seep back into the earth and enhance the groundwater instead of flowing off built-up or sealed areas and causing floods. Groundwater is the purest and most precious form of water we have. Its quantity and quality must be secured against contamination, and it must be available as drinking water. Our surface waters are complex biotopes that stabilize ecological systems. We must therefore prevent man-made substances, especially toxic compounds and those that do not easily decompose, from entering into those natural systems. It is equally important to reduce water consumption drastically. This means that:

—Technologies and products used in industry, agriculture, and private households that endanger the natural water system must be cut back.

—Recycled water systems must be installed in industry, and water-saving techniques must be promoted in private households.

—Regulated rivers must be renaturalized.

*Instruments of Rebuilding*

Cleaning and providing water falls under the responsibility of states and municipalities. But the federal state can provide a legislative framework and financial incentives. This new water policy will entail an amendment of the Federal Law on Management of Water Resources:

—All sources that endanger water (including agriculture) must be registered.

—A complete list of agents endangering water must be compiled.

—The threshold values for drinking water must be immediately adapted to the European Community (EC) Council Directives.

—Sewage treatment must employ the best available technology.

—A ban on discharging sewage must be installed wherever water treatment using the best available technology is ecologically insufficient.

—Persons discharging sewage indirectly through the public sewage system must adhere to the regulations governing the discharge of dangerous substances.

—Just as persons discharging into surface and flowing water must be registered, so must those discharging into the public sewage system; measured in terms of volume and toxicity, indirect dischargers must contribute to sewage treatment costs on the principle of "polluter pays."

### The Soil We Live Off

The soil we live off is only 30–50 centimeters thick. But industrial society treats our most important resource as if it could be exploited infinitely, as if it were resistant against toxins, and as if it could be augmented at will. While the pollution of water and air has already become part of our environmental consciousness, this is not so with regard to soil. Moreover, we are at a much greater loss when it comes to remedying the pollution and depletion of soil. But in many areas the soil has taken all it can take. . . .

Soil is a source of nutrition for plants and is thus the basis of food production. It is an effective filter system against pollutants and helps to replenish and cleanse groundwater. As soil must withstand many different forms of strain (settlement, agriculture, traffic, waste disposal), a soil preservation plan must cover all of these areas:

—Land must no longer be sealed or cut up. In development as well as traffic planning, the value of land should no longer be measured in merely economic terms. Ecological aspects of land use must finally be taken seriously.

—Soil must no longer be poisoned with pollutants. This means that the production of pollutants must be stopped as far as possible at their point of origin. This entails the enforcement of the "polluter pays" principle. Only if this principle is enforced can we go from the present system of environmental repair to a system of damage prevention.

## II. Steps toward an Ecological Economy

### Natural Agriculture and Securing Agricultural Jobs

The accelerated pace of structural change in rural areas and the destruction of small farms costs an estimated 30,000 jobs annually in the Federal Republic. Between 1981 and 1984, the number of farms decreased by 50,000, and there was a 26 percent reduction between 1973 and 1983.

Under the prevailing policy of "grow or give up," the only farms that can survive are those which pursue a stringent rationalization policy with respect to chemicals, technology, and breeding in order to exploit soil, animals, and plants to the highest degree.

The catastrophic damage such a mode of production incurs is already visible. Consolidation of farmland, the cultivation of huge fields, and the trend toward monoculture contribute to the destruction of the landscape, dry out valuable wetland areas, endanger genetic diversity, and thus affect the balance of nature.

*Concepts of the Old Parties*

The prevailing agricultural policy, particularly that of the EC, aims at transforming farms into industrialized agricultural enterprises through various rationalization measures. This implies replacing natural processes with chemical and technological intervention, including genetic and biotechnical manipulation. This policy of pushing prices down forces smaller farms to give up. . . .

*Alternative Concepts*

Green agricultural policy advocates cultural and economic independence for rural areas, a healthy diet, a livable environment, and protecting the jobs on small and medium-sized farms at home as well as in the "Third World." Green agricultural policy starts out with an analysis of the causes of this problematic development and an understanding of the situation of the individual farmer. Farmers employ production technologies with severe consequences for the quality of production and nature itself only because of economic pressure and existential need. Abandoning these technologies and turning toward organic farming can succeed only if the present structure of small and medium-sized farms is secured and if ecological agriculture is recognized as a real alternative.

*Instruments for the Transformation of Agriculture*

—Securing farmers' incomes through producer prices that are differentiated on the basis of structural and regional particularities and that actually pay for the labor expenditures.

—Environmental protection through reducing intensity of production. Producers of mineral nitrogenous fertilizer will be taxed at a rate equivalent to the market price. For farmers using up to 150 kilos of nitrogen per hectare, the cash equivalent of 80 kilos per hectare will be reimbursed. For higher use, no reimbursement takes place. Farmers using less than 8 kilos per hectare will be reimbursed the equivalent of 80 kilos. The amount of dung and liquid manure that each farm produces will be included in calculating the amount of nitrogen to be taxed. This incentive scheme will reduce the use of environmentally destructive nitrogen and will protect the soil from being overly exploited. Giant animal farms are to be banned, as they are cruel to animals and cause enormous ecological problems (manure, Third World fodder-imports). Other cruel forms of raising animals are to be banned as well.

—Promotion of organic gardening, agriculture, and viniculture. The assertion that agriculture based on organic guidelines is unprofitable is wrong, even without taking into consideration the ecological and social costs of conventional agriculture. The higher cost arising mainly from the greater intensity of labor is offset by high-quality products that deserve higher prices and that more and more consumers are demanding in the market. Acceptance of organically grown products can quickly be increased by informing people of the difference between industrial and organically grown food.

## Humane Housing and Cities

### Ecological and Socially Acceptable Rebuilding of Cities

An ecological and socially acceptable transformation of cities requires a democratization of building codes and planning, soil-protection, and emission laws.

We have to stop separating the spheres of housing, work, consumption, culture, and recreation. We have to intersperse monofunctional areas with social and ecological uses. At the same time, neighborhoods must be equipped with special places where cultural, ecological, and urban activities can flourish.

Besides securing existing open spaces in densely populated urban areas, land that is presently covered by concrete and asphalt must be unsealed and the renaturalization of such areas promoted. We have to install forms of energy supply on the neighborhood level that, for example, make use of the waste heat of industrial plants.

Special attention must be devoted to large housing districts built in the 1960s and 1970s, because they suffer most under the existing separation of functions and because the anonymous architecture there has frequently prevented the development of a sense of community.

### Safe, Environmentally Acceptable, and Accessible Transportation

### Instruments of Rebuilding

Rail, Bus and Bicycle Traffic:

—Cut train fares in half, with even greater reductions in local train fares and for commuter tickets. The federal government can make up the resulting loss by increasing the gasoline tax. The expected increase in demand will increase profits, which the Federal Railways can use to extend and improve their services.

—Double investment in public transport. This will permit a qualitative and quantitative extension of surface transportation (trains and buses). Modern streetcars will receive special subsidies, whereas subways will receive them only in exceptional cases. In general, we will subsidize modern public transportation systems and make sure they are accessible to the handicapped.

### Effects

The Umbau program will reduce the domination of the automobile, opening up freedom of choice with respect to alternative transportation systems that are ecologically acceptable. Dismantling financial and other benefits is, of course, unpleasant for those who drive cars, but we regard it as necessary in order to effectively reduce the enormous damage automobiles cause to the public. In return, the conditions for nonmotorized traffic (walking, cycling) and for trains and buses will be vastly improved. Everyone, including car drivers, will benefit from the improved living conditions, fewer accidents, and attractive alternative options. People without cars and those living on main roads (generally low-income people) will benefit more than others. Where automobile use cannot be replaced, we envision compensatory social measures.

The transformation process in the transport sector will be gradual. All in all, the economic viability of public transport will be strengthened, municipal traffic policies will have greater leeway, and dependency on oil imports will be reduced.

### Environmentally Friendly and Renewable Forms of Energy

### Sketch of the Problems

The power industry presents the following problems:

—Enormous dangers for human beings and nature. Nuclear power plants pose the threat of accidents that cannot be technically controlled. Moreover, in their normal operation they emit cancer—causing radiation, and there is evidence that they contribute to the death of forests. The use of nonrenewable energy sources invariably produces carbon dioxide, which is responsible for the global greenhouse effect. Coal liquidization and gasification plants emit large amounts of carcinogenic substances. The present form of hard-coal mining leads to lasting ecological damage.

—Gigantic waste of energy. More than 90 percent of the Federal Republic's power plants squander the waste heat they produce. Their energy efficiency is about 35 percent; the rest—largely in the form of waste heat—is dissipated, putting eco-systems under stress. Insulation in private homes, passive or active use of solar energy, and local/long-distance heating systems are hardly established.

—Large energy corporations with monopolistic power. In conjunction with the established parties, the energy corporations dictate high prices for private households (where energy bills have already reached 6–10 percent of total living costs), but provide industry with energy at prices that are partly below cost. . . . An "unholy alliance" of energy corporations, industry, and the state has stifled attempts at installing a more ecological energy system.

*Alternative Concepts*

The Greens' energy policy advocates full use of energy-saving possibilities. Its priority is the development of renewable energy technologies and the environment-friendly use of domestic energy sources.

Since all past efforts to enforce an ecologically acceptable power industry have failed because of the energy sector's structure, we will need new legal foundations such as a Law on the Regulation of the Power Industry. In concrete terms, this means:

—Re-municipalize energy provision. An energy policy "from the bottom" is necessary because energy-saving and waste-heat resources cannot be transported but have to be mobilized locally. Cities and counties must again become the centers of political decision making with regard to energy. Aside from local supply systems, new forms of cooperation and regionally integrated energy systems based on ecological and energy-saving criteria must be developed. Local energy networks must be re-municipalized.

—Make energy providers service-oriented. Aside from providing energy, energy saving, social acceptability, and ecological soundness will become equally important tasks of the energy corporations. This new type of energy provider will differ from the current model in four ways: (1) principle of need instead of principle of acquisition; (2) use orientation instead of supply orientation; (3) democratization instead of entrepreneurial autonomy; and (4) participation instead of planning from above.

*Instruments of Rebuilding*

—Immediate closure of all nuclear facilities.

—Comprehensive and quick detoxification of all old and new coal-fired power plants.

—Immediate termination of coal gasification/liquidization programs.

—Full use of the waste heat from electricity production. More than half of the energy incurred in electricity production in thermal power plants takes the form of waste heat. This is nearly untapped in the present system. The following measure is necessary. In the future, only those power plants whose waste heat is fully utilized can go into operation. This is usually not possible with large-scale power plants producing more than 300 megawatts, as there are not enough consumers close to the plant.

—No more electric heating; full insulation and economical household appliances. To increase sales, power companies have promoted the spread of electric heating systems in the past few years by offering discounts. Electric heating, however, is a particularly wasteful mode of heating, as energy loss is incurred not only in the power plants themselves but also in transportation and through the process of transforming electricity into heat. Thus, electric heating systems' efficiency is only about a third of normal heating systems'. Nearly all buildings in the Federal Republic are inadequately insulated. Proper insulation would save about 40 percent of heating energy. We therefore advocate a long-term program of building insulation, which should not be used as an excuse for increasing rent. . . . Manufacturers of electric appliances, machines that run on electricity, and electric heaters are obliged to tag their products with the exact amount of energy they use. At the same time, we should promote research and development in this area.

—Prices based on the principle of saving energy. A two-pronged price structure systematically favors electricity-intensive industries and electricity waste (e.g., electricity for the heating market) at the expense of other users. It also causes high losses to the national economy by continuing to direct capital into the creation of additional capacity instead of into energy saving. The two-pronged price structure means that consumers do not have an incentive to save energy.

### Deactivating the Chemical Timebomb

#### Sketch of the Problems

The chemical industry is one of the most important sectors of the economy and the one with the greatest environmental cost. The turnover of the West German chemical industry is presently about 150 billion DM annually, and its employees number more than half a million. Production is capital-intensive and highly concentrated, with a high export quota (50 percent), especially to Third World countries. The chemical industry is also intricately interwoven with other sectors of the economy, as only about 13 percent of its production leaves the plant as a finished product. The industry is the starting point of an increasing chemicalization of production and consumption. This entails great burdens for the environment and for society.

For the environment: chemical production uses the environment as a factor of production far more intensely than other industries: (33 percent of total industrial water consumption goes into the chemical industry, and energy use is 80 percent above the manufacturing industry's average. It also uses the environment as a medium for the production, storage, transport, and disposal of chemical products. Of the 4 million tons of toxic waste generated annually, 60 percent originates in the chemical industry. Pollution occurs during production (gases, sewage, toxic waste), and also during product use: Fertilizers and pesticides pollute foods, lixivate the soil, and threaten groundwater. By way of household chemicals or wood preservatives, toxins end up in people's living rooms. The danger potential is increased by catastrophic accidents in which thousands are killed or injured (Bhopal) and by the long-term effects for future generations (Seveso). As in no other production sector, the chemical industry's employees are highly endangered on a daily basis. Allergies, complicated skin diseases, neural effects (including brain damage), cancer, and chromosomal alterations are part of their workday.

*Alternative Concepts*

1. The Greens' chemical policy aims at transforming existing chemical production to make it more compatible with nature and human health, at abandoning certain problematic production lines, and at developing and promoting a "soft" or natural chemistry.

2. A technical-repair kind of chemical policy is inadequate. The Greens' chemical policy is not limited to post hoc environmental repair but actively intervenes in the process of deciding the what, where, and how of chemical production. This is why substance-related orders and prohibitions, special levies, and conversion measures are an integral part of Green chemical policy.

3. Chemical policy must prevent toxic substances from entering the living space of organisms. Aside from organic and inorganic toxins, substances that cause cancer, effect genetic changes and deformations, or are not degradable (such as nearly all chlorinated hydrocarbons) are also dangerous.

4. A Green detoxification policy has to help break down the myth of "clean" technologies. The computer industry and the perspective of an information society are not about to end the poisoning of human beings and the environment. The chip industry is one of the chemically most problematic industries, as experiences in Silicon Valley have shown.

5. Green politics is directed not only at dismantling problematic production but also at developing a "soft chemistry." This entails systematic research and development of a chemistry that is close to nature and friendly to the environment. The chemical industry is to be guided to produce only chemicals that are not alien to nature and that can decompose in the normal biocycle without damage to human beings and nature. We can already observe some movement in this direction in the area of food, cosmetics, medicine, clothing, and housing. These trends must be promoted.

6. A Green chemical policy also includes measures aimed at democratizing access to information and protecting people endangered by chemical production. This includes a right to inspect records and files on the chemical industry kept by state and federal authorities, a right of legal action by environmental organizations, a right to refuse work in cases of potential health or environmental hazards, and a reversal of the burden of proof in liability cases.

7. Implementing the Greens' chemical policy against the power of the chemical industry will require a strong oppositional force in society. The Greens have to help strengthen the power of citizen initiatives, environmental and consumer organizations, unions, and individuals. Only if this societal pressure if forthcoming will Green parliamentarians be able to implement the necessary changes on the municipal, state, and federal levels.

*Instruments of Rebuilding*
—Ban the production, use, and sale of highly toxic substances
—Extended civil rights and the rights of those affected
—Through a law guaranteeing the right to inspect environmental files and records, give every natural and legal person access to all kinds of official files relating to environmental regulations. This will enable the public to obtain information relevant to health and the environment, such as, for example, emission values, results of official studies, and existing emergency plans.
—Introduce a right to take organizational legal action for environmental and animal protection organizations.
—In liability cases, replace the principle of causality with the principle of plausibility (i.e., a high degree of probability of health impairment will then suffice to claim damages). Hold producers legally responsible even if they have abided by all environmental regulations.
—Introduce a general right to refuse work for situations where workers' health is seriously threatened. Companies do not have the right to endanger people, and even less right to keep damage to health secret.

*Down with Armaments*

*Sketch of the Problem*
Since rearmament in 1955, West German military capacity has steadily increased. Today, about 85 percent of the West German army's procurement occurs through West German companies. The main suppliers of the Third Reich's Wehrmacht, Daimler-Benz, Flick, Krupp, and Thyssen, now produce military goods for the Federal Ministry of Defense.

"Trade with death" is booming, bigger than ever before: tanks, planes, helicopters, submarines, torpedo boats, frigates, ammunition factories, and hand weapons are exported to the Third World with the approval of the federal government. The West German weapons industry ranks as the fifth-largest producer of military hardware in the world.

*Instruments of Rebuilding*
   *Cut back on military expenditure.*
   —Immediately abandon new weapons programs.
   —Reduce personnel according to two procedures: in basic military service, the strength of the *Bundeswehr* (federal armed forces) should be reduced to 340,000 in 1991 (1995: 250,000) by cutting back basic military service to 12 months and using the "natural selection" of present low-birthrate cohorts; in the military bureaucracy, positions that become vacant or that are superfluous are to be cut.
   —Cancel funds for NATO infrastructure.
   —Cancel funds for the "Wartime Host Nation Support Agreement."
   —Reduce national military activities (training) by a third.
   The suggested reductions in military spending would relieve the "defense" budget of 15 billion DM in a year. However, a large portion of these savings will have to be spent to retrain employees in the armament industry and secure their income.
   *Stop the export of military goods.*   Export of military goods to the Third World and into areas of tension is to be stopped immediately.
   *Undertake Military to civilian conversion.*   In the framework of an urgent conversion program, both conversion work groups on the company level and marketable alternative products are to be promoted. During the military conversion process, we should, wherever possible, seek to dismantle existing market concentration and regional economic monostructures.
   The Greens demand a right to refuse work in armaments production for all employees in the armament industry, similar to the right to conscientious objection. Companies must provide their employees with the option of switching to a civilian job within the same company (i.e., offer an equivalent job within one year). Such a personal option would carry the issue of military orders directly into the company. Internal company debates and personal decisions would not take place under the threat of dismissal.

III. Steps toward a Democratic and Social Economy
*Distributing Work Equitably among people and between Women and Men*

*Sketch of the Problem*
   Official unemployment is climbing from peak to peak. In July 1985, 2.3 million people were registered as unemployed in the Federal Republic. Nearly

half of them were women, although their share among the employed is only 40 percent. Moreover, hidden unemployment is now at over 1.3 million people, of whom the majority are women. Apart from women, the elderly, foreigners, the handicapped, and youth are especially hard-hit by unemployment. An increasing number of people are unemployed for more than a year. As "long-term unemployed," they fall into a state of (new) poverty and often have to deal with considerable sociopsychological problems. People who still have a job also feel the effects of mass unemployment: pressure exacted by management increases, and individuals' or unions' scope for action is narrowed.

### Concepts of the Old Parties

The governing coalition and the Social Democrats aim at quantitative and qualitative economic growth by promoting investment, although labor market research has shown that this strategy against unemployment is illusionary and although a continuation of this policy of economic growth is ecologically dangerous. Instead of introducing effective measures against unemployment, they manipulate the unemployment statistics.

The governing coalition opposes all efforts to reduce working hours, especially the working week, which would provide more jobs.

### Alternative Concepts

A quick and effective reduction of mass unemployment will only be possible on the basis of a general and vigorous reduction of working time. This includes a reduction of the working week (the 35-hour week with full financial compensation to start with) as well as a reduction of overtime, qualitatively new part-time jobs, and leave options. The reduction of working time also helps overcome the gendered division of labor, as its goal is the equal participation of men and women in gainful employment as well as unpaid work such as housework and childcare. A further measure in this direction is a 50 percent quota in favor of women for all jobs and training positions. A reduction of working time and temporary leave options also help provide greater individual margins for meaningful work outside of gainful employment: housework and childcare, but also cultural, social, and political activities.

### Instruments of Rebuilding

*Collectively agreed reduction of the work week.* The reduction of the workweek is the element of labor policy that promises to trigger the most new jobs. This is one of the reasons the Greens support union demands for the introduction of the 35-hour week. In order to begin redistributing housework and childcare tasks previously undertaken primarily by women, we must aim at a reduction and redistribution of daily working time.

*Legally regulated overtime reduction.* Whether reductions of total working time will actually provide new jobs as expected depends essentially on whether employers will be able to use counterstrategies, such as increasing overtime to avoid new hirings. Accordingly, our political goal must be the drastic limitation of overtime.

*Collective and individual leave options*

*New patterns of part-time work.* In its present form, part-time work cements the gendered division of labor. Part-time work is usually offered to women, paid less well, insufficiently covered by social security, is low-skill, and without possibilities for further qualification. Nevertheless, many men and women are interested in an arrangement somewhere in between the present norm of full-time work and contemporary part-time work. The practice of part-time work by men is important, as it helps overcome the prevailing gendered division of labor. Qualitatively new forms of part-time work have to be guided by the following criteria: flexible hours; inclusion of part-time workers in collective wage agreements; and gender quotas.

*Quota systems*

—Gainful employment: In order to promote women's access to the labor market and provide them with a secure income, 50 percent of all jobs must be filled by women on all levels. As long as this level has not been reached, women of equal formal qualifications are to be given precedence in hiring.

—Affirmative-action officers and ombudswomen: In order to overcome gendered role models and prejudices, the Federal Employment Office is to undertake research and consulting. A women's commissioner will be installed in all of the Federal Employment Office's agencies. The commissioner's task is to supervise adherence to quota regulations and initiate training seminars on "gender equality" for all Federal Employment Office employees.

—Enforcement. Most probably, legal quotas will not suffice to improve the position of women in the economy. Violations must be financially sanctioned in order to enhance employers' willingness to train and employ more women. Therefore, public orders, subsidies, and loans will depend upon observance of gender quotas.

*Effects*

The reduction of working time is the decisive lever in the struggle against mass unemployment, the dismantling of workers' rights, and the gendered division of labor. A rapid introduction of the 35-hour week could provide 2.5 million new jobs, of which 1.8 million would evolve on the basis of reductions in the workweek and overtime. . . .

*Extending Workers' Rights*

### Sketch of the Problems

The industrial-relations concept of "social partnership" sweeps the contradiction between the interests of capital and labor under the carpet. Decision-making processes in corporations are still hierarchically structured, and although shop stewards are democratically elected, they have no influence on important management decisions.

But integrating workers into the overall interest of individual companies has also led to alliances between capital and labor against the environment. For this reason, the ability to protect environmental interests has to be strengthened on the level of individual companies, too.

### Alternative Concepts

The long-term goal of the Greens' economic policy is the development of grassroots democratic decision-making structures in the economy so that workers may decide what is produced, and where and how it is to be produced. In the short-term, the Greens seek to reveal the contradictions in the interests of capital, labor, and the environment and to extend workers' opportunities for realizing their social and environmental interests more effectively.

Rebuilding the economy requires decision-making competence for employees. They know best what a socially acceptable and healthy workplace should look like; their voices must be heard in the necessary restructuring. The short-term goals follow from these principles:

—Extend co-determination[5] in large corporations to full parity.

—Institutionalize environmental interests on the level of corporate co-determination without weakening the position of workers vis-à-vis capital.

—Make the Workplace Labor Relations Act offer workers a more comprehensive form of co-determination and strengthen their position at the workplace.

—Prevent a weakening of labor union power through modifying Paragraph 116 of the Law to Promote Employment; we demand a legal prohibition of lockouts.

### Instruments of Rebuilding

*A ban on informal exploitative labor markets.*   Inhumane traffic in human beings is commonplace in West Germany. Even within the framework of legally tolerated informal labor arrangements, we can observe many violations of the law. Tax and social security payments are withheld, fictitious agreements on contract work are signed, workers are declared to be subcontractors.

*Changes in the Workplace Labor Relations Act.*   The Greens suggest the following ways to improve and extend the act in the interests of workers and their representatives.

*General institutional changes.*   To strengthen workers' opportunities to participate in the formulation and enforcement of their interests, the following measures are necessary.

—Annul the stipulation binding shop stewards to "fiduciary cooperation" and other provisions that simulate a partnership between business and workers.

—In all company-related, social, and other issues, enable shop stewards to declare themselves competent and give them a right of co-determination.

—Give shop stewards a right to inspect all data collected by the company.

—Introduce equal opportunity schemes for women. These are to be initiated by the shop stewards or newly formed women's committees and must be included in work agreements.

—Freedom of conscience should not end in front of the factory gates. The Greens therefore demand a right to refuse work and a right to strike in cases where people's health is endangered of where weapons are produced.

—Win employees a full right of free expression at work.

*Co-determination with respect to production and products.*   Workers and their representatives must participate in the introduction of new technologies, production processes, products, or comparable changes in the service sector during the planning stage. This is a precondition for adequately taking into account social and ecological criteria. Social and ecological consequences must be ascertained by experts in advance. Shop councils must have the right to consult their own experts.

*Co-determination with respect to personnel and social measures.*   In the face of mass unemployment, protecting and enhancing individual workers' rights with respect to layoffs, transfers, and training, as well as strengthening the shop council in carrying out these tasks are especially important.

*Introduction of independent environmental commissioners in companies whose activities have effects on the environment. . . .*

*Co-determination in management. . . .*

*Regional co-determination. . . .*

*The Steel Crisis: Developing Democratic and Ecological Perspectives*
. . .

*Promotion of Self-Managed Projects and Workshops*
. . .

## Setting Up Regional Development Funds

### Sketch of the Problem

The Federal Republic has developed an intense regional divide, documented, for example, in varying unemployment rates: high rates in Bremen, the Ruhr Valley, the Saarland, Hamburg, Lower-Saxony, and Schleswig-Holstein; low rates in Baden-Württemberg, Hesse, and Bavaria. Industrial structural crises turn into regional crises because economic structures did not diversify soon enough. Industrial and regional policies were used as instruments of an overall growth policy aimed at promoting private investments regardless of the consequences.

### Alternative Concepts

A more sensible industrial and regional policy would, first of all, drop that regional policy has to contribute to overall economic growth. The envisaged structural transformation has to be based on specific regional-historical circumstances and developmental potentials: general product or productivity standards or international competitiveness are not adequate guidelines for a sensible regional policy.

A far-reaching decentralization of regional policies is necessary. We suggest setting up regional development funds, whose task would be to undertake research, inform, consult, and intervene. They could also help coordinate the various specialized policy fields that presently operate parallel or even in opposition to one another: economic, social and cultural, environmental, agricultural, and land-use policies.

In the formation of new economic structures, regional development organizations can also give greater prominence to the issue of democratic and humane workplaces. This will mobilize new potentials by putting an end to the present practice of providing new jobs through a reduction of labor rights.

## Democratization of the Credit Economy

### Sketch of the Problem

In 1982, the banking sector had a total turnover of 2,709 billion DM . Of this, the share of the three largest banks alone was 425 billion DM. By way of widely branched interlocking interests and credit ties, and especially by way of appointments to supervisory, administrative, and advisory boards, the banks control all relevant sectors of the West German economy. With respect to control, the *large* banks are also in the front line: they supply 40 of the banking sector's 55 representatives in the 25 biggest West German companies. This puts banks into a position where they can decide who gets to develop new technologies, which ones will be brought to market, and which sectors of the economy will shrink. They decide in favor of providing credit to the nuclear industry and refuse credit to cooperatives and self-administered businesses. In the past, the banking sector has not granted credits on the basis of a future-oriented policy; as a rule, big corporations and large-scale projects are considered worthy of credit.

Banks also decide on the provision of commercial credit to Third World countries. Enjoying a liquidity surplus in the early 1970s, banks provided generous credits without much consideration for the economic capacities and developmental framework in such borrowing countries. Since liquidity has become a worldwide problem, banks have adopted restrictive credit policies and have attempted to shift their financial burdens and risks onto public and international institutions. The high level of debt and the ensuing high rates of debt service and therefore of exports dramatically limit the amount of goods available within the indebted developing country itself. The International Monetary Fund (IMF), in which the German Federal government has a strong position, enforces this policy in the interests of the international banks. In the last several years, it has become more and more obvious that this policy of tough conditions toward export orientation has not led to a "normalization" of Third World economies. The debt crisis was not eased but only postponed. The possibility of an international bank crash, triggered by the bankruptcy of a developing country and ensuing bankruptcy of one or more credit institutions with international links, can no longer be excluded.

*Alternative concepts*

The Greens are aware that industrial society cannot be rebuilt unless credit provision is brought into line with ecological and social criteria and the financial sector is reorganized more democratically. This debate has just begun within the Greens. Clearly, the role of nonprofit sectors of the finance economy needs to be strengthened and the political-economic influence of large private banks is incompatible with a democratic economy. The consideration of ecological and social criteria when credits are to be extended also makes democratic control of banks necessary.

Because of its decentralized organizational structure, formal requirement of public accountability and an orientation to the public good, and influential position within the credit economy, the savings bank sector presents a good basis for transforming credit policies in accordance with ecological and social criteria. This basis should be used to support specific regional economic policies.

The tough IMF conditions vis-à-vis developing countries with respect to debt repayment are neither humane nor economically justifiable. Apart from the necessary interim step of a moratorium on interest payment, we need a comprehensive cancellation of foreign debts in order to provide a margin of action for domestically oriented development.

*Instruments of Rebuilding*

As first steps toward the transformation of the credit sector, the Greens advocate improving and redirecting public control:

—To better control the structure and the volume of credit, establish a system whereby a minimum reserve (exempting deposits) is coupled to the amount of credit provided. The Law on the Federal Bank offers the option of grading the minimum reserve according to local conditions and bank types. This option should be fully utilized and extended on the basis of labor market and ecological criteria.

—Separate banks and nonbanking companies through a reduction or even a prohibition of equity participation and a prohibition of personal interlinkages via board appointments.

—Forbid stock corporations to use the voting rights of shareholders.

—Make public any credits surpassing 1 percent of the balance sheet total, as well as state credits.

—A precondition for a democratic banking policy is the reduction of concentration. Absolute market shares are an inadequate criterion for antitrust measures. In order to prevent concentration, supplement antitrust laws by a criterion such as "degree to political-economic influence."

—Utilize and if necessary extend the rights of control that the Federal Authority for the Supervision of Banks has at present. This requires regular parliamentary hearings.

## IV. Steps toward Social Security and Justice

### *Rebuilding the Medical System and Emancipating Patients*

*Effects*

The Greens seek to abolish the existing "two-class medical system" (with "private patients" and "public health scheme patients"), support a solidarity-based funding of the health sector, improve the quality and diversity of medical services, provide equal access to all services, including alternative healing methods, and strengthen patients' rights. By introducing uniform statutory health insurance, the insurance payments can be reduced to below 10 percent of a person's gross income for everyone.

. . .

*Those in Need of Care have a Right to a Self-Determined Life Too*

. . .

*Effects*

The measures the Greens propose could create important preconditions for counteracting the incapacitation, isolation, and impoverishment of people in need of care. The financial aid our draft law on care would provide can financially relieve municipalities. Instead of spending public funds on the capital-intensive production of pharmaceuticals and the extension of technical treatment and services, such funds should be redirected into the labor-intensive nursing sector.

## Children Do Not Have to Be a Burden

*Alternative Concepts*

The Greens' family policy is not shaped by the concept of an ideal family and its special worthiness. Rather, its goal is to improve living conditions for children independent of the marital status and income of their parents. It also aims to overcome the gendered division of labor and put an end to the material discrimination against single parents. For this reason, benefits presently linked to marriage are to be cut. Public benefits are to be provided only to children and to those caring for them. Women and men must be given the opportunity to undertake childcare with an adequate income and without fear of losing their jobs. From a legal perspective, childcare must be given the same status as gainful employment.

The Greens' family policy is not restricted to the financial issue of equalizing the "burden" incurred through children. Rather, the Greens' suggestions for policy changes in working time, housing, infrastructure, and other areas all contribute to improving the living conditions of children and those caring for them. State parliaments and city councils should give high priority to enhancing the quality and quantity of childcare institutions. They must also give special support to all kinds of self-help childcare initiatives to counter the tendencies toward compulsory privatization of the childcare sector.

. . .

## Humane Pensions and Income for All

. . .

*Instruments of Rebuilding*

*Basic income maintenance based on need.*   Basic income has to be sufficiently high to cover minimum needs. The present system of social welfare does not meet this standard. This is why, in accordance with the demands of the German Organization of Public and Private Welfare, we advocate a

30 percent increase in social welfare. In addition, there are recurrent payments such as clothing aid, which people are entitled to but are made to beg for. Such aid should be integrated into the regular support system as well as increased by an average of 150 percent.

A needy person's income should not be tied to a work requirement. Simplifications in the new scheme (lump-sum payments rather than special means tests, abrogation of "kinship liability") will make the normal means test less discriminatory. The procedure will become more like a tax declaration. This measure could also help reduce the large number of individuals living below the poverty level because they are ashamed to apply for social welfare or do not want to encumber their children or their parents.

*Securing income for the unemployed.* People who lose their jobs should receive benefits from the Federal Employment Office not only when the legal preconditions for collecting unemployment insurance are fulfilled, but also when they are needy. This means that everyone who becomes needy because of unemployment would receive a guaranteed income from the Federal Employment Office.

—Benefits dependent upon previous unemployment insurance. Under the Kohl/Genscher government, conditions for receiving unemployment compensation or unemployment relief have gotten harder in many ways: eligibility was restricted, duration of payment was cut, and compensation rates were diminished. These burdens have to be undone. The repressive, marginalizing, and discriminatory (for women) provisions of the Law to Promote Employment pertaining to availability and reasonable employment should be abolished.

—Needs-based basic income for unemployed persons. People who are looking for a job and not receiving either compensation or relief, or people whose compensation or relief rates are lower than the level of basic income based on need, should obtain a basic income from the Federal Employment Office. People looking for jobs would thus no longer be dependent upon welfare. Here too, the question of need and the issue of how much basic income a person is eligible for must be decided exclusively on the basis of that person's prior income from gainful employment, his or her personal assets, and his or her income from social security, unemployment benefits, or other transfer payments.

*Securing income for the elderly*

—Eliminating poverty in old age: All persons who have reached the legal retirement age must be guaranteed a basic income. Additionally, they should obtain a supplement of 200 DM, which would make them eligible, on average, for a basic income of 1,200 DM including housing costs (figures for 1986). The elderly will no longer have to seek welfare and will be guaranteed a humane income above the poverty level.

—Independent maintenance for women: Because they have often made no payments or very low payments into the social security and pension funds, women constitute by far the largest group of those living below the poverty line. In order to redress this cause of poverty, payments into such funds by married couples should be imputed equally to each spouse ("payment splitting"), so that the spouse without gainful employment or with only a low income from such employment also becomes eligible for a pension. As a first step, persons undertaking childcare should have their pension insurance payments reimbursed by the federal government for two years per child.

## V. SUMMARY

### What Will the Umbau Change?

#### Reduced Dependency on the World Market

Even powerful industrial nations such as the FRG are affected by the instabilities of the world market and the loss of national scope for action following from global economic integration, though such consequences are not as severe as those affecting most developing countries. Increasing balance-of-trade deficits, the concomitant massive job losses, growing capital export, unavoidable currency devaluation, and inflation have reached unacceptable levels even in the medium term.

Despite this scenario, it would be wrong to conclude that no leeway for domestic economic policy exists. The FRG's present extreme orientation toward and dependency on the world market must not be regarded as "natural"; rather, it is the result of a decades-long policy of promoting and subsidizing the export sector (exchange rate policy, credits backed by the federal government, development of an export infrastructure, etc.). By changing the direction of development as spelled out in this program, dependency could be reduced considerably. This could initiate a foreign economic policy based on a higher level of solidarity with the Third World:

—Building a recycling economy could significantly reduce raw material imports.

—A gasoline tax based on the "polluter pays" principle and the expansion of the public transport system would drastically reduce oil imports, which made up about 15 percent of total imports in 1985.

—An ecological agricultural policy would reduce fodder imports and surplus foodstuff exports to zero in the medium term.

—The government's research and development policy should concentrate on providing solutions to central environmental problems, creating humane working conditions, and the critical evaluation of new technologies (instead of promoting their use regardless of the consequences). This means that a decisive incentive for the present world-market orientation would disappear in favor of an orientation based more on people's needs.

—Reducing imports will increase the purchasing power for domestic products and strengthen the domestic market. If exports and imports are reduced simultaneously, negative effects for the job market will not be forthcoming, contrary to the claims of some world-market ideologues.

These would be first steps toward reducing dependency on the world market. A coordinated policy within the EC could support this policy.

*Greater Third World Independence*

This is not the place to present the Greens' development policies. But we do want to make clear that our economic rebuilding program is not to be paid for by the Third World. Development policies and foreign economic policies must not contradict each other.

The cancellation of Third World countries' debt, which we demand, and the measures set out in this rebuilding program complement each other:

—We demand an end to fodder imports, because we reject mass production of animals. The cancellation of debt will put Third World countries in a position to end fodder production and use land resources to produce domestic foodstuffs.

—We demand an end to arms exports. They mainly serve the profit interests of the West German weapons Mafia and the stabilization of corrupt Third World regimes.

—We demand a radical limitation and selective prohibition of exports of chemical and pharmaceutical products, or, at the very least, that limitations that are effective on the West German market be applied to exports to developing countries as well. The annual death toll of about 50,000 people through the use of pesticides and expensive, unnecessary, or even harmful pharmaceuticals benefits only profiteers.

—We demand steps toward the democratization and decentralization of multinational corporations. This would also reduce their domination of Third World markets. Strengthening workers' rights and reducing export subsidies are only the first steps in this direction.

Even the former chancellor Helmut Schmidt (SPD) has become concerned about the degree of "our" dependency on exports! A rebuilding that enhances our own economic stability and makes us less vulnerable to the instabilities in the world market is good for the Third World, too. The Umbau program is a domestic supplement to the structural changes that are necessary in the context of the world economy. Meaningful development projects in the Third World can be carried out only on the basis of such changes.

### What Opportunities for Action Are Being Used?

In the face of the immense need for ecological and social action, this program advocates using the full range of instruments of intervention the state has at its disposal. This range of possible instruments offers different measures for different tasks.

### Conditions, Orders, and Prohibitions

In life-threatening situations, we cannot employ an instrument whose effect is uncertain; here the state has to issue orders and prohibitions with immediate effect. State intervention that sets standards, threshold values, and conditions should be improved with respect to ecological issues.

Introducing obligatory environmental impact statements and technological impact studies for new and potentially dangerous products and production techniques will make the effects of business activity more transparent, and thereby create a precondition for social change.

### Extension of Civil Rights

Citizens' rights vis-à-vis private corporations and bureaucracies are strengthened considerably by the Umbau program: consumer information and safety, promotion of consumer initiatives, information rights for concerned citizens and for environmental organizations (through public hearings, right to inspect records and files, etc.), as well as rights to object and take legal action for environmental organizations.

### Ecologically Based Costs and Benefits

Financial incentives can have a greater ecological and economic effect than orders or prohibitions when it comes to enforcing a specific economic behavior. The financial incentives suggested in this program take the form of special levies. Such levies have the advantage that they can be raised at the actual point of origin of ecological destruction. They provide incentives to reduce pollution at the point of emission. Special levies also establish a clear-cut legal relationship between the income obtained through the levy and its expenditure for environmental projects. Unlike taxes, levies thus provide a greater degree of transparency, allow more direct control, and enable greater popular participation with respect to public expenditure.

Raising levies sets incentives for developing environmentally compatible technologies and products and stands in contrast to the present orientation toward "technological state of the art," which leads corporations to strive to provide evidence that more stringent environmental standards cannot be fulfilled. The goal is no longer end-of-pipe technology, but emission-free production technologies.

*State-Induced Demand and Economic Activity*

As a direct producer of goods and services as well as a client of private enterprise, the state wields far-reaching influence on production and demand. This opens up many possibilities for an ecological, social, and democratic politics. These too are being used as instruments for the Umbau program. The state should play a vanguard role with respect to the introduction of environmentally compatible technologies and products and should contribute to the ecologization of the economy by a concerted research policy. Moreover, the introduction of citizens' participation and the decentralization of federal and state responsibilities to the municipal level will make economic decision-making processes more democratic.

## How Can the Umbau Be Financed?

There are three ways to fund the Umbau program: cutting ecologically damaging and/or economically wasteful expenditures; introducing earmarked special levies; and raising direct and indirect taxes. A fourth possibility, increasing public debt, is not regarded as necessary, although we do not reject it in principle.

Specific state projects involving destruction and waste have often fostered the emergence of grassroots movements, which have a close relationship to the Green party. Examples of such governmental projects are nuclear facilities (fast breeder, high-temperature reactor, and reprocessing plant), some road and canal construction projects, and military projects.

Money can be saved in other areas as well. The price of pharmaceuticals, for instance, is about 25 percent higher in the FRG than in other European countries, and the pharmaceutical industry employs about 15,000 people in order to maintain the excessive consumption of pills.

A mere cutback in defense expenditure (15 billion DM annually in a four-year period), a limitation of the presently horrific profits of the pharmaceutical industry and of physicians (17 billion DM), and stopping highway construction (5 billion DM) would save 37 billion DM a year, which could be used for other purposes. Implementing the Umbau program would procure 20 billion DM from special levies, although this income would depend on the degree of innovative behavior corporations and households display with respect to alternatives.

The special levies would somewhat reduce present levels of business investment and profits. They could also lead to a marginal reduction of consumer spending. In order to finance the rebuilding measures, this program also advocates selective tax increases. For ecological reasons and in order to enforce the "polluter pays" principle, the gasoline tax has to be increased and a tax on packaging will have to be introduced. Despite these measures, individual households will not experience higher costs if members take advantage of the more extensive and cheaper public transport services that are envisaged.

Charging public income and expenditures will shift financial responsibility between the different levels of government. In the sector of social policy, measures to end poverty and secure a more adequate health care system will subject the federal budget to a greater burden, while municipal budgets will be relieved. A large part of their funds will no longer be tied up by federal laws and will thus become available for ecological transformation. This shift in responsibility will give municipalities a greater margin to decide how to use their funds, particularly for measures whose enforcement can be handled more effectively by the local community than by the state or federal government.

## Mothers' Manifesto (1987)

> For the background and status of these documents, see the introduction.

### I.

It is time for a new women's movement, a movement that represents the reality, the desires, and the hopes of mothers with children with as much determination as it represents the interests of women without children.

The time has come for the majority of women, namely mothers, to represent themselves.

The time is over when other women or even men prescribe to mothers how they should plan their lives, how they should feel about their children and their men, and what attitude they should have towards their job, career, household, society, and childcare.

It is time for the women's movement, the Greens, the left, and conservative forces to begin to deal with the fact that mothers want to fundamentally change the structures of family, neighborhood, jobs, the public sphere and politics. . . .

It is time to grasp that, outside their homes, mothers do not want to be mere workers, wives, and politicians, but also demand room for their children. A society endeavoring to allow children to be taken by the hand requires quite a fundamental challenge to the existing order. Just like the young women in the women's movement 20 years ago, mothers are busy examining everything anew and thereby discovering completely new dimensions.

They are less and less willing to accept the fact that, in professional life, scheduling, meetings, in every form of public event, mothers have no right to participate, or that they are themselves responsible for organizing the preconditions for their participation. They want to take an active part in public life, without paying the high price that many progressive (male and female) full-time politicians or backward "family ideologues" want to force upon them.

What is on the agenda is nothing more or less than the creation of a mother-friendly, child-friendly public sphere, a public "living room," a neighborhood children's room, an overcoming of the narrow family boundaries without having the logic of the pub, the company, or traditional politics pervade all life. . . .

To demand room for mothers and children does not imply a weakening or division of the women's movement. It also does not imply the exclusion of men. On the contrary: only strong and zestful mothers and self-confident children, who feel that there is room for them, can be partners for women who have decided for a life without children and for men who are fathers or not. "Black is beautiful" was the initial slogan of the black movement in the United States; "small is beautiful" strengthened the ecological movement; "motherhood is beautiful" could become the basis for a new self-confidence among mothers, and this could be the breakthrough for a comeback of mothers and children within society. . . .

## II.

United by this strong but also impatient feeling, a congress of about 500 mothers and 200 children took place in Bonn-Beuel on November 22–23, 1986. The Greens had committed themselves to support the congress technically and financially and thus made possible what is decisive for a new women's politics: openness to women from different areas and with different experiences, without trying to bring them into line with party goals. . . . An audience of progressive journalists and critical women accompanied the bustle of this new form of public activity, with some unease and some fear and frustration. It was not only the set up, with interruptions from children's racket, or the occasional screaming baby, not only the fact that some mothers began their statements by pointing out unashamedly that they had one, two, yes four children, or handicapped children, that led to this irritation. Underneath this was the deep and presently unresolvable tension between different lifestyles, the bewilderment of career women with and without children over the expression of a very different mood:

We are, in our current life phase and in our identity, primarily mothers, and glad to be mothers—but we demand conditions so we may live this identity without marginalization, degradation, and constant insecurity. Precisely by living a mother's life, we are sensitized to the needs of the weak as well as the possibilities of transforming many social areas and processes, and we have the competence to develop adequate models of change. Our type of knowledge is absent from this world of antimother, antichildren, and antinature perspectives. We advocate the return of this knowledge into the culture of experts—be they male or female.

The skeptical observers responsible for documenting this congress to the outside world, spoke of mother ideology, of "right-wing" tendencies, of superficial solutions without real perspective. This shows how a narrow concept of politics has implanted itself in the heads of many women, too. . . .

In its struggle with the traditional concept of politics, the women's movement has provided many impulses for dealing in a new way with questions of the private and the public, of power and powerlessness. Today, however, it is clear that mothers, as the largest group among women, have a whole set of quite different impulses, rhythms, organizational forms, and questions reflecting their particular needs. The task we have to tackle in the coming years will be to leave the ghetto of nonmothers as well as the aquarium of career women and begin a new debate about an extended, ecological, and future-oriented concept of emancipation. Reducing women's perspectives to the question of quotas and reproductive rights can never address these dimensions. It is equally inadequate to measure a politics for mothers only by the criterion of overcoming the gendered division of labor. . . . In the end, we have to develop an idea of emancipation that integrates the contents of traditional women's work (i.e., caring for people, acting on behalf of social relations, questioning so-called "objective constraints") as legitimate values and acknowledges them socially, politically, and financially. . . .

## III.

Below, we list some of the goals that came up again and again in various working groups. These can serve as a starting point for further developments:

1. Basic demands underlined with black ink: We want everything! We mothers want to influence and shape developments! We want to participate in decision-making—in all areas!

2. To do this, we need adequate and independent financial compensation for the caring work we undertake now, and for later. In order to obtain

a minimum pension under the present rules, a woman would have to give birth to and raise 35 children! . . . The form this pay should take—minimum income, pension, childcare benefit, or other financial provision—will need to be discussed in the coming years. . . .

3. We also need viable infrastructure for mothers who are temporarily or in the long term primarily mothers and housewives! We need childcare services that are tailored to the needs of all children and women who want to use them, at every streetcorner, in department stores, public offices, and parliaments. These must be open according to our own time schedules. . . .

4. This infrastructure must include neighborhood centers, mothers' centers (open all day), cafeterias, shared meals, and many other things. The goal is to provide as many points of contact as possible where mothers can come together and meet each other in the diversity of their lifestyles and experiences, and where they can support each other with their different skills. . . .

5. We need a working world characterized by a completely new openness. The emerging economic problems should be used to drastically reduce working hours, and also to initiate comprehensive experiments with high-skill part-time work and flexible working hours. We need options to re-enter all jobs and—as a special priority—the lifting of all age restrictions for admission to higher education and occupational training programs. . . .

6. In working life we have grave doubts about a quota system favoring women without children over mothers. We demand additional childcare services at work or nearby, suitable working hours, and adequate wages for typical female jobs. In particular, if quota rules are to be applied at all, we demand quotas that apply to the proportion of mothers within the total group of women: for example, 50–70 percent of all skilled female jobs for mothers! We have to counter the division between women easily exploited by capital and mothers by a determined strategy of creative jobs for mothers. The same goes for the sphere of politics! . . .

7. With respect to political life, the sphere of big words and programs, particularly in the Green Party, this means that work must finally be adapted to mothers' needs! It means drastic working time reductions for full-time politicians, job sharing, and sharing of political mandates, for instance, in the Green Party's federal executive committee. Women's and mother's issues are to have a vanguard and not a straggler position. No votes or resolutions after 11 p.m., an end to the monopoly of opinion based on university student culture, assumption of childcare costs by the public on all levels, including the local. . . .

8. We demand the right for women to fulfill their wishes for children, and not only the right to abortion. Industrial societies render it more and more difficult to lead a life that has anything to do with nature, spontaneous life rhythms, and long-term responsibility. Men increasingly extend their pu-

berty phase to the age of 45 and refuse to take responsibility, together with a woman, for a child. In such a society, it is urgently necessary that women's desire to have children be taken seriously and accepted, rather than cruelly discriminated against, as is increasingly the case. . . .

9. As we are the ones who will in later years take over a large part (over 80 percent) of caring for the elderly, it is also urgently necessary that we be financially supported for this and receive not only suitable living spaces, but also job guarantees and the option to re-enter the working world. . . .

11. We want to cooperate sensibly and fairly with men, the fathers of our children, whether we live together or separately. But we know how difficult it is to create a successful balance in this area. Many lesbians and women without children accuse us of not being zealous enough in forcing fathers to be responsible for their duties. We reject this accusation and turn it around: *we* are the ones that lead daily battles about male support, and we are the ones who tenaciously call on them to contribute their share. . . .

## IV.

A long list of further issues surfaced in the congress's working groups as well as in conversations among mothers. However, we are presently not concerned with presenting a comprehensive catalogue of demands. The point is to give mothers' imaginations free reign so that a common theory and practice may emerge, echoing the experiences of the nearly a hundred initiatives of the mothers' centers' movement and many other groups. . . .

At the present time this means that the Greens should support the regional and nationwide self-organization of mothers through workshops, congresses, and publications as much as they support other important groups. An ongoing Green federal working group on mothers would be a good organizational focusing point for this perspective; opening such a group to non–party members would be a decisive precondition. . . .

## Statement on the Mothers' Manifesto by the Greens' Federal Working Group on Women (1987)

### I.

The publication of the Mothers' Manifesto provoked an intense debate among Green women. Some spontaneously supported the manifesto; others vehemently rejected it.

Many of the problems described in the manifesto are undoubtedly true: for example, the low status of "typically female" work at home and on the job, or the massive discrimination against women with children in the job market. Some of the ideas developed in the manifesto are definitely to be supported.

We also agree that not only the working world but the whole public sphere is structured in a way that makes participation while taking care of children, the sick or the elderly very difficult. It is also correct that a general and broad debate on future and contemporary lifestyles is still needed within the Greens.

Up to now, the consensus among the Greens has been that, unlike other parties, we consider the family to be only one of a variety of legitimate lifestyles worthy of support. After all, the critique of the nuclear family's repressive structures has been a starting point of the new women's movement. Emerging from this perception was the attempt to organize childcare, housework, and living together in a way that differed from that of the traditional nuclear family. . . .

As it is an immense problem for many women to be without jobs or to have access only to unskilled and precarious jobs, and because most women therefore lack the preconditions for a self-determined and independent life, we have demanded quotas for all jobs. Even if the quota principle cannot cover all areas of female reality—is there a single demand that could do this?—for us, it is an essential precondition for an independent life. Whether we like it or not; financial independence for women was and is the linch pin of self-determination.

Of course, quotas by themselves do not alter the present nature of employment, or change antiwomen and antichildren conditions. What we need are ways to orient the working world toward the requirements of the so-called private sphere. This means, for instance, kindergartens and childcare centers in the vicinity of workplaces and working time arrangements that allow men and women to live a life with children. . . .

Equal representation of women in all areas and on all levels of the labor market can surely be no guarantee for such a change, but without female participation, nothing will change at all. . . .

This is why we demand that appropriately qualified women be hired until they fill at least 50 percent of all positions in all areas and on all levels. Since many problems of women with children will not be resolved with this measure, we have presented a number of demands in the last several years that aim to make a life with children easier.

*The Greens demand:*
*—Quotas for all training and employment positions: that is, preferential hiring of women in all areas and on all levels until a 50 percent quota has been reached in all areas in which women have been underrepresented in the past*

—*Radical reduction of daily working time, and full wage compensation for low- and middle-income groups*

—*Legally binding minimum wage above the poverty line*

—*Equal wages for work of equal value*

—*A system of social security and health insurance that includes housewives and women dependent upon "precarious jobs"*

—*Reservation of at least 50 percent of all training positions for women and girls*

—*Abolition of age restrictions for women with regard to training stipends, hiring, and promotion*

—*Further education and training programs for women re-entering the workforce*

—*Childcare benefits and job guarantees for people undertaking childcare in the early years*

—*Sufficient kindergartens and child daycare institutions and their qualitative improvement*

—*Financing for daycare fathers or mothers*

—*Paid leave for the full duration of a child's illness.*

*The Greens advocate:*

—*Freedom of choice with regard to people's lifestyle. All life-styles are worthy of protection, not only married life and family life.*

—*The abolition of "spouse splitting" (i.e., unequal tax imputation for married couples) because this privileges the type of marriage where the housewife stays at home. Tax and social laws must be* neutral *with respect to existing lifestyles.*

(Excerpts from "Reveal Your True Color—The Green Party's Program for the 1987 Federal Election")

*Paragraph 9, Measures to Further the Compatibility of Labor Market and Family Work*

1. In order to compensate for the fact that employees usually perform unpaid work at home and in the family in addition to their job, employers must make arrangements to guarantee the compatibility of their employees' paid work and their family work.

2. For this purpose, employers must draw up plans to secure

—*Daily working time adapted to the needs of employees with children*

—*A reduction in working time of at least four hours a week for family reasons*

—*Eligibility of employees to apply for a maximum reduction of 20 working hours a week for family reasons on all levels of the company or the office while simultaneously guaranteeing their full-time job.*

(Excerpt from Antidiscrimination Law, Article 2, Quota Law)

These demands are surely not sufficient, and we will need to have many more discussions before we can implement improved conditions for a life with children. We support some of the demands formulated in the Mothers' Manifesto, such as, for instance, the demand for cafeterias and childcare places everywhere; the demand for mothers' centers, however, is problematic in our view.

## II.

While we have a lot in common with the singers of the Mothers' Manifesto on the level of concrete demands, there is no overlooking the fact that we can neither support the central tenets of their concept for a future society or their notion of womanhood.

This is not a question of which concept is more radical or which one holds the greater potential for change.

Both the Mothers' Manifesto and the Greens' women's program advocate a mixture of long-term utopian goals as well as short-term demands that can be implemented immediately. We are just as far away from the abolition of the gendered division of labor as we are from a "society which takes children by the hand" (Mothers' Manifesto). Both goals confront existing social structures and deep-seated male values that have been internalized for centuries.

The signers of the Mothers' Manifesto consider their demands to be more realistic than those put forward in the Greens' women's program. We doubt this. We do not see why, on the one hand, a search for "partnership solutions in the private sphere" is considered to be "a phony social perspective" (Mothers' Manifesto), while, on the other hand, the hope that men will one day "take an interest" in participating in a life with children is considered to be more realistic.

The mothers' centers advocated in the Mothers' Manifesto can surely be more easily implemented than quotas in all areas of society. But they are "more realistic" only because they fit into the political landscape better. . . . The Greens' demands for women, on the other hand, may be more difficult to realize (e.g., reductions in working time). However, they are not harder to realize because they are not feasible, but because they do not correspond to existing power structures and to the goals of conservative governmental policy. . . .

As a long-term perspective, our goal of abolishing the gendered division of labor may seem a little worn out by now; but, for us, it still represents an essential piece of utopia. Everyone, men and women, should have the opportunity to earn a living and hence remain free of dependence upon others. Men and women should have enough time to care for children and/or the elderly; this is why we need a radical reduction in daily working time. . . .

We do not consider ourselves to be better, more peaceful, more social, and more humane people. . . . Today, women are still the ones who raise the next generation of little machos and humble, harmony-seeking girls. And it is no secret that motherly love—especially if it becomes a person's only purpose in life—can also be repressive and choking for children.

We regard qualities that are considered to be female, such as empathy, the willingness to adapt time schedules to human needs, to care for the elderly, the ill, and for children, or the ability to show consideration for the weak, to name only a few, as vital and absolutely essential in social intercourse. This is why everyone, men and women, should have these qualities.

But what we reject is the general, uncritical upgrading of motherliness. Alongside the positive aspects many people associate with motherliness, we cannot overlook the fact that for women, motherliness has always meant being determined by motherhood, sacrificing oneself and accepting society's division of roles. Motherliness was never a strictly positive attribute, since it was always simultaneously the term for women's traditional role. . . .

### III.

The constant reference to child*less* women, to "career women," and to "nonmothers" is not only defamatory (because it characterizes women without children as deficient); it also obscures the actual lines of conflict and exploitative conditions in our society.

Although it is undoubtedly the case that women with small children have a much harder position in the labor market than those without children or with older children, this is not the fault of women without children, since they are not usurping the jobs of women with small children. The low labor-market value of mothers still stems from the fact that employers consider them to be a high "risk" and that economists can view necessary childcare work only as raising the wage costs. And it is precisely this brutal calculation that triggers many women's decision against children. . . .

This either-or decision (which men do no have to face) can be extremely ambivalent and painful. Women without children must carry this burden, which is the other side of women's coin. None of this, surprisingly, is recognized by the signers of the manifesto. . . .

IV.

While we deem it important that women with children, who suffer so acutely under the prevailing conditions, speak out self-confidently, we also see that, aside from this common experience, there are massive differences affecting women's opportunities: a socially secure mother has more leeway than a childless woman on welfare, working mothers often have more social contacts than jobless mothers, although those with jobs are then often encumbered with a double burden. And a mother with a well-paying job who can afford a nanny has a whole different set of options.

This is why we object to speaking of mothers *in general* or to dividing women into two groups, "mothers" and "nonmothers/career women," and thereby defaming them. The Mothers' Manifesto has this effect simply by labeling women who, for whatever reason, do not have children, as deficient beings, namely "nonmothers" (by the way, what happened to the fathers and nonfathers?). Those who, as mothers have jobs are immediately branded, "career women." In view of the desire and also the need of many women—with or without children—to have jobs, and in view of the continual conservative attack on working women ("double-income"), we cannot understand why the Greens should create this additional stigma. . . .

Only if one refuses to see employment as women's self-evident right, only if one does not recognize that this society is characterized by enormous social differences that determine women's opportunities, and only if one overlooks the fact that most women in this society are miles away from what is considered to be a "career"—only then might one use such terminology.

We regret that the Mothers' Manifesto associates the legitimate concerns of mothers with a notion of womanhood that we have struggled against for years.

### "Freedom with Security: 16 Theses on Green Legal and Domestic Policy" (1989)

The following theses were developed by the Working Group for Law and Domestic Policy in the Green Federal Parliamentary Group and published in the fall of 1989. The theses reflect political tendencies of the second half of the 1980s, which saw right radical election lists (the "Republicans") succeed in waging xenophobic campaigns against foreign or "guest" workers living and working in Germany. In this document the Greens are attempting to detach the concept of "security" from sensationalist images of evil or foreign elements in society, such as "foreigners," "hostage-takers," "terrorists," "red-green chaos," and floods of other kinds. That they seek to redefine "security" in Green terms, however, reflects the emergent discourse of "risks" in the left, the new social movements, and the Greens.[6] Further, these theses are meant to offer a first statement of Green legal principles, and—given their initiation by the realist-dominated Bundestag group—reflect the increasing state-centeredness of the Greens.

The basic principle of the party since its founding—a critique of the domination of individual and community by state and capitalist market logic—underlies the legal perspective offered here. The theses, however, also address a central contradiction present in the party from its founding—namely, that the Greens are both inheritors of the antistatist, communitarian perspective of the new social movements and advocates of deploying the state for stronger regulation of industry and capital as part of a transition to an ecological society. Liberal critics were quick to point this contradiction out.[7]

While Social Democrats noted sharp reformist tendencies in the theses (such as acceptance of conditions and de facto quotas for the admission of nonpolitical refugees, and acceptance of the sole right of the state to use force in society), conservatives reacted with more vehemence than ever. The idea that the Greens would transfer movement demands into juridical terms hit a raw nerve. The Christian Democratic interior minister, Wolfgang Schäuble, claimed that the execution of such principles would make "chaos a program" and "our democracy defenseless in the face of enemies." In particular, the Greens' call for the abolition of special privileges for German civil servants (*Berufsbeamtentum*), while following "populist trends," would in fact eliminate constitutional administration.[8] The jurist and former defense minister Rupert Scholz argued that demanding a franchise at federal and state level for foreigners meant that the "principle of national identity of a homogeneous legal community" did not exist for the Greens. Hence they stand not for "integration" but for the dissolution and disintegration of the German state.[9]

The document is presented here in abridged form.

Nobody can live in a situation of constant insecurity. Striving for social security is thus a legitimate need of citizens that has to be respected by the polity. But while the population is left alone with a fear of unemployment and threats to their survival, of poisoned environment and foodstuffs, or of technical catastrophes, the state intensifies the "security supply." The state displays ostensible strength and power to act. It collects comprehensive information about its citizens in all areas of life. And it even defines its citizens as objects of suspicion and threat by curbing their rights to self-determination or assembly or other basic democratic rights.

Thus, the present situation is characterized simultaneously by a deep-seated feeling of insecurity among the citizenry and by extensive security measures on the part of the state, which do not, however, lead to more life security or less existential fear.

When the Greens speak of a different kind of security logic, we do not promise a completely secure society, one that is free of risks. *Our question is: What kind of risks does a society think it can handle, what kind of security is necessary, for whom and for what?*

## Thesis 1: Strengthening Individuality, Promoting Solidarity

No law can give or replace the courage to stand up for one's beliefs. The capacity for individuality and emancipation is not only gained by the citizens themselves, but requires social and political conditions. Human rights always have a social dimension.

Freedom is the optimal opportunity to meet individuals' and groups' needs in society while simultaneously respecting the freedom of others. State intervention has to be pushed back wherever it threatens individuals in their personal sphere. Intervention by democratic agencies should be promoted wherever power structures exist that are not democratically legitimized. In this process, the state's activities must always remain judicious and control-lable. We demand priority for the principle of self-determination.

*For citizens to take advantage of their basic rights, they must be able to "afford" political engagement. Their material existence must be secured so that there is room for social and political engagement.* An equitable redistribution of work and an adequate minimum income for all unemployed persons would help bring about such a situation.

## Thesis 2: Realizing the Protection of Privacy

The development of data collection and processing by the private sector and the state has summoned up the spector of the "transparent person." Every citizen has the right to protect his or her personal rights and private domain against state or other social interventions. This includes a *right to seclusion* that no one can forgo without becoming a calculable object to be registered and *stored mercilessly in memory banks* at any time. The Greens advocate subjecting all legislative procedures in parliament not only to a cost estimation but also to an *examination designed to ascertain whether data compilation was undertaken sparingly.* Laws would have to be formulated in such a way as not to restrict the basic right of informational self-determination through extensive data surveys.

## THESIS 3: A TRANSPARENT STATE INSTEAD OF TRANSPARENT CITIZENS AS A PRECONDITION FOR DEMOCRACY

If citizens are to transform themselves from objects of state planning to subjects of political action, the prevailing principle that state action usually takes place in secrecy has to be overcome. It has to be superseded by the *principle of the transparent state*, which is obliged to be public in all areas and can only be exempt from this rule in a few special cases that are narrowly defined and justified.

As a first step, the right to inspect environmental records and files must be enforced. This is a precondition for the efficacy of other rights, such as environmental organizations' rights to initiate legal action.

## THESIS 4: DEMOCRATIC STRUGGLES WITHOUT A FIXATION ON THE STATE

Democracy is not a condition but a method for designing society. It requires an openness to change on the part of the state and the social order. A radical-democratic politics requires an *open discourse* about all imaginable political alternatives, even if they seem far-fetched. If we leave it up to the state and its agencies to define the boundaries of what can be debated, if we allow certain opinions to be disqualified and pushed into a "forbidden sphere" without engaging in a debate about them, we are attempting to secure democracy with antidemocratic means. The present practice of the so-called Federal Office for the Protection of the Constitution has hindered democracy more than it has furthered it.

Dispute and debate between diverging opinions is a better alternative to the "Federal Office for the Protection of the Constitution," which should be dissolved.

## THESIS 5: IN CASE OF DOUBT, SUPPORT DIRECT DEMOCRACY

Since the founding of the Federal Republic, we have had a situation in which Bonn rules and the rest of the country looks on. The parties are not only contributing to the process of articulating political interests, but have secured monopolistic position in the process of political opinion making. Important decisions such as rearmament, nuclear armament, deployment of cruise missiles, and the nuclear program have been taken not only without but against the will of a clear majority. At times, more people have been active in citizen initiatives than in political parties. These people want to be heard and to co-determine decisions. As a fundamental pillar of Green politics, "grassroots democracy" implies the duty to make sure that decisions on important issues are made by those affected by them.

According to the Federal Republic's Basic Law, state power is exercised in "elections and voting." The prevailing interpretation of the Basic Law has so far prevented the granting of direct decision-making and voting rights to the citizens. . . . The Greens demand that we supplement representative democracy by extending direct-democratic rights. A first step would be the introduction of the right to petition for a referendum as well as the introduction of plebiscites on the federal level.

### Thesis 6: Democratic Control of the Executive

Important economic decisions are taken outside of parliament and thus evade democratic control to varying degrees. This is particularly obvious in the sphere of technology—in telecommunication or bio-engineering.

In contrast to other countries, parliamentary powers to control the executive are extremely limited. As long as the executive takes important decisions without the parliament, as long as parliament is reduced to the role of providing party assent for the governing majority, we must at least demand that parliament become a stage for public debate.

The trend toward shifting political decision making to the EC level further disempowers the Bundestag. It must be countered by enhancing national sovereignty in the form of, for instance, *provisos against the ratification of EC decisions* and EC guidelines.

### Thesis 7: Democratizing Parliament

Beyond their constitutional duty of helping to form the political will, political practice and legislation have given political parties a far-reaching monopoly in determining the composition of parliamentary groups and their decisions.

The Greens advocate a *reform of voting laws* in order to provide citizens with greater influence over the composition and sequence of parties' electoral lists, as is already practiced on the municipal level in several states.

Through a *corrective adjustment of the Law Concerning the Financing of Political Parties,* the practice of donations and the influence of industry and lobby organizations must be pushed back. On their ballot, voters should also be able to award a *"citizens' bonus"* to a choice group, party, or citizen initiative, and thus decide which organization should be granted financial assistance for its political work.

### THESIS 9: REFORMING THE ADMINISTRATION

For large sections of the administration, the founding of the Federal Republic in 1949 meant merely a continuation of existing practices within a new constitutional framework.

After 40 years the civil service apparatus[10] has become, under the influence of the political parties, an area of monopolized privileges outside popular control. Social Democracy's welfare state concepts and the conservatives' brand of authoritarian state administration have both promoted the expansion of civil servant privileges and systematized the intimidation of citizens all the way to their degradation into mere objects of planning and administration.

The *abolition of the civil service* and the "special duty of loyalty" is a first step toward a democratic transformation of the administration. Further steps are flattening hierarchy by introducing a collegial form of decision making and putting civil servants on an equal legal footing with public service employees.

A modern administration also needs to discard unnecessary ordinances and to simplify and humanize the language it uses.

### THESIS 10: BASIC RIGHTS HAVE TO BE APPLICABLE TO EVERYONE

Administration and legislation in the area of domestic policy so far have always viewed themselves as instruments for regulating and channelling tensions within society. Particularly in times of crisis and in times of social change and a loss of identity, this administration and legislation have accepted discrimination against minorities and thus gone along with the unreflected need for self-assurance through disassociation held by parts of the population. Foreigners, asylum-seekers, and so-called fringe groups become victims of intensified social control and of the reduction of social services. Finally, they become scapegoats for people's insecure situation and for their fears of competition and pauperization.

Hostility to foreigners and a revival of right-wing radicalism are symptoms of this politics. They consolidate marginalization, they weaken the democratic substance, and they exhaust the capacities for integration and consensus. The liberal quality of a society, however, shows up in the way it treats its minorities and in the rights and liberties it concedes to them.

The aim of the Greens' domestic policy is to direct societal action toward the acceptance of national, ethnic, religious, and *Weltanschauung*-related, sexual, or cultural differences, and strengthening such minorities in their rights.

## THESIS 11: KEEPING THE RIGHT TO ASYLUM INVIOLABLE, STRUCTURING IMMIGRATION BY POLITICAL MEANS

Besides the right of family members to rejoin and the right of immigrants of German origin, the right of asylum is at present the only means available for non-EC citizens to enter the Federal Republic for residential purposes.[11] But we actually became an immigration country long ago for economic reasons, although this has not effected corresponding legal consequences.

The right of asylum is one of the most valuable provisions of the constitution and is inextricably bound to German history. This provision must be defended, extended, and realized according to its original intention, without any restrictions.

We must provide humane and legally adequate conditions for those immigrants and asylum-seekers who have come to us in the past. This entails a *right to residential status for asylum-seekers* who fear persecution in their home country and have come to West Germany on the basis of the Geneva Convention on Refugees. It also includes the option of dual citizenship, an independent right to residential status for women, and the right to vote on the municipal, state, and federal levels for all those foreigners who wish to continue living and working here.

## THESIS 12: RIGHTS FOR FUTURE GENERATIONS

Within the prevailing representative system, even decisions that were taken in a formally lawful manner are recurrently confronted with limits to their enforcement that cannot be overcome even with repressive instruments.

One reason for this lies in the ecological and technical incalculability of the risks that respective regional or social minorities have to bear. Such groups must be protected by special forms of participation and veto rights. Decisions that cannot be revised in the future are fundamentally undemocratic.

We need therefore a societal debate about *new democratic decision-making processes* that can prevent minority action against majority interests or against the interests of future generations.

### THESIS 13: PUBLIC MEDIA AS A PRECONDITION FOR DEMOCRACY

Democratic decision-making processes require a critical public. The private organization of the press has led to a shrinking of the number of independent newspaper editors and a concentration of power in a few corporations. The influence of such private media corporations as well as of the advertising industry is beginning to be felt in radio broadcasting too.

As the importance of the media incorporated under public law has grown as a public sphere and as an instrument of governmental control, leading positions in the media have increasingly been filled according to party preference—usually by the SPD and the CDU.

The function and *composition of the Public Radio Broadcast Councils* have to be questioned more strongly in public debate. Privatizing radio broadcasting and expanding the number of stations are not solutions, since such measures only replace party influence with one-sided profit interests.

*Strengthening the independence of journalists* in their role as the "fourth branch" of the polity requires an "inner freedom of the press"—the right to publish reports against the interest of the publisher, the Broadcast Council, or the broadcasting director, if this appears to be necessary in the public interest.

*Decentralization* and enhancing citizens' influence in the form of direct participation or autonomous local radio projects are steps toward improving media independence.

A deconcentration of media corporations is necessary in order to secure freedom of opinion and freedom of information in the long run.

### THESIS 14: FUNCTION AND LIMITS OF CRIMINAL LAW

Deterrence and atonement as punishment aims are archaic and alien to a modern criminal law policy. On the other hand, rehabilitation and the prevention of recidivism need to be strengthened.

*Criminal laws pertaining to political offences,* such as Paragraphs 129a and 130a of the Penal Code (laws that punish political convictions or opinions) damage the substance of a free society. They are as superfluous and inhumane as the special conditions of imprisonment for politically motivated offenders.

Extending *parole* provisions, *reducing life sentences* to 15 years, and *shortening sentences* for nonviolent property offenses are important steps toward greater efficacy in criminal law.

Legalizing drug use would help drug-users and enhance the prosecution of drug-dealers more than the currently prevailing legal state of affairs.

THESIS 15: POLICE CANNOT REPLACE POLITICS

A major task of the polity is to provide conditions that allow nonviolent regulation of conflicting interests. Claiming a supreme state interest or appealing to a "supralegal emergency" reflects a preconstitutional position, just like a "state monopoly of force" that does not bind itself to the basic rights of the individual. The structure of police forces, their training, and their equipment also shape the structure of the polity in decisive ways. *Lavishly armed police and security apparatuses with comprehensive powers endanger freedom more than they can protect it.*

The domestic arms build-up we have witnessed in the form of new antiterror and "security" laws in the last few years has already led to a comprehensive data network shared by police and secret service institutions. Now it is used as an argument to legalize further steps on the path toward the security state. This process must be stopped. The police should not be misused for tasks that politics has to resolve.

NOTES

1. Available in translation from the Greens' Federal Office, Haus Wittgenstein, Ehrental 2–4, 53332 Bornheim, Germany.

2. See respectively Joachim Hirsch, "Grünes Umbauprogramm—Reformpolitik als Durchstaatlichungsstrategie," *Links,* no. 195 (June 1986) 12–13; and Joseph Huber, "Umbau bei den Grünen," *Die Zeit,* May 2, 1986, p. 31.

3. See *die tageszeitung,* January 19, 1996, p. 7.

4. The next section of the preamble to the Umbau program, "Principles and Perspectives of Green Economic Policies," can be found in Eva Kolinsky, ed., *The Greens in West Germany* (Oxford: Berg, 1989) 252–57.

5. "Co-determination" refers to the system of organized representation of the unions in the executive bodies of industrial firms.

6. See Ulrich Beck's influential *Risikogesellschaft: Auf dem Weg in eine andere Moderne* (Frankfurt am Main: Suhrkamp, 1986), which argues that "postindustrial" society is increasingly replacing confrontation over the distribution of material goods with confrontation over the distribution of (perceived) risks.

7. For example, Herman Rudolph, "Wo die Grünen der Staat drückt," *Süddeutsche Zeitung,* August 17, 1989.

8. "Das Chaos zum Program erhoben," *Frankfurter Allgemeine Zeitung,* August 8, 1989. For the Social Democratic position, see Martin Winter, "Freiheit ist nicht ohne Risiko," *Frankfurter Rundschau,* August 14, 1989.

9. Rupert Scholz, "Der grüne Leviathan", *Die Welt,* August 17, 1989.

10. The "civil service apparatus," in the Prussian tradition of strong state organization carried on in the Federal Republic, reflects the specific role of the German bureaucracy and civil service. The German civil service includes not only the greater part of employees of civil bureaucra-

cies at the federal, state, and local levels, but also members of the military (excluding draftees), all public university, secondary, and primary school teachers, and all police officers.—Eds.

11. The "right of asylum" for political refugees is a constitutional principle of the Basic Law that was vigorously contested in the course of the 1980s and all but undermined by the 1993 Asylum Law.—Eds.

*Bibliographies*

*About the Contributors*

*and Index*

# Selected Annotated Bibliography of English-Language Publications

Bahro, Rudolf. 1982. *Socialism and Survival*. London: Heretic Books. A selection of speeches by Rudolf Bahro from the time he arrived in the Federal Republic up through his participation in the founding of the Green Party. Bahro, like many East German dissidents, proved to be a leftist critic of capitalism as well. His speeches on the "end of the proletariat" were as important as the theses of Andre Gorz for the early Green Party.

———. 1984. *From Red to Green*. London: Verso. The final section of this book of interviews presents Bahro's opinions on the early development of the Greens.

———. 1986. *Building the Green Movement*. Philadelphia: New Society. Essays written from 1983 until Bahro left the party.

Boggs, Carl. 1986. "The Greens," *Our Generation* 18, no. 1, pp. 1–61.

———. 1986. *Social Movements and Political Power*. Philadelphia: Temple University Press.

Bomberg, Elizabeth. 1996. *Green Parties and Politics in the European Community*. London: Routledge.

Bramwell, Anna. 1989. *Ecology in the 20th Century: A History*. New Haven: Yale University Press.

Braunthal, Gerard. 1986. "Social-Democratic–Green Conditions in West Germany: Prospects for a New Alliance," *German Studies Review* 9.

Bürklin, Wilhelm P. 1985. "The Greens: Ecology and the New Left," in Peter Wallach and George K. Romoser, eds., *West German Politics in the Mid-Eighties*, pp. 187–218. New York: Praeger.

Capra, Fritjof, and Spretnak, Charlene. 1984. *Green Politics: The Global Promise*. New York: Dutton. The first English-language book on the West German Greens, written for a popular audience, with some helpful information, but strongly shaped by the authors' own rather American "new age" and "spiritual" orientations.

Chamberlayne, Pre. 1990. "The Mothers' Manifesto over 'Mütterlichkeit,'" *Feminist Review*, no. 35 (Summer) pp. 9–23.

Chandler, William M. and Siaroff, Alan. 1986. "Postindustrial Politics in Germany and the Origins of the Greens," *Comparative Politics* 18, no. 3, pp. 303–25.

Dalton, Russell J. 1992. "Alliance Patterns of the European Environmental Movement," in Wolfgang Rüdig, ed., *Green Politics Two*, pp. 59-85. Edinburgh: Edinburgh University Press.

Dobson, Andrew. 1990/1995. *Green Political Thought: An Introduction*. London: Routledge.

Dominick, Raymond. 1986. "The Roots of the Green Movement in the United States and West Germany," *Environmental Review* 12, no. 3.

Ely, John. 1983. "The Greens: Ecology and the Promise of Radical Democracy," *Radical America* 17, no. 1.

————. 1986. "Marxism and Green Politics in West Germany," *Thesis Eleven*, no. 13.

————. 1988. "The Greens between Legality and Legitimacy," *German Politics and Society*, no. 14.

————. 1992. "Red Green Politics and the German Debate on the New Constitution," *Capitalism, Nature, Socialism: A Journal of Socialist Ecology* 3, no. 1 (March) pp. 6–11.

————. 1994. "Libertarian Federalism and Green Politics: A Perspective on European Unification," in Peter Murphy, ed., *Politics in the Twilight of the 20th Century*. Champagne: University of Illinois Press.

Frankland, E. Gene. 1988. "Green Politics and Alternative Economics," *German Studies Review* 11, no. 1, pp. 111–32.

————. 1988. "The Role of the Greens in West German Parliamentary Politics," *Review of Politics* 50, pp. 99–122.

————. 1989. "Parliamentary Politics and the Development of the Green Party," *Review of Politics* 51, pp. 386–411.

————. 1995. "Germany: The Rise, Fall and Recovery of Die Grünen," in Dick Richardson and Chris Rootes, eds., *The Green Challenge: The Development of Green Parties in Europe*, pp. 23–44. London: Routledge.

Frankland, E. Gene, and Donald Schoonmaker. 1992. *Between Protest and Power: The Green Party in Germany*. Boulder: Westview Press. Solid and informative presentation of the Greens' "confrontation with modernity" following the Habermas/Offe model of a sixties movement that needs to "grow up." Frankland and Schoonmaker argue that the Greens have anticipated problems of democratic governance arising in the next century. They reproach the Greens for "not enough liberalism," but do not deal with their ideas about the economy.

————. 1993. "Disunited Greens in a United Germany," in Russell J. Dalton, ed., *The New Germany Votes*, pp. 135–62. New York: Berg.

Franklin, Mark N., and Wolfgang Rüdig. 1995. "On the Durability of Green Politics: Evidence from the 1989 European Election Study," *Comparative Political Studies* 28, no. 3, pp. 409–39.

Group of Green Economists. 1992. *Ecological Economics: A Practical Programme of Green Reform*. London: Zed Books. This is a translation of Die Grünen, *Die*

*Grünen im Bundestag: Auf dem Weg zu einer ökologisch-solidarischen Wirtschaft.* Bonn: Bundesgeschäftsstelle der Grünen, 1992.

Grünen, Die. 1983. *Programme of the German Green Party.* London: Heretic Books. Translation of the first party program. Another translation is available from Die Grünen in Bonn.

———. 1984. *Against Unemployment and Social Decline: Purpose in Work—Solidarity in Life.* Bonn: Die Grünen. Translation of the economic policy statement of Die Grünen as passed by the federal congress held in Stuttgart-Sindelfingen in 1983.

Hager, Carol J. 1992. "Environmentalism and Democracy in the Two Germanies," *German Politics* 1, no. 1, pp. 95–118.

Hill, Phil. 1985. "The Crisis of the Greens," *Socialist Politics,* no. 4. A shortened version appears in *Radical America* 19, no. 5 (1985) pp. 35–43.

Hirsch, Joachim. 1983. "Between Fundamental Opposition and *Realpolitik:* Perspectives for an Alternative Parliamentarism," *Telos,* no. 56, pp. 172–79.

———. 1983. "Fordist Security State and New Social Movements," *Kapitalistate,* nos. 10/11, pp.75–87.

Hoexter, Michael. 1988. "It's Not Easy Being Green," *New Politics,* vol. 2, no. 1 (Summer).

Hoffmann-Martinot, Vincent. 1991. "Grüne and Verts: Two Faces of European Ecologism," *West European Politics* 14, no. 4, pp. 70–95.

Hülsberg, Werner. 1985. "The Greens at the Crossroads," *New Left Review,* no. 152, pp. 5–29.

———. 1988. *The German Greens: A Social and Political Profile.* London: Verso. This historical presentation of the Greens emphasizes the role of the left in the party, which serves as an antidote to "new age" treatments. The author's reading, however, is rather influenced by his own membership in a Trotskyist group.

Jahn, Thomas. 1993. "Ecological Movements and Environmental Politics in Germany," *Capitalism, Nature, Socialism: A Journal of Socialist Ecology* 4, no. 1 (February) pp. 1–9.

Joppke, Christian. 1993. *Mobilizing against Nuclear Energy: A Comparison of Germany and the United States.* Berkeley: University of California Press.

Kelly, Petra K. 1994. *Thinking Green! Essays on Environmentalism, Feminism and Nonviolence.* Berkeley: Parallax Press. Posthumously published essays illustrative of Kelly's charismatic style of speaking.

Kitschelt, Herbert. 1988. "Left Libertarian Politics: Explaining Innovation in Competitive Party Systems," *World Politics* 40, no. 2, pp. 194–234.

———. 1989. *The Logics of Party Formation: Ecological Politics in Belgium and West Germany.* Ithaca: Cornell University Press. Based on a theory of "left-libertarianism," this empirical study of how green parties "really work" (quite apart from the ideals of grassroots participation) is mostly concerned with the internal organization of the (Belgian and German) Greens, showing how the attempt to create grassroots democracy within green parties has several unintended consequences, among them a weakening of strategic capabilities. The main thesis, however, that left-libertarian parties are and will remain different from the established parties, cannot be sustained.

Kitschelt, Herbert, and Staf Hellemans. 1990. *Beyond the European Left: Ideology and Political Action in the Belgian Ecology Parties.* Durham: Duke University Press. A survey of 256 activists of the Belgian ecology parties AGALEV and ECOLO allows the authors to test some of the hypotheses developed in Kitschelt's 1989 volume and to look more closely at other areas. A wealth of empirical data are presented on the careers, organizational practices, and political beliefs of the activists.

—. 1990. "The Left-Right Semantics and the New Politics Cleavage," *Comparative Political Studies* (Spring) pp. 210–38. Summarizes Kitschelt and Helleman's 1990 book.

Kolinsky, Eva. 1988. "The German Greens: A Women's Party?" *Parliamentary Affairs* 41, no. 1.

—. ed. 1989. *The Greens in West Germany: Organisation and Policy Making.* Oxford: Berg. This anthology of articles on the Greens, mostly by West German political scientists, and largely from the perspective of party sociology, includes a range of opinions from sympathizers to conservative critics, as well as translations of key programmatic statements.

Lagenkejk, Joost. 1991. "West European Red Greens," *Capitalism, Nature, Socialism: A Journal of Socialist Ecology* 2, no. 1 (February) p. 85.

Langguth, Gerd. 1984. *The Green Factor in German Politics: From Protest Movement to Political Party.* Boulder: Westview Press. This descriptive study of the development of the Green Party is written by a one-time member of parliament for the Christian Democratic Party; it is particularly useful for its data on party structure, finances, electoral results, and the like.

Lankowski, Carl. 1990. "One Step Backward, Two Steps Forward? Between '*Antifa*' and *Machtpolitik: Die Grünen* and the German Question," *German Politics and Society* 20 (Summer) pp. 41–56.

Lowe, Philip. 1989. "Gathering Greens," *Marxism Today* 33, no. 8 (September) pp. 14–17.

Markovits, Andrei S., and Philip S. Gorski. 1993. *The German Left: Red, Green and Beyond.* New York: Oxford University Press. This study sees the German Greens as the major innovators in the German left. It defends the realist wing of the party, blaming the fundamentalists for most of the party's problems (while often raising the right questions). It argues that the Social Democrats have been the major implementers but not initiators of green politics in Germany.

Megnin, Donald F. 1993. "Would the Greens Make an Appropriate Coalition Partner after the German National Elections in 1994?" *German Politics and Society* 29 (Summer) pp. 64–86.

Mewes, Horst. 1983. "The West German Green Party," *New German Critique*, no. 28 (Winter) pp. 51–85.

Müller-Rommel, Ferdinand. 1982. "Ecology Parties in Western Europe," *West European Politics* 5, no. 1, pp. 68–74.

―――. 1985. "The Greens in Western Europe: Similar but Different," *International Political Science Review* 6, no. 4, pp. 483–99.

―― ―. 1985. "New Social Movements and Smaller Parties," *West European Politics* 8, no. 1, pp. 41–54.

―――. 1989. "The German Greens in the 1980s: Shortterm Cycle of Protest or Indicator of Transformation?" *Political Studies* 37, no. 1, pp. 114–22.

―――. ed. 1989. *New Politics in Western Europe: The Rise and Success of Green Parties and Alternative Lists.* Boulder: Westview Press. Case studies of West European countries (except the Netherlands) presenting the development of green politics in each country, the parties' organizational structure, electoral support, programmatic profile, and record of government participation, plus a separate chapter on the Greens in the European parliament.

Mushaben, Joyce Marie. 1985–86. "Innocence Lost: Environmental Images and Political Experiences among the West German Greens," *New Political Science*, no. 14.

Offe, Claus. 1983. "'Reaching for the Brake': The Greens in Germany," *New Political Science*, no. 11 (Spring).

―――. 1985. "New Social Movements as a Meta-Political Challenge," *Social Research*, no. 4, pp. 817–68.

Papadikis, Elim. 1984. *The Greens in West Germany.* London: Croom Helm. Contains much information on the Greens broken down into regions and tendencies, though descriptions of the tendencies are not always accurate.

Patterson, William. 1989. "The Greens: From Yesterday to Tomorrow," in Peter Merkl, ed., *The FRG at Forty.* New York: New York University Press.

Pfaltzgraff, Robert L., Jr., ed. 1983. *The Greens of West Germany: Origins, Strategies, and Transatlantic Implications.* Cambridge, Mass.: Institute for Foreign Policy Analysis. A rapidly produced and tendentious treatment by a conservative foreign policy institute. It frequently demonstrates limited knowledge of the milieus and tendencies in the party that it attempts to characterize, and seeks to portray the Greens as caught between "socialist ideology" and "conservative romanticism," a new variation on an earlier politics of "cultural despair" that may threaten stability in Germany and for the NATO alliance.

Pilat, J. F., 1980. *Ecological Politics: The Rise of the Green Movement.* Washington/Beverly Hills: Center for Strategic and International Studies/Sage Publications. A descriptive and helpful characterization of early green politics in West

Germany (with comparisons to France and the United States) asking character-istically conservative questions (about, for example, the danger of terrorism in the antinuclear movement), but offering accurate assessments.

Poguntke, Thomas. 1987. "New Politics and Party Systems: The Emergence of a New Type of Party?" *West European Politics* 10, no. 1, pp. 76–88.

———. 1987. "The Organization of a Participatory Party: The German Greens," *European Journal of Political Research* 15, pp. 609–33.

———. 1990. "Party Activists versus Voters: Are the German Greens Losing Touch with the Electorate?", *Green Politics,* no. 1.

———. 1992. "Unconventional Participation in Party Politics: The Experience of the German Greens," *Political Studies* 40, no. 2 (June) pp. 239–54.

———. 1993. *Alternative Politics: The German Green Party.* Edinburgh: University of Edinburgh Press. Sums up the author's earlier studies of intraparty political culture, the social profile of voters and party activists, and the party's place in the "new politics," without, however, addressing whether the Greens still are a new politics party now that they have dispensed with most of the ideological and organizational features of their early years.

Poguntke, Thomas, and Rüdiger Schmitt-Beck. 1994. "Still the Same with a New Name? Bündnis 90/Die Grünen after the Fusion," *German Politics* 3, no. 1, pp. 91–113.

Richardson, Dick, and Chris Rootes. 1995. *The Green Challenge: The Development of Green Parties in Europe.* London: Routledge. A systematic academic assess-ment of the factors involved in the formation, development, and electoral per-formance of Green parties in Europe, emphasizing the shifting balance of party-political competition.

Rochon, T. R. 1988. *Between Society and State: Mobilizing for Peace in Western Eu-rope.* Princeton: Princeton University Press.

Rosolowsky, Diane. 1987. *West Germany's Foreign Policy: The Impact of the Social Democrats and the Greens.* Westport: Greenwood Press. Explains the predomi-nance of the "neutralist" perspective of the Greens as a result of postmaterial-ism. While sticking predominantly to analysis of programs and missing nuances in party debates, it treats the party in relation to the Social Democratic Party and the Federal Republic's foreign policy.

Rüdig, Wolfgang. 1983. "The Greening of Germany," *The Ecologist* 13, no. 1.

———. 1985. "The Greens in Europe: Ecological Parties and the European Elec-tion of 1984," *Parliamentary Affairs* 38, no. 1 (Winter).

———. 1985–86. "Eco-Socialism: Left Environmentalism," *New Political Science,* no. 14.

———. ed. 1990. *Green Politics One.* Edinburgh: Edinburgh University Press.

———. ed. 1992. *Green Politics Two.* Edinburgh: Edinburgh University Press.

———. ed. 1996. *Green Politics Three.* Edinburgh: Edinburgh University Press.

Rüdig, Wolfgang, and Mark N. Franklin. 1992. "Green Prospects: The Future of Green Parties in Britain, France and Germany," in Wolfgang Rüdig, ed., *Green Politics Two,* pp. 37–58.

Scharf, Thomas. 1994. *The German Greens: Challenging the Consensus.* Oxford: Berg. Case study of the party's involvement in local politics in the town of Mainz, demonstrating that local politics have become more conflictual since the Greens' election to the city council.

Schmid, Carol L. 1987. "The Green Movement in West Germany: Resource Mobilization and Institutionalization," *Journal of Political and Military Sociology* 15, pp. 33–46.

Weston, Joe, ed. 1986. *Red and Green: A New Politics of the Environment.* London: Pluto Press.

Wiesenthal, Helmut (edited and with an introduction by John Ferris) 1993. *Realism in Green Politics: Social Movements and Ecological Reform in Germany.* Manchester: Manchester University Press. In this collection of articles previously published in German (from 1984 onward), the former member of the Greens' executive committee makes his critique of leftist and ecological fundamentalism in the Green movement available to English readers. The last chapter, written specifically for this edition, examines a number of myths associated with the Greens' success.

Wolf, Margareta and Cora Stephan. 1995. "Alliance 90/Greens," *New Politics* 5, no. 3, pp. 152–56.

Women in the Green Party. 1985. *Women in Movement: Current Situation and Activities, Perspectives on International Solidarity.* Bonn: Die Grünen. Brochure produced by the women in the Greens and groups within the autonomous women's movement.

# Selected Annotated Bibliography of German-Language Publications

Besides the writings detailed below, various periodicals have been important forums for Green debate and analysis. The most important is the monthly *Kommune,* published in Frankfurt. Published independently of the party (the Greens have no official intellectual or political magazines or newspapers of note, as do most traditional left parties), *Kommune* carries news, debates, and discussions from all sectors in the Greens and the movements to their left. Published until 1984, the Hamburg journal *Moderne Zeiten* served as a predecessor, though more explicitly "eco-socialist." *Grüner basis-dienst,* published monthly by the Greens' federal office in Bonn, documents position papers by the federal executive and debates at federal congresses. Since the 1994 elections, when Bündnis 90/The Greens returned to the Bundestag, the parliamentary group has published a bi-monthly magazine initially called *Regenbogen* and, as of 1996, called *grün & bündig.* Most of the Green and Alternative parties at the state level also have regular monthly discussion magazines of substance, and individual state party programs are also available from the state party offices. The annual *Grünes & alternatives Jahrbuch,* published by Elephanten Press in Berlin, collects in-depth essays by green activists and sympathetic intellectuals on relevant topics for the party. Much independent left discussion of the party can be found regularly in *Links,* published bi-monthly by the Sozialistische Büro in Offenbach. A good source of current reporting on the party is found in the left daily newspaper, *die tageszeitung.* The quarterly *Forschungsjournal: neue soziale Bewegungen,* initially published with a subsidy from the Greens, deals with the new social movements; and the newsletter *Informationsdienst* of the Institut für ökologische Wirtschaftsforschung provides good sources on economic debates in the party.

Abendroth, Wolfgang, et al., ed. 1983. *Nicht links—nicht rechts? Über Politik und Utopie der Grünen.* Hamburg: VSA.

Adamietz, Axel. 1981. "Grüne im Parlament: Ein Erfahrungsbericht aus der Bremischen Bürgerschaft," *Kritische Justiz* 14, no. 4, pp. 384–401.

Alber, Jens. 1985. "Modernisierung, neue Spannungslinien und die politischen Chancen der Grünen," *Politische Vierteljahresschrift* 26, pp. 210–26.

Antunes, Carlos, Pierre Juquin, Penny Kemp, Isabelle Stengers, Wilfried Telkämper, and Frieder Otte Wolf. 1980. *Für eine grüne Alternative in Europa: Perspektiven der ökologischen und feministischen Linken.* Hamburg: Argument Verlag. Early statement on European green politics, initiated by the "ecological left" in the European parliament

Beckenbach, Frank, Jo Müller, and Eckhard Stratmann, eds. 1985. *Grüne Wirtschaftspolitik: Machbare Utopien.* Cologne: Kiepenheuer & Witsch.

Becker, Egon, ed. 1990. *Jahrbuch für Sozialökologische Forschung.* Frankfurt: Verlag für interkulturelle Forschung.

Berger, Rainer. 1995. *SPD und Grüne: Eine vergleichende Studie ihrer kommunalen Politik: sozialstrukturelle Basis—programmatische Ziele—Verhältnis zueinander.* Opladen: Westdeutscher Verlag.

Bickerich, Wolfram, ed. 1985. *SPD und Grüne: Das neue Bündnis?* Hamburg: Rowohlt. A collection of contributions by major politicians from the right of the SPD to the Green left (including Hermann Rappe, Johannes Rau, Hans-Ulrich Klose, Holger Börner, Peter Glotz, Hans-Jochen Vogel, Otto Schily, Joschka Fischer, Thomas Schmid, Rudolf Bahro, Thomas Rainer Trampert/Ebermann, Jutta Ditfurth) on the question of SPD-Green coalition politics.

Biege, Hans-Peter, et al. 1980. "Die baden-württembergische Landtagswahl vom 16. März, 1980. Spannung nur durch die Grünen?" *Zeitschrift für Parlamentsfragen,* no. 2, pp. 211–22.

Bolaffi, Angelo, and Otto Kallscheuer. 1983. "Die Grünen: Farbenlehre eines politischen Paradoxes," *Prokla* 13, no. 2, pp. 62–105. A detailed, politically sophisticated historical roadmap of early developments in the party.

Braunbehrens, Volkmar. 1983. "Bürgerrechte—eine Frage an 'Die Grünen,'" *Vorgänge,* nos. 2/3, pp. 53–58.

Brun, Rudolf. 1978. *Der grüne Protest: Herausforderung durch die Umweltparteien.* Frankfurt am Main: Fischer.

Bürklin, Wilhelm. 1984. "Ansatzpunkte einer sozialstrukturellen Verankerung der neuen sozialen Bewegungen," in Jürgen Falter, Christian Fenner, Michael Greven, eds., *Politische Willensbildung und Interessenvermittlung.* Opladen: Westdeutscher Verlag.

———. 1984. *Grüne Politik—Ideologische Zyklen, Wähler und Parteiensystem.* Opladen: Westdeutscher Verlag. Empirical materials (polling, tables, etc.) demonstrating that traditional class analyses cannot explain the sources of Green electoral support and offering a complex "path model," with several social and generational factors, seeking to explain this support.

Cohn-Bendit, Daniel, and Thomas Schmid. 1992. *Heimat Babylon: Das Wagnis der multikulturellen Demokratie.* Hamburg: Hoffmann und Campe. Influential text written by Green Party activists in the wake of unification and the rise of rightist violence in Germany. Its emphasis on the domestic "anxiety" produced by immigration and on multiculturalism rather than political participation by those who live and work in the country illustrates the weakness of the democratic concept in postunification Germany.

Diner, Dan. 1985. "Politisierung des Parlaments," *Links*, no. 180 (March) pp. 13–14.

Dinne, Olaf. 1979. *15 Jahre SPD in Bremen, dann Grün: Ein Beitrag zur Bremischen Geschichte jüngerer Vergangenheit.* Bremen.

Ditfurth, Jutta. 1991. *Lebe wild und gefährlich: Radikal-ökologische Perspektiven.* Cologne: Kiepenheuer & Witsch.

Dräger, Klaus, and Werner Hülsberg, eds. 1986. *Aus für Grün? Die grüne Orientierungskrise zwischen Anpassung und Systemopposition.* Frankfurt am Main: ISP-Verlag.

Ebermann, Thomas, and Rainer Trampert. 1984. *Die Zukunft der Grünen—Ein realistisches Konzept für eine radikale Partei.* Hamburg: Konkret Verlag. This book by two of the most prominent representatives of the eco-socialist position has been viewed, both inside and outside the Greens, as the manifesto for the eco-socialist tendency.

Eisel, Stephan. 1984. "Gewalt statt Mehrheit: Zum Demokratieverständnis der Grünen," *Die politische Meinung.* no. 216, pp. 29–34.

Elfferding, Wieland. 1984. "Ist ein Parteienbündnis ohne Vorherrschaft möglich?" *Das Argument,* no. 148, pp. 848–63.

Falkenberg, Gabriel, and Heiner Kersting, eds. 1985. *Eingriffe im Diesseits: Beiträge zu einer radikalen grünen Realpolitik.* Essen: Klartext. A collection of essays offering the most detailed and representative presentation of the Realo position in the party.

Fischer, Joschka. 1984. *Von grüner Kraft und Herrlichkeit.* Hamburg: Rowohlt. Anthology of interviews, reviews, and speeches documenting the odyssey of this one-time rock-throwing "Sponti" who became one of the most "realistic" and important politicians in the Green Party.

———. 1989. *Der Umbau der Industriegesellschaft: Plädoyer wider die herrschende Unweltlüge.* Frankfurt am Main: Eichborn. Arguing that industrial society is our unrecallable destiny, Fischer offers arguments and strategies for implementing the "rebuilding" of this society in democratic and ecological form.

Fogt, Helmut. 1983. "Die Grünen in den Parlamenten des Bundesrepublik: Ein Soziogramm," *Zeitschrift für Parlamentsfragen,* no. 4 (December) pp. 500–517.

———. 1984. "Basisdemokratie oder Herrschaft der Aktivisten? Zum Politikverständnis der Grünen," *Politische Vierteljahresschrift* 25, no. 1, pp. 97–114.

———. 1987. "Die Mandatsträger der Grünen. Zur sozialen und politischen Herkunft der alternativen Parteielite," *Aus Politik und Zeitgeschichte,* no. B-ll.

Fogt, Helmut, and Pavel Uttitz. 1984. "Die Wähler der Grünen 1980–1983: Systemkritischer neuer Mittelstand," *Zeitschrift für Parlamentsfragen,* no. 2, pp. 210–26.

Franken, Michael, and Walter Ohler, eds. 1988. *Natürlich Europa. 1992: Chancen für die Natur?* Cologne: Volksblatt Verlag. A useful round-robin description of green parties throughout Europe, largely from a left-green orientation.

Fromme, Friedrich Karl. 1984. "Parteienlandschaft im Wandel: Protestpartei unter Traditionsparteien—Die 'Grünen,'" *Die politische Meinung*, no. 180, pp. 35–45.

Fücks, Ralf, ed. 1991. *Sind die Grünen noch zu retten?* Hamburg: Rowohlt. Essays by various Green Party functionaries on the unification process.

Golluch, Norbert, and Stano Kochan. 1985. *Die grüne Wende.* Frankfurt am Main: Eichborn. A week before the national elections, a nuclear power plant explodes, bringing the Greens to power. An indispensable green fantasy cartoon book.

Die Grünen im Bundestag. 1983. *Die Grünen entern das Raumschiff Bonn.* Hattingen: Flieter Verlag.

"The Greens enter the Bonn Spaceship" is a collection of speeches, documents, and materials on the work and experience of the first Green faction in the federal parliament.

Die Grünen im Bundestag/AG Frauenpolitik. 1987. *Frauen und Ökologie: Gegen den Machbarkeitswahn.* Cologne: Volksblatt Verlag.

Grupp, Joachim. 1986. *Abschied von den Grundsätzen.* Berlin: Edition Ahrends im Verlag Clemens Zerling.

Guggenberger, Bernd. 1980. *Bürgerinitiativen in der Parteiendemokratie: Von der Ökologiebewegung zur Umweltpartei.* Stuttgart: Kohlhammer.

Hallensleben, Anna. 1984. *Von der Grünen Liste zur Grünen Partei: Die Entwicklung der Grünen Liste Umweltschutz.* Göttingen: Muster-Schmidt.

Hasenclever, Wolf-Dieter. 1982. "Die Grünen und die Parlamente," *Zeitschrift für Parlamentsfragen*, no. 3, pp. 417–22.

Hasenclever, Wolf-Dieter, and Connie Hasenclever. 1982. *Grüne Zeiten: Politik für eine lebenswerte Zukunft.* Munich: Kösel.

Hau, Willi, ed. 1985. *Es geht voran—Erfahrung wird gemacht: Grüne und andere Listen: Eine kommunalpolitische Alternative.* Frankfurt: AZ-Verlag. Discusses green political experiences at the local and municipal level.

Heidger, Ralf. 1987. *Die Grünen: Basisdemokratie und Parteiorganisation: Eine empirische Untersuchung des Landesverbands der Grünen in Rheinland-Pfalz.* Berlin: Edition Sigma.

Heinrich, Gudrun. 1993. *Rot-Grün in Berlin: Die AL Berlin in der Regierungsverantwortung 1989–1990.* Marburg: Schüren Verlag. A case study of the red-green governing coalition in Berlin.

Hirsch, Joachim. 1980. *Der Sicherheitsstaat: Das 'Modell Deutschland', seine Krisen und die neuen sozialen Bewegungen.* Frankfurt am Main: Verlag Neue Kritik. Examines the rise of the new social movements in Germany in terms of the development of the "security state," emphasizing the importance of opposition to the strong German state in explaining the historical specificity and particular significance of the West German Greens.

————. 1985. "Von der Faszination des Staates, oder was bleibt uns außer grünen Amtsinhabern?" *Links,* no. 180 (March) pp. 8–9.

————. 1987. "Unsere postmodernen Grünen," *Links,* no. 204 (March) 14–15.

Hirsch, Joachim, and Roland Roth. 1986. *Das neue Gesicht des Kapitalismus: Vom Fordismus zum Post-Fordismus.* Hamburg: VSA-Verlag. A systematic portrayal of the changes in West German state and society from a "Fordist" to a "post-Fordist" accumulation regime, from the perspective of "regulation" theory. Places the rise of the new social movements and the Greens within a context of systematic structural changes.

Horx, Matthias, Albrecht Sellner, and Cora Stephan, eds. 1983. *Infrarot: Wider die Utopie des totalen Lebens—Zur Auseinandersetzung mit Fundamentalopposition und 'neuem Realismus.'* Berlin: Rotbuch Verlag.

Huber, Joseph. 1983. "Basisdemokratie und Parlamentarismus: Zum Politikverständnis der Grünen," *Aus Politik und Zeitgeschichte,* no. 2, pp. 35–45.

Hubert, Hans-Peter/BAG Frieden und Internationalismus. 1993. *Grüne Außenpolitik: Aspekte einer Debatte.* Göttingen: Verlag Die Werkstatt.

Hugenroth, Reinhild, ed. 1993. *Kein leichter Weg nach Eurotopia: Maastricht—So nicht.* Bonn: Pahl-Rugenstein Verlag. Anthology of issues and positions on European unification by leading members of the Greens and Alliance '90. The first comprehensive discussion of Green positions, largely critical of the Maastricht accord.

Hummel, Dieter, et al., eds. 1986. *Kein Staat mit diesem Staat: Freiheitsrechte, Repression, und staatliche Hilfe in der Demokratie.* Bielefeld: ASTA an der Universität.

Ismayr, Wolfgang. 1985. "Die Grünen im Bundestag: Parlamentarisierung und Basisanbindung," *Zeitschrift für Parlamentsfragen,* no. 3, pp. 299–321.

Jäger, Brigitte, and Claudia Pinl. 1985. *Zwischen Rotation und Routine: Die Grünen im Bundestag.* Cologne: Kiepenheuer und Witsch.

Jäger, Michael. 1984. "Die Grünen im Parlament und das Problem der falschen Fronten," *Kommune,* no. 12, pp. 47–57.

Jahn, Thomas, and Peter Wehling. 1991. *Ökologie von rechts: Nationalismus und Umweltschutz bei der Neuen Rechten und den "Republikanern."* Frankfurt am Main: Campus. Comprehensive study of right-wing ecological politics in Germany. While making clear the overlaps between certain forms of eco-fundamentalism and the German new right, it presents these developments as a feature of the German right, and not central to the (almost exclusively left) Green Party.

Johnsen, Björn. 1988. *Von der Fundamentalopposition zur Regierungsbeteiligung: Die Entwicklung der Grünen in Hessen 1982–1985.* Marburg: Schüren. A historical study of the "short gallop" (not a "long march") from green radicalism to reformism taken by the Hessian Greens once they were faced with the question of governing.

Jun, Uwe. 1993. "Koalition mit Grünen: ein 'Auslaufmodell'? Regierungen von SPD und Grünen in den Bundesländern," *Zeitschrift für Parlamentsfragen* 24, no. 2, pp. 200–210.

Kallscheuer, Otto, ed. 1986. *Die Grünen—Letzte Wahl? Vorgaben in Sachen Zukunftsbewältigung.* Berlin: Rotbuch Verlag. A collection mostly by leading West German left intellectuals on themes such as provincialism in the party, misconceptions about the market, and the issue of the German past.

Kelly, Petra, and Jo Leinen. 1982. *Prinzip Leben: Ökopax—die neue Kraft.* Berlin: Olle & Wolter.

Kelly, Petra, and Joseph Beuys. 1993. *Diese Nacht, in die die Menschen....* Wangen: FIU-Verlag. Interviews with Kelly by Joseph Beuys, one of Germany's most famous postwar artists, illustrating the anthroposophist influence in the Greens and suggesting the role of politicized aesthetics in the party's early development.

Kelly, Petra, and Manfred Coppik, eds. 1982. *Wohin denn wir?* Berlin: Oberbaum Verlag.

Klein, Thomas, Vera Vordenbäumen, Carsten Wiegrefe, and Udo Wolf, eds. 1991. *Keine Opposition: Nirgends? Linke in Deutschland nach dem Sturz des Realsozialismus.* Berlin: Christoph Links Verlag. Attempts to identify oppositional politics in the newly unified Germany.

Kleinert, Hubert. 1992. *Aufstieg und Fall der Grünen: Analyse einer alternativen Partei.* Bonn: J. H. W. Dietz. Written by a prominent member of the realist wing, the book seeks to explain the Greens' failure to pass the electoral threshold in the first all-German elections of 1990 in West Germany. Argues for more professionalization by disposing of the remaining relics of grassroots democracy and encouraging the development of party leadership.

———. 1992. *Vom Protest zur Regierungspartei: Geschichte der Grünen.* Frankfurt: Eichborn. Presents the failures of the Greens during the unification process from the author's realist perspective.

———. 1996. "Bündnis 90/Die Grünen: Die neue dritte Kraft?" *Aus Politik und Zeitgeschichte,* Beilage zur Wochenzeitung Das Parlament B 6/96 (February 2) pp. 36–44.

Klemisch, Herbert, et al. 1994. *Handbuch für alternative Kommunalpolitik.* Bielefeld: AKP.

Klotzsch, Lilian, Klaus Könemann, Jörg Wischermann, and Bodo Zeuner. 1989. "Zwischen Systemopposition und staatstragender Funktion: Die Grünen unter dem Anpassungsdruck parlamentarischer Mechanismen," in Dietrich Herzog and Bernhard Weßels, eds., *Konfliktpotentiale und Konsensstrategien: Beiträge zur politischen Soziologie der Bundesrepublik,* pp. 180–215. Opladen: Westdeutscher Verlag.

Klotzsch, Lilian, and Richard Stöss. 1984. "Die Grünen," in Richard Stöss, ed., *Parteien-Handbuch: Die Parteien der Bundesrepublik Deutschland,* vol. 2, pp.

1509–98. Opladen: Westdeutscher Verlag. A careful and exhaustive summary of the history of the Greens from the beginning up to 1984. An essential reference.

Kluge, Thomas, ed. 1984. *Grüne Politik—der Stand einer Auseinandersetzung.* Frankfurt am Main: Fischer Verlag.

Konkret Literatur Verlag. 1982. *Es grünt so rot: Alternativen zwischen Mode und Modell.* Hamburg: Konkret.

Kraushaar, Wolfgang, ed. 1983. *Was sollen die Grünen im Parlament?* Frankfurt am Main: Verlag Neue Kritik. An important early collection raising questions about parliamentary Green politics including contributions of well-known German left intellectuals (Claus Offe, Joachim Hirsch, Norbert Kostede, Joseph Huber, and Johannes Agnoli), as well as an early statement of the Realo position by Joschka Fischer.

Krieger, Verena. 1991. *Was bleibt von den Grünen?* Hamburg: Konkret Literatur Verlag. A leading feminist within the Greens left the party in 1990, seeing it as no longer an emancipatory force.

Langner, Manfred. 1987. *Die Grünen auf dem Prüfstand: Analyse einer Partei.* Bergisch Gladbach: Gustav Lübbe Verlag. A collection of essays on the Greens by conservative political scientists and politicians (CDU/CSU), notable mostly for a "blame the victim" tendency to explain the Greens as political instigators rather than expressions of new social developments, such as Habermas's conception of the "new obscurity."

Lochner, Axel, ed. 1990. *Linke Politik in Deutschland: Beiträge aus DDR und BRD.* Hamburg: Galgenberg.

Meng, Richard, ed. 1987. *Modell rot-grün: Auswertung eines Versuchs.* Hamburg: VSA.

Mettke, Jörg R., ed. 1982. *Die Grünen: Regierungspartner von morgen?* Hamburg: Rowohlt.

Mez, Lutz. 1983. "Haben die Grünen im Bundestag eine Zukunft?" *Moderne Zeiten,* no. 11.

Möller, Windfried, et al. 1984. "Von der rechtlichen Bindungslosigkeit und der politischen Verantwortlichkeit des Abgeordneten. Ein Beitrag zum Thema Mandatsrotation," *Demokratie und Recht,* no. 4, pp. 367–92.

Müller, Emil Peter. 1984. *Die Grünen und das Parteiensystem.* Cologne: Deutscher Instituts-Verlag.

Müller-Enbergs, Helmut, Marianne Schulz, Jan Wielgohs, eds. 1991. *Von der Illegalität ins Parlament: Werdegang und Konzept der neuen Bürgerbewegungen.* Berlin: Christoph Links Verlag.

Müller-Rommel, Ferdinand. 1985. "Das grün-alternative Parteienbündnis im Europäischen Parlament: Perspektiven eines neuen Phänomens," *Zeitschrift für Parlamentsfragen,* no. 3, pp. 391–404.

———. 1993. *Grüne Parteien in Westeuropa*. Opladen: Westdeutscher Verlag. A cross-national analysis of Green parties in 15 west European nations, focusing on an empirical analysis of the determinants of electoral success at the national level.

Müller-Rommel, Ferdinand, and Helmut Wilke. 1981. "Sozialstruktur und 'postmaterialistische' Wertorientierungen von Ökologisten," *Politische Vierteljahresschrift* 22, no. 4, pp. 383–97.

Murphy, Detlef, Frauke Rubart, Ferdinand Müller, and Joachim Raschke. 1979. *Protest: Grüne, Bunte und Steuerrebellen*. Hamburg: Rowohlt.

Murphy, Detlef, et al. 1981. "Haben 'links' und 'rechts' noch Zukunft? Zur aktuellen Diskussion über die politischen Richtungsbegriffe," *Politische Vierteljahresschrift* 22, no. 4, pp. 398–414.

Neumann, Franz. 1980. "Bundestagswahl 1980—ein verändertes Parteienspektrum?" *Gegenwartskunde,* no. 1, pp. 5–18.

von Oertzen, Peter. 1985. "Zum Verhältnis von 'neuen sozialen Bewegungen' und Arbeiterbewegung: Zur Sozialstruktur des grünen Wählerpotentials," in Gerd-Uwe Bogulawski and Bodo Irrek, eds., *Ohne Utopien kann der Mensch nicht Leben: Beiträge zur Gewerkschaftsarbeit: Eine Festschrift für Hermann Kantelhardt,* 243–61. Göttingen: SOVEC.

———. 1986. "Die Niederlagen bei den Landtageswahlen lösen die Probleme nicht," *Frankfurter Rundschau,* January 13.

Offe, Claus. 1979. "Die Logik des kleineren Übels: Ein Vorschlag an die Sozialdemokraten sich mit den Grünen zu arrangieren," *Die Zeit,* November 9, p.76

———, ed. 1984. *Ende der Arbeitsgesellschaft?* Frankfurt am Main: Campus. Important discussions on the possible end of the "labor society"—that is "work," the labor market, etc.—as a defining character of society. Serves as a model for much Green economic thinking.

Offe, Claus, and Helmut Wiesenthal. 1985. "Die grüne Angst vor'm 'Reformismus,'" *die tageszeitung,* May 31.

Opielka, Michael, Angelika, Fohmann, et al. 1983. *Die Zukunft des Sozialstaats: Materialen zur sozialpolitischen Diskussion der Grünen.* Stuttgart: Die Grünen Baden-Württemberg.

Peters, Jan, ed. 1979. *Alternativen zum Atomstaat: Das Bunte Bild der Grünen.* Berlin: Rotation.

Pohl, Wolfgang, et al., eds. 1985. *Handbuch für Alternative Kommunalpolitik.* Bielefeld: AJZ-Verlag.

Probst, Lothar, ed. 1994. *Kursbestimmung: Bündnis 90/Grüne—Eckpunkte künftiger Politik.* Cologne: Bundverlag. Essays by Green functionaries from the old and the new federal states, dealing with election strategies for the 1995 elections.

Projektgruppe Grüner Morgentau. 1986. *Perspektiven ökologischer Wirtschaftspolitik.*

Frankfurt am Main: Campus. *"Morgentau"* ("morning dew") is a pun based on the accusation of Hermann Rappe, head of the German Chemical Union, that the Greens wanted to put through U.S. Secretary of State Henry Morgenthau's post–World War II proposal for the "pastoralization" of Germany. This large collection offers essays on economic issues from various Green perspectives on a broad array of themes: labor policy, social policy, planning and markets, labor time, foreign trade, and ecological approaches to various industrial sectors.

Raschke, Joachim. 1988. "Bewegung und Partei," *Forschungsjournal neue soziale Bewegungen,* no. 4, pp. 6–16.

———. 1991. *Krise der Grünen: Bilanz und Neubeginn.* Marburg: Schüren. This empirical study of the Green Party provides cogent analysis of why grassroots democracy failed and why the notion of a "movement party" did not work; nevertheless, it concludes with optimism about the future development of the party.

———. *Die Grünen. Wie sie wurden, was sie sind.* Cologne: Bund Verlag. Exhaustive empirical study (959 pages) of the Greens' history and development, drawing on Anthony Giddens' model of "structuration" and including studies of regional differences in the party, internal organization, and relations with other organizations and movements as well as with the media (though it offers no analysis of the Greens' relation to the state). Also includes contributions by other political scientists of differing but engaged perspectives. The best book on the Greens to date.

Raschke, Joachim, and Frauke Rubart. 1983. "Die Grünen und das parlamentarische Regierungssystem," *Gegenwartskunde,* no. 2, pp. 143–57.

Richardson, Elke, and Regina Michalik. 1985. *Die quotierte Hälfte: Frauenpolitik in den grün-alternativen Parteien.* Berlin: Lit Pol.

Roemheld, Regine. 1982. "Minorisierung im Parteien-Wettbewerb: Am Beispiel der Grünen," *Vorgänge,* nos. 5/6, pp. 107–17.

Roth, Roland. 1985. "Neue soziale Bewegungen in der politischen Kultur der Bundesrepublik—eine vorläufige Skizze," in Karl-Werner Brand, ed., *Neue soziale Bewegungen in Westeuropa und den USA: Ein internationaler Vergleich.* Frankfurt am Main: Campus. pp. 20–82.

———, ed. 1980. *Parlamentarisches Ritual und politische Alternativen.* Frankfurt am Main: Campus. A collection of essays (Wolf-Dieter Narr, Claus Offe, Joachim Hirsch, Margit Mayer, Roland Roth, and others) on the opposition of the social movements and citizen initiatives to parliamentary politics at the end of the 1970s, the eve of the Greens' formation.

Rucht, Dieter. 1980. *Von Wyhl nach Gorleben.* Munich: Beck.

Schiller-Dickhut, Reiner, et al. 1981, 1982. *Alternative Stadtpolitik: Grüne, rote und bunte Arbeit in den Rathäusern.* Hamburg: VSA.

Schmid, Thomas. 1986. "Zwischen oder auf den Tankern? Der schwierige Weg der Grünen in die Reformpolitik," *Aus Politik und Zeitgeschichte,* no. B-11, pp. 3–15.

Schmierer, Joscha. 1984. "Radikal und Rational: Seiteneinstieg in die grüne Strategiedebatte," *Kommune,* no. 6, pp. 33–44.

Schöller, Gunhild. 1985. *Feminismus and linke Politik.* Berlin: Quoren.

Schroeren, Michael, ed. 1990. *Die Grünen: 10 bewegte Jahre.* Vienna: Ueberreuter. Includes an excellent in-depth chronology of the Greens between 1977 and 1980, protocol of the founding 1980 Karlsruhe congress, and interviews with founders of the party, many of whom are today no longer in the party (Herbert Gruhl, Rudolf Bahro, Otto Schily) or are in varying degrees disillusioned with it (Thomas Ebermann, Jutta Ditfurth).

Schrüfer, Gertrud. 1985. *Die Grünen im deutschen Bundestag.* Nuremberg: Pauli-Balleis Verlag.

Schultze, Rainer-Olaf. 1980. "Nur Parteiverdrossenheit und diffuser Protest? Systemfunktionale Fehlinterpretationen der grünen Wahlerfolge," *Zeitschrift für Parlamentsfragen* 11, no. 2, pp. 292–313.

Siegert, Jens, et al. 1986. *Wenn das Spielbein dem Standbein ein Bein stellt . . .* Kassel: Weber, Zucht.

Spengler, Tilman, and Karl Markus Michel. 1983. *Kursbuch: Zumutungen an die Grünen,* no. 74. Berlin Kursbuch Verlag. A collection of early essays criticizing the "world-view" ideologies of some early Green tendencies and the mood and discourse of the party in its early form.

SPW-Verlag. 1985. "Rot-grüne Bündnisse—Erfahrungen und Chancen," *Zeitschrift für Sozialistische Politik und Wirtschaft* 8, no. 26. A section of this journal offers several articles discussing the question of coalition between the SPD and the Greens from trade-union and Marxist perspectives.

Stamer, Sabine, ed. 1985. *Von der Machbarkeit des Unmöglichen: Politische Gespräche über grüne Praxis und grüne Perspektiven.* Hamburg: Junius.

Steffani, Winfried. 1983. "Zur Vereinbarkeit von Basisdemokratie und parlamentarischer Demokratie," *Aus Politik und Zeitgeschichte,* no. 2, pp. 3–17.

Steg, Elke, and Inga Jesinghus, eds. 1987. *Die Zukunft der Stadt ist weiblich: Frauenpolitik in der Kommune.* Bielefeld: AJZ-Verlag.

Stober, Rolf. 1983. "Grüne und Grundgesetz," *Zeitschrift für Rechtspolitik,* no. 9, pp. 209–15.

Stöss, Richard. 1979. "Konservative Aspekte der Ökologie bzw. Alternativbewegung," *Ästhetik und Kommunikation,* no. 36, pp. 19–29.

———. 1980. *Vom Nationalismus zum Umweltschutz: Die Deutsche Gemeinschaft/ Aktionsgemeinschaft Unabhängiger Deutscher im Parteiensystem der Bundesrepublik.* Opladen: Westdeutscher Verlag.

———. 1984. "Sollen die Grünen verboten werden?" *Politische Vierteljahresschrift* 25, no. 4, pp. 403–24.

Thaa, Winfried, Dieter Salomon, and Gerhard Gräber, eds. 1994. *Grüne an der Macht: Widerstände und Chancen grün-alternativer Regierungsbeteiligungen.*

Cologne: Bund-Verlag. An essay collection organized by the Society for Political Ecology (a spinoff of the Greens' Federal Foundation Buntstift e.V.) and dealing with Green political themes in the period dominated by *Realpolitik*, such as reform politics in an era of reduced budgets, problems of professionalization, "alternative expertocracy," and constitutional reform.

Thaysen, Uwe. 1978. "Bürgerinitiativen, Parlamente und Parteien in der Bundesrepublik: Eine Zwischenbilanz (1977)," *Zeitschrift für Parlamentsfragen*, no. 9, pp. 87–103.

Tolmein, Oliver, ed. 1986. *Ökorepublik Deutschland: Erfahrungen und Perspektiven rot-grüner Zusammenarbeit*. Hamburg: Konkret Literatur Verlag. Journalistic account documenting and discussing issues of SPD–Green cooperation and tension in cases throughout West Germany and in national political discussions.

Veen, Hans-Joachim. 1984. "Wer wählt grün? Zum Profil der neuen Linken in der Wohlstandsgesellschaft," *Aus Politik und Zeitgeschichte*, nos. 35/36, pp. 3–17.

Veen, Hans-Joachim, and Claus Gotto. 1984. *Die Grünen—Partei wider Willen*. Mainz: Hase & Koehler.

Veen, Hans-Joachim, and Jürgen Hoffman, 1992. *Die Grünen zu Beginn der neunziger Jahre: Profile und Defizite einer fast etablierten Partei*. Bonn and Berlin: Bouvier. Both authors are political scientists connected to the CDU's Konrad Adenauer Foundation. They point out the flaws of *Basisdemokratie* as a countermodel of party organization without explaining why Green activists were so repelled by the formal democratic model of the major parties; they are dismissive of Green programmatic efforts (such as the Umbau Program); and they criticize the Greens' incapacity for "realistic problem solving."

Vollmer, Antje, ed. 1986. *Kein Wunderkind für Alice? Frauen-Utopien*. Hamburg: Konkret Literatur Verlag.

Wasserman, Rudolf. 1984. "Von der parlamentarischen zur Demonstrations- und Widerstandsdemokratie? Zur Ordnung des politischen Kampfes," *Zeitschrift für Politik*, no. 1, pp. 1–10.

Weichold, Joachim. 1993. *Regenbogen, Igel, Sonnenblume: Ökologische Bewegungen und grüne Parteien*. Berlin: Dietz Verlag. Eco-socialist perspective on European ecological movements and green politics.

Welte, Hans-Peter. 1994. *Die Parlamentarisierung der Grünen im Landtag von Baden-Württemberg: Eine Bilanz nach drei Wahlperioden* (1980–1992). Frankfurt am Main: Peter Lang Verlag.

Wielgohs, Jan, Marianne Schulz, and Helmut Müller-Enbergs. 1992. *Bündnis 90— Entstehung, Entwicklung, Perspektiven: Ein Beitrag zur Parteienforschung im vereinigten Deutschland*. Berlin: Gesellschaft für sozialwissenschaftliche Forschung und Publizistik (special issue of *Berliner Debatte INITIAL*). Substantive account of the emergence, development, and characteristics of "Alliance 90" and its subsequent association with the (West German) Greens.

Wiesenthal, Helmut. 1988. "Die Grünen im Bewegungsherbst: Linksradikale Bekenntnispartei oder Konkurrent um die Mitte?" *Gewerkschaftliche Monatshefte,* no. 5, pp. 289–99.

Wischermann, Jörg. 1992. *Anpassung und Gegenwehr: Die Parlamentsbeteiligung der Grün-Alternativen Liste Hamburg und ihre Folgen in der ersten Hälfte der achtziger Jahre.* Frankfurt am Main: Peter Lang Verlag.

Wolf, Frieder-Otto. 1984. "Ausstieg, Umgestaltung oder Umwälzung? Chancen und Illusionen grüner Wirtschaftspolitik," *Das Argument,* no. 146, pp. 225–37.

Wünsch, Roland. 1993. *Das Ende der Alternative: Die Grünen in der Wiedervereinigung.* Bonn: Pahl-Rugenstein. The author argues that the de-alignments caused by unification have been used to eliminate internal critics and thus turn the Greens into a reform party on the lines of the SPD and FDP.

Zeuner, Bodo. 1983. "Aktuelle Anmerkungen zum Postulat der 'Basisdemokratie' bei den Grünen/Alternativen," *Prokla,* no. 51, pp. 106–17.

———. 1985. "Parlamentarisierung der Grünen," *Prokla,* no. 61, pp. 5–22.

———. 1991. "Die Partei der Grünen: Zwischen Bewegung und Staat," in Werner Süß, ed., *Die Bundesrepublik in den achtziger Jahren.* Opladen: Leske & Budrich. pp. 53–68.

Zeuner, Bodo, and Jörg Wischermann. 1995. *Rot-Grün in den Kommunen: Konfliktpotentiale und Reformperspektiven: Ergebnisse einer Befragung von Kommunalpolitikern.* Opladen: Leske & Budrich. On the basis of 1,800 questionnaires filled out by local politicians from the Green and the Social Democratic Parties, the book analyzes the relationship between the two parties and finds them "normal" partners and competitors within the German party system.

# About the Contributors

ALEX DEMIROVIĆ works at the Institute for Social Research in Frankfurt and teaches sociology and political science at Frankfurt University. He is the author of *Nicos Poulantzas: A Critical Analysis* (1987) and co-editor of *Hegemony and the State* (1992).

JOHN ELY received his Ph.D. from the University of California at Santa Cruz and taught in the Program in Cultures, Ideas, and Values at Stanford University. His writings range from the neo-Aristotelian philosophy of Ernst Bloch to alternative and green politics in Europe and the United States.

JOACHIM HIRSCH is professor of political science at the Frankfurt University. His publications include *The New Face of Capitalism* (1986, with Roland Roth), *Capitalism without Alternative?* (1990), and *The National Competitive State* (1995).

LILIAN KLOTZSCH is a political scientist. After working at the Free University of Berlin's Institute for Social Science on the Green Party structure and on local coalition politics of the Greens, she now does research on part-time labor and women for the Senate of Berlin.

KLAUS KÖNEMANN, a political scientist, participated in various research projects on the Greens and local politics directed by Bodo Zeuner at the Free University of Berlin; he now teaches adult education.

MARGIT MAYER teaches political science at the Free University of Berlin. She has written on social movements, urban politics, and state transformation and has frequently compared Germany and the United States in these areas. Her publications include *The Genesis of the American Nation State* (1979), *The New Face of the Cities* (1990), and *Politics in European Cities* (with Hubert Heinelt, 1993).

HORST MEWES teaches political science at the University of Colorado in Boulder. Besides working on problems of modern democracy, he also follows contemporary German politics from an American perspective, teaching at a German university almost every summer. He is particularly interested in the development of the party system and new social movements.

LUTZ MEZ teaches political science at the Free University of Berlin, focusing on environmental policies in western and eastern Europe. His publications include *The Nuclear Conflict* and other writings on energy policies, the role of utilities, and the role of the unions within the energy debate.

DETLEF MURPHY is a political scientist teaching in Berlin and Hamburg. He has published on the Irish party system, British social movements, and the German Greens.

CLAUS OFFE was involved in the founding of the Green Party and has observed its "maturation" process with critical support. He is professor of political sociology at Humboldt University in Berlin. His publications include *Contradictions of the Welfare State* (1984), *Disorganized Capitalism* (1985), and *Modernity and the State* (1996).

CLAUDIA PINL was active with the Greens in Bonn and now works as a freelance writer in Cologne, specializing in women's issues and green politics.

ROLAND ROTH is a professor of political science at the Fachhochschule in Magdeburg, working on critical social theory and political sociology of the FRG. His publications include *Parliamentarian Ritual and Political Alternatives* (1980), *New Social Movements in the FRG* (1987/1991), *Local Politics in Germany* (1994), and *Democracy from Below* (1994).

MICHAEL SCHATZSCHNEIDER is a political scientist and translator living in Bonn, Germany. He has translated for the Institute for Social Research in Frankfurt and has worked for Green MPs in a governing coalition in the state of Hesse and in the opposition in the German Bundestag.

JÖRG WISCHERMANN is researcher and lecturer at the Free University of Berlin. He has worked on problems in the emergence and development of the Greens and new social movements. Currently he is engaged in a research project on local politics in east Germany. His publications include *Adaptation and Resistance: Parliamentarian Participation of the Green-Alternative List Hamburg* (1992) and, with Bodo Zeuner, *Red-Green in Local Governments* (1994).

BODO ZEUNER is a professor of political science at the Free University of Berlin. He has published widely on unions, parties, and social movements. He has directed various research projects on the Greens and on local politics. Out of the most recent one emerged a book, written with Jörg Wischermann, on red-green governing coalitions on the local level.

# Index

3630